Parliament and Parliamentarism

European Conceptual History

The transformation of social and political concepts is central to understanding the histories of societies. This series focuses on the notable values and terminology that have developed throughout European history, exploring key concepts such as parliamentarianism, democracy, civilization, and liberalism to illuminate a vocabulary that has helped to shape the modern world.

Conceptual History in the European Space
Edited by Willibald Steinmetz, Michael Freeden, and Javier Fernández Sebastián

Parliament and Parliamentarism:
A Comparative History of a European Concept
Edited by Pasi Ihalainen, Cornelia Ilie and Kari Palonen

European Regions and Boundaries: A Conceptual History
Edited by Diana Mishkova and Balázs Trencsényi

Basic and Applied Research:
The Language of Science Policy in the Twentieth Century
Edited by David Kaldewey and Désirée Schauz

Democracy in Modern Europe: A Conceptual History
Edited by Jussi Kurunmäki, Jeppe Nevers, and Henk te Velde

Parliament and Parliamentarism

A Comparative History of a European Concept

Edited by
Pasi Ihalainen, Cornelia Ilie, and Kari Palonen

berghahn
NEW YORK • OXFORD
www.berghahnbooks.com

First published in 2016 by
Berghahn Books
www.berghahnbooks.com

Library of Congress Cataloging-in-Publication Data
Names: Ihalainen, Pasi. | Ilie, Cornelia, author. | Palonen, Kari, author. |
Palonen, Kari, 1947- editor.
Title: Parliament and parliamentarism: a comparative history of
a European concept / edited by Pasi Ihalainen, Cornelia Ilie and
Kari Palonen.
Description: New York: Berghahn Books, 2016. | Includes bibliographical
references and index.
Identifiers: LCCN 2015034303 | ISBN 9781782389545 (hardback: alk. paper) |
ISBN 9781785337567 (paperback) | ISBN 9781782389552 (ebook)
Subjects: LCSH: Legislative bodies—Europe. | Representative government and
representation--Europe. | Legislative power--Europe.
Classification: LCC JF501 .P354 2016 | DDC 327.4--dc23 LC record available at
http://lccn.loc.gov/2015034303

British Library Cataloguing in Publication Data
A catalogue record for this book is available from the British Library

ISBN 978-1-78238-954-5 hardback
ISBN 978-1-78533-756-7 paperback
ISBN 978-1-78238-955-2 ebook

Contents

Acknowledgements

This comparative volume on the conceptual history of parliaments and parliamentarism is a product of a five-year international multidisciplinary project involving fourteen countries and twenty-four authors. Kari Palonen took the initiative and invited Pasi Ihalainen and Cornelia Ilie to draft proposals for the planning meetings of the *European Conceptual History* book series. Helpful feedback was received from Michael Freeden (Oxford) and Willibald Steinmetz (Bielefeld) as the series editors as well as from other members of the History of Concepts Group. The Swedish Collegium of Advanced Studies, Uppsala, provided the venue for the first editorial meeting in April 2010. The editors agreed on Pasi Ihalainen coordinating the editorial work, which was loosely divided according to three approaches to parliamentary studies – contributions to historical research to be edited by Pasi Ihalainen, discourse studies by Cornelia Ilie and political theory by Kari Palonen.

Potential authors were invited on the basis of their expertise on national parliaments as institutions or on conceptual history, rhetoric or political theory as analytical approaches to parliaments. The editors want to thank all the contributors not only for having put their expertise at our disposal but also for their patience in the course of a longish project that has involved: writing together, unusually strict word-limited texts, several deadlines, workshops, many stages of editorial feedback and, hence, quite a lot of rewriting as well. Now that the end product is at hand we believe that challenging authors to adopt new approaches, to cooperate closely with other researchers, to summarise their findings to fit in limited space and to subject the texts to several stages of feedback and rewriting has as a whole been a successful strategy.

The first workshop on abstracts for chapters was held at the Finnish Institute in Athens in January 2011, funded by the Academy of Finland Centre of Excellence in Political Thought and Conceptual Change. Comments received from Gonzalo Capellan (Cantabria), Nicola Lupo (LUISS, Rome) and Petros-Iosif Stanganellis (Athens) helped in developing the idea of the book.

The first full drafts of several chapters were presented in connection with the Sixth Jyväskylä Symposium on Political Thought and Conceptual History in June 2011. The editors and authors received feedback from scholars such as Hans-Erich Bödeker (Göttingen), Jonas Harvard (Mid Sweden & Södertörn), Helge Jordheim (Oslo), Rinna Kullaa (Jyväskylä), Ann-Christina Lauring Knudsen (Aarhus), Evgeny Roshchin (Jyväskylä), Alexander Semyonov (St Petersburg), Suvi Soininen (Jyväskylä), Willibald Steinmetz (Bielefeld), Henrik Stenius (Helsinki), Tapani Turkka (Jyväskylä) and Galina Zvereva (Moscow). The symposium was funded jointly by the Centre of Excellence and the two Academy of Finland research projects 'Politics of Dissensus' and 'Parliamentary Means of Conflict Resolution' as well as by the International Office of the University of Jyväskylä. The editorial team next met at the conference 'Parliamentary Discourses across Cultures: Interdisciplinary Approaches' in Bucharest in September 2011.

The final workshop of the project was organized by Pasi Ihalainen at the Department of History and Ethnology in Jyväskylä in August 2012. A lively discussion on the drafts was attended by Willibald Steinmetz as well as by most of the authors. The Academy of Finland projects and the Department of History and Ethnology funded the event, which was planned in cooperation with Taru-Maija Heilala-Rasimov, Teemu Häkkinen, Miina Kaarkoski, Laura-Mari Manninen and Matti Roitto. The Department of History and Ethnology, led by Jari Ojala, also financed the main editorial meeting in Stockholm in July 2013 and paid for the careful language copy-editing by Gerard McAlester. The Faculty of Humanities, led by Petri Karonen, allocated plenty of working hours for Ilona Riikonen, the coordinator of publications of the Faculty, to technical editing. Ville Häkkinen, as Pasi Ihalainen's research assistant, compiled the list of abbreviations. We would also like to thank the three anonymous referees used by Berghahn Books for their constructive criticism as well as the personnel of the publisher, Ann Przyzycki DeVita, Adam Capitanio, Molly Mosher, Chris Chappell and Charlotte Mosedale in particular, for their help throughout the publishing process.

Skype meeting between Abu Dhabi and Jyväskylä, 6 October 2015,
Pasi Ihalainen, Cornelia Ilie and Kari Palonen.

List of Abbreviations

ÅAT	*Åbo Allmänna Tidning*
CAS	*Cortes. Actas de las Sesiones*
CDU/CSU	*Christlich Demokratische Union Deutschlands/Christlich-Soziale Union in Bayern*, Christian Democratic Union of Germany/Christian Social Union in Bavaria
CEDA	*Confederación Española de Derechas Autónomas*, Spanish Confederation of Autonomous Right-wing Parties
CFSP	Common Foreign and Security Policy
CJ	*Commons Journal*
CNT	*Confederación Nacional del Trabajo*, National Confederation of Workers (Spain)
Council	Council (of Ministers) of the European Union
CPSU	Communist Party of the Soviet Union
CW	*Collected Works* (of Karl Marx and Friedrich Engels)
DB	Deutscher Bundestag
DR	Deutscher Reichstag
DSC	*Diario de las Sesiones de Cortes*
DSCCRE	*Diario de Sesiones de las Cortes Constituyentes de la República Española*
DSCGE	*Diario de Sesiones de las Cortes Generales y Extraordinarias*
EC	European Council
ECSC	European Coal and Steel Community
EEC	European Economic Community
EP	European Parliament
ESM	European Stability Mechanism
EU	European Union
FAT	*Finlands Allmänna Tidning*
FRG	Federal Republic of Germany
GDR	German Democratic Republic

KGParl	*Kommission für Geschichte des Parlamentarismus und der Politischen Parteien*, German Commission for Parliamentary History
KPD	*Kommunistische Partei Deutschlands*, Communist Party of Germany
MEP	Member of the European Parliament
MEW	*Marx-Engels Werke*
MP	Member of Parliament (used universally, not only in British context)
NSDAP	*Nationalsozialistische Deutsche Arbeiterpartei*, National Socialist German Workers' Party
ODS	*Ordbog over det Danske Sprog*
PDL	*Partidul Democrat-Liberal*, Democratic Liberal Party (Romania)
PK	Paulskirche
PoIT	*Post- och Inrikes Tidningar*
PSD	*Partidul Social Democrat*, Social Democratic Party (Romania)
PZPR	*Polska Zjednoczona Partia Robotnicza*, Polish United Workers' Party
RSFSR	Russian Soviet Federative Socialist Republic
SAOB	*Svenska Akademiens Ordbok*
SED	*Sozialistische Einheitspartei Deutschlands*, Socialist Unity Party of Germany (GDR)
SPD	*Sozialdemokratische Partei Deutschlands*, Social Democratic Party of Germany
TEU	Treaty of the European Union
TFEU	Treaty on the Functioning of the European Union
UEM	United Europa Movement
UGT	*Unión General de Trabajadores*, General Union of Workers (Spain)
USSR	Union of Soviet Socialist Republics
WRV	*Weimarer Reichsverfassung*

Parliament as a Conceptual Nexus

Pasi Ihalainen, Cornelia Ilie and Kari Palonen

Parliament has for centuries been a central European political institution for expressing dissensus and for conducting debates among the representatives of the citizens in a spirit of fair play. A modern parliament controls government and bureaucracy by claiming the right to make sovereign decisions without appeal. This volume builds on the thesis that deliberation (between opposed points of view in parliament), representation (of the citizens in a parliament), responsibility (of the government to the parliament) and sovereignty (of a parliament within a polity) form the core concepts of parliamentarism and distinguish a parliament from other types of assemblies, making it a unique representative institution. This cluster of distinguishing concepts of parliamentarism creates a clear agenda for the historical, discursive and political analysis of questions that all real parliaments face, more particularly so as each of these dimensions has been fiercely disputed in most European parliaments. Parliament, parliamentarism and the cluster of parliamentary concepts constitute an excellent example of the essentially contested nature of political key concepts. Parliamentarism in any national context has been a product of a series of political disputes and has evolved further as a consequence of an ongoing process of political debate on its nature. It has become such a major feature of most European political cultures that such disputes and the consequent process of transformation in political systems have become tolerated.

This book is divided into three parts, each of which offers perspectives derived from different disciplines that contribute to present-day parliamentary studies, namely historical research (Part I, introduced in more detail in Chapter 1), discourse and rhetorical studies (Part II, introduced in more detail in Chapter 8) and political theory (Part III, introduced in more detail in Chapter 13). The discipline-specific approaches to parliamentary studies will be discussed in these introductory chapters. In this general introduction, we shall define the points of departure of our joint multidisciplinary volume, review the implications of an ideal type of parliament for our research and discuss some central features related to the naming of parliaments. We shall discuss the particularly European features of parliament as an institution, the methodological potential of multidisciplinary parliamentary studies of this type for renewing the research field of conceptual history and the potential of conceptual history for bringing added value to parliamentary studies.

After analysing the four conceptual dimensions of parliamentarism from the perspectives of history, discourse and political theory and drawing together the findings of this multidisciplinary project (which is done at a theoretical level in this introduction and on the basis of empirical studies in Chapters 1, 8 and 13), we should be able to better understand the development of European parliamentarism in long-term comparative and multidisciplinary perspectives. This book explores the mutual relationships between the proposed four dimensions of parliamentarism in various historical periods from the French Revolution to the (re-)parliamentarization of Central and Eastern Europe and the attempted parliamentarization of the European Union through the analysis of national cases, varying from Britain and Finland to Russia and Spain. Side by side with deliberation, representation, responsibility and sovereignty, we also consider other concepts that have played central roles in conceptualizing parliament in modern European history.

The studied period is a long one, covering over two hundred years. From the point of view of conceptual history, parliamentary concepts do not change in successive stages or fashions in a linear way; rather, novelties are frequently combined with actualizations of old topoi. In order to make this recycling of past parliamentary experiences and momentums visible, parliamentary history needs to be studied from a long-term perspective. In present-day parliaments, for instance, we can distinguish different conceptual layers that can only be recognized and understood against the background of an extended time frame and by combining the tools of various disciplines. It is important to identify the political situations to which these layers were originally connected and to see how they have been further developed in differing political contexts. The rhetorical use of concepts by various political agents in the past has opened new horizons for research and debate. Both explicit and highly controversial conceptual changes and less visible and unintended ones in the course of parliamentary history need to be considered in relation to each of the parliamentary dimensions.

In this volume, we focus on debates about the character of parliament and parliamentarism within different European parliaments, countries and genres of writing as one of the first comparative steps in conceptual history. In doing so, we integrate transnational elements into the analysis as far as possible. Eventually, we aim to identify the momentum of parliamentarization in terms of various aspects of parliamentarism in different national contexts – for example, the momentum of extended popular representation in a parliament or governmental responsibility to a parliament – with each momentum initiating a political point of reference for later parliamentary history. We argue that the key periods of parliamentarization in the history of several European countries include the French Revolution, which started in 1789; the parliamentarization of government and the extension of parliamentary suffrage from the 1830s to the last phase of the First World War and its immediate aftermath; the rearrangements that followed the Second World War; and the fall of the Soviet bloc starting in 1989.

On the other hand, the schedule of parliamentarization has varied from country to country, and its 'progress' has been anything but steady. The French Revolution created a break with the tradition of estate assemblies not only in France but also in other countries, offering an alternative to the older British parliamentary and continental estate models for how representative institutions in an increasingly democratic polity should be organized. The period from the mid 1860s to the early 1870s was another period of reform, expressed in the extension of suffrage (Britain and Germany), the parliamentarization of government (France) and the replacement of the estate system with a modern type of parliament (Austria-Hungary and Sweden). The breakthroughs that representative democracy made in several European countries (and not only in newly independent states) during and in the immediate aftermath of the First World War opened entirely new prospects for parliamentary democracy, even if overly optimistic expectations failed to be realized in the nationalistic and often totalitarian atmosphere of the interwar period. After the Second World War, in West Germany, Italy and in Western European countries that had been occupied, the return to parliamentary government with an almost exclusive emphasis on the responsibility criterion was followed without any greater debate on parliamentary principles. Four decades later, the historic changes brought about by the collapse of communism in Eastern Europe in 1989 transformed parliaments in post-communist regimes from pseudo-parliamentary or quasi-parliamentary institutions into key political players as democratically functioning representative and deliberative bodies.

We can, to some extent, build on studies in parliamentary history that have manifested themselves in Europe in recent years. Recent works with a comparative ambition include Christoph Gusy's *Demokratie in der Krise: Europa in der Zwischenkriegszeit* (2008), although it is limited in terms of both its chronological and thematic scope. Two volumes compiled from presentations at conferences organized by the German Commission for Parliamentary History and Political Parties (KGParl) and the historians of the Humboldt University in Berlin have opened a series on comparative parliamentary history in German, discussing parliamentary cultures from a long-term perspective, albeit on the basis of loosely connected cases and bypassing most conceptual, discursive and theoretical aspects of parliamentarism (Schulz and Wirsching 2012; Feuchter and Helmrath 2013). A third volume, based on a conference in The Hague in 2013, is expected to discuss parliamentary ideals from a comparative European perspective.

The study of parliamentary discourse and practices has acquired real interdisciplinary scope only recently as a result of contributions made by scholars from the linguistic sub-disciplines, such as pragmatics, critical discourse analysis and cognitive linguistics, or closely related disciplines, such as rhetoric. Paul Bayley's edited book *Cross-Cultural Perspectives on Parliamentary Discourse* (2004) is a pioneering endeavour that displays the use of several methodological frameworks for the analysis of parliamentary discourses in different countries (Britain, Germany, Italy, Mexico, Spain, Sweden and the United States). A broad spectrum of interdisciplinary perspectives is used in Cornelia Ilie's volume *European Parliaments under Scrutiny: Discourse Strategies and Interaction Practices* (2010a) to examine and problematize the impact of parliamentary debating practices and linguistic strategies on current political action and interaction in parliaments across Europe, including post-communist parliaments.

In political theory, we can speak of a renaissance of studies on the concepts of 'political representation' and 'representative democracy' (e.g., Urbinati, *Representative Democracy: Concept and Genealogy*, 2006), although a tendency to make everything 'representation' and thus to depoliticize the concept is fashionable (see Saward, *The Representative Claim*, 2010). A critique of concepts of governance, depoliticization and a discussion of the 'crisis of representation' is contained in Danny Michelsen and Franz Walter's work, *Unpolitische Demokratie. Zur Krise der Repräsentation* (2013). Nicolas Roussellier's *Le parlement d'éloquence* (1997) and later studies may represent the first initiatives for rehabilitating the parliamentary culture of the French Third Republic and the rhetorical dimension of parliamentary politics in general (see Finlayson, 'Rhetoric and the Political Theory of Ideologies', 2012; Galembert, Rozenberg and Vigour 2014; and Palonen, Rosales and Turkka 2014). The political aspects of parliamentary procedure have also regained interest among scholars (see Clinchamps 2006; Sanchez 2012; Palonen 2014). A renewed interest in parliaments as such, beyond governments and parties, can be seen in more empirical studies in political science, for example in

Germany around the work of Werner J. Patzelt (see 2005, 2012; Patzelt and Dreischer 2009).

However, this is the first work that aims to create a comparative conceptual history of European parliamentarism. Instead of attempting to be completely comprehensive with regard to all European parliaments or all aspects of their conceptual history, this book consists of a selection of representative national and regional case studies written by leading experts in the field. The primary units of comparison are the national parliaments themselves, complemented by a separate chapter on the European Parliament together with some discussion of inter-parliamentary transfers. The selected cases are used to demonstrate central features in the development of parliamentarism as a pan-European phenomenon in key historical periods since the French Revolution. Most of the European great powers were involved in some formative historical period that produced turning points in the history of parliamentarism. Most of the other European regions are represented by illustrative national cases from smaller countries. It goes without saying that not all national histories of parliamentarism can be covered within the confines of this survey volume.

The parliamentarization of representative governments across Europe implies the conceptualization of a definite change in political cultures. This change has taken place rapidly in some national contexts, and it is also applicable to cases such as the replacement of Soviet-style facade assemblies by proper parliaments after 1989. The parliamentary experience, vocabulary, representation and procedures of deliberation to some extent tend to create transnational rather than purely national parliamentary political cultures, and in them the parliamentary language transcends the vernacular 'dialects'. The processes of conceptual transfer and translation concern the relationships between the general parliamentary language and its national 'dialects'. Parliaments use vernacular languages, and they are formed on a national basis, serving as symbols of the transcendence of sub-national particularities. Even if transfers between national parliaments are not self-evident and can imply considerable change in new contexts, parliaments nevertheless have numerous features in common. Supra- and transnational parliamentary assemblies can be expected to have a growing importance in institutions such as the EU and the UN, and this further increases the possibilities for transnational and inter-parliamentary transfers.

Having provided the first expressions of many parliamentary concepts in the past, the British and French parliamentary cultures play, to some extent, a double role in which the national institutions and traditions are mixed with parliamentary ideal types of concepts that serve as models for the latecomers, who have adopted elements taken from these two models. Appropriating the elements of parliamentary culture from these countries and applying them to new contexts have taught the political elites of other countries parliamentary styles of debating. Of course, we should not overemphasize the possibilities for transfer in parliamentary language, as foreign models and references have usually been adopted selectively and even tendentiously in order to serve particular purposes in domestic circumstances (more on this in Chapter 1). Apparent conceptual transfers between parliamentary cultures do not imply that applications necessarily carry similar meanings in different political cultures.

Parliament and parliamentarism remain concepts of dispute. Unlike, for example, the concept of democracy, which has taken on consistently positive (though still contested) meanings in the course of the twentieth century, the concept of parliamentarism has never received universal approval. Not only do its key content and range of reference remain highly contested, but so do its value and its conditions of realization. The phrase 'crisis of parliamentarism' was coined in France at the time of the Third Republic in the late nineteenth century, and since then it has been a recurrent topos evoked from different political corners and for varying purposes (for current challenges to parliamentarism, see the Epilogue in this book). Constant contestation and an atmosphere of crisis have become essential elements of European parliamentarism. Indeed, parliamentarism should perhaps be seen as a long-term discursive process of disputes and crises that moves in time and space rather than a sort of goal that could be achieved at some specific moment in history.

The Ideal Type of Parliamentarism

As was pointed out at the start, our hypothetical point of departure consists in the construction of a four-dimensional ideal type of parliament, comprising a cluster of concepts held together by parliament itself as a political concept. Each of the dimensions has been fiercely disputed among members and constitutes a criterion that distinguishes a parliament from other types of assemblies and institutions. The dimensions of representation, deliberation, sovereignty and responsibility set the agenda for the historical study of the concept of parliament, a concept that is used by political agents and writers on politics alike.

The dimension of representation refers to parliament as a permanent assembly regularly summoned to represent and act in the name of the citizenry and chosen at regular intervals in free and fair elections. The permanence of parliament, the regularity of its sessions, its representative character and the recurrent election of its members together with the freedom and fairness of its elections can be regarded as constitutive criteria for the distinction between parliamentary and non-parliamentary types of representation. The inclusion of the citizenry, the franchise and eligibility of the citizens, the density and rhythm of elections and of the parliamentary sessions, the modes of conducting free and fair elections and so on then constitute the intra-parliamentary range of variation in the parliamentary representation. In addition, we can speak of non-parliamentary modes of representation; these include the old estates, corporative forms of representation, the council type (wards, communes, soviets, etc.) of assemblies, presidential and plebiscitary regimes, and perhaps also the non-elective forms of selecting representatives; for example, by rotation or lottery (see Chapter 13 and the Epilogue for further discussion). Parliaments in this volume are not early modern estate assemblies, debating societies or local or regional assemblies. They are deliberative assemblies based on modern conceptions of the representation of the people. Some other forms of government, such as presidential regimes, have been excluded. Even though the estate assemblies provided the basis on which several modern representative institutions were built, and even though some features of them survived in the upper chambers of many nineteenth-century parliaments, we have chosen not to focus on the analysis of their proto-parliamentary features but have nevertheless paid attention to trajectories in thought and practice derived from the traditions of the representation of the estates.

The dimension of deliberation refers to a characteristic of parliament that is founded on the basic principle of a debating assembly, in utramque partem disputare. The construction of the distinct parliamentary form of procedure consisting of questions dealt with systematically from opposite perspectives and disputed between the members marked a procedural and institutional innovation that was unknown in the ancient and medieval forums of deliberative rhetoric. In a parliament, the opponents sit in the same auditorium; they are insiders, not outsiders – every speech is persuasively structured and every vote is a challenge to existing political configurations. The principles of a free mandate, free speech, freedom from arrest (parliamentary immunity) and free elections are preconditions for the proper functioning of a deliberative assembly. Parliamentary 'government by speaking' (Thomas Babington Macaulay) is opposed to violent confrontation as well as to silent assemblies that have only the right to vote: the parliamentary vote is the last act in the process of deliberation. Parliaments are thus also conceptually opposed to the notion of merely ratifying assemblies.

The main topics of controversies pertaining to the deliberative dimension of parliament are related to such matters as the procedures for setting the parliamentary agenda, the relationship between the government and parliament and the relationship between the plenum and the committees. Further issues can include such topics as the fair distribution of parliamentary speaking times, the powers of the Speaker regarding, for example, the demarcation between free speech and unparliamentary conduct, the rhetorical styles of parliamentary speaking, manners of addressing members in parliament and the recognition of the existence of parties without turning parliament into a mere 'congress of ambassadors' (Edmund Burke).

The sovereignty of a parliament is historically opposed to the royal or presidential prerogatives and to the interpretative power of the courts of law over parliamentary decisions, as legitimized by the doctrine of the separation of powers. The current theoretical debate concerns the compatibility of parliamentary sovereignty with written constitutions and extra-parliamentary vs. intra-parliamentary modes of resolving constitutional disputes. Arguments over parliamentary sovereignty have also arisen in neo-corporative contexts with regard to the imposition of extra-parliamentary decisions (involving labour-market partners and various kinds of lobbyists) on parliaments, leaving it with a merely ratifying role. The intra-parliamentary dimension of sovereignty disputes concerns the demarcation of powers between parliaments. The sovereignty thesis has been applied to national parliaments, while sub- and supranational assemblies have not been treated as parliaments proper by scholars or politicians. With the relativization of national sovereignty in relation to both supra- and sub-national units, the main issue regards the parliamentary forms of deliberation and decision-making in any representative and responsible assembly, and the relations of the parliament to the government and the judiciary. Of special interest here is, of course, the European Parliament, whose increasing powers are, however, far from sovereign (see Chapter 18).

The responsibility of the government to the parliament is the key political issue in the history of parliamentarism in that it distinguishes parliamentary from non-parliamentary regimes. The power to exert budgetary control and to both elect and dismiss a government represent the main steps in the history of the parliamentarization of government. In this respect, parliamentary government is also opposed to plebiscitary procedures, which submit parliamentary decisions to referenda. A majoritarian interpretation of parliamentary government, which holds election results to be decisive, contains a presidential dimension in the election of the prime minister and attempts to reduce the parliament to a merely ratifying institution (acclamatio). Multiparty coalition governments insist on negotiation between parties, which tends to limit the political freedom of members. By contrast, a more deliberative view insists on the parliamentary control and accountability of the administration and the powers of the members of parliament as a counterweight to the government and the administration.

Naming Parliaments

Parliament is usually a common noun and very seldom the proper name of a parliament. The different aspects of the conceptual struggle have been projected onto the names of national parliaments. Parlamentum has been known as a name for negotiations between powerful men since the twelfth century. It, of course, refers to speaking – *parlare* in Italian, *parler* in French – although *parlementaire* originally referred to a negotiator between parties in war and diplomacy. It took a long time for parliaments to evolve from contingent occasions to regular and recurrent assemblies of members and even longer for their members to become elected representatives.

The estate assemblies are called diets, a word derived from the Latin *dies* (day) and originally meaning the day(s) of assembly. The same kind of derivation is still represented today in the German Landtag and Bundestag and the Swedish Riksdag. The Dutch Staten-Generaal and the Spanish Cortes originally referred to the names of estate assemblies but have been retained for the modern parliaments. The nomenclature referring to assemblies – *Assemblée nationale*, *Nationalvergadering*, *Nationalversammlung* and the like – refers to the meeting itself, with an interesting nuance that the Weimar 1919 assembly was at the same time a constituent assembly and an 'ordinary' parliament. The old Scandinavian *ting* – out of which the Danish Folketing, Norwegian Storting, Icelandic Allting (all assemblies composed of 'the people') and Lagting of the autonomous Faroe Islands and the Åland Islands are derived – originally referred to an assembly that debated public affairs and not to a court of law as in later times. The Russian Duma has a similar connotation.

The U.S. House of Representatives refers even more explicitly than national assembly to the 'representative' character of the assembly, as does the Finnish Eduskunta. The names of the chambers refer to those who are represented, although the word 'senate' (derived from the ancient Roman name for the assembly of the nobles, senatus, which literally meant a council of elders – seniores) is still used in the United States, France, Italy and Belgium, for example, and it sometimes even has a higher qualification age than the 'lower house'. The fact that the 'lower' or 'popular' house (sometimes also the 'second' chamber, as in the case of the Dutch Tweede Kamer), as a rule, is more powerful than the higher one (the U.S. House of Representatives is the great exception) is an interesting move of paradiastolic redescription (in the sense of Skinner 2007). Or, in Walter Bagehot's terms, the upper house refers to the 'dignified' and the lower to the 'efficient' aspect of parliamentary politics.

The advisory nomenclature of 'council' is seldom used for parliamentary institutions, although monarchs, in particular, sought to retain them as consultative institutions for a long time. Rather, the vocabulary refers to governmental institutions, including slightly paradoxically the soviets, which originated as workers' councils, *Arbeiterräte*, etc. However, as a result of the rejection of the division between executive and parliamentary powers, the Soviets adopted a title corresponding to the council of royal advisors, and were soon reduced to an advisory position in relation to the party and the state administration.

If we insist on the political control of government and administration, parliament seems a better name than the other alternatives. Using Alfred O. Hirschman's terminology (1970), a parliament expresses a voice, as opposed to exit (non-voting, boycott of parliamentary sittings, used for example by the Sinn Fein members in Britain after 1919) and loyalty (acclamation) as alternative modes of acting.

Analysing Parliamentarism as a Way to Understand Europe

This volume is one of a series titled *European Conceptual Histories*. We argued in the beginning that both parliament as an institution and the parliamentary style of politics are distinctively European. The origins of the parliamentary style of politics lie in the historical formation of specific parliamentary procedures, rhetorical cultures and later forms of government, first in England/ Britain since the early modern period and then in France from the Revolution of 1789 onwards. In some countries (the Netherlands, Sweden, Finland and Poland) the early modern estate diets were transformed into parliaments after the late eighteenth century, and major conceptual revisions and inter-parliamentary transfers were also involved in these processes.

The nineteenth century was a period that saw the introduction and reform of national parliaments throughout much of Europe. By the 1920s practically every European country had had an experience of at least rudimentary parliamentary institutions. The powers of parliaments were fiercely debated both in parliamentary and non-parliamentary regimes, especially during the 'crisis of parliamentarism' in the 1920s and 1930s. The revival of parliaments was, however, a major feature of the breakdown of fascist and communist dictatorships in 1945, the 1970s and from 1989 to 1990. Re-parliamentarization offers a fresh perspective on the comparative conceptual history of the overthrow of dictatorships (see Chapter 12 as well as Ilie 2010b and Ornatowski 2010). Furthermore, the attempted parliamentarization of the EU can also be analysed from this perspective. International networks have also been created recently for the strengthening of parliaments as an inherent part of development programmes: the Europeans continue to export the idea of parliament and parliamentarism beyond their own continent.

The parliamentary regime can legitimately be seen as characteristically European: outside Europe, with the exception of most former British colonies, the presidential model of democracy without parliamentary responsibility and sovereignty prevails, and also the procedure of dissensual deliberation is mostly viewed with suspicion. The debate between parliamentary, presidential or semi-presidential (France) and semi-plebiscitarian regimes (Switzerland) has been one of the main dividing issues in European politics from the nineteenth century onwards.

Most Europeans today share a legacy of government by representation and discussion. Historically, the tacit and gradual formation of a specific parliamentary manner of deliberation, debate and decision-making has created a distinct parliamentary procedure. It has distinguished parliamentary and unparliamentary forms of conduct and speech and created a distinct parliamentary vocabulary by producing new, specifically parliamentary terms and by giving other words and phrases a distinctly parliamentary meaning. The main features of parliamentary procedure are widely shared by all parliamentary regimes and to a large extent by non-sovereign parliaments and assemblies. In short, parliamentary culture(s) with largely shared albeit contested concepts at the same time provide occasions for strategic innovations and national variations in the parliamentary use of these concepts throughout Europe. Parliaments can, furthermore, serve as a model for various fields of political culture with regard to the conduct of meetings and debating. Parliaments are a European cultural feature of primary importance.

Owing to growing collaboration between national and European institutions, the role of national parliaments in the process of consolidating a common European public sphere and the convergence of integrationist goals have been further reinforced. Through institutionally and culturally based communication practices, members of national parliaments and members of the European Parliament contribute to discursively shaping and reshaping their own nations' relationship with past, present and future European values.

Updating Conceptual History through Parliamentary Studies

In the existing conceptual historical lexica such as the German *Geschichtliche Grundbegriffe. Historisches Lexikon zur politisch-sozialen Sprache in Deutschland* (8 vols: Brunner, Conze and Koselleck 1972–97), or in almost any other national project in conceptual history, studies on parliament and parliamentarism have been lacking or hidden behind other concepts such as representation or democracy. Both the traditional history of political thought and social history, which have shaped the existing versions of conceptual history, have shown little interest in parliaments or in the cluster of concepts that define them. However, parliamentarism is for conceptual history, as a highly language-conscious approach to the analysis of political history and theory, a central topic for research, as it has largely been based on speaking and active debate by past political actors. Conceptual history can make visible the dynamics of parliamentary debate as well as the variety of views on the current problematics, which the discursive processes in parliaments have produced.

Histories of parliaments have mainly remained at a national level, bypassing comparisons and transnational transfers and ignoring conceptual aspects, preferring to focus on structures, functions, events, ceremonies and so on. The regime aspect of parliamentarism has tended to be studied rather narrowly in constitutional law and political science, while linguistic, discourse and rhetorical studies have used parliamentary debates mainly to illustrate some general problems of discussion and debate. The emerging new studies on the cultural history of parliaments (especially in the Netherlands) and political communication (especially in Germany), though highly interesting, do not usually focus on parliamentary debate and concepts and their histories.

Based on historical, discourse and political theory analysis, this volume concentrates on the key vocabulary of parliamentary politics in relation to parliament itself as well as its quasi-synonyms and antonyms. It discusses the four conceptual dimensions of parliament delineated in the initial thesis of this introductory chapter, as well as a representative repertoire of concepts and terms indicative of the major controversies relating to the conceptual history of parliament itself. The key concepts of parliamentarism and the repertoire of related concepts have offered us signposts for identifying significant debates on these concepts in parliaments themselves and for searching for exceptional but noteworthy uses of these concepts in parliamentary debates and in parliament-related publications. The relative (though far from complete) similarities between the specific parliamentary concepts across national political cultures make it easier to apply them in a comparative analysis across different languages and official rules and regulations.

Parliamentary debates themselves, especially digitized ones whenever available, serve as primary sources for the conceptual analysis of parliamentarism, whether viewed from the point of view of history, discourse research or political theory. The main advantage of using parliamentary sources in conceptual history is that in parliamentary debates concepts are used as 'moves in argument' (Skinner 1988: 283), and they become topical only when they are disputed. Thus parliamentary concepts are an integral part of controversies about parliamentarism. Conceptual historical studies are part of the rhetorical analysis of debates, but they concentrate on the conceptual controversies, analysing them from historical and comparative perspectives and rendering them explicit (see Ihalainen and Palonen 2009).

The availability of public parliamentary records in most European countries (often in a recently digitized form) offers promising new opportunities for a comparative conceptual history of parliaments. The main 'methodological' problem for conceptual histories of parliament and parliamentary concepts lies in the huge extent of the available primary sources. The subject indexes of the printed works and the search engines of the online textual corpora can, of course, simplify the task. Conceptual historical research based on parliamentary documents requires above all a distinct 'parliamentary literacy' that focuses on the formal and procedural character of parliamentary debate, the item that is being studied, previous debates, key concepts, discursive practices, long-term theoretical debates and the like. Such a literacy provides more general guidelines on what disputes to study, how to read parliamentary sources and how to reflect on this reading in the framework of a conceptual historical study.

Another methodological challenge lies in connecting the case studies (on a national, regional or linguistic areal basis) with the general topoi of parliamentarization. Our aim is to link the case studies to the main problematics both by comparing national similarities and differences with general European trends and by contrasting the studies with those of other national cases – both closely related and highly divergent ones. The objects of comparison can then be national political cultures and historical periods and also the dimensions of the concept of parliamentarism and the three disciplinary aspects (historical, discursive and theoretical) of the analysis of parliamentary politics to which this volume is devoted. Through such contrasts and parallels, the chapters of this book reveal different profiles of the parliamentary concepts and the different rhythms of their historical change, rather than merely presenting national or regional histories with a parliamentary emphasis. The result is, we hope, not a history of national parliamentary institutions in Europe, but a conceptual and rhetorical history of European parliamentarism.

Furthermore, by concentrating as far as possible on parliamentarians' reflection on the character and political role of parliament and parliamentarism, we can search for typical instances of potential conceptual change. Disputes on parliamentary, constitutional and electoral reforms together with votes of no confidence often offer major occasions of debate. Similarly, debates based on governmental statements to parliaments, on the organization of parliamentary procedures themselves and on the status of members of parliament serve as further paradigmatic situations of conceptual dispute that are of particular importance for the conceptual history of parliamentarism. Debates of this character have been regularly, or at least occasionally, conducted in all European parliaments, and they involve the different dimensions of parliamentary politics. On the other hand, any item on the parliamentary agenda can give rise to conceptual debates, and the goal of the various case studies has been to detect some of the most significant controversies relating to parliamentarism.

Complementary to parliamentary debates and documents as sources for the conceptual history of parliament are other contemporary extra-parliamentary texts. In addition to academic, journalistic and literary writings, we can mention textbooks on rhetoric, and 'manuals' like William Gerard Hamilton's *Parliamentary Logic* (1927 [1808]). They can explain the significance of some parliamentary debates or the conceptual struggles involved in them; on the other hand, the conceptual innovations and revisions contained in debates can be better analysed by focusing on the debates themselves. Academic discussions and subsequent studies of parliamentary institutions may be valuable for the conceptualization of parliamentary changes that were not properly understood by the contemporary agents themselves.

Summary of the Idea of the Book

In the following three parts and their respective chapters, the key elements of parliamentarism – representation, deliberation, sovereignty and responsibility – will be analysed by means of empirically oriented research in the disciplines of history, discourse analysis and political theory. Owing to the lack of any existing comprehensive diachronic or synchronic analyses of the conceptual history of parliament and the key parliamentary concepts, the present volume inevitably has the character of an overview. The purpose is both to review existing research and other forms of available information (mainly in parliamentary records) on the conceptual history of parliament in a synthesizing manner, and to reconsider the distinct history and specific political significance of the concept of parliament and thereby open up vistas for further research on the conceptual history of parliament and parliamentarism.

Note on Translations

All translations are by the authors if not otherwise indicated.

References

Bayley, P. (ed.). 2004. *Cross-cultural Perspectives on Parliamentary Discourse.* Amsterdam and Philadelphia: John Benjamins.

Brunner, O., W. Conze and R. Koselleck (eds). 1972–97. *Geschichtliche Grundbegriffe. Historisches Lexikon zur politisch-sozialen Sprache in Deutschland*, 8 vols. Stuttgart: Klett-Cotta.

Clinchamps, N. 2006. *Parlement Européen et droit parlementaire. Essai sur la naissance du droit parlementaire de l'Union Européenne.* Paris: LGDJ.

Feuchter, J. and J. Helmrath (eds). 2013. *Parlamentarische Kulturen vom Mittelalter bis in die Moderne. Reden – Räume – Bilder.* Düsseldorf: Droste Verlag.

Finlayson, A. 2012. 'Rhetoric and the Political Theory of Ideologies', *Political Studies* 60(4): 751–67.

Galembert, C. de, O. Rozenberg and C. Vigour (eds). 2014. *Faire parler le parlement. Méthodes et enjeux de l'analyse des débats parlementaires pour les sciences sociales.* Paris: LGDJ.

Gusy, C. 2008. *Demokratie in der Krise. Europa in der Zwischenkriegszeit.* Baden-Baden: Nomos.

Hamilton, W.G. (1927 [1808]). *Parliamentary Logic, with an Introduction and Notes by Courtney S. Kenny.* Cambridge: Heffer.

Hirschman, A.O. 1970. *Exit, Voice, and Loyalty: Responses to Decline in Firms, Organizations, and States.* Cambridge, MA: Harvard University Press.

Ihalainen, P. and K. Palonen. 2009. 'Parliamentary Sources in the Comparative Study of Conceptual History: Methodological Aspects and Illustrations of a Research Proposal', *Parliaments, Estates & Representation* 29(1): 17–34.

Ilie, C. (ed.). 2010a. *European Parliaments under Scrutiny: Discourse Strategies and Interaction Practices.* Amsterdam: John Benjamins.

Ilie, C. 2010b. 'Managing Dissent and Interpersonal Relations in the Romanian Parliamentary Discourse', in C. Ilie (ed.), *European Parliaments under Scrutiny: Discourse Strategies and Interaction Practices.* Amsterdam: John Benjamins, pp. 193–222.

Michelsen, D. and F. Walter. 2013. *Unpolitische Demokratie. Zur Krise der Repräsentation.* Berlin: Suhrkamp.

Ornatowski, C.M. 2010. 'Parliamentary Discourse and Political Transition: Polish Parliament after 1989', in C. Ilie (ed.), *European Parliaments under Scrutiny: Discourse Strategies and Interaction Practices.* Amsterdam: John Benjamins, pp. 223–64.

Palonen, K. 2014. *The Politics of Parliamentary Procedure: The Westminster Procedure as a Parliamentary Ideal Type.* Leverkusen/London: Budrich.

Palonen, K., J.M. Rosales and T. Turkka (eds). 2014. *The Politics of Dissensus: Parliament in Debate.* Santander: McGraw Hill and University of Cantabria Press.

Patzelt, W. (ed.). 2005. *Parlamente und ihre Macht.* Baden-Baden: Nomos.

Patzelt, W. (ed.). 2012. *Parlamente und ihre Evolution.* Baden-Baden: Nomos.

Patzelt, W. and S. Dreischer (eds). 2009. *Parlamente und ihre Zeit.* Baden-Baden: Nomos.

Roussellier, N. 1997. *Le parlement d'éloquence.* Paris: Sciences-po.

Sanchez, S. 2012. *Les règlements des Assemblées nationales 1848–1851. Naissance du droit parlementaire moderne.* Paris: Dalloz.

Saward, M. 2010. *The Representative Claim.* Oxford: Oxford University Press.

Schulz, A. and A. Wirsching (eds). 2012. *Parlamentarische Kulturen in Europa. Das Parlament als Kommunikationsraum.* Düsseldorf: Droste Verlag.

Skinner, Q. 1988. 'A Reply to My Critics', in J. Tully (ed.), *Meaning and Context: Quentin Skinner and His Critics.* Cambridge: Polity, pp. 231–88.

Skinner, Q. 2007. 'Paradiastole: Redescribing the Vices as Virtues', in S. Adamson, G. Alexander and K. Ettenhuber (eds), *Renaissance Figures of Speech.* Cambridge: Cambridge University Press, pp. 147–63.

Urbinati, N. 2006. *Representative Democracy: Concept and Genealogy.* Chicago: University of Chicago Press.

Part I
The Conceptual History of Parliaments

Chapter 1

European Parliamentary Experiences from a Conceptual Historical Perspective

Pasi Ihalainen

The chapters in Part I of this volume (Chapters 1 to 7) aim at a deeper historical understanding of the formation of parliamentarism as a key concept in modern European political cultures. Their starting point is that the common European tradition of parliamentary political cultures can be better understood through comparative diachronic analyses of parliamentary experiences and the uses of the vocabulary of parliamentarism in political argumentation in various national contexts and in various historical periods since the French Revolution. We aim at estimating the degree of parliamentarism in various historical contexts from the contemporaries' point of view.

The plural form 'parliamentarisms' is used here because a singular form would be oversimplifying for the purposes of historical analysis, given the essentially national character of most parliaments, parliamentary experiences and applications of parliamentarism (cf. Ihalainen, Ilie and Palonen and Chapter 13 in this volume, where a different perspective to the history of parliament by means of the concept of ideal type is presented). Even if our cooperative comparative history in this part aims at generalizations about European parliamentary history based on several contextualized case studies focusing on national contexts, it is important to keep in mind the specificities of various national developments and the versions of 'parliament' and 'parliamentarism' experienced in various times and places. From the point of view of empirically rather than theoretically oriented conceptual history, parliamentarism is not a stable, definable and teleological phenomenon, but rather represents interconnected long-term and multisited discursive processes characterized by contestation. These processes have gradually led to the phenomenon we call parliamentarism today – though the political concept still remains contested and varied in meaning.

Historians – aware of the often unique nature of historical developments and of the context-related meanings of concepts as used in particular arguments in past political discourses – remain suspicious of excessive abstractions and attempts to formulate universal concepts (Haupt and Kocka 2004: 24–26). Hence, they also remain cautious when making generalizations about the history of parliamentarism. Educated and working within the paradigms of national history, they have usually studied the history of one parliamentary institution and may remain unwilling to compare it with others. Given the individualistic traditions of historiography, it is far from easy to integrate the research work and interpretations of even two historians dealing with the same parliament – let alone the analyses of two or more national representative institutions. The assumption of the exceptionalism of every national parliament has been a major hindrance to writing a joint European history of parliamentarisms thus far. Generalizations at the European level need to be based on national cases, to be sure, but it is timely to say something more about the long-term conceptual history of European parliamentarisms as well. Parliamentary history seems, indeed, to be moving more generally towards comparative studies – and hopefully also towards transnational parliamentary history (te Velde 2006; Ihalainen 2013a; Ihalainen and Saarinen 2015; the problems of generalizations and the potential, but in many ways limited, transnational influence of parliamentary models will also be discussed in a future volume on 'The Ideal Parliament', based on a EuParl.net conference held in The Hague in 2013.)

Even if empirically oriented conceptual history cannot be based on any supposedly universal concept of parliamentarism, the ideal typical approach in the theoretical part (Part III) of this work has encouraged us to formulate initial theses on parliamentarisms, the validity of which has then been tested in various national contexts. We do not apply any structural explanations of parliamentarism often favoured in earlier studies, especially in the field of law, or focus on parliamentary culture or communication in general as more recent parliamentary history in several countries has done, but distinctly focus on the linguistic aspects of past experiences of parliamentarisms. We aim at what Quentin Skinner has characterized as 'seeing things their way' (Skinner 2002: vii) – i.e., locating debates among parliamentarians and other participants in discourses concerning the key features of parliament in their proper intellectual and discursive contexts in order to conclude exactly what the speakers were doing in putting forward a certain argument that defined parliament or some of its key features in a particular way. Such a social constructivist point of departure emphasizes an awareness of the essentially contingent nature of the historical development of European representative institutions. However, it needs to be pointed out that parliamentary history as practised by many of the leading experts contributing to Part I has been institutional history and that these authors have been persuaded by the current editor to include conceptual aspects in their analyses. The intention has been to build on existing scholarship on parliaments as institutions and to create a bridge between more conventional parliamentary history and the linguistically conscious approaches used in this volume.

The fact that most present-day European political systems are based on parliamentary democracy should not allow us to presume that this state of affairs is somehow an unavoidable outcome of the development of the last two or three centuries, or that parliamentarisms are now finalized or established. Parliamentarisms should rather be seen as both diachronic and synchronic, discursive and competitive processes with transnational dimensions that have taken place in different times and places and also simultaneously in interconnected contexts: a variety of politicians and theorists have conceptualized parliament, constructing, reproducing and contesting parliamentarisms in interaction with each other and the discursive political process. Competing understandings of parliamentarisms can be seen in the conceptual struggles that are to be found in the primary sources (Skinner 2002: 125, 176–77; Halonen, Ihalainen and Saarinen 2015; Ihalainen and Saarinen 2015).

One way to avoid the application of teleologies and anachronistic terms and interpretations to parliamentary history – in other words, of writing a traditional 'Whiggish' history of the success story of parliamentarism – is to critically estimate in each national case when the past contributors to the debate actually started to use the concept of parliamentarism and related vocabulary – i.e., when they started to talk about representation, sovereignty, responsibility and deliberation in various national languages. Instead of identifying the exact timings of some 'breakthroughs' in national discourses on parliamentarism, however, our goal is to demonstrate general European trends, to compare the pace of change in various national contexts and to estimate influences and transfers between the national systems of parliamentarism. While this general history of the European concept of parliamentarism(s) is constituted by the separate histories of several essentially national institutions, these histories have been interconnected in multiple ways through often tendentious cross references and comparisons in parliamentary discourse and by the selective adaptation of parliamentary models borrowed from other countries.

The history part comprises six national or regional (combining the Low Countries and Scandinavia) case studies of discursive processes that have defined parliamentarisms in some formative historical periods. These cases demonstrate how the initial thesis of this volume, introduced in the introductory chapter, of parliamentarisms being constituted by representation, sovereignty, responsibility and deliberation seems to work in various national contexts, and they reveal which alternative converging or diverging themes and concepts have appeared in the historical debate on parliamentarisms.

Comparative and Transnational History on the Basis of National Case Studies

The comparisons presented here are based on contextualized nation-state-centred studies that provide representative examples of some major trends in the history of European parliamentary experiences. This approach admittedly represents a more traditional way of writing comparative history through collected works on national cases, rather than a project in which the same team explores exactly the same extensive comparative material transnationally. When national cases are analysed separately by individual authors there exists the risk of semantic confusion. We have tried to avoid this by focusing systematically on the features of parliamentarisms defined by the initial thesis of this volume and by discussing the preliminary results based on parallel sources, in a series of workshops and in the course of the editing process. The national cases represent long-term macro-level surveys rather than detailed micro analyses. The explored cases build on a combination of previous research and the use of extensive corpora of parliamentary debates, making it possible to point to specific features in national histories of parliamentary experiences and draw conclusions on the extent and limits of transnational elements of parliamentarisms.

The national cases discussed include the rather unique institution of the English/British parliament between the English and the French Revolutions. The development of the Westminster system is certainly the best-known case internationally, but it has not necessarily provided any dominant model for the formation of parliamentary government in the rest of Europe. British historians themselves have tended to emphasize the exceptional nature of the British form of parliamentarism and its linkage to their particular political culture (see Chapter 9 for the pre-revolutionary period). However, a conceptual analysis of the formation of the seventeenth- and eighteenth-century British conceptions of parliament, placed in a chronology of other parliamentarisms, helps to relate this exceptional institution to a broader European pattern.

The French version of parliamentarism has since the Revolution of 1789 offered an alternative to the British model, even if it has also adopted elements of the Westminster model. A further key national case of parliamentarism is provided by Germany as a relative latecomer. Germany is a country where the contestation of parliamentarism reached particularly high levels and many problems of parliamentarism were concretely felt. Turns in the history of German parliamentarism have, furthermore, also affected other latecomers in Northern and Eastern European countries.

Elsewhere in this volume, the formation of parliamentarisms in Spain, Italy and Central and Eastern Europe are discussed from an historical perspective that is relevant for this part of the book as well. In the rest of the historically oriented chapters we have chosen to focus, side by side with the three European great powers, on three comparisons of national cases that reveal interesting contrasts between culturally related smaller countries or between Western and Eastern European understandings of parliamentarism: the Low Countries, Scandinavia and Russia. The Netherlands and Belgium have experienced two varieties of parliamentarism, which, while interrelated through language, historical experiences and their selective application or rejection of foreign (mainly British and French) models have yet been interestingly different in terms of political culture. The Belgian case has also provided models for other parliamentary reformists to follow. Scandinavian histories of parliamentarism, largely unknown outside the Nordic countries despite their considerable length, deserve attention because of their historical originality and the centrality of the tradition of representative government in the formation of specifically Nordic political cultures. Russia, finally, has conventionally appeared as 'the other' in European political history, and even more so in parliamentary history. It is important to understand what kinds of differing meanings the concepts of parliamentarism have received in Russian political discourse in connection with early and late twentieth-century attempts to introduce elements of parliamentarism to Russia. Such a contrast, if anything, reflects the national nature of parliamentarism in the wider European context and helps to relativize any strictly defined concept of parliamentarism.

Empirical Starting Points

The authors of the historically oriented chapters of Part I (Chapters 1 to 7) analyse the concepts of parliament and parliamentarism on the basis of the political debate that has surrounded and taken place within parliaments. In most of these chapters, parliamentary debates themselves – side by side with other primary texts commenting on parliaments and secondary literature –

have been used for reconstructing a variety of past experiences and conceptions of the institution. Some authors have been able to proceed to the analysis of a more multisited discourse on parliaments, but this has depended on the availability of digitized parliamentary and press sources in each national case. The chapters are meant to provide surveys of the current state of research and to illustrate the main trends in the history of parliamentarisms by means of a few representative examples. They test the potential of conceptual history for future parliamentary history; more extensive empirical analyses have been or will be presented elsewhere.

What distinguishes the approaches of the chapters of Part I from the other parts is that they are based on empirical historical research and written primarily by historians. The chapters build on traditional historical research on parliaments as institutions, although they also address questions that are of interest to linguists and political theorists as well; this is a result of the effect of the linguistic and discursive turns in the human sciences and of an awareness of ongoing theoretical debates on parliamentarism. The different parts of this work thus proceed from empirical research on parliamentary history to analyses of parliamentary discourse and finally to political theories of parliamentarism.

While the parliamentary concepts of sovereignty, responsibility, representation and deliberation have been the starting points for research for the chapters, other important concepts contributing to parliamentarisms – such as publicity – have emerged in the process of research on national parliaments. The authors have discussed these concepts insofar as they have turned out to be relevant for particular national cases. Whereas sovereignty, representation and responsibility have already been discussed to some extent in previous research on constitutional history, focusing on deliberation has given rise to some interesting findings that link the parts of this volume.

The authors were asked to concentrate their analyses on debates concerning more controversial, disputed aspects of parliamentary concepts rather than produce a more traditional constitutional history of the structures, practical functioning or rituals of parliaments, even though previous studies on such themes provide invaluable contexts for the more debate-focused analyses provided here. As far as the history of parliamentary events is concerned, only basic information with direct contextual relevance has been provided. By focusing on the often disputed nature of parliament and parliamentarism, we wish to provide fresh perspectives for future parliamentary and conceptual history. The discursive character of parliamentary processes has not previously been emphasized so much in parliamentary history – even though oratory and debate have traditionally been understood as lying at the heart of parliaments as institutions (see Part II). As far as conceptual history is concerned, we argue that it could be developed into a concrete multidisciplinary research realized in cooperation with discourse studies and political science, and could perhaps thereby be also developed towards genuinely international comparisons and the analysis of transnational processes of cross-cultural transfers as well as hindrances to such transfers.

In the rest of this introduction, the focus will not only be on general trends in European parliamentary history but also on transnational debates and transfers, and transitions and translations of parliamentary concepts between various national contexts. Discussing the shared and divergent features of various European parliamentarisms on a more abstract and generalizing level may reveal alternative forms of development, challenge national historiographies and demonstrate that the national cases are perhaps not quite so unique and self-evident as has been presumed.

Long-term Trends of European Parliamentarisms

The themes uniting most national histories of parliamentarism that deserve attention include: (i) the timing and the central conceptual changes of the transition from early modern estates representing particular interests and based on an imperative mandate, to the representation of the people by sovereign parliaments with a free mandate; (ii) the timing and major conceptual transformations involved in the transition from the notion of the duality of government and parliament to parliamentary democracy based on governmental responsibility to parliament; (iii) the transnational significance of the competing key models of European parliamentarism; and (iv) the relationship between parliamentary deliberation and publicity. I shall next briefly discuss each of these features, drawing on chapters throughout the book but mainly in Part I.

The Timing and Central Conceptual Features of the Transition from Early Modern Estates to the Parliamentary Representation of the People

Owing to its medieval roots and the need to adapt itself to changing historical contexts, the English parliament had to address several key issues of parliamentary government earlier than most other European representative institutions (see Chapter 9). British parliamentary government in the seventeenth and eighteenth centuries was characterized by continuity and a very gradual change in the key concepts that defined it. The notions of the sovereignty and the representation of the people in Parliament remained disputed and ambiguous but tended nevertheless to be increasingly seen as essential features of the institution. While the implementation of parliamentary representation gave rise to questions and suspicion among the public throughout the period, the notion of Parliament as the representative of the people gained ground among parliamentarians from the 1640s onwards, and again in the demands of the reformists after the 1770s. The notion of the accountability of ministers to Parliament also gradually strengthened in the course of the eighteenth century; the 1740s and the 1780s being turning points towards increasingly recognized accountability. And by the 1770s, deliberation had become a further key concept defining the essence of Parliament (Chapter 2).

Since the French Revolution, impulses towards parliamentary government on the European continent have increasingly originated from France; Britain was sometimes seen as a hypothetical model country for criticisms of domestic circumstances but its political culture was rarely regarded as directly applicable to continental countries. The French National Assembly, on the other hand, was not at first called a parliament, and even though prohibited in 1789, the imperative mandate was reintroduced in the spirit of direct democracy in 1793 and remained a possibility in French theoretical debate until the late nineteenth century. Suffrage and thereby representation were widened considerably in France in 1848, but the duality of government was maintained by establishing first a balancing presidency and later an imperial throne (Chapter 3).

The French and the British parliamentary systems became major objects of comparison for German states in the course of the nineteenth century, starting from southern Germany. However, early nineteenth-century German parliaments tended to be characterized by a continuation of the practices of the early modern estate assemblies. Until 1919 and even in the Weimar Republic, the German political system – and many political cultures in the north of Europe – was characterized by the duality of government and parliament, albeit with an emphasis on the executive. The significance of parliamentary assemblies was based on extended representation thanks to the early introduction of universal male suffrage and also on the increase of publicity after 1848. Parliaments were forums for public debate, albeit ones limited by the strong anti-parliamentary tendencies of the Prussian political culture. Even after the parliamentarization and further democratization of the German political system as a consequence of the First World War, the dualism of the political system and anti-parliamentary public discourse survived (Chapter 4).

In Scandinavia, two divergent political traditions coexisted: the Swedish-Finnish model, built on an evolution of early modern traditions of representative government, and Danish absolutism, after the fall of which traditions of representative government needed to be constructed in Norway after 1814 and in Denmark after 1849. Until increasing British and French influences took effect in the late nineteenth century, there was a tendency to avoid calling the national representative institution a parliament. The traditional German model of the duality of government and parliament remained dominant in Sweden until 1919 and also in Finland in the republican constitution after 1919 (Chapter 6).

If notions of representation, parliamentarism and democracy have been effectively nationalized and redefined somewhere, that is certainly the case in Russia. The limited influence of the early twentieth-century imperial Duma was further diminished by the strongly anti-parliamentary views of the Bolshevik revolutionaries, who rejected parliaments as bourgeois institutions. The political role of the new Duma since the 1990s is likewise defined in ways that tend to decrease its parliamentary dimensions in any Western European sense and emphasize a characteristically Russian notion of a national parliament (Chapter 7).

The Transition to Parliamentary Democracy

While the duality of political power in a mixed government has remained a central principle in the British constitution as well, the supremacy of Parliament in relation to the monarchy has become stronger since the late seventeenth century and was rarely questioned after the 1770s (Chapter 2). British nineteenth-century parliamentary history was characterized by a gradual extension of representation and ministerial responsibility, despite simultaneous anti-parliamentary tendencies. British government was parliamentarized in the aftermath of the Reform of 1832 (Chapter 14), but the real democratization of Parliament took place only as a result of the concentration of parliamentary sovereignty in the Commons with the Parliament Act of 1911 and the introduction of universal suffrage with the Representation of the People Act of 1918.

In the French Third Republic, an extensive parliamentary government based on governmental responsibility was established in 1875; parliamentarism was so extensive that the French system became a typical object of anti-parliamentary criticism (Chapter 3). In the Netherlands, the notion of the sovereignty of the people had, following the French revolutionary model, been included in the constitution of the Batavian Republic, and the National Assembly replaced the early modern Staten-Generaal in the late 1790s, but no effective parliamentary sovereignty developed during this short-lived experiment. Later Dutch constitutions and parliamentarians rather emphasized continuity with the old Dutch Republic, never explicitly referred to popular sovereignty and remained suspicious of democracy and the word 'parliament' as well – despite the gradual democratization and parliamentarization of the Dutch polity after around 1900. In Belgium, where the French influence was stronger, the sovereignty of the people was already presented as the supreme authority in the constitution of 1831. Ministerial responsibility was adopted in Belgium in this instrument, earlier than in any other written constitution. Belgian electoral practices and active 'parliamentary' life (explicitly so called) provided innovative models for other European parliaments, especially at the turn of the nineteenth and twentieth centuries (Chapter 5).

In German theoretical and everyday political discourse, it remained difficult if not impossible to reconcile democracy and parliamentarism successfully until the founding of the Federal Republic. Parliamentarism was viewed as a Western export that was inapplicable to Germany. German socialist thinkers saw parliamentarism as having merely an instrumental value, a view that was influential in much of Northern Europe (Chapter 16). Nevertheless, in most countries Social Democrats adopted a more parliamentary strategy during and in the aftermath of the First World War, evidently as a reaction to the Russian Revolution.

In Scandinavia, Norway was an unexpected forerunner in the introduction of parliamentary government in 1884, challenging the Swedish system with which it was in union until 1905. Denmark followed in 1901, and Finland and Sweden in 1917. Until that time the duality of government with its limitations on parliamentary power was strong and overshadowed radical suffrage reforms such as those that were enacted in Finland in 1906, introducing a unicameral parliament and universal suffrage including women (Chapter 6).

The Westminster Model

While England had plenty of interaction with the Continent throughout the early modern period, conceptions of English exceptionalism survived and were strengthened after the Reformation. From the seventeenth century onwards, as a result of repeated confrontations between the monarchy and Parliament (see Chapter 9), which led to regicide and the declaration of a republic, the English political system, too, was increasingly seen as distinct from all continental versions. The English/British parliament was viewed as a unique institution hardly comparable with any other, and, consequently, comparisons between it and the estate assemblies in Sweden or Poland, for instance, were also rare in the eighteenth century and usually only provided warning examples serving the purposes of a particular argument (Ihalainen 2010). In later times, too, the use of transnational models in Britain has tended to be tactical rather than genuinely enthusiastic (Ihalainen 2014). French representative institutions after the Revolution, for instance, provided a point of comparison against which the British deliberative assembly could be defined. This differs distinctly from the role of the British parliament as an object of comparison – though rarely of direct imitation – on the continent. Many continental reformists were inspired by certain procedural features of Britain's parliamentary government and its lively parliamentary political culture as an idealized object of comparison, but they, too, tended to view Britain as exceptional.

The French Model

In continental Europe, the impact of the French model of parliamentary assemblies became considerable after the French Revolution. This impact was not based merely on the obvious cultural (and until 1814 political) dominance of France in many countries but also on the sheer availability of a wide variety of alternative constitutional settlements in France. After the less radical phase of the Revolution, the French parliamentary system began to adopt selected ideas from Britain, including the introduction of bicameralism in 1795 and calls for ministerial responsibility and an emphasis on deliberation after 1815. At the same time, the French model continued to be a trailblazer in reforms such as broadening representation through universal male suffrage and providing remuneration for parliamentarians in 1848. In its republican phases, French parliamentary development was also open to American influences (Chapter 3).

The French model inspired the introduction of representative government in many Italian states in the early nineteenth century, including brief experiments with parliamentary government in 1849, and the gradual extension of parliamentary power in relation to royal government in the late nineteenth century. Even more than in France, Italian parliamentarism remained an object of criticism, seen as an import from Britain and France rather than a result of a national evolution (Chapter 15). Likewise, in early nineteenth-century Spain, many opponents of parliamentary procedures and a new system of representation and ministerial responsibility saw them as being of British or French rather than of national origin; nevertheless, many features of modern parliamentarism were adopted there (Chapter 17). In both Italy and Spain, parliamentary democracies would need to be constructed on a new basis after twentieth-century experiences of fascism.

The Belgian and Norwegian Models

After the late nineteenth century, the Belgian parliamentary model evoked interest among reformers in several European countries, including Romania in 1866 (Chapter 12). According to Marnix Beyen, it was typical of parliamentary discourse everywhere to question rather than to emphasize the importance of foreign precedents and to appeal to (constructed) national traditions of representative government. Those who applied the Belgian model, for instance, might disregard its emphasis on the notion of popular sovereignty (Beyen 2013). Some of the seemingly transnational character of parliamentary discourse may, indeed, be misleading: parliaments provide parliamentarians of other countries with examples that serve their argument in particular domestic debates or that offer a practical model that is applicable to different national circumstances, but such borrowing does not necessarily constitute a transfer between political cultures.

Among the alternative models, that of the Norwegian constitution of 1814, which concentrated legislative powers in a unicameral parliament, should also be mentioned, even though it only had noteworthy impact on the reform debates in the neighbouring Scandinavian countries in the nineteenth and early twentieth centuries (Chapter 6).

The Relationship between Parliaments and Publicity

In Britain, there had been attempts to publish newspaper reports on parliamentary proceedings in the early eighteenth century, but the real breakthrough in parliamentary publicity took place after the 1770s – despite the continued desire of many MPs to protect the parliamentary privileges of secrecy. However, the views of the British political elite changed quite rapidly by comparison with their European counterparts, and Parliament came to be seen as a centre of political debate that was accountable to the public (Chapter 2; Ihalainen 2013b). In France, the first breakthrough of publicity coincided with the declaration of the sovereignty of the people by the National Constituent Assembly. In the nineteenth century, a further extension took place with an increase in the number of public hearings in the 1860s (Chapter 3) and the intensification of parliamentary reporting (Chapter 10). In late nineteenth-century Italy, too, theorists emphasized the need to connect parliamentary representation with increased publicity (Chapter 15).

In Germany, secrecy was dominant in parliamentary debates until the Frankfurt Parliament of 1848. In imperial Germany, the Reichstag, despite its limited powers, played the role of a major forum of public debate, and this media publicity became more extensive in the Weimar Republic, though it tended to lead to disappointment with, rather than respect for, parliament (Chapter 5). In the Netherlands, the publicity of parliamentary proceedings was introduced with the Batavian Republic, but the parliament remained a forum for an educated elite in the nineteenth century and did not become a popular institution among the population at large (Chapter 4). All in all, most Western European models of parliamentarism witnessed an extension of parliamentary representation and the connected growth of critical parliamentary publicity between the late eighteenth and early twentieth centuries. The relationship between parliaments and publicity remains symbiotic yet also characterized by constant tension.

References

Beyen, M. 2013. Comment in the EuParl.net Conference, The Hague, 1 June 2013.

Halonen, M., P. Ihalainen and T. Saarinen. 2015. 'Diverse Discourses in Time and Space: Historical, Discourse Analytical and Ethnographic Approaches to Multi-sited Language Policy Discourse', in M. Halonen, P. Ihalainen and T. Saarinen, *Language Policies in Finland and Sweden: Interdisciplinary and Multi-sited Comparison*. Bristol: Multilingual Matters, pp. 3–28.

Haupt, H.-G. and J. Kocka. 2004. 'Comparative History: Methods, Aims, Problems', in D. Cohen and M. O'Connor (eds), *Comparison and History: Europe in Cross-National Perspective*. New York and London: Routledge, pp. 23–39.

Ihalainen, P. 2010. *Agents of the People: Democracy and Popular Sovereignty in British and Swedish Parliamentary and Public Debates, 1734–1800*. Leiden: Brill Academic Publishers.

Ihalainen, P. 2013a. 'Vertaileva Euroopan historian tutkimus parlamenttihistorian näkökulmasta', *Tieteessä tapahtuu* 31(4): 30–35.

―――――. 2013b. 'Parlamentsdebatten und der Aufstieg ausserparlamentarischer Medien im späten 18. Jahrhundert. Schweden, Grossbritannien und die Niederlande', in J. Feuchter and J. Helmrath, *Parlamentarische Kulturen vom Mittelalter bis in die Moderne: Reden – Räume – Bilder*. Düsseldorf: Droste Verlag, pp. 97–113.

―――――. 2014. 'Prospects for Parliamentary Government in an Era of War and Revolution: Britain and Germany in Spring 1917', in K. Palonen, J.M. Rosales and T. Turkka (eds), *The Politics of Dissensus: Parliament in Debate*. Santander: Cantabria University Press and McGraw Hill, pp. 423–48.

Ihalainen, P. and T. Saarinen. 2015. 'Constructing "Language" in Language Policy Discourse: Finnish and Swedish Legislative Processes in the 2000s', in M. Halonen, P. Ihalainen and T. Saarinen, *Language Policies in Finland and Sweden: Interdisciplinary and Multi-sited Comparison*. Bristol: Multilingual Matters, pp. 29–56.

Skinner, Q. 2002. *Visions of Politics, vol. I. Regarding Method*. Cambridge: Cambridge University Press.

Velde, H. te. 2006. 'Political Transfer: An Introduction', *European Review of History* 12(2): 205–21.

Pasi Ihalainen, Ph.D., is Professor of General History, specifically comparative early modern and modern European history, at the University of Jyväskylä, Finland. He has studied the secularization of the concept of the political party, the modernization of national identities, the redefinition of democracy in constitutional debates in parliaments, and parliamentary conflict resolution in the long eighteenth century, early twentieth century and contemporary history, often in a comparative north-west European perspective. He is a member of the Board of Directors of the research network EuParl.net.

Chapter 2

Key Concepts for Parliament in Britain (1640–1800)

Paul Seaward and Pasi Ihalainen

Although parliamentary debates have frequently been referred to in political history, the evolution of the British parliament has rarely been analysed from a linguistic point of view. In this chapter, we trace shifts in the use and application of key political concepts relating to Parliament and its role and operation during a period of major transformations. By reviewing the use of the terms 'sovereignty', 'parliament', 'representation', 'deliberation', 'responsibility' and 'publicity' in the surviving records of parliamentary debates from 1640 to 1800 (see Chapter 9 for early modern parliamentary rhetoric and Chapter 14 for procedural issues in the nineteenth century), we aim to evaluate changes in their meanings over time and to chart some trends in the formation of the English/British notion of parliament. Rather than attempting to reveal some linear development in a Whiggish sense, we want to analyse the changing and often ambiguous nature of discursive constructions of parliament through time. One problem with this is that before 1771 both Houses of Parliament tried to suppress public accounts of their debates, and therefore they are much less fully reported than later ones. However, some accounts of debates from before 1771, made informally and usually by members themselves, do exist. Moreover, the above-mentioned concepts were also discussed in other contexts, and these discussions and accounts have provided alternative sources for this study.

Despite apparent institutional continuity, Parliament adapted itself to constitutional upheavals and to the rise of critical publicity. As a result, key terms relating to Parliament were used in complex and ambiguous ways, reflecting ambivalence concerning the source and structures of power and authority – as well as the needs of political argument in various speaking situations. Arguments in connection with historical turning points such as the Civil War, the Revolution of 1689, the break with America and the French Revolution meant that the terms defining Parliament became more frequently discussed; their traditional understandings challenged, their inherent ambiguities more exposed and their meanings redefined. Broadly speaking, however, the same terms were used over the entire period and often in similar ways: there was no striking change in parliamentary concepts as Parliament became a more prominent element of the constitution. What did change – especially in the late eighteenth century – was the way that these concepts were used in combination to create a much more elaborate and coherent notion of a parliamentary government that had shed some of the complexities of its relationship with monarchical sovereignty.

Parliament, Sovereignty and Representation during the Civil War

The seventeenth century saw the gradual emergence of notions resembling parliamentary sovereignty (derived from representation) as opposed to monarchical sovereignty (derived from religious ideas). It was already generally appreciated by then that Parliament was in practical terms the most authoritative source of law. Sir Thomas Smith wrote in 1583 that 'the most high and absolute power of the realme of Englande, consisteth in the Parliament' (1583: 34), by which he meant the prince, the Lords and the Commons acting together. This way of thinking gave Parliament some partnership in sovereignty: the monarch was most fully sovereign when he exercised his legislative role in conjunction with the two branches of Parliament. However, the word 'sovereignty' was strongly associated with the personal, indivisible authority of the king. Moreover, the king's acknowledged right to summon and dismiss Parliament and, in certain extreme circumstances, make law without its agreement meant that his theoretical sovereignty was not seriously challenged. Descriptions of Parliament within the constitution approached the question of its authority in an oblique way. One of the most common metaphors for Parliament was that of a 'state physician', an occasional corrective for a diseased state, rather than a permanent partner in government.

The confrontation between the king and Parliament in the 1640s, after an eleven year attempt by Charles I to rule without Parliament, forced many of the ambiguities and unspoken assumptions in this relationship into the open. The arguments of the two years before the outbreak of the Civil War exposed differences over the extent to which the partnership was one of equal elements with equal, 'coordinate' powers, or one in which the king stood outside and above Parliament. The Long Parliament's assertion of its right to ignore the king's veto and the cession by the king in the Triennial Act of 1641 of his right to dismiss it made the idea of a monarchical sovereignty unsustainable. A radical discourse in the 1640s laid claim to Parliament's right to be the 'supreme authority' ('The Humble Petition', 1648), while Thomas Hobbes, in his *Leviathan* of 1651, placed sovereignty unambiguously in the legislative power and derided the notion of power-sharing in a mixed constitution. The scarcity of records of parliamentary debates in the 1640s makes it difficult to determine how soon members began to use the word 'sovereign' in relation to their institution, although during the parliaments of the 1650s some of them certainly did so, including Henry Neville. (Burton's *Diary*, 8 February 1659: 'It is in your power, as the sovereign power of the nation'; and Major Beake, 6 December 1656: 'I conceive the judgment of Parliament is so sovereign, that it may declare that to be an offence, which never was an offence before.')[1]

While it was generally accepted that Parliament's own legitimacy stemmed from its representative status, the nature and meaning of representation were little explored before the Civil War. A more assertive discourse concerning representation was initially a response to the king's rejection of proposed parliamentary legislation on the militia in 1642. Propagandists such as Henry Parker (1643: 20) began to emphasize Parliament's status by referring to it as the 'representative of the people':

> Tis true, the King may be held a representative of the people in ordinary cases, for avoiding of a more troublesome convention, but in extraordinary cases when such a convention is necessary, the Parliament is the onely true representative, and congregated to the King for more perfection sake, or else it were vainly congregated. And because the people cannot be congregated at all, much lesse in any more perfect forme then in a Parliament, therefore the peoples utmost perfection is truly residing in the Parliament. Let not then any private man, Let not the King himselfe undertake to define how far Regall power shall extend in iudiciall or Military affaires (as such a perticular position of things may happen, and according to all emergences) better then the representative body of the Kingdome, which in no respect ought to be held any other thing then the whole Kingdome it self.

Hobbes (2010 [1679]: 268–69) and other royalist polemicists challenged this idea of the representativeness of Parliament, and it was only after the execution of the king in 1649, the declaration of a republic and the abolition of the non-representative element of Parliament, the House of Lords, that Parliament corporately and explicitly identified itself as the representative of the people. The claim invited rejection from some of the people themselves, and there was a precocious but brief debate on the nature of representation within the army during the late 1640s. During the 1650s, the idea that the

House of Commons was the representative of the people became firmly established: the debates recorded in the 1650s concerning the powers of the proposed 'other House' frequently use the term 'representative', emphasizing the representative credentials of the Commons compared to the appointed status of its potential partner (e.g., Burton's *Diary*, Chaloner, Steward and Bodurda, 8 February 1659).

Towards Parliamentary Omnipotence

This debate on representation was largely suppressed after the Restoration, and old ambiguities concerning the place of Parliament within the constitution were restored. It remained rare to associate sovereignty with Parliament on its own: late seventeenth-century debates recorded by Anchitell Grey used the term only to deny the association. Charles II himself, responding to parliamentary intervention in foreign policy on 28 May 1677, argued: 'Should I suffer this fundamental power of making Peace and War to be so far invaded (though but once) as to have the manner and circumstances of Leagues prescribed to me by Parliament, it is plain, that no Prince, or State, would any longer believe, that the Sovereignty of *England* rests in the Crown' (*Commons Journals*, 9: 426).

However, some writers may have been prepared to accord Parliament a more dominant position. Even while he continued to use the idea that Parliament was the state's physician, George Savile, Marquis of Halifax, wrote in *The Character of a Trimmer*, originally published in 1689 (Savile 1989, 1: 197), that the Trimmer

> beleaveth no government is perfect except a kind of omnipotence reside in it, to be exerted upon great occasions. Now this cannot be attained by force upon the people, let it be never so great; there must be their Consent too, or else a nation mooveth only by being driven, a sluggish and constrained motion, void of that life and vigour which is necessary to produce great things. Whereas the virtuall Consent of the whole being included in their representatives, and the King giving the sanction to the united sence of the people, every Act done by such an authority seemeth to be an effect of their choice, as well as a part of their Duty.

This careful formulation suggests a new appreciation of the complexity of the idea of sovereignty. A further series of confrontations between the king and a parliamentary majority in the late 1670s and early 1680s encouraged some radicals to use much clearer language concerning the place of Parliament within the constitution. After the Revolution of 1688–89, even the Tory Party (the political heirs of the Civil War Royalists) reacted to the misgovernment of James II with a stronger recognition of the authority of Parliament, and with Parliament now sitting every year, having an annual rhythm and taking a much more dominant place among governing institutions owing to its routine character and budgetary power, it was difficult to deny its practical supremacy (Dickinson 1977; Kenyon 1977).

Despite Parliament becoming routine, the word 'sovereignty' was still treated with caution. By the 1760s, both Whig and Tory Parties emphasized Parliament's unlimited legislative supremacy in the context of the challenges of Wilkite radicalism and the American colonies (Langford 1991: 152–53), and the notion of 'the omnipotence of parliament' was debated in the press, though it might still be regarded as 'too bold a figure indeed' to describe 'our triform legislature, constituting one indivisible power' (*London Chronicle*, 5 June 1764).[2] William Blackstone, a leading constitutional lawyer, wrote about the 'sovereign and uncontrollable authority' of Parliament in his *Commentaries on the Laws of England* (1765–69, 1: 156). Unqualified associations between Parliament, supremacy and omnipotence became more common from the mid 1770s onwards among both the executive, who opposed the colonists, and opposition speakers, who sympathized with their ideals, and also in the press (*Public Advertiser*, 4 April 1774, 16 May 1774; Parliamentary debates: Charles Pratt, 20 January 1775: 13, 16 March 1775: 83; George Johnstone, 6 February 1775: 161; Edmund Burke, 29 February 1776: 357).[3] According to William Henry Lyttelton, the war in America was intended to maintain 'the inalienable and indubitable rights of the sovereign power of the King, the Parliament, and the nation', who 'in their deliberative or legislative capacity . . . thus united, constituted the sovereign or supreme power' (12 June 1781: 521, 523). However, there were also opposition critics of 'the doctrine of unconditional supremacy' and 'parliamentary supremacy' (Charles James Fox, 1 December 1775: 242; Henry Cruger, 20 February 1776: 337), who insisted that only the people could be truly 'omnipotent' (Goldsworthy 1999: 194, 216, on Richard Price and John Wilkes).

Controlling the Government

One difficulty with the concept of parliamentary power was that in constitutional theory the executive remained firmly under the control of the monarch. The notion of its accountability to Parliament only emerged very gradually: since ministers were appointed by, and reported to, the Crown, they could not be held formally responsible or accountable to the Commons. However, the notion of a controlling, rather than a directing, power – i.e., an ability to audit and check the activities of executive agents – offered a means of formalizing the responsiveness of the king's government to parliamentary pressures.

The idea that it was the function of the Commons to investigate the abuses of royal servants and to bring them to the attention of the king was an ancient one. It was expressed by the early seventeenth-century jurist Sir Edward Coke (1669: 11, 24) when he called the Commons the 'generall Inquisitors of the Realm'. Coke was referring to the 'grand juries' or 'grand inquests' – representative panels established in each county to decide whether individual miscreants should be brought before the judges for criminal trial. Sir Robert Filmer's *Free-holders' Grand Inquest* (1648) made the same analogy between the grand juries and the Commons. 'We are the Grand Jury of the Nation, as the Freeholders are of a county,' one member stated in 1675 (Sir Thomas Clarges in Grey, *Debates*, 3 May 1675). This normally meant that Parliament would address the king for the removal of ministers who were deemed to have been guilty of some misdemeanour. The revival of the medieval practice of impeachment in the 1620s offered a process by which they could initiate and pursue a criminal prosecution of powerful malefactors before the House of Lords, although it was rarely a very effective instrument. Associated with the notion of parliamentary control was the claim, generally accepted after the Revolution of 1689, that ministers had an obligation to 'give an account' to Parliament of matters within their responsibility (Grey, *Debates*, regarding the Attorney General, 24 November 1680, and commissioners of the admiralty, 11 November 1693).

Ministers and parliamentarians in the eighteenth century already regarded it as axiomatic that ministers had a general obligation to provide information to Parliament and could be held accountable to it. By the time of the Sacheverell and Succession Crises in the 1710s, the accountability of ministers to Parliament for their actions was emphasized by several politicians as a principle of 'the fundamental Constitution' (Laurence Hyde, Earl of Rochester, 1710/11: 320; Robert Harley, Earl of Oxford, 1715: 12; Robert Walpole, 1715: 41; Richard Steele, 1716: 86). The political hegemony of Sir Robert Walpole during the 1720s and 1730s, and the more routine conception of 'opposition' that it helped to create, brought about a greater sophistication in defining how parliamentary control over ministers might be exercised (Kluxen 1956; Skinner 1974; Kleinhenz 1991: 63) and in the ways that the MPs understood their role. Walpole recognized that ministers were to some extent accountable to their 'Country' (not expressly 'to Parliament') regarding 'the Counsels they give their Sovereigns' (1738: 307). The opposition leader William Wyndham pointed out that in a free government the executive power was subordinate and accountable to the legislative power, which consisted of an assembly of the people (1739: 240), and Samuel Sandys demanded that as the prime minister had so long acted without being truly accountable, a parliamentary inquiry into his actions was needed (1740: 43). The notion of

the accountability of the executive to the Commons is reflected in an opposition attack in the name of 'the general Voice of the People of England' on
Walpole, as 'a Steward for the Publick' (Alexander Hume-Campbell, 1741:
84; Watkin Williams Wynne, 1741: 93; Velters Cornewall, 1741: 157; William
Pitt, 1741: 170, 211). John Philipps declared that it was the duty of MPs to
be 'jealous of Ministers', as they themselves, as 'Agents for the People' and
'the Representatives of the People', were accountable to the electors (1742:
216, 266). Walpole's resignation, following his failure to secure a majority
in the House of Commons (Langford 2006: 393), was a recognition of the
difficulty of governing without the ability to ensure parliamentary consent.
It suggested a very practical acknowledgement that the power of a minister now rested on his possession of a majority in the House of Commons;
one which would become formalized in the idea of a vote of censure or of
confidence.

By the 1760s, the press maintained the principle of 'the constitutional control, which the people hold over the crown', through 'the representative body
of the people' (*Gazetteer and London Daily Advertiser*, 22 July 1762). The
concept of parliamentary 'control' of the ministers also found its way into late
eighteenth-century procedural tracts (Hatsell 1781: 237). During the crisis
following the defeat in the American War, the notions of ministerial responsibility and parliamentary control became more explicitly stated in parliamentary debates as well. On 20 March 1782, Prime Minister North was forced
to resign as a consequence of military failure (Kleinhenz 1991: 68–69). His
admission that 'it was the right of that House to command; it was the duty of a
minister to obey its resolutions' (4 March 1782: 348) suggested that ministers
no longer regarded themselves as being responsible to the Crown so much as
to the Commons. Charles James Fox likewise conceded that the responsibility of ministers 'balanced the power, and insured to the people that no ill use
would be made of it'; the Commons being appointed 'to check and control'
the use of power (20 November 1783: 85). By the end of our period, the idea
that a minister might be forced to resign by a formal vote of censure in the
House of Commons had become widely recognized. In 1797, Prime Minister
Pitt conceded that 'Ministers were undoubtedly responsible to Parliament
for their conduct; and whenever [Samuel Whitbread, an opposition member]
thought proper to propose a Vote of Censure upon his conduct, he should be
prepared to meet the discussion' (*True Briton*, 10 May 1797).

The opposition remained doubtful about the realities of such responsibility. An anxiety throughout the eighteenth century about how government
could effectively control the Commons through the distribution of offices
and pensions to its members meant that the assertion of the sovereignty of
Parliament implied to many not so much a growth in the power and status of

the representative element of the constitution, but an alarming increase in the effective power of the government.

Parliament and the People: The Complexities of Representation

The recorded parliamentary debates of the late seventeenth century show how deeply members were aware of the representative status of the Commons. They often referred to the constituents whom they represented, particularly on occasions where their consent was uncertain. However, Parliament's supremacy begged many questions about the basis of its power and the real extent and meaning of its representative status. Some of the complexities of 'representation' emerged more fully after 1680 when political divisions were acknowledged under the party labels 'Whig' and 'Tory'. This change encouraged electorates to question whether they were being represented in Parliament in the way they wished. The frequency of elections under the Triennial Act of 1694 encouraged them to believe that they could hold their own representatives properly accountable.

Representation was a dual activity, facing both backwards to the constituents and forwards to the Crown. The use of the word in seventeenth-century parliamentary sources often refers to the function of representation: putting forward a view on behalf of the group to someone qualified to provide redress. The most common use of the word referred to how issues were 'represented' to the king: to represent was to provide the king with information on the basis of which he could make the proper decisions. In December 1678, the House was urged to 'represent to the King the dangerous condition the Nation is in' (Grey, *Debates*, 2 December 1678). Edward Seymour in 1689 told the House: '[I]t is not in our power to remedy the Miscarriages, but it is to represent them to the King to be remedied' (Grey, *Debates*, 14 December 1689).

In a divided political nation, voters could become suspicious that their representatives were not correctly representing the views of their communities. From the 1680s onwards, the relationship between constituencies and representatives could become difficult and contested, with voters claiming that their views were being misrepresented, or demanding that their representatives commit themselves to certain positions through formal instructions. Further friction was caused by petitioning, which constituted a more direct form of popular expression or 'representation' and was often rejected by the 'proper' representatives in Parliament. The presentation of a petition in 1701 urging Parliament to 'have regard to the voice of the people' and to adopt policies to which Tory leaders in the Commons were fundamentally opposed produced a volatile controversy concerning the relationship between the people and their representatives (Bradley 2007: 96; Knights 2009: 42, 51).

The other usage of the word faced towards the origins of the act of representing a community's views, relating to the process by which representatives were chosen and the extent to which the chosen representatives reflected the country itself. The close relationship between the two usages was brought out by Lord Charles Noel Somerset when he defined Parliament in connection with an attempted repeal of the Septennial Act as 'the grand Inquest of the Nation, they are to represent the grievances of the People to their Sovereign; and the People are always to choose proper representatives for that Purpose' (1733/34: 159). In 1745, William Yonge saw a representative as 'the attorney of the people', albeit one who possessed 'full freedom to act as he thinks best for the people' (Rush 2001: 13). However, the link between communities and Members was often tenuous, as rich individuals in practice bought their seats in Parliament, and the effectiveness with which such men really represented their communities was highly doubtful.

The corruption of the representative system by government made the issue a persistent complaint. Campaigners repeatedly attempted to limit government influence within Parliament by means of 'place bills' (disqualifying the holders of various crown offices or government supply contracts from membership) and bills limiting the duration of a parliament and the period between general elections, a process that finally secured elections every three years in 1694. The latter reform was reversed with the Septennial Act (requiring elections only every seven years) in 1716, and the threat of government influence continued to be a preoccupation of opposition parties and 'patriots' well beyond the eighteenth century.

Walpole's government of 1721–42, in particular, was seen to be a threat to the relationship between the electors and the elected. Concern about the influence of the Crown on elections led to suggestions that the Commons might turn into 'a Representative of an Administration, or of one single Minister, but could no longer be a true Representative of the People' (*Protest by Several Lords*, 29 March 1732: 1059). In their attempts to repeal the Septennial Act, the opposition saw the election of representatives as the most essential privilege of the people and called for more frequent elections in order to make parliaments responsible to the electors (John St Aubyn, 1733/34: 143). Calls for parliamentary reform made no serious headway in Parliament before the office of William Pitt the Younger in the 1780s, but the representation of the people had become an established, even if rhetorical, principle of the British parliament.

Deliberation and the Relationship between Parliament, the Executive and the People

By the end of the eighteenth century, concerns about the relationship between Parliament and the executive, and between Parliament and the people, were reflected in the concept of 'deliberation', derived from the rhetorical genre of deliberation pro et contra, already familiar in the early seventeenth-century parliament (Chapter 9). Two arguments encouraged parliamentarians to use 'deliberation' more generally as a description of what Parliament did. One was the need to stress Parliament's distinctive role in relation to the executive and the importance of avoiding corruption thereby. The other was the need to stress the freedom of parliamentarians to come to their conclusions independently of external pressure.

Parliament was regarded as being composed of a mixture of elements, incorporating the Crown as well as the Lords and Commons. In the seventeenth century, the separate roles were often underlined by emphasizing the role of the Commons in providing advice, or 'counsel', to the king. Parliament's debates were often seen as part of a process of producing such 'counsel'. 'Deliberation' was commonly used to emphasize the need to make a particular decision with great care, although its use was also often associated with an attempt to delay a decision or a debate for purely tactical reasons.

By the 1770s, the idea of 'deliberation' was replacing 'counsel' as a description of the essential role of Parliament. Thomas Townshend, an opponent of the American War, regarded the Commons as 'a deliberate body, and one of the branches of the legislature' that had particular privileges, including the power of granting money (1776: 313). In the American crisis, the government was believed to be ignoring parliamentary advice and the separate roles of the executive and deliberative powers, which made the opposition argue for sufficient time for parliamentary deliberation as the very essence of the institution. Townshend, condemning hurry as disgraceful to Parliament, presented 'mere edicts of the council table, or rather the dark machinations of a desperate cabal of ministers' as a counter-concept to 'the laws of free, deliberative assemblies' (7 May 1775: 273). John Hussey-Montagu complained that, through their conduct and use of language, the executive was ignoring Parliament as an essentially 'deliberate body ... a body possessed of discretionary and deliberate powers, who could advise, check, and control the conduct of ministers' (15 March 1781: 268). In the same debate, Prime Minister North responded to the claim that the ministry was manipulating Parliament by recognizing that 'undoubtedly the Parliament had the powers to check and to control the treasury. Having the powers of deliberation, they certainly could rescind any resolution which they had made' (15 March

1781: 269). Thomas Pitt summarized the essential deliberative function of Parliament, connecting it with budgetary power:

> What, Sir, is the Crown but the executive power of Government? What is Parliament but the deliberative? What is this House but the branch of the deliberative power that is trusted with the purse of the People? Sir, it is because these powers are not one, it is because they are disunited, that this Government has obtained the admiration and envy of every other nation ... When the Crown, when the executive power, shall be ill advised and ill administrated, it is for Parliament, it is for the deliberative power, to interpose; and more peculiarly for this House to exert its important privilege, by shutting up the purse with which it is entrusted. (30 November 1781: 74)

By emphasizing the deliberative nature of Parliament, these speakers were underlining the importance of free and unprejudiced debate. The concept of deliberation could also be used to defend the status of Parliament in relation to the people. Deliberation implied that Parliament itself would come to a final decision through a process of calmly weighing the issues at stake, without heat and undue influences. Deliberation among members with a free mandate was the core of parliamentary politics, and it excluded the views of those outside. Parliament was, according to Edmund Burke's famous speech to the electors of Bristol, not 'a *Congress* of Ambassadors from different and hostile interests' negotiating as 'Agents and Advocates' but 'a *deliberative* Assembly of *one* Nation, with *one* Interest, that of the whole' (1775: 28, emphasis in original). Burke's point was an old one, but the strength with which it was expressed in the 1770s and 1780s reflected the growing popular pressure on, and interest in, parliamentary politics. Alexander Murray, the Solicitor General of Scotland, expressly denied the right of extra-parliamentary associations to deliberate on state matters and to redress grievances (8 May 1781: 239). During the radical phase of the French Revolution, leading politicians like Prime Minister Pitt and Foreign Secretary William Grenville began to describe Parliament more generally as the 'deliberative assembly' of the nation. By doing so, they distinguished Parliament from revolutionary assemblies affected by public opinion (Robert Banks Jenkinson, 6 May 1793: 394; Richard Colley Wellesley, 7 May 1793: 437; *Sun*, 18 June 1793; *Sun*, 18 February 1794).

Representing the Public in the Late Eighteenth Century

Although Parliament was maintained to be the representative of the people, its connection with representation was problematic, both in the sense that parliamentarians did not feel obliged to reflect directly the opinion of their voters, partly in view of the fact that, because of the restricted franchise, those who actually voted did not fully represent the population. From time to time, the debate returned to the issue originally raised by seventeenth-century radicals: if Parliament based its legitimacy on the fact that it represented the people, it should represent them and their views as accurately as possible. The mismatch of population and representation was increasingly justified by shifting the basis of representation onto 'interests' as well as communities. Or as Charles Mellish put it: 'Necessity has adopted this fiction of a virtual representation, and it is now become our duty to consult the interest of the kingdom in general, in preference to the advantage of our borough or county' (27 October 1775: 56).

The American crisis pushed the broader question of representation to the forefront of political discourse. Lord Camden saw representation as a 'modern discovery' that constituted the basis of the sovereign power of the legislature (14 March 1776: 247). By the end of the war, parliamentary reform was called for in county petitions complaining that 'the representation of the Commons in Parliament' had 'frequently a separate interest from the people' and was 'unequal to express the general sense of the said Commons' (Petition from Sussex, 22 January 1783: 133). However, despite repeated complaints that virtual representation could not guarantee the people their rights, there was no parliamentary reform in the eighteenth century. Moreover, before the 1770s, the privacy of Parliament's deliberations meant that it was impossible for the wider public to estimate its effectiveness in representing them. Calm deliberation away from the pressure of the people meant deliberation in secret, without public exposure. When the Wilkite radicals demanded the publication of parliamentary proceedings in the early 1770s, members were divided between the defenders of the exclusive privilege of Parliament to discuss politics in secret and the advocates of the right of the people at large to have access to political information. Welbore Ellis considered that the publication of the debates bypassed 'the whole body of the British people' as represented by Parliament, since it allowed anyone to misrepresent the debates of the House (25 March 1771: 121, 126–28). On the other hand, Alderman James Townsend argued that the privileges of the Commons and the people were identical and that discussion of parliamentary debates outside the House should hence be allowed (25 March 1771: 121–22). Attempts to prevent the immediate publication of reports of debates were abandoned shortly afterwards. The result was to strengthen Parliament as the focus of public political discourse. Well before Bagehot's time, the publicity that Parliament brought to political issues became regarded as a self-evident aspect of its role (Ihalainen 2010). Moreover, the simultaneous growth of the press also provided a variety of forums for the expression of dissenting views, challenging the focus on Parliament.

In the aftermath of the French Revolution, expanding parliamentary publicity could already be presented as compensating for the lack of representation: 'The debates in that House were more generally known, and more particularly attended to. Every member knew when he was speaking that his arguments and conduct would be discussed and canvassed by the public at large' (William Adam, 7 May 1793: 489–90). Charles Jenkinson suggested that the publication of parliamentary debates constituted a link between the members and the people and removed any need for universal suffrage: '. . . the very proceedings of the House were continually published, by which the people had opportunities of knowing what was passing daily, which must have great influence on the House, by the opportunities that were afforded to the people of forming their opinions from time to time' (26 May 1797: 689). Though to some extent it was an alibi for representative change, it could be argued that the new publicity given to parliamentary proceedings was a way of making Parliament increasingly accountable to the people.

The Sovereignty of Parliament as the Sovereignty of the People

Much effort had been devoted since the Revolution of 1688–89 to avoiding the implication that – however it was derived – sovereignty lay in the people rather than in Parliament (Dickinson 1977: 46–47, 125–31, 87–90). Opposition Whigs and some Jacobites might invoke the people, recognizing that Parliament's legitimacy was based on its representative function, but they generally avoided the implication that sovereignty resided in the people themselves. The relationship between parliamentary supremacy and its roots in the election of the people remained an ambiguous one.

Towards the very end of the eighteenth century, those ambiguities were exposed and attacked in the wake of the French Revolution. Radical Whigs then controversially used the revolutionary notion of the 'sovereignty of the people' as a synonym for the sovereignty of Parliament – an expression that had been avoided until then. Charles James Fox's extra-parliamentary suggestions that even George III only held the Crown 'by the sacred and solemn Act of Parliament, flowing from the Sovereignty of the People' pushed the notion well beyond contemporary usage, even though he claimed: 'The Sovereignty of the People of Great Britain is surely a thing not new to the language, to the feelings, nor to the hearts of Englishmen. It is the basis of the whole system of our Government' (*Lloyd's Evening Post*, 7 February 1798).

A more extensive confrontation leading to redefinitions of parliamentary sovereignty took place in connection with debates on the union with Ireland (Ihalainen 2010). Benjamin Hobhouse argued that a justification for 'the sovereignty of the people in the last instance' could be found in William Blackstone's recognition of the right of resistance in case the legislature violated the liberties of the people (14 February 1799: 75). Solicitor General John Mitford rejected the idea, arguing that all power had been delegated to the government (*Sun*, 15 February 1799). Foreign Secretary William Grenville described the sovereignty of the people as 'a Jacobinical doctrine', while 'a Part must be always Sovereign, not the whole People'. There was, furthermore, 'no bound to the political . . . competency of Parliament' (*Whitehall Evening Post*, 19 March 1799). Lord Minto claimed that 'the universality of parliamentary power has been characterized by the strong and emphatic title of Omnipotence' (11 April 1799: 419) and that 'the Sovereignty of Parliament' was 'identically and precisely the same with the sovereignty of the people itself, appearing in the only visible, tangible or perceptible form in which it can be recognized in this country'. In the British constitution, 'the authority and sovereignty of Parliament has been established' (11 April 1799: 427) – and thereby popular sovereignty as well. It was unusual for a conservative, such as Minto, to accept the sovereignty of the people – but by treating it as if it was simply another way of expressing the sovereignty of Parliament, Minto was using new and revolutionary notions to reinforce his traditionalist argument.

By 1800, the Westminster parliament was developing a rather more coherent conception of parliamentary government; one made up of the concepts of sovereignty, representation, 'control' (or accountability), deliberation and publicity. At least in principle (if rarely in practice) it could be viewed as an institution based on popular sovereignty realized through representation and deliberating political questions, providing the public with information and what we would call 'political education' through publicity and keeping the executive accountable to the representatives of the people. This does not mean that the unreformed Parliament before 1832 actually embodied such ideals. The debates surrounding Catholic emancipation and the Reform Act (1829–32) would bring about a further development in ideas about Parliament (as, indeed, would some influences from debates about parliamentary systems abroad, especially in France) even though much of this was couched in terms of tactical considerations about the preservation of the system and the removal of abuses, rather than in conceptual change. However, the British parliament, as an evolutionary institution, provided one model for new understandings of the key categories of a parliament – though no longer the only one after the rise of alternative forms of representative institutions in the revolutionary era.

Notes

1 References to the parliamentary diaries of Thomas Burton and Anchitell Grey
   and to the *Journals of the House of Commons* are derived from the electronic text
   provided on British History Online (http://www.british-history.ac.uk/Default.
   aspx), and are indicated as Burton, *Diary*, Grey, *Debates*, and *Commons Journals*.
2 All references to newspapers are based on a digitized version of the Burney
   collection.
3 All references to early eighteenth-century parliamentary debates are from *Cobbett's
   Parliamentary History of England: From the Norman Conquest in 1066 to the Year
   1803* and late eighteenth-century debates from *The Parliamentary Register* as
   available in digital form in The House of Commons Parliamentary Papers. The
   speaker, the date of the debate and the page numbers have been appended.

References

Primary Sources

Blackstone, W. 1765–69. *Commentaries on the Laws of England*, vol. 1. Oxford:
   Clarendon Press.
Burke, E. 1775. *Mr. Edmund Burke's Speeches at his Arrival at Bristol and at the
   Conclusion of the Poll*, 2nd ed. London: J. Dodsley.
Burton, T. 1828. *The Parliamentary Diary of Thomas Burton*. J.T. Rutt (ed.). Retrieved
   from http://www.british-history.ac.uk/subject.aspx?subject=6&gid=45
Cobbett, W. 1806–20. *Cobbett's Parliamentary History of England: From the Norman
   Conquest in 1066 to the Year 1803*. London: R. Bagshaw.
Coke, E. 1669. *The Fourth Part of the Institutes of the Lawes of England; Concerning the
   Jurisdiction of Courts*. London: A. Crook.
Filmer, R. 1648. *Free-holders' Grand Inquest Touching our Sovereigne Lord the King
   and His Parliament*. London: s.n.
Grey, A. 1769. *Debates of the House of Commons, from the year 1667 to the year
   1694*. London. Retrieved from http://www.british-history.ac.uk/subject.
   aspx?subject=6&gid=71
Hatsell, J. 1781. *Precedents of Proceedings in the House of Commons, under Separate
   Titles; with Observations*. Vol. 2. London: J. Dodsley.
Hobbes, T. 1651. *Leviathan, or, the Matter, Form, and Power of a Common-Wealth
   Ecclesiastical and Civil*. London: A. Crooke.
———. 2010 [1679]. *Behemoth, or, The Long Parliament*. P. Seaward (ed.). Oxford:
   Oxford University Press.
Journals of the House of Commons, vol. 9. 1802. London. Retrieved from http://www.
   british-history.ac.uk/subject.aspx?subject=6&gid=43
Parker, H. 1643. *The Oath of Pacification, or a Forme of Religious Accommodation
   Humbly Proposed both to King and Parliament*. London: R. Robstock.
Savile, G. 1989. *The Works of George Savile Marquis of Halifax*, vol. 1. M.N. Brown
   (ed.). Oxford: Clarendon.

Smith, T. 1583. *De Republica Anglorum. The Maner of Gouernement or Policie of the Realme of England*. London: Gregorie Seton.

'The Humble Petition of Thousands Wel-affected Persons Inhabiting the City of London, Westminster, the Borough of Southwark'. 1648. London: s.n.

The Parliamentary Register. Retrieved from the House of Commons Parliamentary Papers database.

Secondary Sources

Bradley, J.E. 2007. 'Parliament, Print Culture and Petitioning in Late Eighteenth-Century England', *Parliamentary History* 26(1): 96–111.

Dickinson, H.T. 1977. *Liberty and Property: Political Ideology in Eighteenth-Century Britain*. New York: Holmes and Meier.

Goldsworthy, J. 1999. *The Sovereignty of Parliament: History and Philosophy*. Oxford: Clarendon Press.

Ihalainen, P. 2010. *Agents of the People: Democracy and Popular Sovereignty in British and Swedish Parliamentary and Public Debates, 1734–1800*. Leiden: Brill Academic Publishers.

Kenyon, J.P. 1977. *Revolution Principles: The Politics of Party 1689–1720*. Cambridge: Cambridge University Press.

Kleinhenz, R. 1991. *Königtum und parlamentarische Vertrauensfrage in England 1689–1841*. Berlin: Duncker & Humblot.

Kluxen, K. 1956. *Das Problem der politischen Opposition. Entwicklung und Wesen der englischen Zweiparteipolitik im 18. Jahrhundert*. Munich: Alber.

Knights, M. 2009. 'Participation and Representation before Democracy: Petitions and Addresses in Pre-modern Britain', in I. Shapiro et al. (eds), *Political Representation*. Cambridge: Cambridge University Press, pp. 35–61.

Langford, P. 1991. *Public Life and the Propertied Englishman 1689–1798*. Oxford: Clarendon.

_____. 2006. 'Prime Ministers and Parliaments: The Long View, Walpole to Blair', *Parliamentary History* 25(3): 382–94.

Rush, M. 2001. *The Role of the Member of Parliament since 1868: From Gentlemen to Players*. Oxford: Oxford University Press.

Skinner, Q. 1974. 'The Principles and Practice of Opposition: The Case of Bolingbroke versus Walpole', in N. McKendrick (ed.), *Historical Perspectives: Studies in English Thought and Society in Honour of J.H. Plumb*. London: Europa, pp. 93–128.

Paul Seaward, Ph.D., is Director of the History of Parliament Trust, London, United Kingdom. His research has focused on mid and late seventeenth-century English politics and political thought and on the English/British Parliament as an institution from the seventeenth century to the present day. He is currently working on the role of parliament in the British imagination, myths and memories in a long-term perspective and on visual representations of parliament. He is a member of the Board of Directors of the research network EuParl.net.

Pasi Ihalainen, Ph.D., is Professor of General History, specifically comparative early modern and modern European history, at the University of Jyväskylä, Finland. He has studied the secularization of the concept of the political party, the modernization of national identities, the redefinition of democracy in constitutional debates in parliaments, and parliamentary conflict resolution in the long eighteenth century, early twentieth century and contemporary history, often in a comparative north-west European perspective. He is a member of the Board of Directors of the research network EuParl.net.

Chapter 3

Discussing the First Age of French Parliamentarism (1789–1914)

Jean Garrigues and Eric Anceau

According to the work of François Furet (1988), the political history of France from the French Revolution to the Third Republic can be seen as a long apprenticeship of parliamentary democracy. Parliamentarism, inspired both by the principles of the Enlightenment (freedom, separation of powers) and the British model (bicameralism, the responsibility of ministers), was gradually introduced into the French political system through a repertoire of thirteen distinctly different political regimes: constitutional monarchies and census suffrage (1789–91, 1814, 1815–48), republican democracies (1792–1804, 1848–51 and 1870–75) and imperial democracies (1804–14, 1815, 1852–70), the alternation of which is evidence of the complexity of the development. This path led to the constitutional laws of 1875, which established a system of a parliamentary nature and were quickly transformed into a real assembly system following the crisis of 16 May 1877. This policy became permanent in the French political landscape until it was ended by the military debacle of 1940.

With regard to an ideal type of parliamentary system, the beginning of the Third Republic embodied the dimensions that define it: sovereignty, deliberation, representation and responsibility. This combination was, however, challenged by contemporaries, and it needs to be analysed. Most significantly, the work of a lawyer called Raymond Carré de Malberg (1861–1935) reflects this uncertainty. In 1920, he considered the Revolution to be the foundation of the modern state built around the notion of national sovereignty. However, in a later work (1931) he recognized a form of perversion under the Third Republic. This controversial evolution of the ideal type model into republican parliamentary democracy is the subject of our reflections: we focus on four major periods using parliamentary debates and works of the time dealing with conceptual issues.

The Invention of National Sovereignty during the French Revolution

The first question that was raised at the time of the Revolution was indisputably that of sovereignty. First put forward in Jean Bodin's *Six Livres de la République* (1576), the concept of sovereignty became the mainstay of the construction of a modern state that took place in the context of an absolute monarchy. Full sovereignty belonged to the king, and it was conferred on him by God. The king was His lieutenant on earth. The French Revolution, born out of a meeting of the Etats Généraux that was summoned to try to resolve the financial crisis that the monarchical state had been struggling with for several years, quickly led to a complete questioning of this principle. The Enlightenment philosophy undermined the idea of absolute monarchy, especially the work of Montesquieu (1748), who sought to reconcile the British parliamentary monarchy and the aristocratic French tradition within a system of balance and mutual control of the three powers.

Sieyès was the first revolutionary thinker to construct a theory of national sovereignty in his *Qu'est-ce que le Tiers Etat?* (1788). His purpose was not only to transfer the sovereignty of the king to the nation as an abstract legal entity but to give jurisdiction embodying this commission to the organs of the nation. However, as Marcel Gauchet explains (1995), the concern of Sieyès was not to give power to the people but to set up a representative power.

This was done on 17 June 1789 when the Third Estate and a few members of the Clergy and Nobility united to form a National Assembly. The king was forced to ratify the legitimacy of the National Constituent Assembly, which adopted this name on 11 July. Subsequently, Article 3 of the *Déclaration des Droits de l'Homme et du Citoyen* (26 August 1789) defined a form of absolutism of national sovereignty in accordance with the law. The constitutional expression of this sovereignty was the subject of endless debates. Monarchists such as Mounier and Lally Tollendal tried to preserve the executive's absolute veto on legislation, while the Patriotic Party was divided between the opponents of any veto (Robespierre and Sieyès) and supporters of a suspensive veto such as Le Chapelier or Thouret, the latter group finally prevailing in the vote on 11 September 1789. However, the key reform was in the passage of the constitution, recognized by the king on 13 September 1791, which established the separation of powers within the framework of a constitutional monarchy, in which the National Assembly, according to the law (Article 3), was the sole possessor of the indivisible sovereignty of the nation. The members of the Assembly were significantly called 'representatives of the nation'. The term 'sovereign', which was still used to describe the king, now 'King of the French', was no longer relevant because he was no longer the 'chief magistrate' of the nation.

However, aside from national sovereignty, another idea emerged from the radical revolutionaries; that of 'popular sovereignty', originating from Jean-Jacques Rousseau's major work *Le Contrat Social* (1762). Pierre Rosanvallon (1998) explains how difficult it was to establish a popular sovereignty that would be as inseparable and absolute as that of the former king. It was a fictional entity – 'the people'– that was now taking the place of Louis XVI. The problem was that at the very moment when the Revolution was giving 'the people' the source of power, the image of 'the people' had never appeared more indistinct.

Even if the two formulas, national sovereignty and popular sovereignty, overlapped for a long time, their essence was radically different, as was shown by Carré de Malberg (1920). The tension between these two conceptions of sovereignty was the true origin of the crisis of the summer of 1792, catalysed by the war against Austria and Prussia and the invasion of French territory. After the fall of the monarchy on 10 August 1792 and the proclamation of the Republic on 22 September, the majority in the Convention held Rousseauesque ideas. The Jacobin constitution of 24 June 1793 actually established popular sovereignty, which, according to Robespierre, could not be delegated. The new Bill of Rights expressed a new distrust of the legislative power, which was now under the control of the primary popular assemblies, and it included the right to oppose their veto on the decisions of their elected representatives.

With the fall of Robespierre, the Thermidorians implemented the constitution of 1795. The main authors were ideologues Daunou and Volney, editors of the newspaper *La Décade philosophique, politique et littéraire*, who promoted the idea of 'enlightened reason', inspired by the Enlightenment. Sovereignty was no longer defined as national or popular but as an expression of the community of 'citizens'. This representative regime was closer to the aims of 1789 and sought to remove any drift towards pure democracy. However, the constitutional weakness of the executive, represented by the Directorate, led to political instability, which in turn led to the seizure of power and the dictatorial coup of 18 Brumaire (9 November 1799) by Napoleon Bonaparte.

The principle of deliberation, which corresponded with the etymology of the word 'parliament' (government by speaking) and had its roots in the regional assemblies of notables at the end of the ancien régime, was manifested in the early days of the French Revolution. The principles of freedom of expression, immunity and public hearings were rapidly being put in place, even against the will of the king, while at the same time deliberation was controlled by the powers of the President of the Assembly and the censorship of speakers.

Representation was also a target of major debate in preparations for the Etats Généraux in 1789, which raised the questions of voting by order (the Clergy, the Nobility, the Third Estate) and doubling the number of deputies of the Third Estate to balance those of the privileged orders. On 8 July 1789, an overwhelming majority of deputies voted for the prohibition of the imperative mandate, which was regarded as 'limiting' by Talleyrand. Freedom of opinion, essential to the decision that provided for the responsibility of the representatives to the sovereign nation, was thereby established.

Subsequently, throughout the duration of the Revolution, a number of questions were raised, touching upon issues such as the appointment of representatives, the manner and procedure of voting, the eligibility threshold, the choice of the best representatives or those who represented society, the nature of the mandate, the number of chambers and the frequency of sessions. Bernard Manin (1995) explains that the debates on the vote in this period showed that representation without social distinctions did not make sense for the majority of voters, who regarded it as necessary that power be associated with competence, expressing the judgment of Montesquieu (1748): 'The people is admirably suited to choose those to whom they have given some part of their authority. But will they know how to direct an affair, recognize places, opportunities, moments, how take advantage of them? No, they will not!' The election procedure of the Legislative Assembly (22 December 1789) had two different categories of 'voters': active citizens who elected members, and passive citizens, excluded from the election according to the criterion of census suffrage. This device corresponded to ideas expressed in particular by Sieyès, who was in favour of an 'elective aristocracy' comprising people who could read and write and also understand politics and who enjoyed sufficient financial independence to enable them to devote themselves to the nation. This notion (formulated by Sieyès) corresponded to a political theory that considered suffrage to be a function, not a right.

The advocates of popular sovereignty were hostile to this form of representative government. They proposed an ideal of direct democracy with an imperative mandate for the representatives of the nation. In the constitutional draft ratified by the Convention on 24 June 1793, the laws passed by the National Assembly were subject to approval by the permanent primary assemblies, which were both electoral and deliberative. However, after the fall of Robespierre, the draft constitution prepared by Daunou and presented by

Boissy d'Anglas on 23 June 1795 was the opposite of the policy of the Jacobin dictatorship in that it introduced bicameralism after the British model. The constitution of 1795 stated that the Conseil des Anciens (the Council of the Elders) and the Conseil des Cinq-Cents (the Council of the Five Hundred) should balance each other. The two assemblies were chosen by the same electorate based on census suffrage. One proposed laws, the other adopted them. As was emphasized by Boissy d'Anglas, 'Absolute equality is a chimera . . . We must be governed by the best, the best are the most educated and the most interested in maintaining the laws' (*Projet de Constitution*).

The Invention of Deliberation under the Bourbon Restoration

The principle of national sovereignty disappeared under the Bourbon Restoration between 1814 and 1830. The 'Préambule de la Charte constitutionnelle' of 4 June 1814, 'granted' by King Louis XVIII to his subjects, implied that the monarch had been called back to the throne, not by the will of the people, but by 'divine providence'. The king, the 'supreme Head of State', was held to be irresponsible and his person was 'sacred and inviolable'. Because of his prominent position, which allowed him to surpass the legislative process (the right of initiative and sanction of the appointment of presidents of the chambers), he was beyond the reach of any opposition.

However, from the beginning of the Restoration, ultra or liberal opponents sought to control the executive power. For example, they used the right to petition in order to establish interaction with ministers, creating a kind of ongoing dialogue between the two chambers and the government. During the 1815 session, the ultras, who constituted the majority, used the debates on amnesty and finance law to fight Richelieu's cabinet. Following the British model, Baron de Vitrolles (1815) stressed the need for ministerial responsibility to parliament as essential for representative government.

As has been underlined by Marcel Gauchet (2007), the Bourbon Restoration marked the start of a liberal period during which the sovereignty of the state and the notion of individualism corresponded to a doctrine of limited representation based on census suffrage. This was a period during which political practice or 'government by discussion' was starting to supersede traditional politics in the form of power from above dominating the social order. Political representation had been the subject of debates since the end of the Empire, when Benjamin Constant published his *Réflexions sur les constitutions* (May 1814) and wrote the ephemeral *Acte additionnel aux Constitutions de l'Empire* during the one hundred days of Napoleon's return in 1815. The liberal royalists, who were united under the name of 'Doctrinaires' behind Royer-Collard (a lawyer), François Guizot (an historian), Baron de Barante and Victor de Broglie, demanded the extension of suffrage to the so-called capacities (see also Chapter 14). This term, which expressed a concept typical of the liberal doctrine, referred to people (especially higher education graduates) who by their professional qualifications were capable of understanding a wide variety of issues, including political ones. However, the ideas held by the Doctrinaires did not fundamentally alter parliamentary representation under the Restoration. By contrast, the deliberative principle was essential to the revival of parliamentary life in that period. The right of address, in other words a text discussed and voted on in response to the Speech from the Throne opening the parliamentary session, was incorporated in the law of 13 August 1814. Debates on finance and weighty bills offered opportunities for deliberation. Subsequently, with the emergence of the interpellation procedure, this field of deliberation substantially increased under the July Monarchy.

A real breakthrough of sovereignty followed the accession of Louis-Philippe to the throne in 1830. His new 'Charte' was revised on 14 August. It was contractually accepted by the king as a condition of his accession. National sovereignty was restored, the monarch being designated as the King of the French people and no longer the King of France. The constitutional text remained silent on any political responsibility of ministers to the assemblies, but it opened the possibility of new practices that eventually enabled this responsibility, which consisted particularly in the right of interpellation, and from 1835 onwards interpellation led to discussing and voting on an *ordre du jour*. This vote had no political significance and was not a vote of confidence in the government, but the appearance of the right of interpellation brought about a new form of technical governmental accountability: the question of confidence. This was first used by Jacques Laffitte on 11 March 1831 on a proposal to create royal obligations.

However, in the absence of any genuine bipartisanship, which meant that there was a solid majority, successive governments allowed Louis-Philippe to impose his concept of institutional balance. The frequent use of dissolution, used six times under the July Monarchy (1831, 1834, 1837, 1839, 1842, 1846), reflected the inability of the Chamber of Deputies to regulate its own tensions. This was one of the reasons for the king's inaction in the face of the electoral and parliamentary reforms that were needed. The Doctrinaires were disappointed with the inadequate expansion of the electorate even though the 1831 law included some capacities: the members of the Institut de France and senior officers. In the 1840s, the opposition demanded both a reform of the electoral system of the Chamber of Deputies and a considerable cut in the number of civil servant members, who constituted more than a third of the assembly (against a tenth in the British House of Commons). According to the liberal Prosper Duvergier de Hauranne (1847), the electoral reform and the parliamentary reform should not have been separated because, for him, 'representative government is in danger' and 'it is corruption that undermines'. A big debate on the expansion of the legal country took place on 15 February 1842 between Prime Minister François Guizot and the poet Alphonse de Lamartine, who became the spokesman for the left wing of the assembly. However, electoral reform proposals presented to both chambers, though very conservative, were systematically rejected. The proposal presented in March 1847 by Prosper Duvergier de Hauranne reflected the state of mind of the liberal opposition, who were distrustful of universal suffrage and considered the mass of the people to be too immature to participate in the election of members. This proposal was meant to reduce the electoral tax and to bring the number of the electorate up to five hundred thousand people. However, the intransigent refusal of the *'moment Guizot'* (the period 1840–48, when Guizot dominated French politics; Rosanvallon 1985), which proved unable to take into account the requirements of political democracy (Ledru-Rollin 1851), led the opposition to continue the discussion outside parliament and to start a campaign of banquets (the only authorized meetings), which led to the Revolution of February 1848.

National Representation under the Second Republic

The turning point for representation was the decree of the Second Republic establishing universal male suffrage on 5 March 1848. The electorate suddenly increased from 240,000 to 9.4 million voters, and the elections thereby became of real consequence, unlike in 1793. This was also a turning point in European history, with the other models, like the British, still adhering to census suffrage. A remuneration was awarded to elected representatives in order to extend the membership of parliament and to justify the title 'representatives of the people'. After the election of the Constituent National Assembly in April 1848, a commission was set up to draft a new constitution. The eighteen members of this commission were strongly influenced by the American example as presented by Alexis de Tocqueville (1835–40). The proposal of the commission, which provided for a single chamber that would elect the executive, was hotly debated in the Assembly from September onwards. Despite Duvergier de Hauranne's pleas for a second chamber as an oligarchic moderator, bicameralism was rejected as a symbol of past monarchies. Elected by universal male suffrage and the ballot list, a single chamber called the National Legislative Assembly, a body that had the sole power to make law and was in permanent session, as during the French Revolution, was established.

It was a consolidation of the principle of national sovereignty exercised by the representatives of the people. However, it required an intervention by Alphonse de Lamartine to overthrow an amendment by Jules Grévy that aimed at controlling or removing the president by the Assembly. This intervention resulted in a constitutional text that asserted national sovereignty. However, this sovereignty was vested not only in representatives elected by universal (male) suffrage to the Assembly, but also in a president who was likewise elected by universal franchise and was not accountable to the Assembly. This separation of powers, inspired by the American model, was of immediate benefit to Louis Napoleon, the heir of Napoleon Bonaparte, who was elected president on 10 December 1848. After his coup of 2 December 1851, which restored the Empire in 1852, Napoleon III did not question the national sovereignty exercised by the representatives of the people in principle, but he did so in his constitutional practice. The constitution of 14 January 1852, strongly inspired by the constitution of 1799, gave him all the constitutional powers, including the initiative and the enactment of laws. It introduced tricameralism; the Corps législatif (Legislative Body) was limited by the Sénat and the Conseil d'Etat (Council of State); and legislation was entirely controlled by Napoleon III and his government. The members of the Corps législatif – who were no longer called representatives of the people since they no longer represented the nation but only an area of the territory – were reduced in number to 261 from 750 in the Second Republic. The electoral practice under the authoritarian Empire denied national sovereignty by giving the advantage to candidates supported by the government.

In the 1860s, pressure from liberals and republicans forced the executive to make a number of concessions. Among the five freedoms required by the leader of the opposition, Adolphe Thiers, in his famous speech of 11 January 1864, were freedom of elections, freedom of national representation and the freedom to ensure that the activities of the executive were directed by public opinion. It was at that time that liberal intellectuals were publishing major works inspired by British and American models, such as *Le Parti libéral* by Edouard de Laboulaye (1864) or *La France Nouvelle* by Lucien Prevost-Paradol (1868). These works advocated the recognition of a true national sovereignty within a structure that could be a republic or a monarchy. This proposal coincided with the gradual evolution of the system itself into a form of parliamentary empire. Changes initiated by the reforms of the imperial decree of 24 November 1860 (the right of address awarded to the two assemblies, expansion of the public hearings of the Corps législatif), the imperial letter of 19 January 1867 (the right of interpellation) and the plebiscite (senatus-consulte) of 8 September 1869 (freedom of amendment, legislative initiative) led at the end of the reign of Napoleon III to a true deliberative system called a 'parliamentary empire' although it was really only a 'semi-parliamentary' system. Emile Ollivier, a great admirer of Benjamin Constant, was even commanded by Napoleon III to establish 'a government representative of the parliamentary majority' in late December 1869 (*Journal officiel de l'Empire français*, 28 December 1869, 1721).

The Introduction of Responsibility during the Third Republic

The Revolution of 4 September 1870 during the Franco-German War and the proclamation of the Third Republic put an end to the ambiguities of the Second Empire, reaffirming the sovereignty of the National Assembly elected on 8 February 1871 by universal male suffrage. The resolution passed on 17 February stated that the National Assembly was only a 'repository of sovereign authority' and that the chief executive (president) performed his duties under its authority. Adolphe Thiers became 'Président de la République' on 31 August 1871, but he was forced by the Assembly to resign on 24 May 1873. His successor, Maréchal de Mac-Mahon, succeeded in getting the Septennial Act passed on 20 November 1873, which extended his term to seven years and removed the responsibility of the president to the Assembly. However, he too was forced to resign on 30 January 1879 after dissolving the Chamber of Deputies in June 1877. The republican model established by the constitution of 1875, the result of a compromise between Orleanists and moderate republicans, confirmed the dominance of the two assemblies, the Chamber of Deputies and the Senate.

The new republican model established the principle of the individual responsibility and solidarity of ministers (as collectively responsible) in both chambers. Deputies and senators could ask questions, make motions and resolutions and interpellations and bring down ministers or governments. For his part, the president held the right to initiate and promulgate laws in conjunction with the assemblies, the right to convene the assemblies and to declare the end of the sessions, and especially the right to dissolve the Chamber of Deputies with the assent of the Senate. We can therefore speak of a dualistic parliamentary republic with power shared between the president and parliament. However, this constitutional balance was soon upset after the crisis of 16 May 1877, in which Mac-Mahon exercised his right to dissolve the Chamber of Deputies to the advantage of the monarchists. From that time on, national sovereignty became the property of the assemblies under the so-called 'Grévy Constitution' (Jules Grévy was the successor of Mac-Mahon). A book on civics written by the renowned historian Ernest Lavisse (the nom de plume of Ernest Laloi) on the centenary of the French Revolution recalled that 'power resides in the assemblies, whose members are elected by the people, and the people are sovereign' (Lavisse 1889: 106).

This first period of the Third Republic has also been described as the golden age of eloquence (see also Chapter 10) following the spirit of the French Revolution. The regulations were formulated more to guarantee the rights of MPs than to ensure the smooth running of debates. In this parliament of law-yers, journalists and teachers, the plenary discussion represented the essence of what we call parliamentary democracy. 'We're wasting too much time with too long speeches', Georges Clemenceau said in 1908. Charles Benoist, head of the right-wing parliamentary reform group, which included 60 members in 1902, wanted to 'turn the unlimited and arbitrary parliamentarism whose excesses discredit the republican regime into a regular and limited parliamen-tarism' (1902). The socialist Léon Blum in 1918 deplored the 'consumption of time, goodwill, illusions', 'discussions without measure', 'amendments without number' and 'speakers extending endless speeches amidst univer-sal apathy'. From the 1920s onwards, the theme of 'parliamentary reform', including the streamlining of parliamentary time, was very much to the fore. On 22 January 1935, for example, a resolution taken at the Conference of Presidents defined the length of any debate on a project or a proposal. This allowed for a more efficient organization of budget discussions between 1936 and 1939. The multiplication of decrees in that period was an expression of the desire to shorten the time for speaking to the detriment of legislative delibera-tion. That change resulted in the system of the Fifth Republic, which reduced the length of parliamentary sessions. The agenda of parliamentary work was set by the government (see also Chapter 14), which had numerous tools avail-able for limiting discussion, including the use of a block vote. This is what the founders of the Fifth Republic under de Gaulle in 1958 called 'rationalized parliamentarism' (Garrigues 2007: 11, 427ff).

The Fifth Republic, however, did not take new cognizance of the main innovation of the Third Republic: the official recognition of governmental responsibility, which is the distinctive difference between systems that are parliamentary and those that are not. From 1880 to 1914, forty-one govern-ments came and went, averaging more than one per year. The longest was that of René Waldeck-Rousseau, who remained in office from June 1899 to June 1902. As stated above, the need for institutional reform to strengthen the executive was expressed around 1900 by Charles Benoist. As Carré de Malberg wrote, the Third Republic came in 1877 when there was a regime of 'absolute parliamentarism'. That was the reason why the founders of the Fifth Republic created a semi-presidential regime, in which the govern-ment's responsibility was framed and balanced by the presidential power of dissolution.

Conclusion

After a process that was the key issue of French political history in the nineteenth century, the assemblies of the Third Republic combined the four elements of parliamentarism: they were sovereign in the full sense of the term, but also fully representative, deliberative and able to overthrow a government by refusing to give it their confidence. We should add a fifth element that belongs to the history of French parliamentarism: the publicity of deliberations. This was included in the first constitution (1791): 'The deliberations of the legislative body are public, and the minutes of its meetings are printed'. After 1814, the openness of the chamber to the public became an index of the democratization of the political system: low in authoritarian regimes such as the First and the Second Empires, and extensive under the July Monarchy and during the Second Republic. A stenographic service responsible for producing a full account of proceedings was set up in 1846 in the Chambre des Pairs (Chamber of Peers) and in 1848 in the National Assembly. After the victory of the supporters of the Republic in 1877, the admission of the public to sessions was imposed in order to advance openness.

The 'Grévy Constitution' turned the Third Republic towards the assembly system, since no president after Mac-Mahon dared to use his right to dissolve the Assembly. The representation of the sovereign nation, an ideal sought from the outset by the Constituent National Assembly of 1789, led to the sovereignty of the national representation. The Chamber of Deputies was all-powerful, but the real nation was not represented.

The term 'rationalization of parliamentarism' dates back to the end of the First World War. It expresses the ideal of a 'scientifically governed society', the first condition for material prosperity. It also refers to various mechanisms proposed to reduce the influence of parliament on government action in order to permit the latter to function more efficiently. The problem is how to reconcile parliamentary sovereignty with government efficiency. The idea of the Gaullist institutional reformists (Debré 1958) is simple: governance does not reside in the parliament. It should be the business of government and the 'forces' of the nation – that is to say, representatives of professional groups, who must meet in an ad hoc assembly.

In 1958, the founders of the Fifth Republic applied various solutions proposed by interwar reformers to ensure the power of the executive. The first solution – at least the most visible one – was the constitution of 1958, which gave the government powers that made it less dependent on parliament, especially with regard to enforcing public policy through legal norms, but which also allowed parliamentary control. In other words, it was meant to establish the tightest boundaries between parliament and the executive power while maintaining the parliamentary principle of collaboration between them.

These solutions were resorted to not only, or at least not primarily, for the reasons imagined by the formulators of the constitution. Indeed, parliament has been at the heart of an unexpected modernization of political life: the emergence of clear parliamentary majorities has created governmental stability. The parliamentary history of the Fifth Republic has established 'majority rule'. The polarization of political forces – which has accompanied the implementation of majority rule – has been combined with a duality governing the devolution of power (the legislative and presidential elections). This has characterized the Fifth Republic, and it also produces brand new situations in French politics called 'alternance' (between right and left governments) and 'cohabitation' (between a leftist President of the Republic and a rightist government, or vice versa). In this way parliament has regained a central position, albeit in the absence of real power.

References

Primary Sources

Benoist, C. 1902. *La Réforme parlementaire*. Paris: Plon-Nourrit.

Blum, L. 1918. *Lettres sur la réforme gouvernementale*. Paris: B. Grasset.

Bodin, J. 1576. *Six Livres de la République*. Paris: Jacques Du Puys.

Carré de Malberg, R. 1920–22. *Contribution à la théorie générale de l'Etat Moderne, spécialement d'après les données fournies par le droit constitutionnel*, vol. 2. Paris: Recueil Sirey.

_____. 1931. *La Loi, expression de la volonté générale. Etude sur le concept de loi dans la Constitution de 1875*. Paris: Recueil Sirey.

Constant, B. 1814. *Réflexions sur les constitutions, la distribution des pouvoirs et les garanteis, dans une monarchie constitutionelle*. Paris: H. Nicolle.

Debré, M. 1958. *Refaire une démocratie, un Etat, un pouvoir*. Paris: Plon.

Duvergier de Hauranne, P. 1847. *De la réforme parlementaire et électorale*. Paris: Paulin.

Laboulaye, E., de. 1864. *Le Parti libéral, son programme, son avenir*. Paris: Charpentier.

Lavisse, E. 1889. *La première année d'instruction morale et civique. Notions de droit et d'économie politique*. Paris: Armand Colin.

Ledru-Rollin, A. 1851. *Du Gouvernement direct du peuple*. Paris: Impr. de Prève.

Montesquieu. 1748. *De l'esprit des lois*. Geneva: Barillot & fils.

Prevost-Paradol, L.-A. 1868. *La France Nouvelle*. Paris: Michel Levy frères.

Projet de Constitution pour la République française et discours préliminaire au nom de la commission des onze. Paris: Imp. Nationale, Messidor an III.

Rousseau, J.-J. 1762. *Le Contrat Social*. Amsterdam: M.M. Rey.

Sieyès, A.E.J. 1788. *Qu'est-ce que le Tiers Etat?*

Tocqueville, A., de. 1835–40. *De la démocratie en Amérique*, vol. 2. Paris: Ch. Gosselin.

Vitrolles, Baron de. 1815. *Du Ministère dans le gouvernement représentatif.* Paris: Dentu.

Secondary Sources

Furet, F. 1988. *Histoire de France, Tome 4. La Révolution: 1770–1880.* Paris: Hachette.

Garrigues, J. (ed.). 2007. *Histoire du Parlement de 1789 à nos jours.* Paris: A. Colin.

Gauchet, M. 1995. *La Révolution des pouvoirs. La souveraineté, le peuple et la représenta-tion 1789–1799.* Paris: Gallimard.

_____. 2007. *La Révolution moderne. Vol 1 de L'Avènement de la démocratie.* Paris: Gallimard.

Manin, B. 1995. *Principes du gouvernement représentatif.* Paris: Calmann-Lévy.

Rosanvallon, P. 1985. *Le Moment Guizot.* Paris: Gallimard.

_____. 1998. *Le Peuple introuvable. Histoire de la représentation démocratique en France.* Paris: Gallimard.

Jean Garrigues, Ph.D., is Professor of Contemporary History at the University of Orléans, France, and Lecturer at the Institute of Law at the University of Paris-1 Panthéon-Sorbonne. His research focuses on French politics between the nineteenth century and today and on the relations between political and economic power, political parties and pressure groups and parliamentary life. He has been President of the Comité d'histoire parlementaire et politique since 2002, and he is Vice President of the International Commission for the History of Representative and Parliamentary Institutions and a member of the Board of Directors of the research network EuParl.net.

Eric Anceau, Ph.D., is Lecturer in Nineteenth-Century History at the University of Paris-4-Sorbonne and Sciences Po Paris, France. In his research, he has specialized in the overall history of politics and in French political and social history in the period 1789–1940, particularly from the point of view of the history of elites. He is associated with the Centre de recherches en histoire du XIXᵉ siècle and is Vice President of the Comité d'histoire parlementaire et politique.

Chapter 4

From Monarchical Constitutionalism to a Parliamentary Republic

Concepts of Parliamentarism in Germany since 1818

Andreas Biefang and Andreas Schulz

Germany's parliamentary development in the nineteenth and twentieth centuries was marked by territorial reorganization and political regime changes. These alterations in external conditions had considerable influence on how contemporaries debated about parliamentarism, the tasks they attributed to it and the hopes and fears they associated with it. The political circumstances defined to a great extent the topics that could or could not be discussed in parliament or in public at any given time. These limitations on discussion could be defined very differently for different individual German states or for the whole nation state, for the constitutional monarchy or the parliamentary republic. This chapter attempts to do justice to this situation by linking a systematic analysis of central concepts of parliamentarism with some elucidation of chronological questions and issues relating to constitutional systems (for parliamentary discourse, see Chapter 11, and for theoretical debates, see Chapter 16).

The Monarchical Principle instead of Sovereignty of the People: Parliaments in Individual German States in the Period 1818–48

Modern parliamentarism arose in Germany at the level of the states that emerged from the multiplicity of member states in the Holy Roman Empire. It evolved within the political and legal framework of the German

Confederation, founded in 1815. The Confederation was an association of states founded to establish a new political order following the end of the French occupation. In terms of domestic policy, it was driven by the dread of revolution, aiming to prevent this by a mixture of jointly exercised police control and preventive reforms. Article 13 of the Confederation constitution became the most important element in this strategy; it laid down that the member states must enact their own 'representative constitutions', entailing a limited form of representation based on the social estates. Modern German parliamentarism thus did not start with a revolution; on the contrary, it was a strategy to avoid revolution.

The Kingdoms of Bavaria and Württemberg and the Grand Duchies of Baden and Hesse-Darmstadt did indeed receive constitutions of this type in the first wave of constitutionalization, 1818–20. A second wave in the early 1830s – triggered by the July Revolution in Paris – included a number of other states, the most important of these being the Kingdoms of Hanover and Saxony and the Electorate of Hesse (Brandt, Kirsch and Schlegelmilch 2006: 640–977; Daum 2012: 781–1040). In most cases, these constitutions were negotiated between princes and assemblies, but then imposed unilaterally. With the exception of the Electorate of Hesse, the representative assemblies consisted of two chambers: an upper chamber and a people's chamber. In concept and in their institutions, the parliaments built to some extent on the traditional social estates that had emerged in the Holy Roman Empire and which had ceased to exist in 1806. That applies, for example, to the concept of representation, which guaranteed that representatives of the different social estates would be assured of a quota of places even in the people's chambers (Stollberg-Rilinger 2008). This idea was symbolically expressed in the plenary chambers (with the exception of Baden) with their hierarchical rectangular seating arrangements. The dress regulations for the representatives specified different styles for different social groups, giving a visible form to this surviving premodern idea of the social order.

However, the fact that the principle of abstract representation was applied for the first time had more weight than the surviving elements of the traditions mentioned above: the great majority of parliamentary seats were assigned through elections. The elections were indirect and in most cases took the form of an open ballot. The electoral law strongly favoured the property-owning classes. The largest numbers of people entitled to vote were in Württemberg and Bavaria, where around two-thirds of all men over twenty-five years of age possessing local citizenship rights could cast their vote at elections by direct suffrage. The regulation that elected representatives should not represent the interests of their estate but those of the whole population 'according to their own convictions' (constitution of Baden) was also in accordance with the concept of abstract representation.

The modern elements of the constitutional orders were modelled on French examples, specifically the 'Charte constitutionnelle' of 1814. Despite differences in detail, these early forms of constitution fall into the category of monarchic constitutionalism, in which the Crown remained predominant (Kirsch 1999). The 'monarchical principle' that the prince was the sole possessor of sovereignty remained intact. The parliaments were granted above all the right to approve taxes and budgets. They took part in the legislative process but had neither the right to initiate legislation nor the authority to set the agenda for plenary sessions. State control also restricted the publication of proceedings, heavily in some cases, severely limiting the extent to which the state assemblies could become political forums. Fundamental issues of parliamentarism were therefore mainly dealt with in the form of journalism, for example in the *Staatslexikon* edited by Karl Rotteck and Karl Theodor Welcker, who were elected representatives in Baden. The importance of the *Staatslexikon* for the development of political language can hardly be overestimated (Werner 2010). Sessions lasting a total of a few weeks per year were sufficient for the parliaments to fulfil their intended tasks, but this was by no means enough for the development of a parliamentary environment and sociability. Despite this, the leading 'people's men' acquired some popularity in their states.

As time went on, parliamentary practice gradually undermined the strict dualism between the executive and a legislature in which the chambers understood themselves to be the overall representatives of the people; instead, an informal parliamentarism developed in which groups of representatives who supported the government and those who opposed it confronted each other (Brandt 1987; Götschmann 2002; Fehrenbach 2007; Becht 2009). Looking at Germany as a whole, the early constitutional parliaments had limited power to shape the culture, particularly because the Kingdom of Prussia and the Habsburg Monarchy had no constitutions and therefore no modern parliaments (Obenaus 1984). Overall, the German Confederation and its member states did not succeed in satisfying the people's growing desire for political participation, particularly in relation to the national issue. The revolutions in spring 1848, therefore, were not restricted to individual states, and they culminated in a national revolution.

Sovereignty of the People and the Parliamentary Form of Government: The Conceptual Laboratory of the Revolution of 1848–49

The revolutions in individual German states led to changes of government and revisions of constitutions, without, however, abandoning the principle of the constitutional system. At the national level, on the other hand, things developed differently: the groups supporting the revolution went much further. The revolutionary interlude served as a conceptual laboratory for a constitutional development that continued to be characterized by monarchical constitutionalism up to 1918. Demands for the creation of a 'German national parliament', often referred to as a 'people's assembly', and a national constitution were part of the standard repertoire of the agendas of the revolutionary people's assemblies in March 1848.[1]

To initiate the necessary steps, a pre-parliament made up of 574 'trusted men' of the people met in Frankfurt am Main on 31 March 1848. The pre-parliament was legitimized by revolutionary law and made the case for a 'National Assembly' to be elected in 'free people's elections' in order to develop the constitution to which they aspired. In doing so, they declared themselves in favour of the concept of abstract representation, which was considered essential for the creation of political legitimacy (Botzenhart 1977).

The election laws were enacted in cooperation with the German Confederation's organs so that legal continuity was formally maintained. The conduct of the elections themselves was the responsibility of the states, leading to considerable differences in the actual form of the election regulations; for example, in relation to the question of whether the elections were direct or indirect (Obermann 1987). The elections took place in accordance with the principle of 'universal and equal suffrage', which in some states, however, was linked to economic conditions such as economic 'independence', a criterion that was defined in very different ways in different states. Overall, however, the number of those entitled to vote was always at least 75 per cent of adult men. By the standards of the time, this could be adjudged a success in terms of the people's representation (cf. France in Chapter 3).

Regardless of the formally preserved legal continuity with the German Confederation, the National Assembly (*Nationalversammlung*) decided not to seek the princes' approval for the constitution, but to enact it autonomously.[2] In doing this, they showed de facto their commitment to the concept of 'the sovereignty of the people', although the term was rarely used and was still viewed with suspicion by many 'constitutional' liberals. For example, Heinrich von Gagern, later Speaker of the National Assembly, who can be regarded as belonging to the centre right, had already argued in the pre-parliament that 'the sovereignty of the people' and 'the principle of monarchy in the state' were not mutually contradictory. The creation of a national executive in late June 1848 also took place through the sovereign exercise of the National Assembly's power; in this process, it was intended that the heads of the 'Reich's ministries' should be responsible to the parliamentary majority, in practice if not formally. The term 'parliamentary form of government' soon became commonly used by the elected representatives (Botzenhart 1977: 54–70, 163–76; cf. Steinmetz 1998: 1089–138). The National Assembly's reclaiming of power in this way was undoubtedly made easier by the fact that there was no established monarchic power to oppose it at the national level. The revolutionary act was counterbalanced by the appointment of the Austrian Archduke Johann as a provisional 'Imperial Regent'. A preliminary decision was thus taken in favour of a monarch as head of state, whereas the left-wingers would have preferred a republican solution with a president or a directorate.

Within one year, the National Assembly prepared a complete constitution for a national federal state. Their comprehensive catalogue of fundamental rights came close to American and French models. Controversies about the constitution were the visible signs of a hidden conflict, however. 'This divergence was added to the social issue', as Karl Stedman, the representative for Cologne, had already stated in the pre-parliament: either one spoke in favour of an open order relying on the widest possible level of participation, as supported by the republican left wing of parliament, or one favoured a socially restricted, exclusive rule, as preferred by the right-wing monarchic constitutionalists in the parliament. However, fundamental compromises were still possible thanks to the fluid 'centre ground' in the house. In this way, an imperial constitution was enacted in March 1849. The compromise kept to the lines already drawn, linking the head of state, now dynastically defined as the 'Prussian hereditary monarchy', with a 'democratic parliament' elected by general, equal, secret and direct ballot.

The National Assembly experiment was forcibly terminated in the summer of 1849 by the counter-revolution. The restoration of the German Confederation meant that achievements such as the sovereignty of the people, parliamentary government and the catalogue of fundamental rights were lost for decades. Nevertheless, the Revolution had brought a qualitative leap forward in the conceptualization of parliamentarism. Many of the principles that had been discussed both in parliament and in public and set down in the Imperial constitution were seminal for future developments and were reflected in the constitution of the German Reich (Kühne 1985; Pollmann 1985). This applies, for example, to the concept of parliamentary autonomy, according to which the parliaments regulated issues of internal organization and public representation on their own responsibility, to the principle of unlimited parliamentary publicity and to the right of legislative initiative. Politically, the linking of the Prussian hereditary monarchy and a freely elected national representative body proved to be particularly influential: a significant result of the revolution was the constitutionalization of Prussia, which – unlike Austria – was now able to catch up with parliamentary development.

Monarchical Constitutionalism in the Nation State 1867–1918

Democratic Electoral Practice instead of Sovereignty of the People

A form of national parliamentary government was finally established in Germany with the founding of the German Reich, as the state form was named, in 1871. Prussia's military success in the war leading to the German Reich's foundation enabled Prussia to increase its territory by annexations and to take its place at the head of a German federal state. The anti-legitimist 'revolution from below' against the German Confederation in 1848 was replaced by the 'revolution from above' in 1867–1871. Although the position of the Kaiser was bound to the Prussian monarchy, the Reich had no historical dynastic status. The title of Kaiser, too, was initially hardly more than the name of the office that the Prussian King held in his function as director of the *Bundesrat*, the federal council of the Reich. The new state was imposed against considerable resistance in the southern German, Catholic-dominated regions, and, in order to ensure its long-term stability, it was essential to give it additional national democratic legitimation. This was achieved by referring to the law on general, direct, secret and universal suffrage of 1849. This concept of suffrage served as 'an appeal to all classes and estates, to the members of all states of the German nation, to participate equally in the creation of a great new German state', as Johannes Miquel, a National Liberal, put it at the constitutive Imperial Diet.[3]

Universal male suffrage was elevated to constitutional status and was further developed in a law echoing that of 1849. It became a decisive factor in politicizing broad sections of society. The general public increasingly perceived the Reichstag as the place where vital issues were debated and decided. Both the central role of parliament in the legislative process and the public ritual of election campaigns contributed to this perception (Anderson 2000; Biefang 2008). The sheer number of active participants, the diverse forms of action and the wide reporting in the media made election campaigns an experience that aroused an emotive sense of community in the cause of democracy among large parts of the population. This exercise in democratic practice, along with the progress in safeguarding the institution of the secret ballot and the presentation of the act of casting a vote as a citizen's honourable duty, strengthened the Reichstag's claim to speak in the name of the people. Universal suffrage had, furthermore, an enormous impact on the development of parties and the party system.

Parallel to the development of the party organizations, a new type of politician evolved: the professional parliamentary representative, a versatile politician who devoted his entire energy to politics and increasingly relied on politics for his financial livelihood. This form of professionalization provoked violent political and intellectual criticism, mainly directed against the Social Democrats. Robert Michels, a sociologist, coined the phrase 'the iron law of the oligarchy' in 1911 (Bluhm 2012).

Publicity and Representation

Since the end of the eighteenth century, parliament and publicity had been seen as conceptual twins by the liberals and democrats, whose ideas had been influenced by the Enlightenment (see also Chapter 2 on Britain and Chapter 3 on France). Both were viewed as organs of a political process that was determined by the citizens in free debates. The press was allotted the role of an intermediary between voters and elected representatives, although initially it was not clearly recognized that the press was also an autonomous actor in the formation of opinions. The battle against press censorship and for the freedom of parliamentary reporting was the main topic in many debates and accelerated the formation of political associations. The freedom of parliamentary reporting was de facto established during the Revolution of 1848–49, although it was another two decades before it was guaranteed in the constitution. Only when the German Reich was founded was the symbiotic link between parliament and publicity guaranteed permanently (Biefang 2012).

In the early phase of constitutionalism, the parliaments had little scope to strengthen their role in the political system owing to the dominance of the monarchy (Knauer and Kümmel 2011). The publication of parliamentary proceedings was regulated by the executive. Press reports were subject to censorship. The parliaments were barely perceptible as independent institutions. With the exception of the Grand Duchy of Baden, they did not even meet in newly built premises but in existing buildings that had been adapted for the purpose. The construction of parliament buildings only began when the nation state was founded (Biefang 2002; Cullen 1999).

During the Reich, systematic publicity activity at the Reichstag was in its infancy. It included the production of leaflets reporting on how the Reichstag worked and the issue of biographical handbooks about the elected representatives, known as 'parliamentary manuals'. The Reichstag's most important contribution was in guaranteeing access to journalists and artist-reporters, including press photographers after 1900, and providing a suitable infrastructure. The provision of a visitors' gallery and visitors' service also demonstrates the Reichstag's general openness. In the daily papers, a great deal of space was allotted to the reporting of parliamentary debates. Parliamentary presence in the media was supported by the representatives' and candidates' image awareness and presentation strategies; it was in their own interest to cooperate increasingly with the press. The leading politicians, at least, became well-known through the media and enjoyed nationwide fame. They formed a new national political elite that took its place alongside the established aristocratic, military and bureaucratic elites. All in all, the public representations of parliamentarism contributed to strengthening the Reichstag's claim to legitimacy and to increasing its power.

Increasing Power without Parliamentarism

After the interlude of the Revolution, Germany had returned to the monarchical principle. The parliamentarization of the political system – i.e., the appointment of the government through the majority factions in the Reichstag – did not occur until 1918. The chancellor was appointed and dismissed by the Kaiser alone. The chancellor had to take 'responsibility' for the entire government vis-à-vis the Reichstag, albeit initially only in a legal sense. The relevant legal theory was provided by teachers of constitutional law, the majority of whom were conservatives, and even those who had more liberal inclinations supported the strict dualism between parliament and the executive in their adherence to anti-pluralistic opposition Rousseauism, which saw the parliament as representing the totality of interests vis-à-vis the monarchy. The teachers of constitutional law did little to advance parliamentary development (Schönberger 1997; see also Chapter 16).

However, the Reichstag and the parliamentary parties also exerted little pressure in this direction. The left-wing Liberals were the only party to form a more or less united front advocating parliamentarization (Rauh 1973; Kühne 2005). The Social Democrats basically viewed parliamentarization as progress, but they preferred to concentrate on overcoming bourgeois parliamentarism (Pracht 1990). The majority of the Catholic Centre Party and the National Liberals supported the appointment of the chancellor's government by the Kaiser, partly for power-political reasons, since the existing system mainly benefited the parties of the centre, whereas the majority situation in the Reichstag could result in Social Democrat participation in government if parliamentary rule were established. For the parties to the right of the Social Democrats, the concept of a parliamentary government was in power-political terms a questionable option. Accordingly, discussions on this topic were not very intense; this was also because the Reichstag was hardly a place where debates on the principles of constitutional reforms could be held. The concept of parliamentary government could not be implemented until after the upsets caused by the First World War and the military defeat in October 1918. At that point, the monarchy was beyond saving. The Revolution gave birth to the Republic.

Parliamentary Democracy in Germany

Weimar Parliament

The German national parliament that emerged from defeat and the Revolution was elected by men and women according to the rules of democracy. It met in the theatre of a small town in central Germany. The provisional government's move from Berlin to Weimar symbolized the deep breach with the Wilhelminian Reich. Through the democratic change to the constitution, parliament became the central political actor for a decade.[4] Although the Reichstag soon returned to its former seat in Berlin, the town where Germany's parliamentary democracy was founded remained present in historical memory: whereas the state was officially called the German Reich, as before 1919, the 'Weimar Republic' and the 'Weimar Parliament' became established after 1929 as derogatory terms in the language of politics, initially in the vocabulary of the anti-parliamentary factions.[5]

From the start, there was a profound contradiction between the external changes to the form and constitution of the state and the weak emotional commitment to the political order – a discrepancy that prompted even contemporaries to voice the exaggerated diagnosis of a 'republic without republicans'. Another factor that contributed to the lack of identification with the Weimar state was the National Assembly's (Nationalversammlung) predetermined commitments in constitutional law, which made it more difficult to anchor parliamentary democracy in society (see also Chapter 16). Owing to a lack of trust in a democratically elected parliament, the Weimar constitution (Gusy 1997) established a strong president as a 'non-partisan' counterweight, following the nineteenth-century constitutionalist tradition of a government responsible solely to the monarch. The direct election of the president by the people which was implemented in the Weimar constitution offered the parties an escape route from political responsibility. The idea behind this decision, which was also supported by some members of the parliamentary left wing, was the concept of a unified 'overall interest' or 'the people as a whole', symbolized by the head of state as a *pouvoir neutre*. In case of an undefined 'emergency', the president had the authority to act through emergency regulations without parliament's agreement (Weimar constitution, Art. 48, see Mosler 1988: 5). An additional plebiscitary corrective to the parliamentary conflict of particular interests was introduced in the form of a popular petition or referendum directly addressed to the sovereign. In order to avoid the danger of possible 'parliamentary absolutism', the parliamentary democracy voluntarily adopted the fetters of a plebiscitary-authoritarian constitutional structure.

For all its limitations, parliament was the central constitutional organ in the new republican order. The members of the Reichstag influenced society to accept the republic through the legislative process and even more so through the publication of parliamentary proceedings. Parliament's public image was therefore an important factor in legitimizing and stabilizing democracy. The parliamentary actors were overwhelmed by extreme expectations from associations and groups that were not appropriate to parliamentary procedure and were not in line with the members' professional self-image. Thus the members of the Weimar Parliament were confronted from the very start with massive demands that they were expected to balance out in the course of the legislative process. Demands for 'equal' and 'just' representations of interests were issued from all sides. The idea behind these claims was the image of parliament's 'popular' character, in which the members should act as agents for all relevant social classes and professions. This people's representation was supposed to be egalitarian and to represent the whole of society while at the same time being personified in a selection of the best members of the people. Their skill, efficiency, expertise and professionalism were taken for granted; on the other hand, the members themselves considered that they were judged by moral behavioural criteria such as truthfulness, honesty and selflessness. They perceived their everyday professional life in the activities of parliament as being determined by the functional logic of external constraints. However, none of them could escape the pull of normative expectations, and therefore the internal discourse of the Reichstag was often dominated by the same moralizing rigour and denunciatory tones that also characterized media reporting about Weimar parliamentarism. It is characteristic of parliamentarism that this communication is public, national and takes place via the media. A parliament is considered to be the representation of the 'general will', an authority providing legitimation and a national political sphere of communication.

Representation of the 'General Will'
Universal suffrage as enshrined in the Weimar constitution satisfied for the first time the principle of the equality of social claims to participation – this now concerned the entire adult population since women were entitled to vote for the first time. Great expectations as well as deep fears were linked to the idea of universal and equal suffrage. However, the assumption that the numerical superiority of group or class interests would dominate the parliamentary legislative process was not fulfilled.

The pictures and photomontages of George Grosz and John Heartfield (1926) memorably expressed the idea that the people's representatives were subject to external control by powerful groups outside parliament – the actual 'pillars of the system'. Parliament did not reflect the economic and social structure of the population, nor did its members act as the people's delegates. The bourgeois, educated, property-owning classes endorsed this professional, materialistic point of view, particularly because they had lost their last political bastion when universal suffrage was extended to the municipalities and the three-class suffrage was abolished in Prussia. They expected the bourgeois parliamentary parties to ensure that their material claims were represented. The result of this general demand that interests be 'equally' represented was the 'Reich Economic Council' provided for in Article 165 of the Weimar constitution. The bourgeois parties viewed the Council, which was organized to represent the professions, as an 'economic parliament', while the left-wing parties aimed to use it as a 'workers' chamber' and a political instrument of the councils (*Räte*). Whether viewed as a professional grouping or a democratic council, the introduction of the Reich Economic Council was nothing less than a vote of no confidence in parliamentarism. Overall, the parliamentary representational principle was primarily interpreted in terms of political interests: instead of serving as the delegates of the whole nation, the representatives were expected by many to feel a duty towards their social constituency and the manifesto of the party group that had nominated them. When priority was given to rigorous adherence to particular interests, it was almost impossible for members to convince their party or electoral public that the parliamentary deliberation and negotiation process made it essential in practice to modify or give up positions laid down in the manifesto. Theodor Heuss, a liberal member of the Reichstag, complained in 1930 that the parliamentary 'party particularism' made it difficult to build bridges, even between bourgeois parties (Dorrmann 2008: 378). On other occasions, however, he, too, reviled political concessions to parliamentary competitors as symptomatic of the 'disgusting state of German parliamentarism' (Dorrmann 2008: 428).

Despite all the capacity for cooperation, particularly evident in the first half of the 1920s between the parties of the left centre, social backing for the 'Weimar coalition' remained fragile. Overall, the parliamentary elite found it difficult to acknowledge the equality of political demands and thus the democratic plurality of values as indispensable prerequisites of a parliamentary system. Over time, pragmatic cooperation developed among Reichstag members merely in order to enable them to 'carry on' (Mergel 2012), but there was no firm consensus in principle on the fundamental aspects of representative democracy. As social conflicts intensified after 1929, parliament was dominated by the politically narrow perspective of segmented social constituencies and the influence of powerful interest groups. Under these conditions, the anti-parliamentary alternative concept of the *Volksgemeinschaft* (national community; Bajohr and Wildt 2009), for which the extreme right wing constantly campaigned, became increasingly attractive.

Not until the racist and totalitarian potential of the Volksgemeinschaft policy was finally recognized did a fundamental redefinition of the principle of parliamentary representation take place. The general acceptance of the equality, in principle, of social interest groups became an essential precondition of the success of the democratic new beginning after 1945. The parliamentary reform of 1969, therefore, also focused on strengthening the rights of the opposition in order to ensure that divergent opinions were heard. 'The state consists of all political powers', as a Liberal member put it – an insight that had matured among members of the Bundestag (Born 1969: 212). He went on to say that only parliamentary systems have the ability to balance competing interests and to reconcile social conflicts. Since then, the recognition that this is the essence and task of parliamentarism has been part of the fundamental democratic consensus of the Federal Republic of Germany.

Parliament as an Authority Providing Legitimation

The transition from the monarchical German Reich to the Republic reveals the importance parliamentarism had gained under the constitutional monarchy. The abolition of the monarchy took place in early October 1918 through the appointment by the Kaiser of a parliamentary government responsible to the Reichstag, not to the monarch. Even after the outbreak of the November Revolution, the actors did not lose sight of the necessity of a parliamentary basis for the legitimation of political action. The revolutionary council of the people's representatives and their supporters in society in 1918 adhered to the aim of a constituent assembly legitimized by elections. Although they had authorized the revolutionary movement to act autonomously, their political leaders stated that they felt 'legitimacy scruples'. They therefore carried forward the transition to parliamentary democracy initiated in October 1918 with the call for elections to a national assembly.

Despite public criticism, the Weimar Republic preserved not only its legal authority but held its position as a generally accepted institutional centre of political power in the Republic. Even in the transition from a parliamentary to a presidential republic in the early 1930s, constitutional procedures were strictly followed as the Reichstag was 'disempowered' by an emergency decree. Hitler's appointment as chancellor took place within the existing constitutional framework, and even after completely taking over power the National Socialist regime did not dispense with the formal legitimation of the legislative process by the Reichstag of the 'uniformed extras' (Lilla 2004). The German Democratic Republic (GDR), founded in 1949, also practised a formally democratic legitimation procedure; their *Volkskammer* (People's Chamber) was both the constitutional legislature and an irrelevant, powerless parliament in political terms. On the other hand, this parliamentary 'approval machine' gained unexpected importance in the process of winding up the one-party rule of the socialist regime 1989–90. The 'Round Tables' had fulfilled their revolutionary function in controlling power and participating in government. They stepped down in favour of the Volkskammer, which introduced democracy by instituting elections and thus giving the revolution a legitimate political basis. The voluntary abdication of the Citizens' Committees and Round Tables in 1990 resembled the Workers' and Soldiers' Councils' transfer of power to the National Assembly 1918–19 – and it was more than a formal resemblance: in both cases, parliament was required as an authority for legitimating the revolution (Weil 2001).

Finally, the Bundestag became the central constitutional organ of parliamentary democracy in the West German Federal Republic. It was unchallenged as the source of legitimation for the state legislative process and was only bound to the 'timelessly' valid normative basic rights expressed in the constitution and the Federal Constitutional Court's scrutiny of legislation. The 1968 extra-parliamentary opposition movements, which claimed to unmask parliamentarism as merely an apparently democratic performance to cover the 'true' (i.e., economic) power structures (Roth and Rucht 2008), proved unable to challenge the Bundestag's claim to be the authority for the legitimation of political action. In contrast, the increasing criticism of the parties' extra-constitutional position of power in the 1970s and 1980s received considerable support. This critical sentiment embodies the view that when the consultative and decision-making monopoly of parliament is transferred to party headquarters or coalition committees, the Bundestag is degraded into a mere formal rubber stamp for registering extra-parliamentary decision processes. This concern received additional weight as the European Union institutions were deepened. Supranational demands for sovereignty created political sensitivity to the necessity of updating the legitimating concept of parliamentary democracy (see also Chapter 18).

'A Medium of the People' – Parliament as a Sphere of Communication

In a representative democracy, there is a functional relationship between parliament and the people; the elected representatives and the voters. This led to several misinterpretations and profound illusions about parliamentary practice, especially among left-wing political scientists such as the Marburg scholar Wolfgang Abendroth. In his understanding, the idea of the sovereignty of the people implied an 'identity of the governing and the governed' (Abendroth 1968; see also Chapter 16) and thus should not only be relevant in terms of democratic theory but become part of a political reform agenda. While similar conceptions have been widely discussed within the so-called '1968 movement', the parliamentary system of the German Federal Republic clearly developed as a mere representative democracy where the accord between the governing and the governed is fulfilled in the communication between parliament and the public. A member of the Bundestag as an elected representative communicates the political will of his or her constituency in parliament. In the constituency, he or she gives an account of parliamentary decisions and presents them in public through the media. The originally close communicative relationship between representatives and their constituencies is still reflected in the image of the 'popular speaker' and 'populist'. In the nineteenth century, 'speaking to the people' meant confronting a (local) election meeting in person and assessing its mood. In the central parliaments of modern nation states, the increased distance has been bridged by the media. In this way, parliament has since the nineteenth century developed into a 'sphere of communication' (Schulz and Wirsching 2012) with the triple constellation of parliament, the media and the public (Dieckmann 1981: 208–45). The incongruence between the 'real' communicative relationship and the ideal of a direct people's democracy has often produced overblown expectations and conspiracy scenarios. According to one political metaphor in common currency since the nineteenth century, the parliamentary stage was a theatre of illusions, while in 'dark rooms' backstage secret negotiations were held and decisions taken on political issues affecting the fate of the nation.

In complete contrast to this sinister image, the Weimar Reichstag and the preceding parliament of the German Reich stood in the bright light of increasing media publicity. Never before had reports about parliamentary practice been more comprehensive and controversial. Members could be heard and seen everywhere; the reporting of the spoken word was uncensored and reproduced acoustically, although the Weimar Reichstag initially made very little use of this possibility (Braun 2011: 29–59). Most attention was focused on the plenary debates; they determined the image of parliamentarism as a whole. In wide swathes of the population, plenary debates were perceived as an expression of irreconcilable party quarrels, with no intention of approaching an idealized political general will, or even worse, as a deceptive performance that was intended to conceal the actors' 'real' intentions (see Chapter 11). Ruth Fischer, the fierce agitator of the Communist Party, referred to this popular idea when she opened her parliamentary inaugural speech with the words, 'Honourable shadow theatre! Honourable dream figures!' (*Verhandlungen des Reichstags*, 2 June 1924). The general public, too, showed little sympathy with a culture of conflict structured by a dialectical dialogue and framed in parliamentary procedures and internal party-political rhetoric.

The Reichstag did not succeed in communicating a realistic image of the division of work in the parliamentary process, and therefore the fact that the Weimar parties' ability to compromise was sometimes impeded seemed to express a fundamental dysfunctionality of the parliamentary system. This was another reason why the contrasting anti-parliamentary concept of a Volksgemeinschaft under unified, authoritarian leadership gained appeal as an apparently ideal embodiment of the political will of the whole people, particularly because this idea could be linked to both right-wing and left-wing ideas. Under the authoritarian regime, the 'managed' parliament of the National Socialist state claimed to be the 'true' expression of the identity of the people and their political leaders. According to the propaganda, the will of the people was carried out in the unanimous acclamation of legislative drafts presented to it; discussion and action were harmonized at last (see also Chapter 11). In the end, the proclaimed unity of the people, the Fuehrer and the people's representatives proved to be mere propaganda; the people's representation was simply an instrument to legitimize an authoritarian system.

Even so, after 1945 the ideal of the people's self-rule was by no means considered invalid. The democratically elected representatives in the Federal Republic also encountered anti-parliamentary feelings. They were often faced with abstract moral and political demands, and their actions were judged according to criteria such as transparency, objectivity and authenticity. However, unlike the Weimar Republic, the parliament in Bonn was more successful in adapting its working style and communication to the expectations of the people. The political style of a 'new objectivity' and sobriety manifested itself in the parliamentary practice of the Bonn republic. The glassy transparency of the architecture of the Bonn parliament was a powerful symbol. The permeability expressed in the political symbolism of parliament's architecture was also a guiding principle of the Federal Republic's conception of parliamentary reform. Parliamentary decision-making processes were to become more transparent, and the communication between the Bundestag and society made easier. One Bundestag member appealed to his colleagues: 'If you make committee meetings public, you increase the value of parliamentary activity and raise a veil which conceals parliament and its activity from many people in our country!' (*Verhandlungen des Deutschen Bundestages*, 18 June 1969: 13305). Not all members of parliament were in favour of this vision of making parliamentary consultation processes entirely public and organizing the Bundestag as the 'medium of the people', as a kind of resonance chamber of public communication. Critics of the transparency concept considered that the 'economy of time' and the need for the efficient organization of parliamentary working procedures were factors weighing against it. For example, the 'facultative openness' of the committees, enacted by the Bundestag in 1969, delayed the parliamentary discussion of important legislation.

The attempt to reorganize the sittings of the Bundestag into a forum for speech and discussion was only partly successful in a parliament based on the division of labour. For example, the obligation to engage in free speech, which the representatives considered 'a core element of parliamentary negotiation' (*Verhandlungen des Deutschen Bundestages*, 18 June 1969: 13298), could only be implemented at the price of a strictly regimented debating order. In order to break up the monotonous sequence of prepared speeches, the new rules of procedure subjected parliamentary dialogue to the authority of the Speaker, who from then on determined the order of speakers.

Notes

1 Examples can be viewed digitally at: http://sammlungen.ub.uni-frankfurt.de/1848/
2 The deliberations (*Verhandlungen*) of the German Constituent National Assembly in Frankfurt am Main 1848–49 are available in digital form at: http://daten.digitale-sammlungen.de/~db/ausgaben/uni_ausgabe.html?projekt=1182243493
3 The stenographic Reichstag reports can be viewed in digital form at: http://www.reichstagsprotokolle.de/index.html
4 The entire text of the Weimar constitution is available online from the Deutsches Historisches Museum & Haus der Geschichte der Bundesrepublik, *Die Verfassung des Deutschen Reichs vom 11. August 1919*, at: http://www.dhm.de/lemo/kapitel/weimarer-republik/innenpolitik/reichsverfassung-1919.html
5 'Bonn is not Weimar!' was the self-reassuring catchword in the early days of the Federal Republic.

References

Primary Sources

Mosler, H. (ed.). 1988. *Die Verfassung des Deutschen Reiches vom 11. August 1919*. Stuttgart: Reclam.
Verhandlungen des Deutschen Bundestages, 5. Wahlperiode. Stenographische Berichte, Vol. 70, 240th session.
Verhandlungen des Deutschen Reichstags, 2. Wahlperiode. Stenographische Berichte, Vol. 381.

Secondary Sources

Abendroth, W. 1968. *Antagonistische Gesellschaft und politische Demokratie. Aufsätze zur politischen Soziologie.* Berlin: Luchterhand.

Anderson, M.L. 2000. *Practicing Democracy: Elections and Political Culture in Imperial Germany.* Princeton: Princeton University Press.

Bajohr, F. and M. Wildt (eds). 2009. *Volksgemeinschaft. Neue Forschungen zur Gesellschaft des Nationalsozialismus.* Frankfurt am Main: Fischer Taschenbuch Verlag.

Becht, H.P. 2009. *Badischer Parlamentarismus 1819 bis 1870.* Düsseldorf: Droste.

Biefang, A. 2002. *Bismarcks Reichstag. Das Parlament in der Leipziger Straße. Fotografiert von Julius Braatz.* Düsseldorf: Droste.

———. 2008. 'Die Reichstagswahlen als demokratisches Zeremoniell', in A. Biefang, M. Epkenhans and K. Tenfelde (eds), *Das politische Zeremoniell im Deutschen Kaiserreich 1871–1918.* Düsseldorf: Droste, pp. 233–70.

———. 2012. *Die andere Seite der Macht. Parlament und Politik im "System Bismarck" 1871–1890,* 2nd ed. Düsseldorf: Droste.

Bluhm, H. (ed.). 2012. *Robert Michels' Soziologie des Parteiwesens. Oligarchien und Eliten – die Kehrseiten moderner Demokratie.* Wiesbaden: VS Verlag für Sozialwissenschaften.

Born, W. 1969. 'Große, kleine oder außerparlamentarische Opposition? Zur Rolle der Opposition im parlamentarischen Regierungssystem', in E. Hübner, H. Oberreute and H. Rausch (eds), *Der Bundestag von innen gesehen.* Munich: Piper, p. 212.

Botzenhart, M. 1977. *Deutscher Parlamentarismus in der Revolutionszeit 1848–1850.* Düsseldorf: Droste.

Brandt, H. 1987. *Parlamentarismus in Württemberg 1819–1870. Anatomie eines deutschen Landtags.* Düsseldorf: Droste.

Brandt, P., M. Kirsch and A. Schlegelmilch (eds). 2006. *Handbuch der Europäischen Verfassungsgeschichte im 19. Jahrhundert,* Vol. 1: Um 1800. Bonn: Dietz, pp. 640–977.

Braun, B. 2011. *Die Weimarer Reichskanzler. Zwölf Lebensläufe in Bildern.* Düsseldorf: Droste, pp. 29–59.

Cullen, M.S. 1999. *Der Reichstag. Parlament – Denkmal – Symbol.* Berlin/Brandenburg: be.bra.

Daum, W. (ed.). 2012. *Handbuch der Europäischen Verfassungsgeschichte im 19. Jahrhundert,* Vol. 2: 1815–1847. Bonn: Dietz, pp. 781–1040.

Dieckmann, W. 1981. *Politische Sprache, politische Kommunikation.* Heidelberg: Carl Winter Verlag.

Dorrmann, M. (ed.). 2008. *Theodor Heuss – Bürger der Weimarer Republik. Briefe 1918–1933.* Munich: De Gruyter.

Fehrenbach, E. 2007. *Verfassungsstaat und Nationsbildung 1815–1871,* 2nd ed. Munich: Oldenbourg.

Gusy, C. 1997. *Die Weimarer Reichsverfassung.* Tübingen: Mohr Siebeck.

Götschmann, D. 2002. *Bayerischer Parlamentarismus im Vormärz. Die Ständeversammlung des Königrichs Bayern 1819–1848.* Düsseldorf: Droste.

Kirsch, M. 1999. *Monarch und Parlament im 19. Jahrhundert. Der monarchische Konstitutionalismus als europäischer Verfassungstyp – Frankreich im Vergleich.* Göttingen: Vandenhoeck & Ruprecht.

Knauer, M. and V. Kümmel (eds). 2011. *Visualisierung konstitutioneller Ordnung (1815–1852).* Münster: Rhema.

Kühne, J.D. 1985. *Die Reichsverfassung der Paulskirche. Vorbild und Verwirklichung im späteren deutschen Rechtsleben.* Frankfurt am Main: Luchterhand.

Kühne, T. 2005. 'Demokratisierung und Parlamentarisierung: Neue Forschungen zur politischen Entwicklungsfähigkeit Deutschlands vor dem Ersten Weltkrieg', *Geschichte und Gesellschaft* 31(2): 293–316.

Lilla, J. 2004. *Statisten in Uniform. Die Mitglieder des Reichstags 1933–1945.* Düsseldorf: Droste.

Mergel, T. 2012. *Parlamentarische Kultur in der Weimarer Republik. Politische Kommunikation, symbolische Politik und Öffentlichkeit im Reichstag,* 3rd ed. Düsseldorf: Droste.

Obenaus, H. 1984. *Anfänge des Parlamentarismus in Preußen bis 1847.* Düsseldorf: Duncker & Humblot.

Obermann, K. 1987. *Die Wahlen zur Frankfurter Nationalversammlung im Frühjahr 1848.* Berlin (GDR): VEB Deutscher Verlag der Wissenschaften.

Pollmann, K.E. 1985. *Parlamentarismus im Norddeutschen Bund 1867–1870.* Düsseldorf: Droste.

Pracht, E. 1990. *Parlamentarismus und deutsche Sozialdemokratie 1867–1914.* Pfaffenweiler: Centaurus.

Rauh, M. 1973. *Föderalismus und Parlamentarismus im Wilhelminischen Reich.* Düsseldorf: Droste.

Roth, R. and D. Rucht (eds). 2008. *Die sozialen Bewegungen in Deutschland Seit 1945. Ein Handbuch.* Frankfurt am Main and New York: Campus Verlag.

Schulz, A. and A. Wirsching (eds). 2012. *Parlamentarische Kulturen in Europa. Das Parlament als Kommunikationsraum.* Düsseldorf: Droste.

Schönberger, C. 1997. *Das Parlament im Anstaltsstaat. Zur Theorie parlamentarischer Repräsentation in der Staatsrechtslehre des Kaiserreichs (1871–1918).* Frankfurt am Main: Vittorio Klostermann.

Steinmetz, W. 1998. '"Sprechen ist eine Tat bei euch". Die Wörter und das Handeln in der Revolution von 1848', in D. Dowe, H.G. Haupt and D. Langewiesche (eds), *Europa 1848. Revolution und Reform.* Bonn: Dietz, pp. 1089–138.

Stollberg-Rilinger, B. 2008. *Des Kaisers alte Kleider. Verfassungsgeschichte und Symbolsprache des Alten Reiches.* Munich: C.H. Beck.

Weil, F. 2001. *Verhandelte Demokratisierung. Die Runden Tische der Bezirke 1989/90 in der DDR.* Göttingen: V & R Unipress.

Werner, E.M. 2010. 'Das Rotteck-Welckersche Staatslexikon', *Jahrbuch Forum Vormärz-Forschung* 15: 205–19.

Andreas Biefang, Ph.D., is Researcher at Kommission für Geschichte des Parlamentarismus und der politischen Parteien, Berlin, Germany. He is a specialist on national organizations and the political citizenship of the elites in mid nineteenth-century Germany and on the Reichstag of the era of Bismarck. His current projects concern parliament and publicity with particular reference to visual representations of parliamentarism between the late eighteenth and early twentieth centuries.

Andreas Schulz, Ph.D., Professor of Modern History at the Goethe University, Frankfurt am Main, and General Secretary of Kommission für Geschichte des Parlamentarismus und der politischen Parteien, Berlin, Germany. His research has focused on the Napoleonic Rheinbund and elite and bourgeois culture in modern Germany. He has edited a volume on parliamentary cultures in Europe (together with Andreas Wirsching), and currently he is working on a project on the criticism of parliamentarism in Germany and France. He is a member of the Board of Directors of the research network EuParl.net.

Chapter 5

Passion and Reason

Modern Parliaments in the Low Countries

Marnix Beyen and Henk te Velde

The early modern Dutch Republic had known an elaborate system of representation, and so had, to a lesser degree, the Habsburg Netherlands. However, the modern parliaments that emerged in the Netherlands and Belgium at the end of the eighteenth and the beginning of the nineteenth century were to a large extent copies of foreign examples. The parliament of the independent Batavian Republic, which was founded in 1796 after French revolutionary troops had overthrown the Dutch Republic, was largely a copy of the French Revolutionary National Assembly. Furthermore, the parliament of the United Kingdom of the Netherlands and Belgium (1815–30), which came into being after the fall of Napoleon, was inspired by the prestigious British model of constitutional monarchy and a bicameral system, but in practice it followed French examples closely.

In both countries, the imported system has proved to be very stable, and the Dutch and Belgian parliaments even lived through the crisis of parliaments in the 1930s without any fundamental problems. Since 1945 hardly any serious politician has ever publicly wanted to abolish the parliamentary system. If we look at it in that light, the similarities between the Belgian and Dutch parliaments easily outweigh the differences. This similarity is also a result of the fact that the two countries were parts of one united kingdom precisely during the formative years of the parliamentary systems as they still exist in the Low Countries today.

Nevertheless, from the perspective of this comparative volume, there are also very interesting differences. It could be argued that the Dutch parliamentary system has borne the marks of the politics of the early modern Dutch Republic, a liberal regime based on a lively civil society and a rather large bourgeois elite, but without a very vigorous political life. Formal politics has consisted first and foremost of administration and the rule of law, and only last and least democracy in the sense of active popular participation, let alone popular sovereignty. There was a notion of popular sovereignty in the brief Batavian parliament, but it disappeared and has not been included in the Dutch constitution since 1814. Even today the monarch is formally still a member of the government. The Belgian parliamentary system, on the other hand, originated in a revolt against the rather authoritarian Restoration regime of the Dutch King William I and still bears the traces of its revolutionary origins. Its first constitution was based on the sovereignty of the people, and it was the most liberal one in Europe at the time. Even though sovereignty at first did not really imply popular participation, parliamentary politics has always been livelier in Belgium than in the Netherlands, and Belgian constitutional experiments with universal male suffrage were an inspiration for other countries around the turn of the twentieth century (Barthélemy 1912).

In this chapter, we will show how these different origins of representative government led to different forms of self-presentation and divergent political styles. We will also examine the influence of the different starting points on the use of the basic concepts of parliamentarism by the members of parliament in both countries. We have profited from recent digitizing projects that have rendered accessible and searchable the debates of the two parliaments in public databases. Although the websites www.plenum.be and www.staten-generaaldigitaal.nl are technically conceived in different ways, they nevertheless facilitate comparative research on the use of concepts in parliamentary sessions.

Self-presentation and Parliamentary Styles

The divergent self-images of the Belgian and the Dutch parliaments are apparent from the way the institutions presented themselves to the public. In the Netherlands, continuity with the ancien régime was emphasized. The national representative body was not referred to as 'the parliament', but as the 'States General' (Staten-Generaal). This was the name of the central representative institution of the republic, and in fact it operated rather as an executive committee, and the several provinces of the federal state were represented in this central committee. Estates existed on the provincial level, but rather than the classic three estates, they represented the towns and to a certain extent the nobility. When the term 'parlement' was used in the Second Chamber (*Tweede Kamer*), it first denoted the British House of Commons. Only as late as 1847 did the Liberal representative Luzac hesitatingly but approvingly conclude that 'the Netherlands, in this assembly, possesses its parliament' (*Handelingen der Staten-Generaal*, 3 May 1847: 234).

The suggestion of continuity was ambiguous: the parliament of the Dutch-Belgian kingdom of 1815 resembled the parliament of 1796 more than the States General of the Dutch Republic. Before the Dutch-Belgian Union of 1815, however, the Netherlands had for one year just one chamber, which was not open to the public, held hardly any real debates and had procedures resembling those of the States General. The word used for the 1796 unicameral parliament, the National Assembly (*Nationale Vergadering*), was not used again because of its revolutionary connotations. Even in the National Assembly, the word parlement had hardly been used, and it suggested an advisory body or even a powerless talking shop rather than a sovereign national assembly (Oddens 2013).

The neutral, uncontroversial term *volksvertegenwoordiging* (representation of the people) was used in everyday speech and in the parliament. In recent times, the parliament has mostly been referred to as 'the Chamber', meaning the Second Chamber or the Dutch House of Commons. This reflects the fact that the Second Chamber is the heart of the national representation; the First Chamber is a senate that is constituted through indirect elections and has a secondary role in the legislative process. It was first conceived as a sort of House of Lords, but it developed into a *chambre de réflexion* that was appointed by the king until 1848 and afterwards indirectly elected. Until 1917, its members had to belong to the category of rich citizens.

The Belgian parliament, by contrast, presented itself as a modern representative institution. French was the only parliamentary language in the newly independent state, and Belgian politicians used the language of the French parlement. Although the constitution of 1831 referred to *les Chambres* rather than to a parliament – following the example of the French Charte constitutionnelle of 1814 and 1830 in this respect too – the latter term immediately entered common political parlance. Members of both the House of Representatives and the Senate called themselves *parlementaires* (parliamentarians), and when from 1844 onwards full-text versions of the plenary discussions were published, they were entitled *Annales Parlementaires* (Parliamentary Proceedings; cf. in France: *les Archives Parlementaires*).

This difference was not only a question of self-labelling; it also betrayed different ideals about the nature of verbal interactions, which, according to all MPs, were at the heart of parliamentary politics. However, if we compare the formulas used for these interactions – i.e., those formulas preceded by a possessive pronoun in the first person plural – striking differences appear. These kinds of self-reflexive formulas seem to appear much more frequently in the Belgian than in the Dutch parliamentary proceedings.[1] If we reduce this comparison to all the expressions denoting non-antagonistic 'deliberations' (*beraadslagingen* / *deliberaties* / *deliberatiën*), the proportion between

Belgium and the Netherlands is 'only' three to one (2,049 as against 647). However, for those expressions signifying more antagonistic verbal interactions such as 'our debates' (*onze(r) debatten / nos débats*) or 'our discussions' (*onze(r) discussiën / onze(r) discussies/ nos discussions*) this proportion rises to more than ten to one (3,347 as against 328).

It seems that Belgian MPs debated in order to convince their opponents, while their Dutch counterparts were looking for a rational or businesslike common ground. This is corroborated by the higher and earlier frequency in Belgium of martial metaphors such as 'parliamentary struggle' (*parlementaire strijd / lutte(s) parlementaire(s)*) or 'parliamentary arena' (*parlementaire arena / arène parlementaire*).[2]

In a similar vein, parliamentary eloquence, like the art of persuading the audience and fellow MPs, was more fashionable in Belgium than in the Netherlands. During the Dutch-Belgian kingdom it appeared that Belgian MPs were better at oratory than their Dutch counterparts, who argued more calmly and were good at finding compromises behind the scenes (Van den Berg and Vis 2013: 222). Later Belgian MPs publicly sang the praises of parliamentary eloquence (cf. Hymans 1914: 243–64). Politicians such as the Catholic, formerly Liberal, MP Edmond de la Coste in 1851 regretted the alleged waning of this eloquence. De la Coste most notably deplored the fact that the Liberal government had decided on a certain case without seriously consulting parliament. According to him, this was not a parliamentary but a military fashion of proceeding: everything was decided in the headquarters of the governing party, at the expense of parliamentary deliberation and eloquence:

> Deliberation having no influence whatsoever anymore on the result, it will be nothing more than a vain rattle of words. Parliamentary eloquence – we do have an eloquence which is typical of our country – will cease to exist because, if one does not have the hope of persuasion, the word ceases to have either resilience or power. Life, in a word, will retreat from parliament. (*Annales de la Chambre des Représentants*, 23 June 1851: 1, 496)

Parliamentary eloquence should avoid violence and aggression, but not passion. The Dutch, on the other hand, did not like passionate parliamentary eloquence. Even Abraham Kuyper, an icon of charismatic leadership in Dutch political history, at times praised self-restraint instead of fierce partisan opposition when he was prime minister. Thanks to this attitude, deliberations had 'at certain moments provided us with the joy of a parliamentary eloquence that would honour and adorn the best parliament in Europe' (*Handelingen der Staten-Generaal*, 24 February 1904: 1356).

These differences were already obvious to contemporary observers. In the 1880s Auguste Reynaert, a Belgian MP, wrote a comprehensive overview of 'discipline' in European parliaments. He did so in order to understand the unrest that reigned in Belgian and other houses of representatives, especially in the British House of Commons at the time of the Irish obstructionism. Reynaert awarded the prize for the most well-behaved and most calm parliament to the Netherlands. Dutch debates seemed to be a continuous civilized conversation about technical matters. Even though the Dutch parliament has also known its periods of unrest – in particular during the interwar period and also in recent years (Geert Wilders) – it has retained its sober nature. In Aristotelian terms, 'logos' was valued, in particular if supported by an 'ethos' of professional and, until the 1960s, juridical and detached dignity. 'Pathos' was abhorred (Reynaert 1884: 286, 323–28). Even the Dutch conception of the parliamentary proceedings reflected this attitude. The official shorthand service, which was installed in 1849, ignored everything that happened in the meeting except the spoken word itself. Utterances of emotions or hilarity were not recorded.

The parliamentary culture in Reynaert's own Belgium, on the other hand, resembled more closely its French counterpart with its strong emotions, oratorical exploits and theatrical gestures (see Chapter 10) – most of which were carefully recorded in the proceedings. In particular after the entry of socialist MPs into the House of Representatives in 1894, these features would often be accompanied by verbal and, at times, even physical violence. This tendency culminated in two fights involving most of the house during the 1930s, but even after the Second World War the Belgian parliament would retain a more theatrical and febrile character than the Dutch one (Deferme 2004: 11–30; Beyen and Röttger 2003: 337–83). The former Social Democrat Prime Minister Willem Drees wrote that businesslike argumentation was more successful in the Dutch parliament than emotional and compelling oratory. He also suggested that its calm nature made the Dutch parliament even more 'democratic' than the sometimes turbulent British parliament (Drees 1975: 142–44, 160). This difference reflected perhaps partially and indirectly the difference between the predominantly Protestant Netherlands and Catholic Belgium. More directly, however, these different communicative patterns can be traced back to different ideals about the constitutional and political role of parliament. The following sections will show that these differences were also manifested in the use of central political concepts.

Sovereignty of the People and Democracy

J. de Bosch Kemper, a Dutch constitutional lawyer and moderate MP, supported the crucial constitutional reform of 1848 but denied that it was based on the principle of popular sovereignty, which he claimed was

> an absurdity that cannot exist and that, if it existed for a moment, would have the most catastrophic consequences – as the example of France shows us; however, I don't find this principle in the constitution. On the contrary, it is excluded, as long as the king and the members of the States General swear the oath not to govern according to the popular will, according to what the often erring popular masses say, but according to what their conscience tells them to be good for the fatherland. (*Handelingen der Staten-Generaal*, 3 October 1848: 917)

The Dutch constitution of 1848 made no mention whatsoever of popular sovereignty. During the nineteenth century, especially in debates about the change of the constitution (in 1848) and ministerial responsibility (in the 1860s), popular sovereignty was almost exclusively used in a negative sense, in warnings about the 'un-Dutch' dominance of the lower classes or the foreign principles of the French Revolution. The first modern political party was the Neo-Calvinist 'Anti-Revolutionary Party' (1879). It was called anti-revolutionary because it fought against popular sovereignty and other principles of the French Revolution. Its leader, the aforementioned Abraham Kuyper, called himself a democrat, but he vehemently rejected the 'principle' of popular sovereignty (see e.g., *Handelingen der Staten-Generaal*, 13 May 1896: 1083).

Dutch nineteenth-century politics sought to steer a middle course between popular sovereignty and absolute monarchy in a kind of mixed constitution, in which power was shared between the four Cs – the Crown, the cabinet, the chambers and the constituency. The balance between the four Cs shifted over time as the king lost most of his power and the political parties gave a voice to the constituencies, but this did not lead to a more favourable attitude towards popular sovereignty. Around 1900 'democracy' was adopted as a slogan and a platform by several parties – the Socialists, the left-wing Liberals and to a certain extent the Neo-Calvinists – but popular sovereignty was neither a battle cry nor a programme.

In the Belgian constitution, political sovereignty was explicitly located in the people. According to Article 25, '[a]ll [constitutional] powers emanate from the nation'. This formula was ambiguous, since it evoked the abstract, transhistorical 'nation' rather than the concrete *pays réel* – and thus could be used to defuse the explosive notion of popular sovereignty. Nonetheless, the clause shows that the Belgian political elites did not reject popular sovereignty as their Dutch colleagues did. Although Belgian MPs also tended to emphasize the moderate character of the Belgian parliamentary system, they did not stress the absence of absolute monarchy and popular sovereignty but described their 'democratic kingship' as 'the free expression of the . . . sovereignty of the people' (*Annales de la Chambre des Représentants*, 14 April 1848: 512; Van Schoor, a Liberal, during a discussion on the war budget). Both advocates and opponents of the principle seemed to recognize that Belgium was 'a country in which the sovereignty of the people is the basis of the institutions', as the Catholic MP Barthélemy Dumortier asserted in 1853. In such a country, 'the will of the people, whose rights one always proclaims, should also be taken into account' (*Annales de la Chambre des Représentants*, 13 April 1853: 1057).

Three years later, Dumortier used an almost identical phrase to criticize the Liberal MP De Lexhy, who in spite of his 'truly advanced principles' had labelled petitioners as members of the 'ignorant classes': 'We are sitting here by virtue of the sovereignty of the people; when we speak of the people, we have to listen to them respectfully' (*Annales de la Chambre des Représentants*, 17 December 1856: 332). Dumortier seemed to be quoting words that the prominent Liberal and freemason Théodore Verhaegen had used barely one month before. He tried to counter Catholic pretentions to express the popular will by quoting the criticism of the sovereignty of the people by the prominent Catholic politician Ernest de Gerlache – 'the sovereignty of the people by whose virtue we are sitting here!' (*Annales de la Chambre des Représentants*, 27 November 1856: 153).[3] Nearly eight years later, de Gerlache's pamphlet would again be quoted by the Liberal Louis De Fré in order to prove the unreliability of the Catholics on the question of popular sovereignty (*Annales de la Chambre des Représentants*, 11 June 1863: 513).

These examples show that the notion of 'sovereignty of the people' functioned very differently in Belgian and Dutch parliamentary discourses. Dutch MPs enhanced the legitimacy of their arguments by dissociating themselves from the concept of the sovereignty of the people, but their Belgian colleagues had to use the opposite strategy. Conversely, opponents could be delegitimized in the Netherlands by accusing them of supporting popular sovereignty; in Belgium, on the other hand, it was more advantageous to denounce them as betrayers of popular sovereignty. This difference had serious consequences for the way the concepts of (ministerial) responsibility and representation functioned in Belgian and Dutch parliamentary discourses.

Ministerial Responsibility

Ministerial responsibility was already an item of discussion during the early days of the United Kingdom of the Netherlands and Belgium, but it had not yet been implemented, even though the ideas of Benjamin Constant, for instance, were well known (van Velzen 2005). However, it became one of the central tenets of the Belgian constitution of 1831. Article 63 stated that 'the king is inviolable, the ministers are responsible'. This suggested that ministerial responsibility was introduced to limit the sovereignty of the king by making him incapable of acting politically. Leopold I, Belgium's first king, certainly tried to create manoeuvring space for himself, but the theoretical predominance of 'popular sovereignty' was so deeply entrenched in Belgian political culture that the limits to the king's sovereignty seemed self-evident and the notion of ministerial responsibility therefore was not a crucial concern for Belgian MPs.

When the notion 'responsibility' was used in Belgian parliamentary discourse, it was much more an expression of the need for ministers to be accountable to the people and its representatives in parliament, not only for their own acts but also for those of their department. As such, the concept appeared throughout the nineteenth and twentieth centuries, particularly in the wake of dramatic events. From a landslide in a train tunnel in 1846 to the so-called Heysel tragedy (the death of thirty-eight football supporters resulting from crowd violence before a European Cup Final in Brussels) in 1986, the question was whether the responsible minister should resign because of errors made within his area of responsibility. Even the possibility of the resignation of the minister concerned was not addressed in the Dutch parliament in debates about the disastrous flood of 1953 that killed two thousand people (van Baalen and Ramakers 2001: 218–32).

In the Netherlands, the constitution of 1814 did not yet mention a king but a 'sovereign' monarch or prince, and later there were debates about the (at least formal) sovereignty of the king. Therefore, invoking the concept of 'responsibility' aimed most often at limiting precisely the king's power. Until the 1840s, Dutch ministers remained to a certain extent servants of the king. In the 1848 constitution, ministerial responsibility was introduced with the exact same words as in the Belgian constitution of 1831: '*De koning is onschendbaar; de ministers zijn verantwoordelijk*' (The king is inviolable; the ministers are responsible).

At the time, this was hardly controversial: the debates about the constitution of 1848 mainly revolved around the (much feared) introduction of direct elections instead of the complicated system of indirect elections that had until then hampered the real representation of the people. Conservatives and liberals alike wanted ministerial responsibility and inviolability of the king, but they did not mean the same thing. During the nineteenth and even part of the twentieth century, ministerial responsibility was not a clear, explicit rule; the ideal was rather to reach a balance between the different powers within the constitution (Slijkerman 2011). In the nineteenth century, most parliamentarians still supported a certain political role for the king in order to avoid the omnipotence of parliament – and thus popular sovereignty. Especially when in opposition, the Liberals tended to emphasize the role of the parliament, and after long debates in the 1860s ensuing in repeated dissolutions of parliament, the conclusion was that a government had to resign if the parliament had lost faith in it, regardless of the arguments that were used. In the 1880s, the radical Liberal Samuel van Houten famously declared that the Crown was an 'ornament' rather than the 'foundation' of the constitution (*Handelingen Verenigde Vergadering 1883–1884*, 1 August 1884: 9). However, in the 1930s the Neo-Calvinist Prime Minister Hendrikus Colijn still formed a 'royal' cabinet, which was supported by Queen Wilhelmina but not by the Second Chamber. It is true that the Chamber immediately rejected the new government, which accepted this decision and resigned, but only after 1945 was ministerial responsibility really interpreted as an absolute rule that implied a passive monarch.

While in exile in London during the Second World War, Queen Wilhelmina appointed a new cabinet when the old one did not seem to be able to cope with the circumstances of the war. This was possible because the parliament had immediately ceased to meet when the Germans attacked the Netherlands in May 1940 and did not reconvene until after the war. The Belgian parliament not only remained in session during the German invasion but also tried to meet in exile. When the chips were down, Dutch politics were apparently about administration, not about representation. Even after the war, which ended in the Netherlands in May 1945, the Second Chamber did not meet until September, and new elections – the first after 1937 – did not take place until 16 May 1946, a year after the liberation. One of the first things the Belgian government did after returning from exile was to account for its deeds before the united chambers of parliament (on 19 September 1944, only two weeks after the liberation of the Belgian territory). The king, for his part, had made his own position impossible by not going into exile and trying to play an active role in opposition to the government and the parliament during the war. After a long and violent struggle (the 'Royal Question'), he was forced to abdicate in favour of his son in 1950.

Representation

During the nineteenth century, the concepts of representation of the Dutch
and Belgian parliamentary elites resembled those of doctrinaire liberals elsewhere, such as François Guizot in France (see Chapter 3). However, the concepts had different meanings depending on the discursive contexts in which
they functioned. In the Netherlands, Johan Rudolf Thorbecke, the leader
of the Liberals, who was also the main architect of the 1848 constitution,
provided the standard interpretation of 'representation'. He argued that the
independence of the representatives vis-à-vis their constituencies distinguished a representative system from 'democracy' – which he still saw as a
sort of direct democracy. Just like De Bosch Kemper in the passage quoted
above, Thorbecke emphasized that MPs were not directly accountable to 'the
people' but that they must act and decide independently, as they should in a
political system without popular sovereignty.

In Belgium, on the other hand, the 'liberal' concept of representation ran
into difficulties much sooner. In the Netherlands, representation had more to
do with the representatives than with the represented, but in Belgium 'to represent' came to mean 'to express the popular will'. In such a context, a political competition could easily arise over who expressed this will most faithfully.
The concept of popular sovereignty became a powerful weapon in the party
struggle that exploded in the 1840s, after the 1830s alliance of Catholics and
Liberals against the Dutch king had broken down.

'Representing the people' became nearly synonymous with 'defending
the party ideology' or, during the twentieth century, implementing the party
programme – which was then also the case in the Netherlands. The dominance
of the concept of 'popular sovereignty' gave strong impetus to the development of political parties, which appeared in the nineteenth century as the
main vehicles of democratization, but which would become some of its main
obstacles at the end of the twentieth century. More than the Netherlands,
Belgium would become and remain a 'partitocracy'.

These differences remained visible when all over Western Europe the
liberal notion of representation gradually gave way to a democratic one.
According to this conception, parliament ought to reflect or mirror society.
Sometimes the metaphor of the 'photograph' was used to describe what representation meant (Loots 2004; te Velde 1999: 138, footnotes 83–84). If until
the 1960s people criticized the form of representation, it was mainly because
it had not reflected societal groups well enough – in particular, during the
interwar years many people rejected the 'atomistic' system of representation
that gave the vote to individuals rather than groups. The Dutch and Belgian
parliaments debated a more 'organic' or corporatist type of representation

that would reflect the separate groups that constituted the national community more adequately (cf. Chapter 4 on Germany).

Given its relatively democratic character, it was not surprising that late nineteenth-century Belgium served as a pioneer of universal suffrage. Universal male suffrage was introduced in 1893, with an experimental system that gave more than one vote to men of certain groups in society. The influential D'hondt system of proportional representation was not only elaborated theoretically but also tried out in political practice after 1899. In the Netherlands, both of these innovations would only follow as a result of the constitutional reforms of 1917, but then the democratization of the Dutch system was more radical. Proportional representation was combined with the introduction of a single national constituency (in Belgium local constituencies were maintained) and in 1919 the suffrage was extended to all women; in Belgium female suffrage would only be introduced at the national level in 1948.

A partial explanation for these different trajectories of democratization can be found in the relative strengths of the political parties. It could be argued that the strong political parties had at first stimulated but then hijacked the democratic potential of the Belgian system because they wanted to extend or protect their electoral basis rather than advance a democratic system that would endanger their position. In the Netherlands, the democratization of the system and certainly the introduction of proportional representation also defined political parties as expressions of organized societal groups – so-called *zuilen* (pillars). However, precisely because the liberal conception of representation survived longer, these parties posed less of a threat to the idea of a fairly homogeneous 'national representation'.

It goes without saying that the language question was a divisive factor in Belgian politics. Since the 1970s it has even torn the national political parties apart, giving rise to a highly centrifugal form of federalization. That this had such an impact was once more partly due to the conception of popular sovereignty. For a growing number of MPs, the sovereign people were the Flemish section of the population alongside but sometimes instead of the Belgian nation. For that very reason, from 1895 onwards a growing number of them started speaking Dutch in parliament, thus rendering the idea of a homogeneous nation ever more fictitious (Lauwers 2013). If more liberal notions of representation had prevailed, the linguistic dualism could perhaps have been neutralized by the political elites. In a deliberately 'democratic' Belgium, on the contrary, these same elites even acerbated its divisive nature (Beyen 2011: 17–28).

Meanwhile, the Netherlands had experienced its third and possibly even its fourth democratic wave. The first abortive one had been in the last years of the eighteenth century. Democracy was then really popular, if one can put it that way, and the National Assembly had mobilized a lot of democratic energy. The first constitution was written in 1798, and a representative system had emerged. After being modified, this system had ended with the introduction of Napoleon's brother as king in 1806 and then the annexation by the French Empire in 1810, to which Belgium had belonged since 1794. In 1814 the unitary state and the idea of a written constitution were kept, but the spirit of politics had radically changed.

The second wave was the emergence of religious and socialist parties at the end of the nineteenth century, which would determine the progress of Dutch democracy for a century. Parliament became more or less a continuation of party politics. Then the late 1960s and early 1970s saw a new wave of democratization, this time in the form of 'participatory democracy', in universities, factories, government institutions and in an exuberant youth culture that transformed Amsterdam into the European capital of counterculture. This type of democracy did not care much for formal parliamentary democracy, which was mainly seen as the world of bureaucrats. Democracy was much more than voting and representation. However, left-wing parties gained a larger number of seats in parliament, and politics became much more popular. The boom ended with the economic crises of the 1970s, and in the 1980s and 1990s administrative politics took over once more.

The year 2002 arguably marked the start of the fourth democratic wave. First Pim Fortuyn and later Geert Wilders stormed the citadel of established politics in the name of 'the people'. According to their populist arguments, the 'elite' did not listen to the people and had only their own interests at heart. It could be argued that popular sovereignty was becoming more popular in the Netherlands than it had been since the last years of the eighteenth century. According to the new populism, the people longed for a homogeneous society without too many strangers or too much Europe. The onslaught at first left established politicians speechless and then unsure of how to respond. Did they still understand the people they were supposed to represent? Meanwhile, perhaps more than ever, the parliament has become the centre of democracy. Political parties have lost their function of social movement, and ideas of democracy in other domains than formal politics have largely disappeared. Populist demands for a new sort of democracy – more direct democracy, less 'backroom politics', and, if necessary, less rule of law – have centred on the parliament. Even the nature of parliamentary debates has changed: they have become less respectable, less calm and more populist. The parliament has lost much of its power to control the government, which was one of the strong aspects of the Dutch Second Chamber, but it has become more of a national forum than it used to be.

In Belgium, the continuing hold of the parties on the political system and the ever-growing claims by subnational movements not only prevented democratizing tendencies from fully developing in civil society, but they also inhibited the renewed popular legitimacy of the parliament, as sometimes seems to have been to a certain extent the case in the Netherlands. Even more than the Netherlands with its populist unrest, Belgium seems to have become the victim of what the Indian political scientist Sunil Khilnani has called 'the self-devouring capacities of modern democratic politics' (Khilnani 1993: 189–205).

Conclusion

We have discussed two parliamentary traditions that have had so much in common, yet have also differed so much ideologically and 'climatologically'. Where does the comparison leave us? First of all, it demonstrates the relevance of history or tradition for a parliament, and, more particularly, the choice of a relevant past. The Dutch parliament could have followed the example of the National Assembly of 1796, and in fact it did adopt a number of its constitutional rules, and it also occupied its assembly hall. However, after 1813 the elite chose to follow the spirit of the politics of the early modern republic. The path dependency of Belgian politics, on the other hand, followed the revolutionary origins of the country, its modern constitution of 1831 and the inspiration of French oratory and ideas about popular sovereignty. The nineteenth century – the parliamentary century par excellence – to a large extent determined the nature of both parliaments.

Secondly, parliamentary systems tend to ossify after some time and need reinvigorating. This reinvigoration was provided at the end of the nineteenth century by the new political parties that gave both parliaments a broad legitimacy, though not the prestige the British House of Commons had around 1900. These days, most people in both countries tend to think that parliaments and political life are declining, but this could be deceptive. It is hard to say something definitive about the long-term development of democracy and the representative system in liberal countries such as Belgium and the Netherlands. It could be argued that Belgium – except at the end of the eighteenth century and perhaps during the 1960s and 1970s – was more 'democratic' than the Netherlands, but what does that mean? The atmosphere of the Belgian parliament has been less formal, its rhetoric more exuberant and the conception of its duties less 'governmental' and more popular. On the other hand, it is possible that the calmer or even duller Dutch parliament, which did not often attract popular attention, has (until recently) been better able to influence government (Gerard 2011: 90), and this is a crucial duty of parliaments.

Viewed in that way, the comparison illustrates the tension between the representative and controlling functions of parliaments. To a certain extent, it could perhaps also serve to illustrate another tension between the dialectical and rhetorical functions of parliamentary debates. The Dutch parliament with its austere logos conception of debating could at least in the second half of the nineteenth century be seen as almost an ideal type of forum of pure discussion without much regard for the audience in the (small) public galleries. In that regard, it seems to resemble a Scandinavian parliament such as the Swedish one (cf. e.g., Ilie 2004: 45–86). Neglecting the public is, however, impossible in the long run. The Belgian parliament already demonstrated in the nineteenth century that parliamentary debates normally have two faces: a dialectical one and a rhetorical one. Parliamentary politics demands that MPs look for the right balance anew in each period.

Notes

1   More precisely, when we added the bigrams *onze(r) debatten / nos débats, onze(r) beraadslagingen / onze(r) deliberatiën / onze(r) deliberaties, onze(r) discussiën / onze(r) discussies / nos discussions*, we counted 5,399 instances in the Belgian parliamentary proceedings, as against only 1,023 in the Dutch proceedings. It should be noted that the figures indicate the number of debates in which the bigram appeared and that they may have appeared more than once in some or several of these debates.

2   The latter term appeared for the first time in the Dutch proceedings in 1937 and would appear seven times afterwards. In Belgium, it had appeared (at least) fourteen times between 1844 and 1922, and would appear only three times thereafter.

3   The Liberal Théodore Verhaegen against the Catholic Etienne de Gerlache, the author of *Essai sur le mouvement des partis* (1852) who called popular sovereignty a 'dogma . . . irreconcilable with order and peace and with every form of regular government' (65).

References

Primary Sources

Annales de la Chambre des Représentants, retrieved from www.plenum.be

Handelingen der Staten-Generaal, retrieved from www.statengeneraaldigitaal.nl

Handelingen Verenigde Vergadering 1883–1884, retrieved from www.statengeneraal digitaal.nl

Secondary Sources

Baalen, C. van and J. Ramakers (eds). 2001. *Het kabinet-Drees III (1952–1956). Barsten in de brede basis*. The Hague: SDU.

Barthélemy, J. 1912. *L'organisation du suffrage et l'expérience belge*. Paris: Giard and Brière.

Berg, J.Th.J. van den and J.J. Vis. 2013. *De eerste honderdvijftig jaar. Parlementaire geschiedenis van Nederland, 1796–1946*. Amsterdam: Bert Bakker.

Beyen, M. and R. Röttger. 2003. 'Het streven naar waardigheid. Zelfbeelden en gedragscodes van de volksvertegenwoordigers', in E. Gerard et al. (eds), *Geschiedenis van de Belgische Kamer van Volksvertegenwoordigers*. Brussels: Kamer van Volksvertegenwoordigers, pp. 337–83.

Beyen, M. 2011. 'Tragically Modern: Centrifugal Sub-nationalisms in Belgium, 1830–2009', in M. Huysseune (ed.), *Handelingen van het Contactforum 'Contemporary Centrifugal Regionalism: Comparing Flanders and Northern Italy', 19–20 juni 2009*. Brussels: Koninklijke Vlaamse Academie van België voor Wetenschappen en Kunsten, pp. 17–28.

Deferme, J. 2004. 'Van "burgerlijke afstandelijkheid" naar "volkse betrokkenheid". De politieke cultuur van enkele socialistische mijnwerkers in het Belgische parlement, 1894–1914', *Brood & Rozen* (1): 11–30.

De Gerlache, E. 1852. *Essai sur le mouvement des partis en Belgique, de 1830 jusqu'à ce jour*. Brussels: Decq.

Drees, W. 1975. *Het Nederlandse parlement*. Naarden: Strengholt.

Gerard, E. 2011. Review of H. te Velde, 2010. *Van regentenmentaliteit tot populisme: Politieke tradities in Nederland, BMGN – Low Countries Historical Review* 126: 90.

Hymans, P. 1914. 'L'éloquence au Parlement'. *La Belgique artistique et littéraire*, 16 February, 243–64.

Ilie, C. 2004. 'Insulting as (Un)parliamentary Practice in British and Swedish Parliaments', in P. Bayley (ed.), *Cross-Cultural Perspectives on Parliamentary Discourse*. Amsterdam/Philadelphia: John Benjamins, pp. 45–86.

Khilnani, S. 1993. 'India's Democratic Career', in J. Dunn (ed.), *Democracy: An Unfinished Journey, 508 BC to AD 1993*. Oxford: Oxford University Press, pp. 189–205.

Lauwers, K. 2013. 'De grenzen van de hoffelijkheid. Het vroege gebruik van het Nederlands in de Belgische Kamer van Volksvertegenwoordigers (1888–1910)'. Unpublished master's thesis. University of Antwerp, Belgium.

Loots, J. 2004. *Voor het volk, van het volk. Van districtenstelsel naar evenredige vertegenwoordiging*. Amsterdam: Wereldbibliotheek.

Oddens, J. 2013. *Pioniers in schaduwbeeld. Het eerste parlement van Nederland (1796–1798)*. Nijmegen: Vantilt.

Reynaert, A. 1884. *Histoire de la discipline parlementaire*, vol. 2. Paris: Durand and Pedone-Lauriel.

Slijkerman, D. 2011. *Het geheim van de ministeriële verantwoordelijkheid. De verhouding tussen koning, kabinet, kamer en kiezer, 1848–1905*. Amsterdam: Bert Bakker.

Velde, H. te. 1999. 'Van grondwet tot grondwet. Oefenen met parlement, partij en schaalvergroting, 1848–1917', in R. Aerts, et al. (eds), *Land van kleine gebaren. Een politieke geschiedenis van Nederland 1780–1990*. Nijmegen/Amsterdam: SUN.

Velzen, P. van. 2005. *De ongekende ministeriële verantwoordelijkheid. Theorie en praktijk 1813–1840*. Nijmegen: Wolf Legal Publishers.

Marnix Beyen, Ph.D., is Professor of Modern Political History at the Department of History and member of the Power in History Research Centre for Political History at the University of Antwerp, Belgium. In his research he focuses on the cultural – historical, literary, linguistic, scientific, visual – representations of nations as well as on the history of parliamentary cultures in Western Europe during the nineteenth and twentieth centuries. His research projects include one on the personal interactions between MPs and 'ordinary' citizens in Belgium and France between 1890 and 1940.

Henk te Velde, Ph.D., is Professor of Dutch History at Leiden University, the Netherlands. His research concentrates on political culture, national identity, political transfer and comparison, especially in the Dutch context. He has discussed subjects such as Dutch and European parliamentary culture in the nineteenth century, parliament as a theatre of politics and constitutional history and bourgeois culture in the Netherlands. He is now writing a book on British and French parliamentary cultures in the nineteenth century.

Chapter 6

The Formation of Parliamentarism in the Nordic Countries from the Napoleonic Wars to the First World War

Uffe Jakobsen and Jussi Kurunmäki

This chapter analyses the conceptual clusters that have been formed in the debates over parliamentary government in Denmark, Finland and Sweden. The aim is to bring forth a transnational view by paying attention to the ways in which the parliamentary life of other countries was referred to and commented on in the examined countries. Our discussion extends from the age of post-revolutionary constitution-making in the early nineteenth century through the debates over the introduction of the principle of parliamentarism to the breakthrough of parliamentary democracy in the early twentieth century.

The Nordic countries had been made up of two kingdoms that were partly imperial and to a great extent conglomerate in character. They were more in conflict with each other than in a state of some politically conceived togetherness. What tied these countries together, however, was their more or less similar Scandinavian languages, the Lutheran state religion, and some shared political and legal institutions that emanated from the Swedish and Danish realms. Importantly, in the 1930s and after the Second World War, these countries shared a widely held conviction emanating from an often reiterated narrative of a common 'Nordic democracy'. This narrative was based on the legacy of the Viking-Age-style governance by an assembly, with the *ting* as the central institution 'which ties the history of Nordic democracy together' and explains 'why democracy has found such a firm footing in the Nordic nations of today' (Líndal 1981: 40–41; cf. Andersson 1949; for a critical analysis see Kettunen 1999; Jakobsen 2009; Kurunmäki and Strang 2010). This, of course, is just one among several narratives concerning the origin and development of democracy in Denmark (Jakobsen 2010) and Sweden (Premfors 2000: 115ff). Moreover, some tend to see it as more or less applicable to the whole of Northern Europe's development from "assembly democracy" to parliamentarism (Dahl 1998: 17ff; Keane 2009).

Despite shared cultural characteristics and political experiences, the Nordic countries display different ways and rhythms of parliamentary democratization. The Napoleonic Wars changed the geopolitical conditions of Northern Europe. Sweden lost its eastern part, Finland, to the Russian Empire in 1809, to which the country belonged as a grand duchy until 1917. The diet of 1809 in Finland, at which Alexander I promised to maintain the Swedish laws, has been retrospectively regarded as the founding moment of the Finnish political nation. In 1814, Norway became independent of Denmark as a consequence of the Treaty of Kiel, which ended the Danish-Norwegian hostilities with Britain, and it immediately adopted its first constitution. The so-called Eidsvoll constitution of 1814 introduced a bicameral system of political representation, which was inclusive with regard to the standard of the times, although suffrage was far from universal, applying only to male owner-occupier peasants, officials and the urban bourgeoisie (Sandvik 2011). Later that year, Norway was forced into a personal union with Sweden, which lasted until 1905.

Norway was the trailblazer of parliamentary democratization not only in terms of parliamentary representation but also of parliamentary government. The question of parliamentarism became a national issue in Norway during the latter part of the nineteenth century, when the country belonged to the personal union under the Swedish Crown. In 1884, the Swedish king had to give way to the demand of the majority of the Norwegian parliament over a question of the right of the Norwegian ministers to take part in the procedures of the parliament. In practice, this wrangle meant that the Norwegian parliament came to have the decisive word in the formation of a government. In 1905, the union with Sweden came to an end after a long-lasting dispute over the right of Norway to have independent representation abroad. In 1898, men over twenty-five years of age gained the right to vote. In 1913, universal suffrage was introduced, which made Norway the first independent country in the world to have universal and equal suffrage for both sexes.

After the ceding of Norway, the Danish realm was made up of the Kingdom of Denmark and the Duchies of Schleswig and Holstein. The Danish Assembly of the Estates of the Realm was, in accordance with the Treaty of Kiel, to be established in Holstein because Holstein was a member of the

German Confederation. However, this did not happen until 1830, when the Danish king decided that Assemblies of the Estates of the Realm should be set up in all parts of Denmark (one in Holstein, one in Schleswig, and two in the Kingdom of Denmark). These assemblies were only advisory bodies, but they became forums of debate and criticism of the absolute monarchy and paved the way for a movement that in the 1840s would demand a free constitution and the abolition of absolutism. The Danish absolute monarchy collapsed in 1848, and a constitution was adopted on 5 June 1849, following the work of a constitutional assembly in 1848 and 1849. The 1849 constitution transformed Denmark into a constitutional monarchy with a bicameral parliamentary assembly, the Rigsdag, which contained an upper house, the Landsting, and a lower one, the Folketing, which was elected by all male heads of household (*husbond*) over thirty years of age. The king reserved the power to appoint and dismiss governments even though there were hefty debates over the right of a majority in the Folketing to decide on the formation of the government after the 1866 revision of the constitution. Parliamentarism was introduced de facto in 1901 and de jure in 1953, and universal suffrage for elections to the Folketing was introduced in 1915 for men and women over the age of twenty-five (cf. Jakobsen 2008).

The Swedish constitution of 1809 marked the end of the absolutist rule of Gustav III and Gustav IV Adolph, a period that had followed the regime of the Estates of the Realm, the so-called 'Age of Liberty' (1719–72). The constitution of 1809 was based on the idea of the separation of powers between the monarch, whose domain included the Council of State (*Statsrådet*), which made up the government, and the Riksdag, which maintained control over the state budget. It was presented as a dualistic system. The Riksdag Procedure of 1810 did not change the existing system of political representation, which was based on the four estates – the nobility, the clergy, the burghers and (importantly) the peasantry (Brusewitz 1913: 127–50; Sundin 2009: 129). The reform of political representation finally took place in 1866, when the estates were abolished and a bicameral parliament was introduced. By the early twentieth century, the question of universal suffrage was subordinated in Swedish public discourse to that of parliamentary government (Kurunmäki 2008b). It was more important for the Liberals and the Social Democrats to introduce universal male suffrage in the elections to the lower chamber than to enfranchise women at the same time, despite the fact that the issue of suffrage had set the political agenda towards the turn of the century. The principle of parliamentary government was accepted by the king in 1917, and in 1918, in the shadow of the collapse of the German monarchy, the upper chamber of the Riksdag was no longer able to block universal and equal suffrage.

In contrast to Norway, Denmark and Sweden, Finland constituted a country which had for a long time lagged behind in the realization of representative government but where the democratization of voting rights was abrupt and early. After 1863, the Finnish diet, which was of the early modern Swedish type, had become more a symbol of national autonomy than a centre of political power. The dependence of Finnish parliamentary life on the autocratic rule of Russia blocked any significant enhancement of the formal status of the diet, but that, in fact, opened up a possibility for a radical reform of suffrage in 1906. Finnish women were the first in Europe to gain universal voting rights (Kurunmäki 2008a). However, it became possible to put the principle of parliamentary government into practice only in 1917, when the Russian Empire was terminated in two revolutions.

In common narratives, the origin of parliamentary democracy in the Nordic countries derives from the Viking Age assemblies, the tings. This imagined Viking Age democracy and the narratives of a specific 'Nordic' democracy related to the Viking Age assemblies came to the fore in the nineteenth century and again in the 1930s, and they also flourished in the immediate aftermath of the Second World War and during the Cold War (Jakobsen 2010; Kurunmäki and Strang 2010). This took place to a great extent through the dissemination of publications from the different cultural institutes of the Nordic countries (Koch and Ross 1949; Lauwerys 1958; Allardt et al. 1981) and also in the context of broader cultural debates.

In the first drafts of the Danish constitution made by members of the government, the two chambers were referred to as the First and the Second Chamber. However, at the meeting of the Council of State on 2 August 1848 these were changed to Landsting and Folketing respectively on a proposal by the leading figure of the liberal movement, Orla Lehmann, apparently without much debate. However, parliament as such was named the Rigsdag on a proposal of Prime Minister A.W. Moltke (*Statsrådets Forhandlinger* 1954: 408). During the debate in the Constituent Assembly, there were suggestions to change Rigsdag to Daneting (*Beretning om Forhandlingerne paa Rigsdagen* (*Beretning*), 2: col. 2735 and col. 3624), but the proposal was not adopted.

By suggesting the old Nordic term *ting* for the chambers of parliament, Lehmann was making a conceptual connection between the past, the present and the future: the 'free constitution', parliament and parliamentarism were presented as a return to times before absolutism in order to emphasize continuity. The new assembly concerned 'the people' more than the monarch. By naming the chambers *ting*, the constitution could be seen as a restoration of the old Nordic democratic tradition with deliberating assemblies as the central institution and not necessarily welcoming modernity (Stevnsborg 1999).

The restitution of the people, the imagined historical legal tradition of the Folketing and the historization of absolutism were part of both scholarly and popular historical writings in the 1840s, exemplified by two related articles in the very first issue of the Danish *Historisk Tidsskrift* (Larsen 1840a, 1840b) and publications such as *Haandbog i Fædrelandets Historie* (Allen 1840) and *Illustreret Danmarkshistorie for Folket* (Fabricius 1853) among others, which contained detailed descriptions of the constitutional system of the Viking Age society.

In the thirteenth century, the Latin term 'parlamentum' was used in official documents for national assemblies where the king met and negotiated with representatives of the aristocracy and the clergy – parlamentum generale danorum (Larsen 1840a). From the eighteenth century onwards, however, 'parliament' was mainly used (e.g., by Fredrik Sneedorf (ODS: Parlament)) for the British and French legislative and judicial institutions. This was also the case throughout the debates in the Constituent Assembly between 1848 and 1849, apart from the adjective 'parliamentary' with reference to parliamentary rules, order, tradition, behaviour, forms, negotiations, tactics, rights and the like (cf. *Beretning*). Only late in the nineteenth century did 'parliamentarism' become more common in debating domestic matters, especially with reference to parliamentarism in the lower chamber (*folketings-parlamentarisme*) (Hørup 1898: 264ff).

The Early Semantics of 'Parliamentary Government'

In the Swedish constitution of 1809, any influence of the Riksdag on the composition of the Council of the State was denied, but the individual ministers were nevertheless made judicially responsible to the representative institution. However, their responsibility was limited to the advice they gave to the monarch. A minister could absolve himself from judicial responsibility by registering a reservation in the records (Andersson 1917: 1–8; Tarschys 1990: 224; Ruin 2009: 318). Towards the 1820s, the principle of parliamentary government gained ground among the critics of King Karl XIV Johan. The 'opposition', mainly in the Noble Estate, elaborated a view of parliamentary government that was based on the idea of a politically accountable ministry and on the role of 'opinion' in politically restricting the monarch. The inspiration came from British parliamentary politics and also from Benjamin Constant, whose distinction between *pouvoir royal* and *pouvoir exécutif* was adapted to Swedish circumstances. The ideal was a 'constitutional monarchy' (Andersson 1917: 37–39, 60–64). The opposition papers began to describe its position in terms of 'parliamentary government', an expression that was soon in common use (e.g., PoiT, 7 May 1838).

Towards the 1840s, the demand for a parliamentary government took on a more principled character than before and became associated with the idea of the sovereignty of the people (Andersson 1917: 37–39, 60–64, 118–26; von Sydow 1997: 43). The conservatives, however, were against any adjustment of the principle of the separation of powers. According to them, the ministers should be regarded as advisors of the monarch. In their rhetoric, calls for parliamentary government were seen as foreign imitations; as inherently liberal and incompatible with Swedish circumstances (e.g., PoIT, 28 February and 11 April 1846). In 1848, revolutionary sentiments in Europe had their repercussions in Sweden, too, causing some violent demonstrations and an alarmed reaction among the authorities. In this context, the king prepared a proposal for reform of the Riksdag, which, however, did not gain support, as it was deemed at the same time too radical and too conservative. In 1849 and 1850, two popular meetings took place in which the demand for universal male suffrage was presented, before the 1850s saw a downward conjuncture of political radicalism.

In Finland, any public conflict between the monarch and an opposition was out of the question. After Finland became a part of the Russian Empire in 1809, the diet was not summoned again until 1863. This alone made any attempt to create a parliamentary government unrealistic in the Finnish circumstances. Moreover, the executive organ, the Senate, was composed of high-ranking bureaucrats without any formal or practical political link other than to the imperial government in St Petersburg. In such circumstances, even descriptive news items about political life in other countries were of crucial importance with regard to the importation of political ideas and the formation of political language. When viewed in the light of the reception of parliamentarism in news about foreign countries and the early modern tradition of the estates, 'parliamentary government' as a concept did not come to Finland late by European standards. There were quite early and fairly plentiful references in the Finnish press to parliamentary affairs in France and Britain. The official Swedish-language paper published reports from London dealing with demands for parliamentary reform in Britain (*Åbo Allmänna Tidning* (ÅAT), 4 and 6 February 1817) and criticisms of ministers in the name of the people (ÅAT, 11 March 1817). A wide range of phrases containing the word 'parliamentary' emerged in the 1830s: 'freedom of parliamentary debates' (*Finlands Allmänna Tidning* (FAT), 9 April 1829), 'parliamentary sovereignty' (FAT, 31 December 1831), the 'finest example of parliamentary eloquence' (FAT, 5 September 1834) and 'parliamentary government' (FAT, 1 March 1839).

Meanwhile, in Denmark, the Assemblies of the Estates of the Realm had become a forum for criticism of the monarchy. Eventually – almost thirty-five years after the Norwegian Constituent Assembly had adopted the Eidsvoll constitution in 1814 – a Constituent Assembly met in order to negotiate a 'free constitution' for the country. It marked the end of absolutism and a new constitution, the June constitution of 1849 (*Junigrundloven*). The Norwegian constitution was a recurring object of reference during the debate in the Danish Constituent Assembly. In particular, the question of the separation of powers was discussed with reference to the Eidsvoll constitution. According to the Norwegian constitution, legislative power was vested in the parliament. One member of the Danish Constituent Assembly, however, could not accept the idea that the representative assembly of the people should usually have legislative power, as was the case in the Norwegian constitution but not in 'many other' constitutions. Another member pointed to the Belgian constitution in the same vein. Eventually, legislative power was vested in the king and parliament conjointly in the adopted Danish constitution. During the sessions of the Danish Constituent Assembly, lively discussions took place on whether the veto of the king should be suspensive as was the case in Norway. However, an 'absolute veto' was adopted to preserve the power of the king vis-à-vis the parliament. During these debates, the imagined legacies of Viking-Age forms of government were invoked when a member of the assembly used the argument that the legacy from the 'old days in *Norden*' (the Nordic countries) included the notion of the king as a 'man of action', and this was difficult to reconcile with parliamentary government or the principle of parliamentarism (*Beretning*, 2: col. 2292). However, this time the Viking-Age tradition was put forward as an argument in favour of a continuation of the king's central role in decision-making and not in favour of parliamentary deliberations of the representatives of the people or the principle of parliamentarism.

The Language of 'Parliamentarism'

The term 'parliamentarism' entered political language in Sweden and Finland in the 1850s (cf. Stjernquist 1995: 9). *Svenska Akademiens Ordbok* (SAOB, 'The Dictionary of the Swedish Academy') refers to a mention in a small liberal weekly in 1853, in which it was held that 'parliamentarism is completely possible in Sweden, but not required according to the constitution' (SAOB: *parlamentarism*). A few years later, the official paper of the government (*Post- och Inrikes Tidningar*) associated parliamentarism with British self-government but also with the need to stand against demands for unlimited reforms stemming from the parties and the press (PoIT, 15 January 1857). In Finland, the actual expression 'parliamentarism' surfaced in a report in which it was held that the coup by Napoleon had liberated the French merchants from parliamentarism (FAT, 16 January 1852). Some years later, the rapid legislative procedure in the French National Assembly was contrasted with the 'unending' parliamentary speeches and party conflicts that characterized parliamentarism (FAT, 27 May 1858).

However, the most topical concept in Swedish and Finnish politics towards the 1860s was 'representation'. In Sweden, a strong press opinion – in which bureaucratic reformism, pan-Scandinavian sentiments and a pro-Garibaldi kind of national liberalism merged – pushed for reform. The 1866 Riksdag Act abolished the estates and introduced a bicameral body of representation. The chambers were equal in power but composed according to different economic criteria (Kurunmäki 2000: 11–41). The reform was not meant to introduce parliamentary government. However, many opponents of the reform bill feared that the future would belong to political parties and to a system in which the government would be dependent on the support of these parties. In short, they were concerned about the future of the balance of powers – i.e., the dualism between the king's government and the representative institution – and rejected 'the government of ministers' (*ministerstyrelse*) (see e.g., *Preste-Ståndets Protokoll*, 1865–66, 3: 230–31). Foreign experiences were used as arguments on both sides. For example, it was held that the power of the king had decreased in Denmark because the 1849 constitution had strengthened the parliament. For the advocates of the bill, the Norwegian Storting was the main exemplary case. The British parliamentary system was also presented in a positive light, although the 'aristocratic' character of the House of Lords was pointed out (e.g., *Preste-Ståndets Protokoll*, 1862–63, 1: 147.) For the conservatives, a suitable political system was a 'constitutional monarchy', which meant that the monarch would have the right to decide independently on governmental issues after listening to the members of the Council of State (Södergren 1865: 51–52). What is noteworthy is that the proponents of the bill did not really push for the principle of parliamentary government. It was clearly considered politically too risky a goal in a situation where the king only reluctantly accepted the reform plan that was issued in his name.

The centre of political power in Sweden changed after the reform. Two mutually contrary arguments were soon developed in order to make the de facto leading minister prime minister (*statsminister*). The reform that took place in 1876 was supported by arguments according to which the parliamentary reform had made parliament stronger vis-à-vis the government and thus a readjustment was needed so that the dualistic constitution would not be violated (Ruin 2009: 326). On the other hand, it was held that a prime minister was needed because the Riksdag had already gained an elevated position and therefore the only way to go forward was to confirm the existence of parliamentarism (*Riksdagens Protokoll, Andra kammaren*, 1872, 3: 500; see Ruin 1990: 94–97; Ruin 2009: 327).

The Swedish parliamentary reform was well-known in Finland, where a considerable liberation of political life had taken place after the accession to the throne of Alexander II in Russia in 1855. The diet was summoned in 1863 after more than fifty years in abeyance. The debate that emerged between the nationalist Fennomans with their policy of promoting the Finnish language and culture and the more or less Swedish-minded Liberals concerned the applicability of foreign examples to Finnish parliamentary politics. The Liberals tried to present the Swedish reform issue as exemplary for Finland, too, and registered their sympathy for British parliamentarism. However, the implementation of their principles was problematic, since they defended the idea that there was a valid constitution in the country, which meant that they also supported the existing estates as well as the semi-absolute Swedish constitution of 1772 (Kurunmäki 2003). The 1869 Diet Act maintained the existence of the estates although the Constitutional Committee had claimed that the estate privileges had lost their foundation. The Diet Act stated that the diet represented 'the people of Finland' rather than the estates or any other privileged bodies. The principle of an imperative mandate was also denied in the document (Pohjantammi 2003: 376–77).

In the 1870s, the public debate on parliamentarism gained considerable momentum in Denmark, too. Various factions in the lower chamber formed a party group called the United Left with the main purpose of introducing the principle of parliamentarism. At the 1872 election, the party gained a majority in the lower chamber. In 1873, the lower chamber submitted an address to the king demanding a government 'in conformity with a chamber based on general suffrage' (*Rigsdagstidende*, 1872–73: 1853ff). When this was denied by the upper chamber and the king, the so-called 'constitutional struggle' started. In 1873, Henning Matzen, a professor of law, issued an attack on parliamentarism and published a series of newspaper articles on 'the constitution and parliamentarism', later issued as a pamphlet (Matzen 1873a, 1873b), and followed them with a 'reply' to his critics a year later (Matzen 1874). In these writings, Matzen developed a quite extraordinary theoretical defence of what later became the actual policy of the government, which was supported only by the upper chamber.

The campaign for parliamentarism in the lower house in Denmark in the 1870s and, most importantly, the establishment of parliamentary government in Norway in 1884 inspired the advocates of parliamentarism in the other Nordic countries as much as they fuelled critical concern among those who were against the implementation of the principle. In Denmark, the government that was appointed by the king was opposed by the majority of the Folketing. Citing the more democratic electoral system of Folketing elections, the Folketing proclaimed that the Landsting should 'be neither its superior nor its equal' (Hørup, quoted in *Morgenposten*, 31 December 1878) in forming governments, thus developing the concept of Folketing parliamentarism or so-called 'lower chamber parliamentarism'. The democratic movement under the battle cry of 'none above and none next to the Folketing' managed to force through the 'system change' in 1901 so that the principle of parliamentarism was de facto accepted.

In Sweden, some critical voices viewed the Danish attempts to promote parliamentarism as an infraction of the constitution (*Kalmar*, 16 April 1877) and as leading to anarchistic and despotic parliamentary politics (*Dalpilen*, 2 February 1883). However, it was quite naturally more common in Sweden to discuss the Norwegian struggle over parliamentarism, since it directly concerned the powers of the Swedish king. Being also the monarch of Norway, the king of Sweden had actually experienced parliamentary government in practice since the year 1884, a fact that could be used both in favour of and against the demands for parliamentarism in Sweden (see e.g., *Göteborgs Weckoblad*, 10 June 1880; *Norra Skåne*, 13 June 1884). For the Swedish conservatives, the Norwegian parliamentarism threatened to dissolve the monarchical union between the two countries, whereas the Norwegian advocates of national independence and their liberal supporters in Sweden favoured parliamentary government (Stråth 2005: 25).

By the turn of the century, the opponents of parliamentarism seemed to be on the defensive, except in Finland, where parliamentarism was discussed on a principled level rather than as an issue that was directly related to domestic circumstances. In Sweden, the concept of parliamentarism had become so important that one of the leading conservatives in the country, Pontus Fahlbeck, a professor of political science, presented in 1904 a Swedish version of parliamentarism in contrast to the commonly held concept that he described as 'English parliamentarism'. Fahlbeck held that the Swedish system was based on 'dual parliamentarism', in which there was a separation of powers between the governing monarch and the representative institution, but where there was also a traditional practice whereby joint committees dealt with parliamentary matters (Fahlbeck 1904: 104–49, 175–219). In other words, he attempted to give the existing system of government the name 'parliamentarism' without abandoning any of its non-parliamentary elements.

In general, the conservatives associated parliamentarism with the influence of the unreasoning masses and the existence of party conflicts (e.g., Kjellén 1902: 197–99). However, the negative picture that was given of parliamentarism did not necessarily refer to its British form as such. The rhetorical strategy in Swedish criticisms of parliamentarism was often based on the argument that the parliamentary government may have had its undeniable merits in the context of Gladstone and Disraeli, but it was impossible to imitate it in other places and times (e.g., *Riksdagens Protokoll, Första kammaren*, 1906, no. 48: 76–77). According to the historian Carl Hallendorf, contemporary parliamentarism in Denmark and Norway displayed a warning of the lack of validity of such 'imitated parliamentarism', since parliamentary government in these countries was occasionally based on 'a majority of one man' in parliament and they suffered from the absence of any united opposition that could overthrow the government (Hallendorff 1911: 392–95).

However, it was the domestic political contest over parliamentary democratization that triggered criticism against parliamentarism in Sweden. The issue of parliamentarism was entangled with the question of reforming voting rights and the electoral system. The left (the Liberals and the Social Democrats) aimed at a majoritarian electoral system in order to achieve a strong enough mandate in the lower chamber, whereas the right preferred a proportional vote so as to secure their majority, which would be based on the upper chamber and on a notable minority in the lower chamber. The Liberal leader and prime minister (1905–06, 1911–14) Karl Staaff as well as the leading Social Democrat Hjalmar Branting openly supported 'lower house parliamentarism' in Sweden. The purpose was to make the lower chamber of the Riksdag strong enough to combat the existing coalition between the upper-chamber conservatives and the monarch. It was not difficult to identify this goal as being inspired by the British model, although Staaff wanted to present his view as being based on the development of a domestic constitutional tradition (*Riksdagens Protokoll, Första kammaren*, 1906, no. 48: 42–43; *Riksdagens Protokoll, Andra kammaren*, 1906, no. 57: 11).

In Finland, the late nineteenth-century vocabulary of parliamentarism contained different levels of specification with regard to political goals. 'Parliamentarism' sometimes referred just to the constitutionally guaranteed meetings of the diet (e.g., *Morgonbladet*, 4 January 1878). At the same time, 'parliamentarism' was also discussed in quite an elaborate manner when it was treated as a political principle not applicable to the Finnish situation (e.g., Palmén 1878: 265–69). A more openly proclaimed stand in favour of parliamentarism was associated with 'the liberals' of the 1860s, who were often regarded as idealistic but unrealistic owing to their enthusiasm for foreign models (e.g., von Born 1885: 29; Palmén 1887: 418).

While the question of governmental power had priority over suffrage amongst the Swedish Liberals and Social Democrats in the early twentieth century, the Finnish parliamentary democratization dealt with the inclusiveness of the demos (Kurunmäki 2008b). The Russian Revolution of 1905 opened up a 'window of opportunity' for the advocates of a suffrage reform in Finland, and under the pressure of a general strike and the influence of the discourse of national unity, the reform turned out to be more radical than most of its advocates could have imagined (Kurunmäki 2005, 2008a). Universal suffrage, including women, and a unicameral parliament were introduced in 1906. The most consistent defence of parliamentarism came from the Social Democrats, who became the largest party in the new parliament, the Eduskunta (_Sosialistinen Aikakauslehti_ 1906: 121–23, 145, 171–73). However, their conception was closer to an idea of a governing parliament than of parliamentary government.

Parliamentarism and Democracy

The concept of parliamentarism was not necessarily associated with democracy in the nineteenth century. A recurring argument was that parliamentarism could not be applied to the conditions in which universal (male) suffrage prevailed (e.g., FAT, 17 April 1877). However, the concepts increasingly merged with each other towards the end of the century (e.g., Palmén 1895: 205; Danielson 1898: 88, 97). In Sweden, the Liberal Prime Minister Karl Staaff made a distinction between 'the rule of authorities' (_herremakt_) and 'the rule of the people' (_folkmakt_) when he defended parliamentarism in the lower house in 1906 (_Riksdagens Protokoll, Andra kammaren_, 1906, no. 57: 11). In the discourse of the Social Democrats, the concept of parliamentarism was sometimes interchangeable with 'popular self-government' and 'democracy', although their relationship with parliamentarism was somewhat complicated owing to the socialist criticism of 'bourgeois democracy' (Branting 1948 [1911]: 86). However, in 1917, the Social Democrats, whose far-left faction formed a party of its own and became communists, joined a cabinet that was led by the Liberals. It was during the formation of this cabinet that the Liberal leader Nils Edén demanded that the king should not go behind the back of the cabinet with his unofficial advisers, as he had done in 1914 in his famous 'castle yard speech', in which he publicly took a stand against the anti-militaristic policy of the government. In 1917, the king promised not to act publicly against his cabinet, and it has been common to view this moment as the breakthrough of parliamentarism in Sweden (e.g., von Sydow 1997: 60, 117).

However, the exact date of the breakthrough of parliamentarism is always a matter of retrospective evaluation. In the Swedish case, the abolition of the graded voting rights in the elections to the First Chamber (Första Kammaren) and the inclusion of women in the electorate were decided upon in November and December 1918 at an extraordinary session of the Riksdag. The debate over voting rights took place after the fall of the German monarchy and during a revolutionary uprising in Germany that had its repercussions in Sweden in the form of mass demonstrations and the threat of a general strike (Andræ

1998: 13–14, 281). While the king's acceptance of parliamentary government also took place under the shadow of the Bolshevik Revolution in Russia, the democratization of suffrage was timely, especially in view of the revolutionary situation in Germany.

The leader of the right in the First Chamber, Ernst Trygger, tried to object that the government was about to change the constitutional balance between the two chambers by introducing universal suffrage in municipal elections (which functioned as electoral organs for the First Chamber) and thereby radically change the constitution at an extraordinary session of the Riksdag (*Riksdagens Protokoll, Första kammaren*, 1918, no. 5: 4–9). However, the majority of the right had already recognized the principle of universal suffrage. In the language of Prime Minister Edén, political events in other countries, particularly in Germany, and a general wave of democratization across Europe were contrasted with 'Swedish democracy'. It was as if 'Swedish democracy' was an already existing factor whose will merely had to be fulfilled (*Riksdagens Protokoll, Första kammaren*, 1918, no. 5: 9–19).

In Finland, the collapse of the tsarist regime in Russia in March 1917 added momentum to the movement towards parliamentarism. As in the case of universal suffrage (1905–6), the sudden decline of the imperial power was exploited by the Finnish political elite. Three overlapping processes can be discerned to have taken place in 1917: the reform of parliamentary procedure, the declaration of parliament that it possessed supreme power in internal affairs (the so-called Power Act (*Valtalaki*)), and the proposal for a new constitution in which the principle of parliamentarism would be combined with a strong presidency. It was commonly held amongst the political parties that the political link between parliament and the Senate (government) should be made stronger and independence from the provisional government in Russia increased. In spring, both national interests and theoretical debates spoke in favour of parliamentarism (Lindman 1935: 16–23). The real topic of debate was not whether there should be a parliamentary government but whether parliament was to be given the right to appoint the members of the government. The Social Democrats, who held a single majority in parliament, strove for a system in which the parliament would nominate the members of the government. Their ideal was, after all, a ruling parliament rather than parliamentary government (Lindman 1935: 22–23; Pohjantammi 2003: 399). Although this view was not included in the Parliament Act, the law in itself was quite exceptional, as the principle of parliamentarism had previously been mentioned in a foundational law only in Turkey and Venezuela (Ståhlberg 1927: 16).

While the Parliament Act, quite surprisingly, touched upon the constitutional relationship between the parliament and the government, and the

Power Act attempted to put the principle into practice in a radicalized form in the context of rising political antagonism, the question of the constitution was formally taken up by the Constitutional Committee. The point of departure was the principle of the separation of powers between parliament and parliamentary government on one hand, and the president on the other (Lindman 1935: 30–32). The constitution drew to a considerable degree on new French constitutional theories that were critical of the way in which parliamentary government functioned in France and which would also influence the making of the Weimar constitution (Lindman 1935: 33). However, the Finnish reform was still unfinished when the society became embroiled in a violent domestic conflict in 1918. After the Civil War, the constitutional model of the majority of the victorious non-socialist side was a strong monarchy – a model that was not realized as a result of the collapse of the Wilhelmine regime in Germany. The republican constitution of July 1919 was built on the principle of parliamentary government and, at the same time, considerable executive powers for the president. With this constitution, Finland, too, became a parliamentary democracy of the Nordic type, although it kept a presidency that was politically more powerful than the monarchies in the other Nordic states.

References

Primary Sources

Åbo Allmänna Tidning (ÅAT), retrieved from http://digi.kansalliskirjasto.fi/sano malehti/secure/query.html

Allen, C.F. 1840. *Haandbog i Fædrelandets Historie*. Copenhagen: C.A. Reitzel.

Beretning om Forhandlingerne paa Rigsdagen: vol. 1–2. 1848–49. Copenhagen: Bianco Luno.

Dalpilen, retrieved from http://magasin.kb.se/searchinterface/title.jsp?id=kb:42269

Danielson, J.R. 1898. 'Kansanvalta ja perustuslaillisuus', *Valvoja* 11(2): 88–102.

Fabricius, A.K. 1853. *Illustreret Danmarkshistorie for Folket*, vol. 1. Copenhagen: Gyldendalske Boghandel Nordisk Forlag.

Fahlbeck, P. 1904. *Sveriges författning och den moderna parlamentarismen*. Lund: C.W.K. Gleerups Förlag.

Finlands Allmänna Tidning (FAT), retrieved from http://digi.kansalliskirjasto.fi/ sanomalehti/secure/query.html

Göteborgs Weckoblad, retrieved from http://magasin.kb.se/searchinterface/title. jsp?id=kb:33801

Hallendorff, C. 1911. 'Parlamentarism', *Svensk tidskrift* 1: 391–401. Retrieved from http://runeberg.org/svtidskr/1911/0003.html

Högvördiga preste-ståndets protocoll vid lagtima riksdagen i Stockholm åren 1862 & 1863. 1862–64. Stockholm. (Preste-Ståndets Protokoll 1, 1862–63).

Högvördiga preste-ståndets protocoll vid lagtima riksdagen i Stockholm åren 1865 &
1866. 1865–67. Stockholm. (Preste-Ståndets Protokoll 3, 1865–66).

Hørup, V. 1898. 'Folketingsparlamentarisme', in V. Nielsen (ed.), *V. Hørup i Skrift*
og Tale. Udvalgte Artikler og Taler, vol. 3. Copenhagen: Gyldendal, pp. 264ff.

Kalmar, retrieved from http://magasin.kb.se/searchinterface/title.jsp?id=kb:33801

Kjellén, R. 1902. 'Döda bokstäver i Sveriges gällande regeringsform: II',
Statsvetenskaplig Tidskrift 5(3): 181–200.

Larsen, I.E. 1840a. 'Om Rigsdage og Provindsialforsamlinger samt Rigsraadet i
Danmark fra det 13de Aarhundrede indtil Statsforandringen 1660. Grundtræk af
en historisk-statsretlig fremstilling', *Historisk Tidsskrift* 1: 241–333.

_____. 1840b. 'Om de Danske Kongers Personlige Deeltagelse i Retspleien fra de
Ældste Tider indtil den Nuværende Tid', *Historisk Tidsskrift* 1: 334.

Matzen, H. 1873a. 'Grundloven og Parlamentarismen', *Dagbladet,* 15, 16, 17 and 19
May 1873.

_____. 1873b. *Grundloven og Folkets Selvstyrelse.* Copenhagen: Gyldendalske
Boghandel.

_____. 1874. *Til Gjensvar.* Copenhagen: Gyldendalske Boghandel.

Morgenposten.

Morgonbladet, retrieved from http://digi.kansalliskirjasto.fi/sanomalehti/secure/
query.html

Norra Skåne, retrieved from http://magasin.kb.se/searchinterface/title.jsp?id
=kb:38124

Palmén, E.G. 1878. 'Mietteitä puolueista 1877–1878 vuoden valtiopäivillä. VII.
Loppukatsahdus', *Kirjallinen Kuukausilehti* 12: 265–73.

_____. 1887. 'Käänne Suomen puolueoloissa', *Valvoja* 7(11): 415–27.

_____. 1895. 'Parlamentarismi ja puolue-elämä pohjoismailla', *Valvoja* 15(4):
204–24.

Post- och Inrikes Tidningar (PoIT), retrieved from http://magasin.kb.se/searchinter-
face/title.jsp?id=kb:226761

Rigsdagstidende. Copenhagen: Bianco Luno.

Riksdagens protokoll vid lagtima riksmötet år ..., Andra kammaren. 1867–1948.
Stockholm: Riksdagen.

Riksdagens protokoll vid lagtima riksmötet år . . ., Första kammaren. 1867–1948.
Stockholm: Riksdagen.

Södergren, J.A. 1865. *Satser angående det från riksdagen 1862–1863 hvilande Förslag*
till national-representationens ombildning. Stockholm: A.L. Norman.

Sosialistinen aikakauslehti.

Statsrådets forhandlinger 1848–1863. 1954. H. Jørgensen (ed.), vol. 1: 24. Januar – 15.
November 1848. Copenhagen: Munksgaard.

Secondary Sources

Allardt, E., et al. (eds). 1981. *Nordic Democracy: Ideas, Issues, and Institutions in*
Politics, Economy, Education, Social and Cultural Affairs of Denmark, Finland,
Iceland, Norway and Sweden. Copenhagen: Det Danske Selskab.

Andersson, I. 1917. '*Oppositionen*' *och ministeransvarigheten. Parlamentariska strömningar i svensk politik 1809–1840.* Uppsala & Stockholm: Almqvist & Wiksells Boktryckeri.

_____. 1949. 'Äldre demokratisk tradition i Norden og dess fortsatte utformning i Sverige', in H. Koch and A. Ross (eds), *Nordisk demokrati.* Copenhagen: Westermanns Forlag, pp. 5–39.

Andræ, C.G. 1998. *Revolt eller reform. Sverige inför revolutionerna i Europa 1917–1918.* Stockholm: Carlssons.

Born, V.M. von. 1885. 'Något om parti-benämningar', *Finsk Tidskrift* 1: 29–35.

Branting, H. 1948 [1911]. 'Parlamentarism eller förmynderskap', in R. Edberg (ed.), *Demokratisk linje.* Stockholm: Tidens Förlag, pp. 82–86.

Brusewitz, A. 1913. *Representationsfrågan vid 1809–10 års riksdag. En inledning till representationsreformens historia.* Uppsala: Akademiska Boktryckeriet.

Dahl, R.A. 1998. *On Democracy.* New Haven: Yale University Press.

Jakobsen, U. 2008. 'The History of Parliamentary Democracy in Denmark in Comparative Perspective', in K. Palonen et al. (eds), *The Politics of Democratization in Europe: Concepts and Histories.* Farnham: Ashgate, pp. 301–14.

_____. 2009. 'The Conception of Nordic Democracy and European Judicial Integration', *Nordic Journal of Human Rights* 27 (2): 221–41.

_____. 2010. 'Inventions and Developments of Democracy: The Approach of Conceptual History', *European Political Science* 9(3): 316–27.

Keane, J. 2009. *The Life and Death of Democracy.* London: Simon & Schuster.

Kettunen, P. 1999. 'A Return to the Figure of the Free Nordic Peasant', *Acta Sociologica* 42(3): 259–69.

Koch, H., and A. Ross (eds). 1949. *Nordisk demokrati.* Copenhagen: Westermanns Forlag.

Kurunmäki, J. 2000. *Representation, Nation and Time: The Political Rhetoric of the 1866 Parliamentary Reform in Sweden.* Jyväskylä: University of Jyväskylä.

_____. 2003. 'The Reception of Political Concepts in the Wake of Finnish Parliamentary Life in the 1860s', in K. Palonen and J. Kurunmäki (eds), *Zeit, Geschichte und Politik / Time, History and Politics. Zum achtzigsten Geburtstag von Reinhart Koselleck.* Jyväskylä: University of Jyväskylä, pp. 291–310.

_____. 2005. 'A Parliament for the Unity of the People: On the Rhetoric of Legitimisation in the Debate over Finnish Parliamentary Reform in 1906', in L. Landgrén and P. Hautamäki (eds), *People, Citizen, Nation.* Helsinki: Renvall Institute, pp. 116–31.

_____. 2008a. 'The Breakthrough of Universal Suffrage in Finland, 1905–1906', in K. Palonen, T. Pulkkinen and J.M. Rosales (eds), *The Ashgate Research Companion to the Politics of Democratisation in Europe.* Farnham: Ashgate, pp. 355–70.

_____. 2008b. 'Different Styles of Parliamentary Democratisation in Finland and Sweden: An Analysis of Two Debates over Parliamentary Reform in 1906', in S. Soininen and T. Turkka (eds), *Parliamentary Style of Politics.* Helsinki: Finnish Political Science Association, pp. 106–28.

Kurunmäki, J. and J. Strang. 2010. 'Introduction: "Nordic Democracy" in a World of Tensions', in J. Kurunmäki and J. Strang (eds), *Rhetorics of Nordic Democracy*. Helsinki: Suomalaisen Kirjallisuuden Seura, pp. 9–36.

Lauwerys, J.A. 1958. *Scandinavian Democracy: Development of Democratic Thought and Institutions in Denmark, Norway and Sweden*. Copenhagen: The Danish Institute, The Norwegian Office of Cultural Relations, The Swedish Institute, The American-Scandinavian Foundation.

Líndal, S. 1981. 'Early Democratic Traditions in the Nordic Countries', in E. Allardt et al. (eds), *Nordic Democracy: Ideas, Issues, and Institutions in Politics, Economy, Education, Social and Cultural Affairs of Denmark, Finland, Iceland, Norway and Sweden*. Copenhagen: Det Danske Selskab.

Lindman, S. 1935. *Parlamentarismens införande i Finlands statsförfattning*. Uppsala & Stockholm: Almqvist & Wiksell.

Ordbog over det danske sprog (ODS), retrieved from http://ordnet.dk/ods

Pohjantammi, I. 2003. 'Edustus', in M. Hyvärinen et al. (eds), *Käsitteet liikkeessä. Suomen poliittisen kulttuurin käsitehistoria*. Tampere: Vastapaino.

Premfors, R. 2000. *Den starka demokratin*. Stockholm: Atlas.

Ruin, O. 1990. 'Statsministerämbetet: från Louis De Geer till Ingvar Carlsson', in *Att styra riket: regeringskansliet 1840–1990*. Stockholm: Allmänna Förlaget, pp. 92–135.

_____. 2009. 'Kung och statsminister', in M. Brundin and M. Isberg (eds), *Maktbalans och kontrollmakt. 1809 års händelser, ideer och författningverk i ett tvåhundraårigt perspektiv*. Stockholm: Sveriges Riksdag, pp. 315–40.

Sandvik, H. 2011. 'Gender and Politics Before and After the Norwegian Constitution of 1814', in P. Ihalainen et al. (eds), *Scandinavia in the Age of Revolution: Nordic Political Cultures, 1740–1820*. Farnham: Ashgate.

Stjernquist, N. 1995. 'Varför behövs nordiskt samarbete kring parlamentarismforskning?', in N. Stjernquist (ed.), *Parlamentarismen i de nordiska länderna. En egen modell?* Stockholm: Riksbankens Jubileumsfond & Gidlunds Förlag, pp. 9–17.

Ståhlberg, K.J. 1927. *Parlamentarismen i Finlands statsförfattning*. Helsinki: Holger Schildt.

Stevnsborg, H. 1999. 'Folk, regent og retshistorie', *Fortid og Nutid* June: 91–115.

Stråth, B. 2005. *Union och demokrati. De förenade rikena Sverige och Norge 1814–1905*. Nora: Nya Doxa.

Sundin, A. 2009. 'Att öppna ett fönster – och lämna det på glänt', in M. Brundin and M. Isberg (eds), *Maktbalans och kontrollmakt. 1809 års händelser, ideer och författningsverk i ett tvåhundraårigt perspektiv*. Stockholm: Sveriges Riksdag, pp. 113–36.

Svenska Akademiens ordbok (SAOB), retrieved from http://g3.spraakdata.gu.se/saob/

Sydow, B. von. 1997. *Parlamentarismen i Sverige. Utveckling och utformning till 1945*. Stockholm: Gidlunds Förlag.

Tarschys, D. 1990. 'Regeringens styrformer', in *Att styra riket: regeringskansliet 1840–1990*. Stockholm: Allmänna Förlaget, pp. 222–46.

Uffe Jakobsen, Ph.D., is Associate Professor in political theory and comparative politics at the Department of Political Science at the University of Copenhagen, Denmark. He has previously worked as Vice Rector at the University of Greenland, Nuuk. His current research interests include conceptual history and theories of democracy and processes of democratization in Denmark and in Europe more generally, with special reference to the development of parliamentary democracy and the role of democracy in European integration, and nation-building and state-formation in Greenland.

Jussi Kurunmäki, Dr Soc. Sc., has worked as Associate Professor and Lecturer at the Department of Political Science, Stockholm University, Sweden, and is currently a senior research fellow at the University of Helsinki, Finland and Södertörn University, Sweden. He has published on parliamentary democratization in Sweden and Finland in the late nineteenth and early twentieth centuries, the rhetoric of democracy in the Nordic countries and on the methods of conceptual history and rhetorical analysis. He is a member of the Board of Concepta – International Research Seminars in Conceptual History and Political Thought.

Chapter 7

The Conceptual History of the Russian State Duma

Irène Herrmann

On 27 April 2011, a major international conference took place at the Tauride Palace in St Petersburg to celebrate the 105th anniversary of the Russian State Duma. This event, and its timing, is extremely interesting since this celebration did not mark 'an actual centenary'. The chairman of the State Duma, Boris Gryzlov (2011), acknowledged this fact himself. One is led to infer that it was organized specifically to transmit political messages to the audience and the Russian citizenry at large, and three of these messages seem particularly relevant.

The most obvious message was the indisputably close link between the first Imperial Duma and its modern counterpart. Not only was this connection expressed through the date and location of the celebration, which occurred exactly at the same place and on the same day as the opening of the first Duma, but it was also vehemently stressed by the various orators, in whose view there was no doubt that the imperial institution was the direct ancestor of its post-Soviet homonym. In fact, the event was even labelled the '105th anniversary of Russian parliamentarism' (Deklaraciya 2011).

For most commentators of this event, the first Imperial Duma itself had very ancient roots. They linked its existence and democratic endeavours to medieval and early modern, supposedly deliberative assemblies, such as the Veche (Ponomaryov 1988), the Zemsky Sobor or the Boyars' Duma. The orators' (not necessarily conscious) purpose was twofold: to stress the purported length of the Russian democratic tradition, and then in turn to disqualify any foreign political legacy. In other words, by establishing an historical continuity between various Russian representative institutions they created a truly Russian sort of (exercise in) democracy.

Within this framework, or so the second message went, the Duma was considered a true (lower house of) parliament, and its creation the true start-ing point of Russian parliamentarism. However, this very parliamentarism was considered not only compatible with the classical tradition of Western parliaments but also best suited for the specific case of Russia. In other words, the third message forcefully suggested that Russian parliamenta-rism was special (Stenograph, 22 April 2011). The specificity of the Russian democratic institutions was altogether proven and mirrored by the concepts that the Chairman of the Duma, Boris Gryzlov, used and explained in his jubilee speech. He mentioned Russia's current 'sovereign democracy' as a mere translation of its far older *Samoderjavnoe narodovlaste* – i.e., autocratic people's self-determination (Shkel' 2011). This concept sounded truly old and authentic. More importantly, the very use of the old Slavic word 'Duma' simultaneously underlined the intrinsic differences between Russian and foreign parliaments and expressed both the Duma's comparability and its uniqueness.

From the perspective of the conceptual history of parliaments, this ambi-guity is extremely telling and fascinating. Globally, it raises three sorts of issues, firstly pertaining to the history of the Duma and the remains of the tsarist autocratic regime in the present Duma. Secondly, issues related to its compatibility with the present-day Western general acceptance of what a true parliament should be like, encompassing the way it fits the criteria of rep-resentation, deliberation, sovereignty and responsibility as formulated in the starting hypothesis of this volume. Finally, issues concerning the perception of the Duma and how it is influenced by the word that designates it. Let us start with the history of the Duma.

Power(lessness) from the Tsars to the Soviets

In order to give his manifold message any effectiveness, Gryzlov had to conceal several historical elements, three of which might seriously have weakened his argumentation and hence its expected positive political effect. He did not mention that the name of the Duma was not a consen-sual one, guided by the desire to continue and improve the legacy of the Imperial Duma. Actually, its name was the result of a linguistic fashion and an historical compromise between two contradictory, parliamentary and Soviet-style forms of representation (*Current Digest of the Post-Soviet Press*, 1987–91).

From the end of the 1980s onwards, several assemblies, be they gatherings of citizens (*Moskovskie Novosti*, 19 November 1989), political institutions (*Izvestia*, 29 January 1990) or even newspapers (*Pravda*, 5 April 1990), called themselves Dumas, without it meaning any specific form of organization, let alone a decision-making organ. At the very beginning of the 1990s, the political actors who wanted a new parliament for the Russian Soviet Federative Socialist Republic (RSFSR) thus rather smoothly and logically adopted the same word to designate the lower house (Rumanciev 2007–09, 1: 145, 377; 2: 354).

In any case, and unlike Gryzlov, they were careful not to underline any close link between the old imperial institution and the post-Soviet parliament that they wanted to establish. Their discretion seems puzzling as the political use of history is one of the best ways to legitimize the introduction of novelties (Herrmann 2011: 13–14), and the Russian audience was enthusiastically rediscovering its imperial past (Ferretti 2002; Scherrer 2006). Actually, their silence reflects the embarrassment caused by the political struggle between the promoters of parliaments and the defenders of soviets; it also mirrored the internal uneasiness of most social actors, who were unwilling to deny their entire communist past for a new capitalist future, and it was admittedly also influenced by the bad reputation the Imperial Duma had in Soviet society (*Izvestia*, 7 June 1989).

The third edition of the *Great Soviet Encyclopaedia* (1969–78), which is a valuable source of mainstream information for the end of the Soviet era, notably depicted the Imperial Duma as a powerless institution that merely aimed to support a 'bourgeois monarchy'. Despite its indisputable ideological bias, the article was not totally wrong, and it quite rightly stressed the decisive role played by the events of the year 1905, when the defeat against Japan and the Revolution compelled Tsar Nicholas II to make several political concessions, including the creation of a State Duma (see also the case of Finland in Chapter 6). Unlike the older institutions bearing the same name, the new State Duma was a parliament-like organ in that it was elected and had the power to enact laws.

That being said, like the Boyar Dumas and, later on, the municipal Dumas and the contemporary German Reichstag, the State Duma had only restricted power or, more to the point, only the amount of power the monarch allowed it. The emperor had the right to appoint his ministers, to veto the laws issued by the Duma and to dissolve the Duma itself whenever he wanted to. This situation rapidly led to conflicts, and after the dissolution of two Dumas, Nicholas II tamed his 'legislature' by astutely settling the problem of representation that had long been discussed during the nineteenth century (Semyonov 2009a, 2009b). As of 1907, the elections took place in a 'curial' way, allotting deputies according to the voters' 'estate': while 120,000 workers could elect one deputy, it required only 230 landowners to achieve the same result (Kyr'yanov 2006).

In 1917, the situation understandably changed. Given the February Revolution and especially the abdication of the emperor, several members of the Duma formed a provisional government with the intention of assuming power and organizing the transition to a true constitutional regime. The very progressive laws that it issued were hardly implemented, since the provisional government's power was decisively challenged by another institution: the Petrograd Soviet. Like the State Duma, the latter was created in the wake of the Revolution of 1905 out of strike committees and, like the provisional government, it was (re)activated as a result of the First Revolution of 1917. Now, it operated according to totally different principles and quickly became an example to emulate, purportedly (or supposedly) building on the models of soviets formed during the Paris Commune.

The soviets were (at least ideally) spontaneous gatherings that elected their representatives to meet at a superior level while retaining the imperative mandate and the power to recall them, thereby removing the possibilities for independent deliberation. More importantly, there was no separation of powers. Cooperation with the provisional government was thus difficult and became impossible after the Bolsheviks seized power, gradually adopting the exclusive political model of soviets and disseminating it throughout the (communist) world. According to Lenin's quite consistent views, parliaments were to be used for propaganda and to challenge the bourgeois system from within. In Russia, parliamentarism had been temporarily maintained to show the 'backward classes' its true character: ensuring the power of the rich while pretending to care for the concerns of the poor. Only this experience could convince the workers and peasants of the superiority of soviets (Lenin 1920). Within this theoretical framework, Soviet institutions unsurprisingly showed no obvious (or at least no consciously assumed) sign of parliamentarism.

This does not mean, however, that the Soviet system totally differed from the Duma. From a practical point of view, the soviets, whatever their level, were directed by the party, so their real power was almost non-existent. They were mere symbolic decorations, just as the Duma had once been. At a higher level of abstraction, both the capitalist and communist regimes shared some common concerns. They notably wanted their respective systems to function and consequently to be supported by the majority of their citizens. This is why the 'parliamentarization' of Soviet politics began before the fall of the USSR and even before parliamentarism had ceased to be considered one of the main hallmarks of the regime's arch-enemy. Conversely, it also explains why the creation of a parliamentary institution was seen as particularly vital once the Soviet Union had collapsed. From this perspective, the Duma was not only a political tool but also the symbol of an ideological change, although its reintroduction seemed to be more of an (admittedly abrupt) evolution than a real break with the past.

Representation from Gorbachev to Yeltsin

When Gorbachev came into power in 1985, he analysed the poor economic situation as being the indirect result of civic disengagement. His reflection led him to open up public debate and leave unprecedented space for the expression of political opinions and knowledge. In addition, he launched several political reforms aimed at opposing corruption and reviving the citizens' interest in politics: the famous policy of perestroika. Both programmes included better political representation.

The first of these programmes clearly opposed Brezhnev's legacy. In order to gain uncontested support, the latter had given more power to regional elites. In the early 1980s, it was thought that the aging and almighty local elites would paralyse any attempt to develop the country. Gorbachev proceeded to replace them and established new political actors; however, while these were rather young, dynamic and more in touch with the people's concerns, they were fortuitously mostly Russian as Gorbachev paid no real attention to their nationality (Lapidus 1989: 92–108).

The second programme was even more ambitious, as it encompassed the reform of the ruling political system. These fundamental changes occurred in two main interconnected stages, respectively focusing on the redefinition of the role of the Communist Party of the Soviet Union (CPSU) and the reshaping of the Soviet Union's deliberative organs. In January 1987, Gorbachev launched the policy of *demokratisaciya* (democratization), aimed at revitalizing the party by challenging its old sclerotic ruling elite. He accordingly called for multi-candidate elections to take place for the Communist Party in the localities and the soviets. In June 1988, he gave this programme more publicity and increased its effect. A more decisive step was taken in early 1990, when Section 6 of the 1977 constitution, which stipulated the leading role of the CPSU, was replaced by a new version that guaranteed multipartyism (Constitution 1977).

This radical change took place and was especially effective in the context of Gorbachev's power reorganization. In order to challenge the 'old communist guard', the first secretary had also decided to change the old structures and, on 1 July 1988, launched the so-called Congress of People's Deputies of the Soviet Union (Gorbachev 1988), a 2,250-member body whose function was to elect the Supreme Soviet. Although it was meant to revive the old system of soviets and actually added an additional stage in the designation process of the Soviet legislative assembly, some observers consider it to have been a parliamentary-like assembly (Magun 2007: 66ff). It did acquire some of the power formerly devolved to the party and gained better control of the executive. Also, its sessions were supposed to last several months, which allowed for true discussions. Above all, two thirds of its members were elected by the people from among several candidates of different political persuasions.

According to a well-known historical mechanism, the result of the first election, in March 1989, displayed vast support for Gorbachev and his moderate reformism; however, the election of the new Congresses of People's Deputies at the federal level, on 4 March 1990, showed that within one year different forms of opposition had coalesced and all those who had lost their trust in Gorbachev started to back other political forces such as the so-called Radical Reformists or the Nationalists. The latter had gained influence notably because of the growing dissatisfaction with the Russian elites installed by Gorbachev in his fight against corruption. Multipartyism ultimately supported this trend and provided the Nationalists' claim for independence with an official basis.

There had been more and more nationalist movements and demonstrations from 1986 onwards, and they had gradually intensified. In this process, the election of the local Congresses of People's Deputies acted as a powerful trigger for nationalistic forces by inciting an increasing number of republics to declare independence from the Soviet power. This process mainly concerned peripheral regions, such as the Baltic States (1990) and Georgia, but it also appealed to the newly elected Russian authorities and especially their leader, Boris Yeltsin, who, in the summer of 1990, declared his republic's independence in a nationalistic and demagogic way. In June 1991, he even became Russia's first elected president, not least in order to challenge Mikhail Gorbachev.

The latter took several steps to preserve his power and the supremacy of the Soviet Union. He sent troops to the Baltic States and held a referendum to display the support he enjoyed, but he was also forced to prepare a new Union Treaty that yielded a large degree of autonomy to the republics. One day before its signature, Soviet conservatives decided to pre-empt the event by seizing power. Yeltsin played a key role in the failure of this coup and instantaneously gained enormous popularity as a result. His newfound fame allowed him to supersede Gorbachev, who resigned in December 1991, just as the collapse of the Soviet Union was officially ratified.

The irony is that Gorbachev's introduction of novel electoral rules and better representation into the ossified Soviet structures had decisively worked against him, his projects and even the preservation of the USSR. It allowed long-restrained nationalisms to reappear on the political agenda and to seduce not only national minorities but also a huge Russian majority that followed Yeltsin's wishes to build a Russian state on the still-smouldering ruins of the Soviet Union. That being said, while Yeltsin's 'dissolving [of] the Soviet Union may have been his most important achievement' (McFaul 2000: 50), much remained to be done with regard to the parliamentarization of the new country.

Responsibility under Yeltsin

At first, there was genuine interest in laying down democratic rules for Russia. From 1990 onwards, at a time when there was still no Russian state, a constitutional commission gathered to provide the country with new legislative institutions (Fond konstitucionnykh reform 1990–93). After the collapse of the Soviet Union, when its work was becoming crucial, serious rifts appeared among its members regarding the way this restructuring was to be managed, the degree of centralization and the respective powers of the legislative and the executive.

In this debate, Yeltsin first advocated a balance of power that was not that unfavourable to the projected parliament (Moore 1995). During the process of constitutional elaboration, the Congress of People's Deputies gave its president extraordinary powers. He was thus able to launch decisive economic reforms, which he considered more important than any political reorganization. If this conviction prevented him from authoritarian moves, it also prevented him from developing new institutions that would have unfailingly backed him. Sometime after the liberalization of prices, in January 1992, the Congress of People's Deputies opposed most of Yeltsin's suggestions as a result of an increasing distrust of his economic reforms, rendering the president unable to prevail and eventually leaving the Russian Federation ungovernable.

This outcome stemmed (at least partly) from the unresolved question of responsibility. Although this issue was mentioned during constitutional discussions (Rumanciev 2007–09, 1: 786), it was not clearly solved: Yeltsin apparently understood his extraordinary powers to mean that he had carte blanche to act as he wished, while the Congress still considered itself to be above the president. As of the end of 1992, this struggle for pre-eminence developed into a fierce conflict that resorted to constitutional tools, such as referenda or declarations of unconstitutionality, before eventually making use of real weapons. In the autumn of 1993, violence broke out against the background of a severe economic crisis. MPs called for their supporters to storm the Moscow television tower. The next day, Yeltsin replied by having troops open fire on what was considered to be the Russian parliament.[1] In doing so, he showed the entire world how little responsibility the government had vis-à-vis the parliament.

This turn of events had several consequences for the new parliamentarian institutions created by Yeltsin to replace the Congress. In fact, the very necessity of their existence, their global character and denomination had long been decided by the above-mentioned constitutional commission. The commission had supported a bicameral system right from the start and agreed very early on that the lower chamber should be named the 'Duma' (Rumanciev 2007–09, 2: 406). The 1993 coup decisively shaped the institution, notably on issues pertaining to responsibility. On one hand, the violent outbreak convinced Yeltsin to strengthen the government's power over the new parliament. For instance, the President was given the right to dissolve the Duma. He could also initiate/veto legislation or issue decrees with the force of law. Moreover, since he was not constitutionally required to choose his government from the parliamentary majority, the Duma did not bear any responsibility for the country's policy (Remington 2008: 111).

On the other hand, possibly because of the demonstrations of democratic goodwill that Yeltsin was compelled to display – after all, he was backed by the Russian democratic forces and even more so by most of the Western states – the Duma was not entirely powerless. Its 450 members were elected in a fairly democratic way, by a system combining proportional/majority representation, which gave it indisputable legitimacy. It also enjoyed several rights that constitute a true parliament: it issued laws (which had to be ratified by the upper house), and the individual chosen as prime minister had to be approved by it. It could rely on several additional tools such as the Audit Chamber or the right to organize hearings and even to impeach the president. In short, the Duma could remind the president that he was accountable to his parliament.

In the context of painful economic changes, the war in Chechnya and, above all, the lack of a majority in parliament, the first Dumas often used their power to challenge the president, and from 1998 to 1999 the Duma initiated an impeachment procedure against Boris Yeltsin.[2] This decision was obviously spectacular and possibly dangerous, as the president could have responded with legally sanctioned violence, as he had in similar circumstances in 1993. This time, though, he did not do so and instead agreed to resign peacefully at the end of the millennium. The Duma's impeachment procedure was indeed first and foremost a symbolic reminder: despite all the public gesticulations, Yeltsin and the Duma had been able to cooperate, manage the Soviet legacy and initiate the country's democratization and parliamentarization (Remington 2008: 118) in a way that is tellingly reflected in the notion of deliberation.

Deliberation from Yeltsin to Putin

The Duma and the Congress of People's Deputies were both undoubtedly considered true loci of deliberation. It is thus not really surprising that the constitution of 1993 provided for three readings at the Duma, although the discussions had probably not been expected to be so animated and acerbated; at first, the lower house was a place of sometimes violent disputes that ignored true parliamentary discourse, and personal attacks, directed less at a member's political ideas and stance than at his or her past or origins, occurred often enough. On 23 December 1994, the deputy of the Liberal-Democratic Party of Russia (a far-right patriotic party) E.Ju. Loginov tellingly complained: 'I protest against . . . the accusation of anti-Semitism. Tomorrow, some person with schizophrenia will accuse me of zoophilia or eating babies'.[3] He received the following answer: 'If he [Loginov] is not an anti-Semite, then I am [the famous Soviet prima ballerina] Maya Plisetskaya'.[4] The parliamentary rhetoric nonetheless improved progressively, and by the turn of the millennium unparliamentary discourse had become rare.

This evolution may have had various causes. Firstly, the changing attitudes within the Duma may be seen as evidence of Russian democratization. In most parliamentary systems, the use of adequate discursive techniques shows the integration of a code of dispute resolution that attempts to respect the view of one's opponent. It would seem only natural for Russian parliamentarism to follow in the same tracks. Indeed, the mastering of such parliamentary discourse coincided with the introduction of new institutional rules that were at least officially meant to enhance the Russian legislative system.

In 2000, newly in power, Putin launched significant reforms in the functioning of Russian federalism and hence the upper house of parliament. The 1993 constitution was silent on how to choose the two deputies who were to represent their 'subject' (administrative regions or members of the federation) in the Federation Council, so that as of 1995 this position was held by the heads of the local executive and legislative organs. In order to officially avoid these dual mandates and better respect the separation of power, Putin decided that the members had to be full-time representatives. Although the latter were supposed to be designated by their regions, the process of designation was actually mostly supervised by Moscow. The Kremlin's monitoring strengthened in 2004 following its adoption of an antiterrorist and anti-corruption law stipulating that the governors of the subjects would not be elected by local voters but appointed by the government itself (Remington 2008: 121).

At approximately the same time, in the wake of the terrorist attack on Beslan, the wave of reforms also reached the lower house. Here again, changes were officially presented as being in the interest of democracy. It was decided that the Duma would be exclusively elected by proportional representation, which actually prevented all typically regional and/or independent candidates from sitting in parliament. Furthermore, all candidates had to be party members, even as it was becoming increasingly difficult for parties to obtain an official status, as the authorities allegedly feared fantasy candidatures (Patze 2011: 166). Finally, the minimum threshold for any party to be represented in parliament rose from 5 to 7 per cent. This measure was officially meant to strengthen the party system by reducing the number of parties (Stone 2009: 21–22).

The result of these decisions was indeed remarkable. The number of parties sank from eleven in 1993 to four in 2007 and 2011. More importantly, the absence of independent candidates strikingly reduced the ideological diversity of the lower house and consequently the richness of its debates. This trend had admittedly older conceptual roots. Already in 1994, some MPs had claimed that the Duma sessions were not meant for political debates (Stenographs, 13 January 1994; 19 January 1994). This point of view was somehow reiterated a decade later by Gryzlov himself; however, it took another four years for journalists and the public sphere to comment on the chairman's alleged utterance that the Duma was not being a place for discussion. This commentary reveals that around 2007 parts of Russian society started to feel and resent the undemocratic evolution of the Duma. At least since 2007, the novel rhetorical discipline displayed by the deputies has had little to do with democracy and more to do with the hidden agenda of democratization and the evolution of the Duma's sovereignty.

Sovereignty from Putin to Medvedev

The Duma's sovereignty has never been that of a classical parliament. Although the lower chamber's sovereignty was obviously crucial for the first MPs, they did not compare it with Western standards but with their Soviet, pre-perestroika legacy (Stenographs, 20 May 1994). This reference allowed Yeltsin to give the Duma a little leeway vis-à-vis the executive power, which he did mainly in order to avoid it having any resemblance with the Congress of People's Deputies that he had come to hate so much. That being said, such an interpretation is only partially true as this policy continued despite the change of president and the blossoming economy from the early 2000s on. Putin did not alter the previous trend. In fact, all his democratizing measures had self-reinforcing side effects. Under the cover of Western parliamentary ideals, these measures favoured the president's party and control within and over the Duma. Putin's new 'democratic' rules of the game excluded all minor parties and typically local candidates; the designation of governors of the subjects was a way to control the Duma indirectly. Even the shift from semi-direct to entirely proportional representation occurred in a media land-scape that was dominated by his party, so that his electoral reform was only a means to dominate the political arena even more (Patze 2011: 196ff). Under the cover of democratization, the Duma could no longer meet all the criteria that constitute a true parliament.

Admittedly, Medvedev undertook to improve this situation. As soon as Putin handed over power to him in 2008, the new president showed a will-ingness to distance himself from his mentor prime minister by adopting pro-parliament measures. He notably re-established the threshold of 5 per cent and facilitated the registration of parties; however, on most points, such as the appointment of governors of the subjects, he shared his predecessor's views. Moreover, he extended the length of term of office in the Duma from four to five years. Above all, he actively contributed to the blurring of the sep-aration of executive and legislative powers by allowing Putin to head 'United Russia', the overwhelmingly dominant party in the Duma, at the same time as the latter chaired the cabinet of ministers.[5]

As a result of Putin's and Medvedev's policy on the parliament, the Duma lost (almost) all of its sovereignty and became a mere 'house of approval' (Remington 2008: 126). Accordingly, it no longer played its institutional role. Most political decisions were made before being submitted to the Duma by people who had little to do with it. The Duma was reduced to a rather deco-rative rubber-stamping role. The latter criticism has been levelled ever since Putin took power if not before (Meier and Zarakhovich 2000), and it has even become more noticeable since 2005 with the Duma's increasing loss of sover-eignty. Indeed, Russian citizens even contributed to the trend by massively voting for the government party.

Such an attitude has not gone unnoticed. Most authors have attributed it to the enhancement of the economic situation, which the ever-rising prices of hydrocarbons from the beginning of the new millennium have made possible. Some scholars have also stressed other causes, such as the fear of terrorism, the excesses of the so-called 'Yeltsinian' democracy or merely the lack of a true political alternative (Stone 2009; Colton and Hale 2009). These expla-nations all seem plausible and even confirmed a contrario by the demon-strations that took place in December 2011 after the election of the sixth post-Soviet Duma. The new middle-class generation that had emerged was asking for more than economic and physical security. Thousands of Russian citizens could then show their discontent publicly, but their demands did not focus on the Duma. The only parliamentary issue of note that these dem-onstrators indirectly tackled was that of representation, as they demanded new and fair elections and better representation of the opposition parties. As for the actual functioning of parliament encompassing the notions of responsibility, deliberation and even sovereignty, it was hardly ever mentioned.

Admittedly, the people's silence on this may have stemmed from a conviction that better representation would progressively lead to functional enhancements. One may also argue that the demonstrators did not believe that the Duma per se needed immediate changes and that there were more important issues at stake. These suppositions are not contradictory; instead they suggest that the Duma, despite the timing of the demonstrations, was not a top priority.

Conclusion

Against all odds, the political demonstrations that took place in early December 2011 indirectly and unwillingly confirmed some claims made about eight months earlier during the celebration of the 105th anniversary of the Duma. The very fact that they did not demand radical democratic improvements in the Duma – whatever the reasons for their silence might be – suggests that they agreed with Gryzlov or, at least, did not consider it a true Western-style parliament. Of course, it may be that they did not see the shortcomings of the Duma or care about them. Most probably, though, their attitude also expressed their belief that this institution did not really or immediately need to fit Western parliamentary criteria, as it was a specifically Russian version of parliament. In other words, they somehow shared Gryzlov's repeatedly asserted belief in the genuine 'national' character of the Russian political system.

If the demonstrations that followed the 2011 election did not deny the specificity of the Russian case per se, they took place after gross electoral frauds in Russia had been manifested to the entire world (Assemblée parlementaire du Conseil de l'Europe 2012). Hence, one must infer that the people understandingly did not want to be labelled as stupid by their own government and, consequently, did not want their specificity to consist in being credulous. They obviously felt ridiculed, and their mass reaction sheds light on the role they assigned to their parliament. Judging by the slogans of December 2011, the Duma was supposed to play first and foremost a highly symbolic role. It was not meant to represent the population so much as to show the world and themselves that the population was taken into account.

This statement has at least two – historical and conceptual – consequences. It suggests that Gryzlov's reference to history was both unexpectedly and indirectly right. The specific, and mostly symbolic, understanding of the role of the current Duma is highly reminiscent of the Imperial Duma, as the early twentieth-century deputies were both powerless and emblematic of the Tsar's goodwill. In other words, the link between both Dumas was maybe not their specific (non-)parliamentarian functioning, as Gryzlov inaccurately claimed, but rather their particular function of dignifying Russian society. When the Kremlin ignored this minimal but by no means negligible expectation, the population felt humiliated and clearly neglected.

From this perspective, the demonstrations would indicate that the understanding of the Duma's history influenced Russian society. While the past was variously interpreted and hence given different weight by different social actors, its importance was indubitably reinforced by the use of the very word 'Duma'. Moreover, the term not only designed but also moulded the concept by generating understandings and expectations that were not exactly parliamentarily oriented but nonetheless strong. Apparently, the concept of the Duma comes across as a specific expression of the population's fundamental wish to be taken into consideration, of which the concept of parliament then appears to be another formulation.

Notes

1　The death toll has yet to be agreed upon.
2　This procedure lasted roughly from June 1998 until May 1999 (sources: Stenographs).
3　'Я выражаю протест . . . (Алла Гербер) обвинила меня в антисемитских высказываниях. Завтра какой-нибудь шизофреник . . . обвинит меня в зоофилии или поедании младенцев' (Stenographs, 23 December 1994).
4　'Если он не антисемит, то я вообще тогда Майя Плисецкая', А.А. Osovcov, Fraction Russia's Choice (reformists) (Stenographs, 23 December 1994).
5　Significantly enough, the 29 April 2011 issue of the *Parlamentskaya Gazeta* presents this specificity as one of the key achievements of the Russian parliamentary system.

References

Primary Sources

Constitution. 1977. Retrieved 28 June 2012, from http://constitution.garant.ru/history/ussr-rsfsr/1977/zakony/185465/

Current Digest of the Post-Soviet Press. 1987–2011. Retrieved from http://www.east viewpress.com/Journals/CurrentDigest

Deklaraciya. 2011. 'Декларация Международной конференции, посвящённой 105-летию парламентаризма в России'. Retrieved 26 June 2012, from http://www.parlament-club.ru/articles,special,1,866.htm

Fond konstitucionnykh reform. 1990–93. Retrieved from http://www.rfcr.ru/archive/

Gorbachev, M. 1988. 'On Progress in Implementing the Decisions of the 27th CPSU Congress and the Tasks of Promoting Perestroika: Report to the 19th All-Union Conference, June 28, 1988'. Moscow: Novosty Press Agency.

Great Soviet Encyclopaedia, 3rd ed. 1969–78. Retrieved from http://slovari.yandex.ru

Gryzlov, B. 2011.'Тезисы Выступления Председателя Государственной Думы Бориса Грызлова на Международной Конференции, Посвященной 105-Летию Парламентаризма В России'. Retrieved 26 June 2012, from http://www.parlament-club.ru/articles,8,special,1,861.htm

Lenin, V.I. 1920. 'Speech on Parliamentarism'. Retrieved 28 February 2013, from http://www.marxists.org/archive/lenin/works/1920/jul/x03.htm#fw5

Rumanciev, O.G. (ed.). 2007–09. *Из истории создания Конституции Российской Федерации. Конституционная комиссия: стенограммы, материалы, документы (1990–1993 гг.)*, vols. 1 and 2. Moscow: Fond konstitucionnykh reform.

Shkel', T. 'Запад ни при чем', *Rossiyskaya Gazeta*, 28 April 2011. Retrieved 26 June 2012, from http://www.rg.ru/2011/04/28/parlamentarizm.html

Stenographs (of the Duma). 1994–2011. Retrieved from http://transcript.duma.gov.ru/

Secondary Sources

Assemblée parlementaire du Conseil de l'Europe. 2012. *Observations des élections législatives dans la Fédération de Russie*. Retrieved 30 December 2012, from http://assembly.coe.int/ASP/Doc/XrefViewPDF.asp?FileID=12924&Language=FR

Colton, T.J. and H.E. Hale. 2009. 'The Putin Vote: Presidential Electorates in a Hybrid Regime', *Slavic Review* 68(3): 473–503.

Ferretti, M. 2002. 'Le stalinisme entre histoire et mémoire. Le malaise de la mémoire russe', *Matériaux pour l'Histoire de Notre Temps* 68: 65–81.

Herrmann, I. 2011. 'Introduction sous l'angle suisse', *Revue Suisse d'Histoire* 61(1): 4–21.

Kyr'yanov, I.K. 2006. *Российские парламентарии начала XXв.: новые политики в новом политическом пространстве*. Perm: Permskoe knizhnoe izdarel'stvo.

Lapidus, G.V. 1989. 'Gorbachev's Nationalities Problem', *Foreign Affairs* 68(4): 92–108.

Magun, A. 2007. 'The Post-Communist Revolution in Russia and the Genesis of Representative Democracy', *Redescriptions, Yearbook of Political Thought and Conceptual History* 11: 61–77.

McFaul, M. 2000. 'Yeltsin's Legacy', *The Wilson Quarterly* 24(2): 44–58.

Meier, A. and Y. Zarakhovich. 2000. 'Putin Tightens His Grip', *Time World* (29 May). Retrieved 28 June 2012, from http://www.time.com/time/world/article/0,8599,2050649,00.html

Moore, R. 1995. 'The Path to the New Russian Constitution: A Comparison of Executive-Legislative Relations in the Major Drafts', *Demokratizatsiya* 3(1): 44–60.

Patze, P. 2011. *Wie demokratisch ist Russland? Ein tieforientierter Ansatz zur Messung demokratischer standards*. Baden-Baden: Nomos.

Ponomaryov, V. 1988. 'The Nodvorskaya Veche' – What are the "Friends" of Restructuring Calling on Young People to Do?', *Sobesednik* 44: 12–13. Retrieved 13 December 2010, from http://dlib.eastview.com/browse/doc/20014473

Remington, T.F. 2008. 'The Russian Federal Assembly, 1994–2004', in D.M. Olson and P. Norton (eds), *Post-Communist and Post-Soviet Parliaments: The Initial Decade*. Oxon and New York: Routledge, pp. 110–30.

Scherrer, J. 2006. 'Idéologie, identité, mémoire. Une nouvelle "idée russe"?', *Transitions* 44(2): 123–38.

Semyonov, A. 2009a. 'The Real and Live Ethnographic Map of Russia: The Russian Empire in the Mirror of the State Duma', in I. Gerasimov, J. Kusber and A. Semyonov (eds), *Empire Speaks Out: Languages of Rationalization and Self-description in the Russian Empire*. Leiden, Boston: Brill, pp. 191–228.

————. 2009b. 'Revoliutsiia 1905 goda: uskol'zaiushchaia liberal'naia al'ternativa', in I. Prokhorova et al. (eds), *Antropologiia revoliutsii*. Moscow: Novoe Literaturnoe Obozrenie, pp. 101–26.

Stone, S. 2009. 'Over-Managed Democracy: Evaluating Vladimir Putin's Presidency', *Cddrl Working Papers* 113. Retrieved 27 June 2012, from http://iis-db.stanford.edu/pubs/22526/No_113_Stone_Overmanaged_Russia.pdf

Irène Herrmann, Ph.D., is Associate Professor of Transnational History of Switzerland at the University of Geneva, Switzerland. She has also worked at the universities of Laval, Moscow and Fribourg. Her fields of expertise include conflict management, the political use of the past, conceptual mechanisms and the reception of politics in Switzerland and post-Soviet Russia. She is a board member of Concepta – International Research School in Conceptual History and Political Thought.

Part II

The Discourse and Rhetoric of Modern Parliaments

Chapter 8

Parliamentary Discourse and Deliberative Rhetoric

Cornelia Ilie

While there is wide agreement that government based on democratic deliberation is the most viable and legitimate form of government in modern societies, recent and current societal developments are continually raising our awareness of the constant challenges facing parliamentarism and parliaments, which are meant to foster democratic modes of public debate, opinion-building and decision-making in the public sphere. Deliberation is generally considered necessary in decision-making across a broad and diverse political spectrum whenever there are reasons for deciding on one course of action but also equally compelling reasons for choosing another. This fundamental parliamentary function derives from one of the principles of classical rhetoric, masterfully summed up by Aristotle: 'We deliberate not about ends, but about the means to attain ends'. The rhetorical underpinnings of the political process of deliberation can certainly explain the growing scholarly interest in the role of parliaments as dynamic institutional mechanisms of representative and deliberative democracy based on multiparty dialogue. This multiparty dialogue is nowadays recognized as an important prerequisite for ensuring a plurality of perspectives and a polyphonic parliamentary deliberation that is both undergoing and bringing about substantial sociopolitical changes across temporal and spatial boundaries.

As we saw in Part I, parliamentary debates have acquired greater transparency and visibility over time, and these have contributed to a stronger impact on electors' perceptions and consequently on the development of public affairs. The rhetorical patterns of parliamentary deliberation display various ideological visions, party affiliations, institutional positions and political agendas of the members of parliament as representatives of citizens in terms of their social, professional, gender and ethnic backgrounds. Since parliamentary dialogue is audience oriented – i.e., it is enacted by and among fellow parliamentarians before a wide (present and virtual) audience – it involves not only parliamentarians, but also members of the electorate, the general public and the media. Nowadays the growing impact of this dialogue is due to widespread and effective use of multimedia and the Internet as important means of stimulating citizens' input and active participation. As parliaments and parliamentarians are taking an increasingly central role in media reports and current debates, it has become imperative to understand the parliamentary uses and misuses of language, discourse-shaped power and gender relations, as well as the interplay between patterns of parliamentary interaction and the participants' political agendas. Especially so as the scope of parliamentary discourses stretches beyond parliament (through extra-parliamentary dialogue: the media, lobby groups) and beyond national borders (through inter-parliamentary dialogue).

The Rhetoric of Parliamentary Pros and Cons

If we are to understand the particular role of parliamentary rhetoric in articulating political motives and legitimating political action, we need to take a closer look at the struggle over the use of language as a concrete manifestation of the struggle for power: acquiring political power, challenging it, competing for it, or defending and consolidating it. In socio-historical periods marked by significant paradigm shifts and political polarizations, parliaments have played a decisive role in benchmarking current societal issues and exposing party-political agendas by debating the pros and cons of alternative political solutions (Van Dijk 2003). In the course of often heated debates, political adversaries have to be proved wrong, or at least neutralized. This is why the strength of parliamentary rhetoric lies in its agonistic spirit, according to which there are always at least two sides to each political issue, which can therefore be debated for and against. By debating ideas and opinions, proposals and counterproposals, parliamentarians are discursively problematizing and (re)shaping current conceptualizations of values, identities and relationships that lie at the basis of collective decision-making. After all, the end goal of parliamentary debates is to affect the audience's beliefs and opinions in order to motivate them to act in a certain way with regard to real-life issues.

In many societies, the aftermath of crucial sociopolitical events has repeatedly confirmed Chantal Mouffe's claim (1993) that politics is not simply about reaching consensus but is, rather, about the possibility of manipulating dissensus within the framework of an established agreement on how to conduct affairs. Therefore, it is essential to understand the double-sided nature of parliamentary rhetoric: parliamentary debates display both a rhetoric of

dissensus, involving confrontation and adversariality, and a rhetoric of consensus, involving compromise and solidarity (Ilie 2003b). Consequently, the
rhetorical and argumentative strategies used by parliamentarians are best
studied at both micro and macro levels: at the micro level from the perspective
of discursive patterns of cooperation, competition, domination and/or relations of subordination between interlocutors, and at the macro level as shaped
by institutional mechanisms (e.g., political and sociocultural traditions, moral
norms of conduct and interaction) that involve both opportunity (acquiring and maintaining power and influence by imposing one's own rhetorical
speaking style) and constraint (having to comply with norms of interaction,
avoiding prohibited behaviour and forbidden words or expressions).

A paradoxical phenomenon regarding parliamentary deliberation is worth
exploring in greater depth. Throughout history, parliamentary debates have
been undergoing a process of increasing conventionalization, while at the
same time there is a growing tendency to renew or update certain procedures;
for example by adopting a more informal speaking style. In general, parliamentary discourse exhibits a mixture of features belonging to both the institutional genre (= monitored, agenda-centred and audience oriented) and the
conversational genre (= spontaneous, improvised and interlocutor oriented).
Whereas the language of parliamentary debates is conventionalized to a large
extent (including the use of specialized terminology and ritualized forms of
address (see Chapters 11 and 12)), its rhetorical force, indicated by the construction of pathos and the co-construction of ethos, relies very much on
spontaneous interventions, hilarious remarks, heckling, etc., which are likely
to appeal to both the insider audience and the public at large. The unpredictable combination of two discourse genres – institutional and conversational
– often renders parliamentary rhetoric irresistibly engaging and captivating.

Oral vs. Written Parliamentary Rhetoric

Parliaments typically display distinctive rhetorical communication genres that
are on the one hand associated with the oral tradition (e.g., extemporaneous
speeches), and on the other, with the tradition of the written word (e.g., legislative texts). Parliamentary dialogue takes shape as an oral performance that is
meant to be eventually written down in the official records. As early as the late
eighteenth century, the English 'parliamentary culture of gentlemanly orality
began to negotiate a relationship with an increasingly dominant culture of
print' (Reid 2000: 122; see also Chapter 2 on parliamentary publicity). Due to
culture-specific literacy traditions, parliaments differ in terms of the priority
given to the written or the spoken word. In the British House of Commons,
for example, the reading of prepared speeches and an overdependence on

written notes have long been banned as unparliamentary practices, whereas French parliamentarians have for a long time followed the tradition of reading speeches like literary pieces, in line with the Latin rhetorical tradition (see Chapters 9 and 10). Since parliamentary oratory is histrionic by its very nature, it is not surprising that in democratic parliaments the debates are enacted as stage performances, displaying a range of culture-specific theatrical characteristics (see Chapter 10 on perceived differences between French and English types of parliamentary theatricality).

Strategic Uses of Parliamentary Forms of Address

Several discourse-analytical and rhetorical studies have provided evidence that the strategic uses of interlocutor-oriented and audience-oriented forms of address in parliamentary interaction are dependent on in-group membership, out-group positioning, institutionally hierarchical status and overall political goals. They can be seen as ritualized ways of manipulating perceptions of parliamentary relations and the political power balance. For example, the default form of address in the British parliament is the third person, 'a deferential and distance-marking form of address, which enables them [members of parliament] to make straightforward and forceful statements in their interaction with fellow MPs, while upholding a safe institutional distance from each other' (Ilie 2010). Historically, this particular linguistic use is motivated by the officially endorsed convention, according to which parliamentarians are not supposed to address each other directly, but only through the Speaker of the House or the President of Parliament. This ritualized form of address plays an important role in mitigating, to a certain extent, the negative effects of aggressive parliamentary confrontation and adversarial behaviour, including unparliamentary, even insulting, speech acts (Ilie 2001, 2004). While Westminster-type parliaments display the same default form of address in the third person, some European parliaments, such as the Swedish Riksdag, recommend, but do not consistently reinforce, the use of third person address. Other European parliaments, such as the French and the German ones, prefer the use of the second person plural form of address, which is seen to activate the rhetorical ethos of interpersonal politeness. In communist-era parliaments, such as the Romanian and Polish chambers and the GDR Volkskammer, there was a marked preference for the first person plural 'we', in an attempt to avoid the expression of individual commitments in the first person singular 'I'. The standard nominal form of address in these parliaments was the ideologized 'comrade', which, for obvious reasons, became one of the first things that changed after 1989, at the outset of the new post-communist parliamentary sittings (Chapters 11 and 12).

Contextualizing and Recycling Parliamentary Topoi

As institutional language users, parliamentarians are constrained by discourse practices, while at the same time they can use the resources of language both to undermine and to underpin the effectiveness of these very practices. This is achieved in different ways, depending on the politicians' actual power positions, motivations and goals, the degree of freedom of expression and action, as well as the overall environment of a given sociopolitical system. When taking the floor, parliamentarians rely heavily on rhetorical commonplaces (topoi) to single out and contextualize particular metadiscursive representations that are culturally familiar and relevant to their audiences. Beginning in the second half of the nineteenth century and throughout the twentieth century, a number of recurrent topoi were consistently used across Western, Central and Eastern European parliamentary discourses to attract and mobilize public support.

One of the most influential was the topos of the nation state, which had a high popular appeal, since it was built on emotions and highlighted major related concerns – i.e., national language, national culture and national identity. During the years of the French Revolution, the rhetoric of leading orators of the successive assemblies (e.g., Mirabeau's use of pathos or Robespierre's ethos) promoted the idea of the nation state, associating it with rights, the people and sovereignty (Chapter 10). In the Paulskirche speeches, the German nation state was frequently metaphorized in hyperbolic terms based on a figurative conceptualization according to which 'the state is a building' (Chapter 11), whereas in Romanian and Polish parliamentary discourses the idea of a nation state was more often than not associated with an historical ideal of nation-building and national sovereignty rooted in the past and projected into the future (Chapter 12; see also Chapter 6 on Scandinavia).

The Rhetorical Challenges of Unparliamentary Language

Parliamentary conventions are both a prerequisite and a challenge for members of parliament, who are expected to comply with institutional norms (i.e., parliamentary order), while at the same time attempting to circumvent these very norms (i.e., parliamentary disorder). This is why institutional practices and principles of conduct can often be most clearly revealed through violations and disruptions of normative forms of politeness and through negotiated claims about these violations. Polemic debates involve systematic face-threatening acts manifested by unparliamentary language and behaviour. These acts cover a continuum that ranges from milder/mitigated acts, such as reproaches, accusations and criticisms, to very strong ones, such as insults. By challenging certain ideas and attitudes, unparliamentary forms of language and behaviour at the same time reinforce particular values and beliefs. In examining the cognitive and rhetorical functions of insults in the British and Swedish parliaments, Ilie (2001, 2004) has found that such unparliamentary uses of language provide a rich ground for the study of interpersonal dynamics, the unpredictable changes in the power balance and the reasoning fallacies underlying verbal controversies.

The aim of abusive language and insulting behaviour is to call into question the addressee's ethos – i.e., credibility and moral profile, while enhancing the speaker's own ethos in an attempt to strike a rhetorical balance between logos and pathos appeals. What is generally referred to as 'unparliamentary use of language' represents instances of institutionally ritualized confrontational interaction. Cross-cultural comparisons are particularly enlightening in this respect, since verbal abuse involves evaluative statements grounded in specific social and cultural systems of moral values. The debates in the House of Commons display endless instances of unparliamentary language, which can sometimes be double-edged – i.e., intended to hit two targets simultaneously, as in the following excerpt:

> Charles Kennedy (LibDem, Ross, Skye and Inverness, West): Which does the Prime Minister [Tony Blair, Lab] consider the voters of London will view as more offensive: the Conservatives' disgraced mayoral candidate or Labour's discredited selection system? (Hansard Debates, 24 November 1999: column 611)

The rhetorical disjunction, which is obviously meant to emphasize the insulting speech act above, represents a recurrent argumentative fallacy, namely that of the false dilemma, whereby the speaker deliberately restricts the interlocutor's choice to two equally unacceptable alternatives. With regard to institutional regulations against unparliamentary language, some Western parliaments, notably the House of Commons and the Swedish Riksdag, prohibit parliamentarians from accusing fellow parliamentarians of lying, or using particular insulting words. However, rhetorically skilful MPs usually manage to find equally effective alternatives. Winston Churchill, when asked to withdraw the word 'lie', is reported to have replaced it with the phrase 'terminological inexactitude'. Other parliaments, such as the German, the Romanian and the Polish ones, do not enforce such a prohibition. Why are (explicit or implicit) parliamentary insults so frequent, and how do they succeed in having such a strong impact on the audience? According to Ilie (2004), the most probable reason is that they call into question the parliamentarians' very prerequisites for participating successfully in the debates, namely outstanding rhetorical skills. Indeed, in the House of Commons, as in other democratic assemblies, one of the highest parliamentary skills is to outsmart political adversaries by giving quick and witty replies and by displaying a sense of humour.

The Co-performance of Parliamentary Disorder

In order to make an impact and score political points, parliamentarians resort to pathos appeals by widening or narrowing the scope of linguistic images, minimizing or maximizing the degree of merit/accountability of their fellow parliamentarians, challenging statistical data, and last but not least, by redefining key institutional concepts (e.g. British 'consensus' vs. Swedish 'samförstånd' in Ilie 2007). In many cases metadiscursive statements convey simple, double or multiple messages through echoing, quoting and ironizing, to name but a few rhetorical strategies (Ilie 2003a). Parliamentary dialogic confrontation exhibits an ongoing co-performance of debating parliamentarians and consists of the interplay between orderly discourse (speeches, interpellations, oral/written questions, question time sessions, etc.) and disorderly discourse (disruptive acts, such as interruptions, heckling, laughter). A prototypical instance of disorderly discourse is constituted by parliamentary interruptions, which, although often perceived as histrionic acts, may affect a speaker's ongoing process of argumentation, as is often the case in the House of Commons:

> The Prime Minister [Tony Blair, Lab]: . . . What is happening in Zimbabwe is absolutely appalling, but I do not think that anyone is suggesting that we take military action there. [Hon. Members: '*Why not?*'] Perhaps some people are. (Hansard Debates, 4 Jun 2003, column 169)

Linguistic and Rhetorical Studies on Parliamentary Discourse

In spite of a growing interest over the past few decades in the theoretical study of parliamentarism and the empirical analysis of parliamentary discourse practices, the study of parliamentary discourse has acquired truly interdisciplinary scope only recently, as a result of several significant contributions made by scholars from the linguistic sub-disciplines, such as pragmatics, critical discourse analysis, and cognitive linguistics, or closely related disciplines, such as rhetoric, which have developed and used multidisciplinary approaches to the study of parliamentary debating norms and practices. Relatively recent interdisciplinary studies by scholars of political discourse analysis dedicated to parliamentary dialogue have pointed out significant institutional and linguistic aspects of parliamentary debating strategies, emphasizing the interplay between parliamentary procedures, rhetorical traditions and political discourse styles (see Biryukov et al. 1995 on parliamentary discourse in present-day Russia; Ilie 2000 on the argumentative role of clichés in parliamentary metadiscourse in the House of Commons; Pérez de Ayala 2001 on politeness and impoliteness strategies during Question Time in the House of Commons; Burkhardt 2003 on rhetorical usages of language in German parliamentary interaction; Grad Fuchsel and Martín Rojo 2003 on 'civic' and 'ethnic' nationalist discourses in Spanish parliamentary debates; Carbó 2004 on parliamentary disruptions in Mexican parliamentary debates; Sivenkova 2008 on question-asking in the British and Russian parliaments; Archakis and Tsakona 2009 on critical aspects of biased media reporting of parliamentary debates in Greece; Bruteig 2010 on Czech parliamentary debates during communist and post-communist times; Marques 2010 on the effects of deictic usages of the first person pronoun in Portuguese parliamentary debates; Ornatowski 2010 on the linguistic and behavioural changes undergone by Polish parliamentary discourse after 1989; Zima, Brône and Feyaerts 2010 on the functions of unauthorized interruptions in Austrian parliamentary debates).

The Parliamentary Case Studies in Part II

In countries like Britain, France and Belgium, parliamentary eloquence achieved great popularity among both experts and laypersons through books and essays on political, literary and epistolary rhetoric (Chapters 5, 9 and 10). Later on, parliamentarism became very successful as a result of the gradual transition from carefully prepared epideictic speeches to deliberative forms of dialogue, including improvised speeches, spontaneous interventions and humorous interruptions from the floor – the latter being notoriously frequent in the British parliament and widely quoted in extra-parliamentary circles (Ilie 2005). As has been noted by Guilhaumou (1989) (cited by Bouchet (Chapter 10)), the French political revolution was accompanied by a parallel linguistic revolution in the form of new semantic associations and innovative conceptualizations. Throughout its history, French (as well as British and German) parliamentary rhetoric has influenced and, in its turn, been influenced by the eloquence of journalists (who have followed and reported the debates) and of lawyers (many of whom have gained reputations as career politicians) (see also Bösch 2012). While the German parliamentary style started on a rather solemn and polite note (the Paulskirche rhetorical style) with short and relatively rare interruptions, it gradually took on stronger pathos and became instead over-metaphorical, as noted by Burkhardt (Chapter 11). A parallel can be drawn with the initial debating culture in the earlier stages of the Romanian parliament (in the second half of the nineteenth century), when there were hardly any interruptions, but rather a prevalence of lengthy epideictic speeches, which served as pro et contra interventions conveying divergent opinions (Chapter 12). However, this situation gradually changed, and a confrontational debating style, with occasional disorderly interventions, became the norm.

Throughout their (longer or shorter) histories, most European parliaments have undergone several more or less dramatic metamorphoses, which are explicitly singled out in historians' periodization and labelling systems (Chapters 9, 10, 11 and 12). While each individual parliament exhibits its own oratorical preferences and specific debating styles, a closer look at their institutional evolution reveals comparable dialectics of interconnectedness between patterns of parliamentary continuity and change, and sometimes even of continuity in change. In Eastern Europe, this is significantly instantiated by the commonalities and differences displayed by Romanian and Polish parliamentary rhetorics. During the communist rule, both countries experienced non-democratic parliamentary substitutes, labelled by Ilie and Ornatowski (Chapter 12) as a 'pseudo-parliament' in the Romanian case and a 'quasi-parliament' in the Polish case. The difference between the two coinages points to an important difference between the two communist-type parliaments: while the Romanian Great National Assembly served mainly as a political platform for the Romanian Communist Party during the time of Ceaușescu's personality cult, the Polish parliament was actually more than a mere rubber stamp, especially throughout the 1980s. The GDR Volkskammer represented still another case of a communist-type parliament, symbolically labelled an 'acclamation parliament' by Burkhardt (Chapter 11). Common to all these parliaments was strongly reinforced ideological propaganda that was meant to suppress individual expression by manipulatively imposing a distorted representation of reality. There were no actual debates, but rather well-rehearsed speeches followed by applause on command. After experiencing a relatively similar political system during the communist era, the democratic parliaments that have recently emerged in the fledgling democracies of Central and Eastern European countries display a range of distinguishing characteristics in terms of institutional (re)structuring and (re)organization, as well as preferred/adopted debating styles. These countries started the process of democratization at approximately the same time, but they had different starting situations owing to different political cultures and different parliamentary traditions. At the same time, they have undergone similar processes of reinvention and reactivation of their respective parliaments, by removing communist 'pseudo-parliamentary' constraints, reactivating historical parliamentary practices, rituals and traditions and reinventing new (post-communist) parliamentary norms and conventions (Chapter 12).

The country-specific analyses of parliamentary rhetoric featured in Part II focus on the transfer, transition and translation of key concepts across time and space. Debatable and controversial aspects of historically determined conceptualizations have been closely examined diachronically by means of contextualized interpretation of parliamentary records. The authors show that a preference for certain topoi is rooted in particular political traditions, such as higher or lower levels of competition and conflict tolerance, or greater or less political control of societal developments. By investigating the rhetorical uses of topoi expressed by means of recurrent key words in both parliamentary and extra-parliamentary discourses, the authors of the following chapters provide us with deeper insights into the historical transformations that have taken place over time in several representative Western, Central, and Eastern European parliaments.

The chapters in Part II provide extensive evidence that parliamentary debates do not only reflect political, social and cultural configurations in an ever changing world, but they also contribute to shaping these configurations discursively, cross-rhetorically and cross-culturally. The authors have identified and singled out, in a diachronic perspective, the relevant cognitive, cultural and institutional key concepts that characterize the context-specific evolution of parliamentary rhetoric, at both macro and micro levels, in several European countries, and they offer representative case studies of the parliaments in England, France, Germany, Romania and Poland. A major aim of the authors has been to identify the ways in which deliberative strategies in the parliaments under consideration are affected by patterns of continuity and change in sociopolitical systems, historical and culture-specific institutional constraints such as traditional forms of political dialogue, a preference for consensus-seeking strategies vs. confrontation-seeking strategies, and specific deliberation conventions stipulated by parliamentary norms.

Some of the main questions that prompted the research of the authors of the ensuing chapters are the following: What is the role of rhetorical communication in parliamentary debate and decision-making? To what extent do parliaments contribute to fostering an ongoing public dialogue based on pro et contra argumentation? How are social continuity and change articulated rhetorically in terms of different parliamentary norms and traditions? What are the relevant historical concepts associated with the evolution of various parliamentary institutions in Europe? What kind of similarities and dissimilarities can be found across these parliaments? Based on linguistic and rhetorical approaches, the added value of micro-level investigations of parliamentary discourses consists in providing analytical depth and interdisciplinary breadth through the cross-fertilization of discourse analytical theory and rhetorical scholarship on the one hand, and content analysis and historical conceptual analysis on the other.

Concluding Remarks

The increasing complexity and gradual modernization of parliamentary practices have taken place as a result of the interplay between a gradual ritualization of parliamentary language usage through institutionalization processes and a diversification of parliamentary rhetoric through conversationalization processes. It is the varying linguistic and rhetorical patterns of parliamentary discourses that enable us to trace back, distinguish and compare successive stages in the evolution of parliamentary institutions in premodern and modern history.

The case studies presented in the following chapters foreground the interdependence between language-shaped facts and reality-based language ritualization and change. The linguistic and rhetorical perspectives on the dynamic of sociocultural and political phenomena associated with parliamentary change and continuity contribute substantially to highlighting the ways in which parliamentary language affects and is affected by the scope and depth of historical transformations, political upheavals and societal evolution in general.

References

Primary Sources
Hansard 1803–2005, http://hansard.millbanksystems.com/

Secondary Sources
Archakis, A. and Tsakona, V. 2009. 'Parliamentary Discourse in Newspaper Articles: The Integration of a Critical Approach to Media Discourse into a Literacy-based Language Teaching Programme', *Journal of Language and Politics* 8(3): 359–85.
Biryukov, N., Gleisner, J. and Sergeyev, V. 1995. The Crisis of 'Sobornost': Parliamentary Discourse in Present-day Russia. *Discourse & Society* 6(2): 149–75.
Bösch, F. 2012. 'Parlamente und Medien. Deutschland und Grossbritannien seit dem späten 19. Jahrhundert', in A. Schulz and A. Wirsching (eds), *Parlamentarische Kulturen in Europa. Das Parlament als Kommunikationsraum*. Düsseldorf: Droste, pp. 371–88.

Bruteig, Madzharova Y. 2010. 'Czech Parliamentary Discourse', in C. Ilie (ed.), *European Parliaments under Scrutiny: Discourse Strategies and Interaction Practices*. Amsterdam: John Benjamins, pp. 265–302.

Burkhardt, A. 2003. *Das Parlament und seine Sprache. Studien zu Theorie und Geschichte parlamentarischer Kommunikation*. Tübingen: Niemeyer.

Carbó, T. 2004. 'Parliamentary Discourse when Things Go Wrong: Mapping Histories, Contexts, Conflicts', in P. Bayley (ed.), *Cross-cultural Perspectives on Parliamentary Discourse*. Amsterdam: John Benjamins, pp. 301–37.

Grad Fuchsel, H. and Martín Rojo, L. 2003. '"Civic" and "Ethnic" Nationalist Discourses in Spanish Parliamentary Debates', *Journal of Language and Politics* 2(1): 31–70.

Guilhaumou, J. 1989. *La Langue politique de la Révolution française. De l'événement à la raison linguistique*. Paris: Klincksieck.

Ilie, C. 2000. 'Cliché-based Metadiscursive Argumentation in the Houses of Parliament', *International Journal of Applied Linguistics*, 10(1): 65–84.

————. 2001. 'Unparliamentary Language: Insults as Cognitive Forms of Confrontation', in R. Dirven, R. Frank and C. Ilie (eds), *Language and Ideology, Vol. II: Descriptive Cognitive Approaches*. Amsterdam: John Benjamins, pp. 235–63.

————. 2003a. 'Discourse and Metadiscourse in Parliamentary Debates', *Journal of Language and Politics* 1(2): 269–91.

————. 2003b. 'Histrionic and Agonistic Features of Parliamentary Discourse', *Studies in Communication Sciences* 3(1): 25–53.

————. 2004. 'Insulting as (Un)parliamentary Practice in the British and Swedish Parliaments', in P. Bayley (ed.), *Cross-cultural Perspectives on Parliamentary Discourse*. Amsterdam: John Benjamins: 45–86.

————. 2005. 'Interruption Patterns in British Parliamentary Debates and Drama Dialogue', in A. Betten and M. Dannerer (eds), *Dialogue Analysis IX: Dialogue in Literature and the Media. Selected Papers from the 9th IADA Conference, Salzburg 2003*. Tübingen: Niemeyer, pp. 415–30.

————. 2007. 'British "Consensus" versus Swedish "Samförstånd" in Parliamentary Debates, in G. Garzone and C. Ilie (eds), *The Use of English in Institutional and Business Settings: An Intercultural Perspective*. Bern: Peter Lang, pp. 101–25.

————. 2010. 'Strategic Uses of Parliamentary Forms of Address: The Case of the U.K. Parliament and the Swedish Riksdag', *Journal of Pragmatics* 42(4): 885–911.

Marques, M.A. 2010. 'The Public and Private Sphere in Parliamentary Debate: The Construction of the Addresser in the Portuguese Parliament', in C. Ilie (ed.), *European Parliaments under Scrutiny: Discourse Strategies and Interaction Practices*. Amsterdam: John Benjamins: pp. 265–302.

Mouffe, C. 1993. *The Return of the Political*. London: Verso.

Ornatowski, C.M. 2010. 'Parliamentary Discourse and Political Transition: The Case of the Polish Parliament after 1989', in C. Ilie (ed.), *European Parliaments under Scrutiny: Discourse Strategies and Interaction Practices*. Amsterdam and Philadelphia: Benjamins, pp. 223–64.

Pérez de Ayala, S. 2001. 'FTAs and Erskine May: Conflicting Needs? – Politeness in Question Time', *Journal of Pragmatics* 33: 143–69.

Reid, C. 2000. 'Whose Parliament? Political Oratory and Print Culture in the later 18th Century, *Language and Literature* 9(2): 122–34.

Sivenkova, M. 2008. 'Expressing Commitment When Asking Multiunit Questions in Parliamentary Debates: English-Russian Parallels', *Journal of Language and Social Psychology* 27(4): 359–71.

Tsakona, V. 2009. 'Humor and Image Politics in Parliamentary Discourse: A Greek Case Study, *Text and Talk* 29(2): 219–37.

Van Dijk, T.A. 2003. 'Knowledge in Parliamentary Debates', *Journal of Language and Politics* 2: 93–129.

Zima, E., G. Brône and K. Feyaerts. 2010. 'Patterns of Interaction in Austrian Parliamentary Debates: On the Pragmasemantics of Unauthorized Interruptive Comments', in C. Ilie (ed.), *European Parliaments under Scrutiny: Discourse Strategies and Interaction Practices*. Amsterdam: John Benjamins, pp. 265–302.

Cornelia Ilie, Ph.D., is Professor of Business Communication at the College of Business, Zayed University, Abu Dhabi, the United Arab Emirates. She has previously worked as Professor of English Linguistics at Malmö University, Sweden. Her main research interests include the discursive practices of institutional dialogue – particularly in the media, political discourse and parliamentary debates – argumentation analysis and cross-cultural rhetoric. She is the founder of EPARDIS (Europe and Parliamentary Discourses), a cross-European network for the interdisciplinary study of parliamentary practices, and the President of ESTIDIA (European Society for Transcultural and Interdisciplinary Dialogue).

Chapter 9

Rhetoric, Parliament and the Monarchy in Pre-revolutionary England

Markku Peltonen

When on 11 April 1606 Francis Bacon defended in the House of Commons the king's right to impose import duties to regulate trade, Thomas Hitchcock strongly opposed it. The next speaker, John Savile, noted that 'for my owne Parte . . . I was by the Speech of the learned Gentleman that first spake [meaning Sir Francis Bacon] almost transported to the other opinion until I now upon hearing more have further considered on the Matter'. Savile concluded his oration with 'a merrie conceite': 'When I was a Boy I heard them say Mercury was a Thiefe, at which I marvailed in regard they also said he was a God, but since I came to better Judgement I perceive it meant that Eloquence whereof Mercury was esteemed God, is the Thiefe' (Willson 1931: 120).

Savile's comment suggests that eloquence could wield considerable power in early modern parliaments. Bacon's eloquence had apparently first moved Savile to support impositions, but Hitchcock's speech quickly prompted him to reconsider his position and to move to the opposite side. Although clear and hard evidence of the power of individual speeches to provoke MPs to change their mind is relatively scarce, there is abundant evidence to suggest that eloquence played a crucial role in early modern parliaments. Secretary of State Thomas Wilson wrote in 1570 that Demosthenes provided an important model 'to make an English man tel his tale praise worthily in any open hearing either in Parlament or in Pulpit' (Demosthenes 1570: *jr-v). Henry Peacham Jr, a schoolmaster, who travelled widely in Europe and published *The Compleat Gentleman* as a result of these extensive travels, still believed in the propaedeutic values of such an indigenous institution as Parliament. If a gentleman, Peacham asserted, was intent on teaching himself to become a powerful orator, he should, in addition to frequent visits to Star Chamber and other law courts, purchase 'separates' of parliamentary speeches (Peacham 1622: 53).

What is the historical significance of such observations? What is, in other words, the point we can make if we are able to show that the art of rhetoric was seen as central to early modern parliamentary work, and that MPs' speeches, for instance, could help someone to learn the art of rhetoric; or when are we able more specifically to demonstrate that numerous MPs made full use of their grammar school and university education in their parliamentary speeches?

Earlier scholarship on the history of the pre-revolutionary parliaments of the Tudor and early Stuart periods suggests at least two widely contrasting answers. The older scholarship associated this link between the *ars rhetorica* and parliamentary work with the wider exceptionalism of early modern England. The central role rhetoric played in Tudor and early Stuart parliaments was said to be an indication of progress towards modern, liberal and parliamentary democracy (Redlich 1908). The other answer suggested by earlier scholarship is the strongly contrasting one that there is no real point in studying rhetoric and speech-making in Elizabethan and early Stuart parliaments. On the contrary, it is futile and hence a waste of a historian's time because early modern parliaments were engaged in business rather than politics (Elton 1986; Russell 1990).

Both accounts have something to commend themselves. However, both can also be criticized for failing the test of anachronism: the former for not recognizing the major differences between early modern and twentieth century political participation; the latter for not taking sufficient heed of the early modern emphasis on the importance of rhetoric in parliamentary work.

The aim of this chapter is to offer an account of rhetoric and its role in the Elizabethan and early Stuart parliaments that avoids both of these problems. It argues that rhetoric was indeed central to these parliaments, and that without taking account of it their character is difficult to understand. At the same time, it also argues that we cannot read the current assumptions of parliamentary democracy into Elizabethan and early Stuart parliamentary rhetoric. My argument falls into two parts. (For some earlier examples for which I am greatly indebted, see Mack 2002 and Colclough 2005.) First, I examine the role of deliberative rhetoric in parliamentary debates and argue that deliberative rhetoric was central to Parliament not only in the construction and delivery of speeches but also in conditioning parliamentary work in fundamental ways. Second, I seek to argue that deliberative rhetoric enables us to interpret certain key developments and debates in their proper historical contexts. I will briefly examine the growing conflict between James I and his first English parliament and argue that deliberative rhetoric played an important role in it.

Uses of Deliberative Rhetoric in Elizabethan and Early Stuart Parliaments

Thomas Wilson, John Savile and Henry Peacham were not alone in suggesting that rhetoric was important in Parliament. The journals of early modern parliaments habitually talk about eloquence and persuasion, and when early modern Englishmen associated rhetoric and Parliament, they did not emphasize the powerlessness of parliaments. Elizabeth I acknowledged as much in 1571. She commanded Nicholas Bacon, Lord Keeper of the Great Seal, to explain to both houses her views about the way in which subsidies had been granted. 'Her Highness knoweth very well', Bacon pointed out, 'that before her time theise manner of grantes have sundrie times passed not without great difficultie, with long perswasions and sometimes sharpe speeches. But this contrariwise without any such speech or other difficultie hath bynn freely and frankelie offered and presented' (*Proceedings in the Parliaments of Elizabeth*, 1: 189). Indeed, when Bacon's youngest son, Francis Bacon, contended in 1593 that it was 'against the orders of the House that in a publique bill any advocates or councell should be allowed on either side to use perswasive or contrary speaches' he was quickly overruled (*Proceedings in the Parliaments of Elizabeth*, 3: 132). The members of the House of Commons, when they sent the Speaker to carry their message to the king in 1628, specifically urged him to use his rhetorical training. 'Every particular head', a diary states, 'was read in the House and voted that they be *verbatim*, presented to the King by the Speaker only, and that the Speaker have power to put them in his own method, he still retaining the substance' (*Proceedings, 1628*, 2: 433).

Although epideictic and judicial rhetoric could be important, it was of course deliberative or political rhetoric that was most central to parliamentary work. There were two elements of deliberative rhetoric that were directly relevant to parliamentary debates – the subjects discussed and the forms of argument used. Cicero's *De inventione* and the anonymous *Ad herennium* assumed an intensely political context for deliberative rhetoric, but in Renaissance Anglophone manuals deliberative rhetoric was mostly dealt with within the private sphere. Thomas Wilson, for instance, wrote that in a persuasive speech we intend to 'aduise our neighbour to that thing, whiche we thynke most needful for hym or els to cal him backe from that folie, which hindereth muche his estimacion' (Wilson 1553: 16r). When we turn to grammar-school textbooks, however, we find an overwhelmingly political account of deliberative rhetoric. While these textbooks also used Roman treatises in their accounts of deliberative rhetoric, they relied even more on Aristotle's *Rhetoric*, which listed five subjects for deliberative orations. These were, as the 1637 English translation listed them, 'Of levying of money', 'Of peace and Warre', 'Of the safeguard of the Countrey', 'Of Provision' and 'Of making Lawes' (Aristotle 1637: 9–12). Practically all English school text-books (in Latin) offered this list as the range of deliberative topics. They maintained, as Charles Butler did in his *Oratoriae* (1629), that in private matters the area of deliberative rhetoric was limitless, but in 'public causes' it consisted of five topics: 'wealth, war and peace, guarding of regions, those which are brought in and carried out, proposing laws' (Butler 1629: H4r).

Given that pre-revolutionary Englishmen were accustomed to making deliberative speeches on political topics, it should be no news that they had also been trained to use rhetorical arguments in them. Even the most elementary training in rhetoric taught that in deliberative rhetoric the orator could invoke the characteristics of honesty and utility. All rhetoric manuals agreed that in addressing an audience of the common people the most potent argument was usefulness. However, there was a noticeable difference between Anglophone and Latin manuals. Whereas the former merely discussed utility in general terms, the latter guided schoolboys to a political analysis of utility. If the orator addressed a well-educated audience, all rhetoricians concurred that the orator should then appeal to the honesty and therefore to the virtuous nature of his cause (Peltonen 2013: 70–79).

The relevance of deliberative rhetoric to parliamentary work emerges in subsidy debates. Although Elizabeth was convinced that it was far better if subsidies were granted without recourse to the powers of eloquence, this did not prompt her councillors to renounce rhetoric and rely simply on the MPs' benevolence. On the contrary, the councillors and their so-called men of business were ready to promote subsidies with carefully constructed deliberative orations. For example, in 1566, Ralph Sadler, a Privy Counsellor, made a full-scale deliberative speech in support of subsidies. Although Sadler appears not to have had a university education, he had entered Thomas Cromwell's service as a teenager, and his patron had ensured that he had an excellent education in Latin and Greek. On 18 October 1566 this education stood him in good stead when he defended subsidies. According to his own notes, Sadler began by establishing his ethos and appealing to the emotions of his audience, saying: 'I will with your favour in few words say my poure mynde and opynyon'. When he moved to his arguments, he emphasized above all 'the benefite and common weale of my countrey' (*Proceedings in the Parliaments of Elizabeth*, 1: 141). Walter Mildmay, a Privy Counsellor and Chancellor of the Exchequer, was the main spokesman for subsidies for much of the reign. Educated at Christ's College, Cambridge and Gray's Inn, Mildmay emphasized the importance of education, founding Emmanuel College, Cambridge in the 1580s. He was the main speaker for subsidies in every parliament from 1576 until his death in 1589, and his speeches circulated widely as model orations (Peltonen 2013: 141–43; Neale 1953: 346–48).

Recourse to the power of rhetoric was not limited to Privy Counsellors and their men of business. Those who opposed the council's policies similarly endeavoured to use the *ars rhetorica* to drum up support. Henry Jackman made a particularly strong oration opposing subsidies in 1589. Jackman was a cloth merchant from London, but he had been educated at Magdalen College, Oxford and the Inner Temple. Perhaps the most elaborate piece of rhetorical invention took place in May 1626 when the Commons presented their charges against the Duke of Buckingham. There were no less than eight MPs who registered the charges, and their statements could be read either as eight distinct speeches or as one large oration. It is indicative that Dudley Digges and John Eliot, who were both educated at Oxford and who gave the first and last speeches respectively, were imprisoned for their orations. They were perhaps Buckingham's most avowed enemies amongst the speakers, but it was they who gave those parts of the joint oration – the *exordium* and the *peroratio* – where the strongest emotional appeal could be made (*Proceedings, 1626*, 3: 190–224).

MPs did not endeavour to persuade just other MPs; they also made full use of rhetoric in concerted efforts to persuade the monarch. Perhaps the most interesting example comes from 1572, when a conference of both houses decided to persuade Elizabeth to act against Mary Stuart and the Duke of Norfolk. As an anonymous journal describes their collective attempt at rhetorical invention: 'It was agreed that every man sholde set downe in writing sutch reasons as he thought were best able to move the Queen herin'. Specific forms of rhetorical invention were ascribed to specific men. Bishops were expected to invent 'reasons moving the conscience'. Those whose task was to invent arguments based on 'reasons of pollicie' were advised to use the figure prolepsis (foreseeing and forestalling objections). The conference came to the conclusion that they should tacitly answer 'such obiections as the queen were able to make for the not procedinge in the first bill'. Civil lawyers were thought to be the fittest to find out 'reasons *pro et contra*'. It was surmised that a wide range of arguments would be invented, and it was therefore decided that a strict selection should be made and that only 'the most principall reasons shold be chosen'. These arguments were to be presented to the queen in writing rather than orally, because a written text – in this the conference concurred with numerous rhetoricians – was more potent than an oral speech. Oral arguments 'move for the time, yet it is gone strait, and the reasons sone forgotten', but once they are on paper, 'thei are read with pawsinge and are considered upon, and so the better imprinted in the minde, and therby so mutch the more do move' (*Proceedings in the Parliaments of Elizabeth*, 1: 331–32). Clearly, the queen, the councillors and the MPs believed in the potency of rhetoric.

Far from being futile to parliamentary work, contemporaries saw rhetoric as an integral and important part of it. So, it seems to be the case that Elton and others were wrong when they claimed that we can ignore rhetoric and orations in our analyses of pre-revolutionary parliamentary work.

The Art of Rhetoric in Parliamentary Work

Is this all, or can the Renaissance *ars rhetorica* help us understand early modern parliamentary work in a more specific way? In what follows, I endeavour to demonstrate that the art of rhetoric enables us to acquire a better historical understanding of the profound change in the relationship between the monarch and Parliament at the beginning of the seventeenth century. As numerous scholars have demonstrated, compared to Elizabethan parliaments, Jacobean ones were marked by controversial debates and growing conflicts between the king and some leading members of the House of Commons. Of course, there are several factors that account for this change. The lack of effective management and the length of the sessions were important factors (Kyle 2012: 13–35), as was the range of new topics, which included most importantly the Union between England and Scotland and impositions to raise royal revenue (Russell 2011: 72–73, 31–32, 37–38).

Yet another factor, and one which has been overlooked but which is of considerable importance, is the role of the *ars rhetorica*. The difference between Elizabeth's and James's style of address was striking. Practically all Elizabeth's speeches in Parliament were replies to Parliaments' demands, mainly with regard to marriage and the succession, but from the very beginning of his reign James addressed his parliaments on his own initiative. Historians have mostly focused on the elevated notion of absolutist royal power in these speeches, which had of course been largely absent from his predecessor's addresses. What I want to highlight instead is their rhetorical character and the broader rhetorical context in which they took place. In his speeches, James often not only wanted to make clear what kind of policy he preferred but also, at the same time, he made a powerful case for this policy. And he made this in full-blown deliberative speeches. This made him, willy-nilly, a participant in a rhetorical debate, which had profound consequences. In order to understand this fully, we need to explore briefly some central aspects of the Renaissance *ars rhetorica*.

Renaissance rhetoric was above all an art of power and persuasion. 'The vse of *Retorick*', Francis Bacon wrote in 1595, 'is . . . in effectuall movinge of the minds of them to whome your speech or wrytinges are directed'. The ability to persuade one's listeners or readers and thus to move their minds, Bacon maintained, 'makes yow raigne ouer the wills and affections of men, which is the greatest soueraignitye that one man can haue over an other' (Stewart and Knight 2012: 659). Schoolboys learned a similar message. At the very beginning of their rhetoric classes they were taught that the main aim of rhetoric was to persuade or win the listeners over to their own side. As Butler's *Oratoriae* put it, 'The end of oration is to persuade: that is to lead auditors to our opinion' (Butler 1629: BIv). The Renaissance *ars rhetorica* was adversarial and agonistic in character. This adversarial nature of communication already emerged in the teaching of letter-writing. Epistolary manuals advised schoolboys to pay attention to 'the person of our aduersarie', the epistolary 'enemie' and 'the aduersary party' (Fleming 1576: Biiir; Verepaeus 1592: 91; Macropedius 1580: Aviir). When schoolboys reached the uppermost forms and learned more about the art of rhetoric, the world started to be seen in terms of a stark polarity between ourselves and our adversaries. Practically all textbooks on rhetoric were constructed from the point of view of this dichotomy. The orator, from the invention of arguments to the delivery of the speech, needed to assess everything not only from his own but also from his adversary's point of view (Peltonen 2013: 65–66).

Underlying these aspects of the art of rhetoric was the conviction that speaking *in utramque partem* – on both sides – is a defining character of the *ars rhetorica*. Crassus declares in the third book of Cicero's *De oratore* that the orator 'must have the intelligence, power and art to speak *in utramque partem* on virtue, duty . . . utility, honour, disgrace . . . and similar matters' (Cicero 1942: 3.27.107). Antonius concurred and emphasized that this ability applied above all to judicial and political speeches (Cicero 1942: 1.18.84–19.85). This was not lost on Renaissance rhetoricians and schoolmasters, and it seems that from the very beginning of their training in rhetoric schoolboys were instructed in the importance of speaking *in utramque partem*. Erasmus's *De conscribendis epistolis* devoted particular attention to the proficiency in writing and speaking on both sides. Schoolboys could write 'for and against learning, wealth, the monastic life, languages, matrimony, and monarchy' (Erasmus 1985 [1521]: 43–44). John Brinsley, a schoolmaster from Ashby-de-la-Zouch and an important author of educational treatises and a translator of school texts, likewise taught schoolboys that once they had written on a theme they should 'shew, what any of them can obiect against it; or if it be true, what absurdities and inconueniences will follow from it; and also some of them to answere the obiections and inconueniences' (Brinsley 1612: 178–79).

In the domain of rhetoric there were thus no self-evident truths, and everything could be questioned. Erasmus explained that to sharpen their pupils' wits schoolmasters could give them such 'disreputable subjects' to defend as poverty, ingratitude and tyranny. Even they could be defended, Erasmus observed, because 'nothing is so inherently good that it cannot be made to seem bad by a gifted speaker' (Erasmus 1985 [1521]: 145–46).

These features of the *ars rhetorica* were commonly understood to be central to parliamentary work. Those who kept journals constantly referred to 'persuasion' or 'eloquent persuasion'; as Fulke Onslow's journal reported in 1572: 'After much debating it was agreed in respect of the credite that the House gave to Sir Fraunces Knowles' persuasion' (*Proceedings in the Parliaments of Elizabeth*, 1: 314). In his famous description of the Elizabethan polity, Thomas Smith, a humanist and diplomat, emphasized the adversary character of parliamentary debates. Of course, debates were conducted in a 'mervelous good order' because MPs never addressed one another but always the Speaker so that they avoided attacks against the adversary's person. However, Smith emphasized even more strongly that they argued vehemently and violently against one another: 'With moste doulce and gentle termes, they make their reasons as violent and as vehement the one against the other as they may' (Smith 1982 [1583]: 82–83).

The conduct of parliamentary business was commonly seen as an example of speaking *in utramque partem*, and in 1593 the House of Commons formally ruled that this was the way in which debates should be conducted (for a discussion on the longer-term development of parliamentary procedure see Chapter 14). The debate about the subsidy bill was exceptionally intense, with several MPs trying to catch the Speaker's attention at the same time. The Speaker, Edward Coke, then 'propounded it as an order of the Howse in such a case for him to aske the partyes that would speake on which side they would speake, whether with him that did speake next before, or against him, and the partye who speakes against the last speaker is to be heard first; and so yt was ruled' (*Proceedings in the Parliaments of Elizabeth*, 3: 110–11).

A Royal Orator and His Opponent in Parliament

We can now return to James I's speeches. Of course, when the king addressed Parliament, the MPs fully understood that they were not being addressed by one of their fellows. Whether they thought the king to be one of the three estates, the MPs never thought of themselves as being on a par with him (see Chapter 2 for later developments). James concurred. Those MPs who dared

to question him, the king noted, 'must give me their king a lie', which was
the worst possible insult (*Proceedings in Parliament, 1614*: 44). The Earl of
Salisbury also pointed out that it was 'not ordinary' that 'the King in parliament should give an answer in *genere deliberatiuo*' (*Proceedings, 1610*, 1: 211).

Nevertheless, the MPs had learned in grammar school that any view, however noble, could be argued against and refuted. They had also learned that
speaking *in utramque partem* was the proper way of participating in debate in
the House of Commons. Moreover, it is possible that they had learned to see
the king, at least when he spoke in the deliberative genus, as a participant in a
rhetorical debate. One epistolary manual contained a princely letter on peace
and war, in which the prince defended war by a standard set of deliberative
arguments, maintaining that war 'is iust, honest, and profitable, the which
we shall proue as well as by reasons as to depresse oure aduersarie' (Fulwood
1571: Miiir–v).

The accession of James VI of Scotland to the thrones of England and
Ireland as James I in March 1603 effectively created the Union of the Crowns
– a personal or dynastic union between England and Scotland. James and
many close to him wanted to cement this personal union with a firmer one,
which the king called the 'perfect Union'. Quickly, however, the king yielded
and adopted a more limited programme, which commissioners from both
kingdoms negotiated in 1604. The result, the Instrument of Union, made
four proposals: the abolition of mutually hostile laws, the abolition of the separate legal status of the Border region; the freeing of trade between England
and Scotland and mutual naturalization. The Instrument was debated in
the third session of James's first English parliament, which was opened in
November 1606 by the king's 'Eloquent and very long Speech' (Willson 1931:
185).

The main aim of this deliberative speech was to advise or exhort Parliament
to proceed with the Instrument of the Union. James commenced with an
exordium, which endeavoured to win his listeners' attention and support by
reminding them of their joint deliverance from the Gunpowder Plot almost
exactly a year earlier. In the second part, the *narratio*, James carefully followed Cicero's suggestion and simply declared that 'the greatest and weight-
iest Matter of all is this Matter of the Union' (*Commons Journal* (CJ), 1: 314;
Cicero 1949: 1.19.27). The *divisio*, the third part of the oration, followed,
and James announced that he would take the *confirmatio* and *refutatio* in the
reverse order (CJ, 1: 314–15). When James moved to the *confirmatio*, his
arguments, as befitted a deliberative speech, were based on *honestas* and *utilitas*. If Parliament failed to accomplish a firm Union, it would be an embarrassment for both himself and the people before 'the Eye of all the World'. All
'the Reasons of his Desire', the king also assured his listeners, were 'directed

to the Commonwealth of both Kingdoms', which 'every Man must acknowledge to be commodious' (CJ, 1: 315).

Delivering such a deliberative speech in Parliament made the king a participant in a rhetorical debate. This is evident from the Commons' reactions; they insisted that they should 'openly dispute, and discusse' the matter. Nicholas Fuller hoped that 'every man would declare his minde; No man to be silent, but every man to speake though it were but five words' (Willson 1931: 190). What Fuller was in effect suggesting was that instead of simply following the king's exhortation and thus embracing his arguments the MPs should debate it *in utramque partem*. Before the Christmas break, many in the Commons criticized the commercial provisions of the Instrument (Galloway 1986: 98–103). This meant of course that they were arguing against the royal 'reason of Desire', which had argued for these commercial provisions. Similarly, after the break in February, when naturalization became the focal point, many in the Commons revived old arguments against the Scots. When Christopher Pigott 'entered into' an 'Invective against the Scotts and Scottish Nation, using many Words of Scandal and Obloquy', James, on receiving the news of the speech, was furious and demanded immediate punishment. The king reminded the council that he was also a Scot; Pigott, in other words, had directed his invective against the king. The Commons sent him to the Tower, but also excused themselves for having allowed him to speak by belittling the importance of speechmaking. Quoting Seneca, they pointed out that 'light troubles speak, vast ones are silent' (CJ, 1: 355–56; HMC Salisbury, 19: 59).

The royal reaction to Pigott's invective did not stop MPs questioning the naturalization of the Scots and thus arguing directly against the king. Thomas Wentworth argued against naturalization in a judicial oration (CJ, 1: 336, 1015), and Fuller, who had been educated at Christ's College, Cambridge and Gray's Inn, questioned the king's use of emotional arguments in his 'long Speech against general Naturalization' by questioning the king's wisdom. 'A wise Owner', he maintained, 'will not pull down the Hedge' separating fertile and bare pastures, but would only build gates. If the hedge were demolished, 'the Cattle will rush in in Multitudes, and much against their Will return'. Fuller also resorted to *utilitas*, arguing that naturalization would cause serious difficulties for English merchants. He further employed the figure erotesis or erotema – posing a question, the answer to which is implied. This figure gave 'great strength and a coragious countenance', and Peacham 'compared it to the point or edge of a weapon, wherewith the Champion defendeth himself, and woundeth his enemie' (Peacham 1593: Qiv). If Mary and Philip had had a son who would have become the 'King of Spaine', 'had it been fit to naturalize those Subjects?' The king was clearly Fuller's 'enemie' (CJ, 1: 334–35, 1013).

Until early March the opposition to both naturalization and the Union had the upper hand in the Commons. The situation changed, however, when a large majority of the leading judges of the land reached a decision that allegiance to the king came before the law. This decision worked in favour of naturalization and prompted those opposed to the royal policy to reconsider their position. The mastermind behind this reconsideration was Edwin Sandys, who had been educated at Merchant Taylors' School and Oxford. The headmaster of Merchant Taylors' School, Richard Mulcaster, was one of the leading humanists and schoolmasters in Elizabethan England.

Mulcaster's views on a humanist education were somewhat contradictory. He was alert to the differences between 'a fré citie' and 'a hole monarchie'. 'Popular gouernementes', he maintained, 'did yeald so much vnto eloquence, as one mans perswasion might make the whole assembly to sway with him'. But in 'a *Monarchie*' language aimed to 'please'. Consequently, there was no one in England who could 'proue a *Tullie* [Cicero] or like to *Demosthenes*'. Whereas in popular governments 'the toungue' was imperial bycause it dealt with the people', in a monarchy it 'must obey, bycause it dealth with a prince'. Nevertheless, Mulcaster cherished no illusion about the qualities, inherited or otherwise, of the prince, who as a child was 'as other children be, for soule sometimes fine, sometimes grosse'. As a student, the prince was 'no lesse subiect, then his subiectes be'. Similarly, gentlemen were no different from the commonalty – 'their witts be as the common, their bodies oftimes worse'. However, gentlemen had 'some choice of peculiar matter . . . bycause they be to gouerne vnder their prince in principall places' (Peltonen 2013: 25–26, 220–21).

There is no direct evidence as to whether Mulcaster's views had an effect on Sandys, but judging from the fact that Sandys spent six years at Merchant Taylors' School and ten years at Oxford, this humanist schooling must have been a formative period. Little wonder then that he made an adroit use of the art of rhetoric in reconsidering the Commons' position against royal policy and in finding a new line of argument. Having opposed the Instrument, Sandys now suddenly embraced the initial and much bolder royal proposal for a perfect Union. Of course the perfect Union Sandys was upholding was not the kind of perfect Union James had been proposing. It could be said that Sandys was employing the figure of redescription – paradiastole (see Skinner 2002, 3: 87–141). James and many around him had initially talked about a perfect Union and in his opening speech in November 1606 James had emphasized that the ultimate aim was to have both countries 'united, and subjected both to One Rule and to One Law' (CJ, 1: 315). In a joint conference between the Lords and the Commons on 7 March, the defenders of the Instrument of the Union continued to use the same vocabulary, the Earl of

Salisbury talking about 'a perfect Union' and the Earl of Northampton about 'a perfect universall Union'. Sandys seemed to be following them when he distinguished between an imperfect Union, where both 'Kingdomes remaine distinct in their Natures, and agree in the Heade', and a 'perfect Union' where 'the Scottish Nation be ruled by Our Lawes, and participate all Benefitts with us' (Willson 1931: 219–20; CJ, 1: 1027–28). He echoed the king's words, arguing that 'the perfect Union' was 'a Coniunction under one Law, and Gouvernment' (Willson 1931: 2224–25). For James, one rule referred to himself and one law to a future union of laws. For Sandys, however, one law referred to the Scots becoming subject to English law and one government to the Scots being represented in the English parliament. In Sandys's scheme of a perfect Union, in other words, Scotland would become part of England. With the help of paradiastole, he re-described the king's perfect Union in such a way that England and Scotland were far from being equals.

The argument *in utramque partem* came on 31 March, when the king addressed both houses. James was not content to speak in Parliament; he took the extraordinary step of having a version of his speech printed (James 1607). Again, the king's speech was a complete deliberative oration, which endeavoured to exhort Parliament to support the Instrument of the Union. In his *exordium*, he disparaged his rhetorical skills, comparing his oration (which announced the Easter recess) with 'the worst Wine proposed in the end of the Banquet'. He next moved to the *narratio*, in which he carefully explained the slow progress of the Commons' proceedings; in his divisio he announced that the speech had four topics (James 1994 [1607]: 159–61). The king dwelt long on the definition of the perfect Union, but he also censured his adversaries, clearly singling out Fuller and Sandys, about whom he said: 'Euery honest man desireth a perfect Vnion, but they that say so, and admit no preparation thereunto, haue honey in the mouth, gall in the heart' (James 1994 [1607]: 164–65). After a long *refutatio*, the king returned to the benefits of the Union. Again, they consisted of utility but also of honour and 'greatness' (James 1994 [1607]: 176–77).

The king's oration did not stop the Commons from debating the Union. After Parliament reconvened in late April, Sandys gave 'a long learned speech', which was a straight reply and rebuttal of the royal speech. Again, his humanist education stood him in good stead. Of course, the king was not present when Sandys spoke, but it is arguable that it was precisely the nature of parliamentary debate *in utramque partem* that enabled Sandys to refute the royal oration and get away with it.

Perhaps the clearest indication of what Sandys was up to was his prooemium. It is a typical instance of the type of *exordium* called *insinuatio*, which the orator used in defending a disreputable or obscure cause. Dissimulation was the chief means used in such an indirect opening. Sandys praised James's speech and its rhetorical potency of moving the Commons (Willson 1931: 256–58; CJ, 1:1035–36). Moreover, explaining his interpretation of the perfect Union, Sandys began by quoting James, stating that 'there be *Unus Rex, Unus Grex, Una Lex*'. While there was already one king, there was no unus grex 'untill the whole doe ioyne in makeing Lawes to governe the whole'. That is to say, a perfect Union required one parliament. Similarly una lex required 'One Parliament', because 'though Scotland would give up their Lawes and take Ours, yet it were not one Law, but the like': 'Therefore One Parliament is necessary' (Willson 1931: 258–59; CJ, 1: 1036). Necessity was thought to be the most potent argument in deliberative rhetoric.

In his *confirmatio*, Sandys insisted that his perfect Union was 'behoofefull and desirable'. He first emphasized the benefits the king would reap from his perfect Union. For both kingdoms, it was above all a question of 'Strength' – they would be 'encreased' by the Union (Willson 1931: 259–60). Next, Sandys refuted the arguments of his adversary, focusing on those related to Scotland. It was possible to argue that the Union would reduce Scotland 'but to a Northerne Parte of Our Kingdome'; however, England would likewise become 'but a Southerne Parte'. Moreover, the king would be absent from Scotland, but Sandys countered this by emphasizing the negative consequences of royal 'Purveyance'. A bold conclusion followed: 'So with the Kings Presence immediately doe follow many Burdens and Grievances' (Willson 1931: 260). Sandys also argued, closely following rhetoricians, that his type of Union was 'more easy to be effected' than the Instrument (Willson 1931: 260).

Those in the Commons who opposed Sandys's proposal endeavoured to refute his arguments but did not fail to appreciate his rhetorical skills. Bacon insisted that Sandys's proposal was 'but *Digressio*', but gave credit to his dazzling eloquence; the speech showed 'much Arte' (Willson 1931: 269). The real oration *in utramque partem*, however, came on 2 May, when James once again gave a long deliberative oration to both houses. In his *exordium*, he appealed for his listeners' favour and benevolence. In his *divisio*, he promised to talk about three things: to interpret his earlier words, to refute his adversaries' arguments and to offer guidance to Parliament on how to proceed. The king first rebutted Sandys's interpretation of his own royal words. But instead of answering Sandys he ridiculed him and thus ignored the rule that in Parliament attacks against the adversary's person should be avoided. James identified Sandys as one of 'Fools', who had no 'solid Argument'. This amounted to the use of the figure diasyrmus, where 'the arguments of an aduersarie are either depraued or reiected' (Peacham 1593: Giiijr). Later the king again used diasyrmus, comparing his adversaries' speeches to 'gilded

Pills' that were neither 'wise, nor honest'. The seriousness of the royal use of diasyrmus emerges when we remember that, according to Peacham, 'in all graue and weightie controuersies it ought to keepe silence, as in solemne disputations . . . except there be the greater cause to vrge it' (Peacham 1593: Giiijv).

James also poked fun at Sandys's argument about the residence of the monarch by using epitrope (ironical concession), noting that 'it is good to be sometimes far from the Princes's Court'. Peacham had warned that an orator who uses this figure 'is to take heed that it be not vsed where ignorance and simplicitie not percyiuing the figure, may take the meaning according to the words' (Peacham 1593: Qiiijv). In view of Sandys's thorough training in rhetoric, James did not have to worry that he might miss the irony. The king finished with a dire threat: 'I pray you, do not too far move me to do that which my power may tempt me unto' (CJ, 1: 366–68).

Rhetoric as a Subject and Medium of Political Struggle

James's oration on 2 May ended the debate about the Union. The whole debate reveals several important points about the role of the *ars rhetorica* in Parliament. First, rhetoric was clearly not superfluous paraphernalia. On the contrary, most MPs and even the king deemed it worth their while to make full use of the art. And they did so, just as any rhetorician would have told them, to persuade their listeners and win them over to their own side. The fact that James fully participated in these rhetorical battles had significant consequences. It made him a participant in a rhetorical debate with the MPs and thus allowed them to argue against their king – to question his views and arguments. As the contemporary definitions of some of the figures that they employed indicate, both the king and his adversaries were ready to use the strongest weapons of the *ars rhetorica*.

This chapter has illustrated a broad application of major rhetorical tools both classical and those constructed in Renaissance rhetorical culture, as well as those constructed in a distinct parliamentary environment. The five Aristotelian topoi of deliberative oratory, repeated in grammar school text-books also shaped the agenda-setting of parliamentary politics and of the power struggles with the monarchs. Honesty and utility were the main criteria for judgment and decision in parliamentary deliberations. The classical stages of orations were widely applied in parliamentary speeches. Renaissance rhetorical culture possessed a broad repertoire of tropes and figures, both ancient ones and those invented by contemporary rhetoricians, such as prolepsis, diasyrmus or epitrope, and they were frequently used in parliamentary debates. The deliberative genre continued to predominate over epideictic and forensic ones in parliamentary debates, and James I tried to exploit it even in royal speeches. We can speculate whether he would have been more successful by sticking to epideictic declarations or whether his adoption of deliberative rhetoric was already a concession to parliamentary powers.

References

Primary Sources

Aristotle. 1637. *The Briefe of the Art of Rhetorike*. London.

Brinsley, J. 1612. *Lvdvs literarivs*. London.

Butler, C. 1629. *Oratoriae*. Oxford.

Cicero. 1942. *De oratore*. 2 vols. London: Loeb.

———. 1949. *De inventione*. London: Loeb.

Commons Journal (CJ).

Demosthenes. 1570. *The Three Orations of Demosthenes*, trans. Thomas Wilson. London.

Erasmus. 1985 [1521]. *On the Writing of Letters*, trans. Brian McGregor, in *Collected Works of Erasmus*, 25:1–254. Toronto: Toronto University Press.

Fleming, A. 1576. *A Panoplie of Epistles*. London.

Fulwood, W. 1571. *The Enimie of Idlenesse*. London.

HMC Salisbury Mss.

James VI & I. 1607. *His Maiesties Speech to Both the Houses of Parliament*. London.

———. 1994 [1607]. *Political Writings*. Cambridge: Cambridge University Press.

Macropedius, G. 1580. *Methodus de conscribendis epistolis*. London.

Peacham, H. 1593. *The Garden of Eloqvence*. London.

Peacham, H. Jr. 1622. *The Compleat Gentleman*. London.

Proceedings in Parliament, 1610. 1966. E. Foster (ed.). 2 vols. New Haven: Yale University Press.

Proceedings in Parliament, 1614 (House of Commons). 1988. M. Jansson (ed.). Philadelphia: American Philosophical Society.

Proceedings in Parliament, 1626. 1991–92. W. Bidwell and M. Jansson (eds). 4 vols. New Haven: Yale University Press.

Proceedings in Parliament, 1628. 1977–83. M.F. Keeler, M. Jansson Cole and W.B. Bidwell (eds). 6 vols. New Haven: Yale University Press.

Proceedings in the Parliaments of Elizabeth. 1981–95. T. Hartley (ed.). 3 vols. London: Leicester University Press.

Smith, T. 1982 [1583]. *De Republica Anglorum*. Cambridge: Cambridge University Press.

Stewart, A. and H. Knight. 2012. *The Oxford Francis Bacon 1 Early Writings 1584–1596*. Oxford: Oxford University Press.

Verepaeus, S. 1592. *De epistolis latine*. London.

Willson, D.H. 1931. *The Parliament Diary of Robert Bowyer 1606–1607*. Minneapolis: University of Minnesota Press.

Wilson, T. 1553. *The Arte of Rhetorique*.

Secondary Sources

Colclough, D. 2005. *Freedom of Speech in Early Stuart England, 1603–1628*. Cambridge: Cambridge University Press.

Elton, G.R. 1986. *Parliament in England 1559–1581*. Cambridge: Cambridge University Press.

Galloway, B. 1986. *The Union of England and Scotland, 1603–1608*. Edinburgh: J. Donald.

Kyle, C. 2012. *Theater of State*. Stanford: Stanford University Press.

Mack, P. 2002. *Elizabethan Rhetoric*. Cambridge: Cambridge University Press.

Neale, J. 1953. *Elizabeth I and Her Parliaments*, vol. 1. London: Jonathan Cape.

Peltonen, M. 2013. *Rhetoric, Politics and Popularity in Pre-revolutionary England*. Cambridge: Cambridge University Press.

Redlich, J. 1908. *The Procedure of the House of Commons*, trans. A. Ernest Steinthal. 3 vols. London: A. Constable & Co.

Russell, C. 1990. *Unrevolutionary England, 1603–1642*. London: Hambledon Press.

———. 2011. *King James VI & I and his English Parliaments*. Oxford: Oxford University Press.

Skinner, Q. 2002. *Visions of Politics*, vol. 3. Cambridge: Cambridge University Press.

Markku Peltonen, Ph.D., is Professor of General History at the University of Helsinki, Finland, and Academy of Finland Professor. His research interests include the history of political thought, especially the history of classical republicanism in early modern England, the history of politeness and customs and the development of natural philosophy in the early modern period. His project as Academy of Finland Professor focuses on the history of early modern political participation and the early stages of representative democracy.

Chapter 10

French Parliamentary Discourse, 1789–1914

Thomas Bouchet

The destiny of the revolutionary and post-revolutionary political history of France seems to be mainly parliamentary – and Parisian – with the heart of the country beating where the parliamentary rostrum and benches lie (see Chapter 3). Looking back, one might be tempted to describe nineteenth-century French parliamentary history as a succession of political battles with highly controversial debates and strong ideological positions, and with a long-term victory of parliamentarism obliterating a series of short-term defeats. On the eve of the First World War, all leading French politicians were not only great parliamentarians but also skilled orators. Does that mean that a parliamentary way of ruling the state goes along with the successful elaboration of a parliamentary way of acting through words, which consequently gives birth to a specific parliamentary style? Do parliamentarians find new ways of arousing emotions or persuasion by deliberating, arguing pro et contra, negotiating or even engaging in harsh agonistic debates? In fact, the so-called autonomy, centrality and sovereignty of French parliamentary discourse can be questioned. For that purpose, the strength and depth of the prevailing political representations of discursive practices and rhetorical strategies developed in parliamentary debates will first of all be estimated in the following sections of this chapter. It is, however, also necessary to reconsider these representations: French parliamentary discourse is partly made up of legacies from earlier ages and influences from elsewhere, with continuities and static phases. Its rhetorical and oratorical devices are shaped by political discourse generally, but they also influence it. And it cannot be regarded as unquestioned, or established once and for all: parliamentary discourse continues to be challenged.

Orators in Battle, Orators in Power

The periodization generally adopted in the history of parliamentary discourse follows the chaotic destiny of the state and the nation, ranging from periods of strength to periods of parliamentary weakness, the latter roughly corresponding to imperial dictatorships. The following key periods have traditionally been identified: the first period (1789–95); the second period (1848–51); and the third period (after the 1870s). During all these periods, two opposing oratorical styles characterize the discourse: calm and proud deliberative speeches – supposed to lead to rationally founded political decisions – and vehemently agonistic ones expressing everlasting tensions. With the process moving from the passionate speeches of Mirabeau and Danton to the powerful and self-confident parliamentarism on the eve of the Great War, it seems that deliberation finally prevailed (Garrigues 2007; see also Chapter 3 in this volume).

During the years of the French Revolution (1789–95), pathos and ethos were omnipresent in the speeches of the leading orators of the successive assemblies (Constituante, Législative, Convention), as the establishment of political and social foundations was considered an absolute priority. Emphasis – with a frequent use of stylistic figures such as anaphora, hyperbole and hypotyposis – accompanied meticulously prepared and often completely pre-written discourses that allowed no room for improvisation. Political revolution and linguistic revolution in word associations or definitions of concepts were seen as intimately related (Guilhaumou 1989). The insistence on principles with the omnipresence of notions such as 'rights', 'nation', 'the people' and 'sovereignty' went along with the oratorical actio and rhetorical passion, personified by different actors, as in Mirabeau's pathos or Robespierre's ethos. Solemn statements abounded, as when Volney exclaimed when emphasizing the universality of the debates: 'Until now, you have debated in France and in the name of France, but henceforth you will be debating in the whole world and in the name of the world' (*National Constituent Assembly*, 17 May 1790). The postures of the orators became less hieratic as time passed, but they remained a trademark of the period.

The history of parliamentary discourse entered a new period after the Directorate and the silence of the Consulate and the First Empire; from 1814 onwards, during the reigns of Louis XVIII, Charles X and Louis-Philippe I, the questions of order and liberty and the opposition of political models permeated the whole of French political life and language. The Constitutional Monarchy (1814–48) is often described as the heyday of a highly elaborate discourse built on classical models. It has been remarked, for instance, that in the debate of 7–19 January 1839 on the address to King Louis-Philippe I, the use of prosopopeia is frequent, with seventeen occurrences from Lamartine, Passy, Thiers and others (Girard et al. 1976: 216). Highly educated and autonomous deputies and peers with similar positions in society used roughly the same procedures and techniques, which resulted in repetitiveness. Even great names – the classical François Guizot or the more inventive Adolphe Thiers – followed this trend.

During the Second Republic (1848–51), following the Revolution of February 1848 and the fall of the July Monarchy, parliamentary life was characterized by a tension between radical (full of vehemence, anger or enthusiasm) and moderate (pragmatic, self-controlled) models. The question of representation was reconsidered when universal male suffrage was first adopted (March 1848) and then restricted (May 1850). Relations between the executive and the legislature were complex. The Assembly was shaken by numerous political battles in which the shadows of the revolutionary debates are perceivable.

The centrality of parliamentary eloquence is emphasized, sometimes ironically, by Louis de Cormenin (writing under the pen name 'Timon') in his famous *Etudes sur les orateurs parlementaires* (1836), republished in 1842 under the title *Le Livre des orateurs* (1842). Later on, fighting – verbally – against Louis-Napoleon Bonaparte after the coup of December 1851 and the dissolution of the Assembly, Victor Hugo looks back and contrasts dictatorship and parliamentarism: 'For the past sixty years, the French rostrum has been the open mouth of the human spirit' (*Napoléon le Petit* [1852], quoted in Stein 2007: 7).

After the violent interruption of parliamentarism following Bonaparte's coup of December 1851 and throughout the first ten years of the Third Empire, parliamentary debate reappeared, embodied by monarchist, Bonapartist, liberal or republican orators, in connection with political instability, noticeably in the lower chamber (Corps législatif in the 1860s, Chambre des députés in the 1870s). A new generation of leaders – Jules Ferry, Léon Gambetta, Ernest Picard and others – emerged and engaged in direct and lively debates in the context of the military collapse of the Empire in 1870 and with regard to questions about the nature of the following regime.

At the end of the Second Empire, Gustave Flaubert ironically evokes the high reputation of parliamentary discourse in nineteenth-century France: his *L'Education sentimentale*, published in 1869 but essentially dealing with the 1840s, has as its protagonist a young man called Frédéric Moreau, who dreams of success and glory during the reign of Louis-Philippe I. First, Moreau sees himself as a famous lawyer, and then, above all, 'in the Chamber, as an orator with the salvation of a whole people on his lips, drowning his opponents in his prosopopeia, crushing them with a retort, his voice filled with thunderbolts and musical intonations, ironical, pathetic, passionate, sublime' (Flaubert 1972 [1869]: 105).

Finally, the thirty-five years of a stable Third Republic after 1880 manifested themselves as a term of parliamentary apprenticeship with two chambers – the Chambre des députés and the Sénat – controlling the government, dealing with current issues or facing major crises, on their way to professionalization. The sovereignty of the legislative power was rarely challenged. Nuance and negotiation predominated; individual eloquence was muted by the collective voice of the political parties, which were officially recognized by the law of 1901 and by parliamentary groups (1910). The durability of the regime led to the stabilization of political forces. Except at times of major threats to the regime – Boulangism at the end of the 1880s, followed by the Panama scandal and then the Dreyfus affair – deliberation reigned supreme.

The above succession of clear landmarks, with a shift from the age of innovations to the age of accomplishment and maturation, is a leitmotiv of the analyses that flourished at the end of the nineteenth century, especially in the 1890s. The history of French parliamentary discourse inherited an interactional framework set up in republican circles. Joseph Reinach exemplifies this process. A republican follower of Léon Gambetta in the early days of the Third Republic, he published in 1894 *Le 'Conciones' français. L'Eloquence française depuis la Révolution jusqu'à nos jours*, a collection of mainly parliamentary examples of oratorical bravura from forty-four orators, starting with Mirabeau and ending with Ferry, and with Danton and Gambetta as complementary outstanding figures. The central part of the book, entitled 'Political eloquence', is accompanied by examples from other institutions (the bar, the pulpit, academies and universities). *Le 'Conciones' français* is not only a compilation. Analysing the characteristics of eloquence and considering the Third Republic as an achievement for political rationality, Reinach writes: 'We are not fond of flame anymore, but of light'. Approximately one third of the texts he selects come from the revolutionary years, but what he praises most is the prominence of the deliberative over the agonistic, the virtues of reasoning, of moderate debating, first burgeoning under the Constitutional Monarchy, and then flourishing with the Third Republic.

Continuities and Routines

In his examination of parliamentary discourse, Jean Starobinski insists on a close link between novelty and continuity: that there was a rupture is unquestionable ('1789 marked the birth of French parliamentarism'), but before 1789 the history of French political eloquence was not a blank page: it was the fruit of a centuries-long rich tradition of clerical (*la chaire*) and legal (*le barreau*) practices (Starobinski 1986: 440). According to him, taking a face-value approach – and seeing little more than a century of cumulative experiments and chaotic progress – could lead to undervaluing phenomena that are not necessarily immediately apparent. The history of parliamentary discourse is much more than an expression of political history (or even of parliamentary history) with a specific configuration for each regime or period. In fact, partly inherited and imported, it is often a routine, a revival of experiments. The tempo of the history of oratory can be very slow.

The heritage of eminent Greek and Roman orators, and more generally the *ars rhetorica*, shaped parliamentary eloquence until 1914, and indeed thereafter. The influence of classical rhetoric did not die with its masters (from Aristotle to Quintilian): its treatises, its methods (the centrality of the actio, the devices of docere-movere-delectare), its practical training in the educational system – in the lycées of the nineteenth century, where young men were taught how to speak as Demosthenes or Cicero did – lived on. With busts of Greek and Roman orators decorating the Conseil des Cinq-Cents (Council of Five Hundred) during the Directorate (1795–99), the sessions were attended by Solon, Demosthenes, Lycurgus, Brutus, Cato and Cicero. Throughout the nineteenth century there were orators who did not hesitate to quote from Latin, even if familiarity with that language was tending to lose ground. 'Vare, redde me legiones!': in his charge against the supporters of the late Napoleon III on 22 May 1872, the duc d'Audiffret-Pasquier gave a new life to Augustus, who is supposed to have uttered these words after the military disaster of Varus's armies in 9 AD (quoted in Guislin 2005: 48), and the orator continued with a very classical device, the anaphora of '*rendez-nous . . . rendez-nous*'.

Pre-1789 French eloquence, especially religious eloquence, is easy to identify in nineteenth-century French oratory – throughout the nineteenth century, Bossuet was widely read and sometimes quoted in sessions. Oratory studied in the colleges of the Old Regime and the art of conversation praised during the eighteenth century remained relevant. Before 1914, social talk and parliamentary discourse cannot be completely distinguished (Joana 1999: Conclusion). Many deputies could be encountered in the salons of Madame Dosne or Madame de Lieven during the July Monarchy, or in the salon of Princess Trubetskoy during the Third Republic: 'Yesterday, the princess advised Gambetta not to heckle the foreign secretary about the Eastern Question. Gambetta replied that his friends had no intention of voicing any objections on that matter' (Police report, 3 November 1876, quoted in Joana 1999: 224). This case clearly demonstrates the connections between the hemicycle and the salon.

Throughout the century, British parliamentary discourse offered a complementary model for many French orators and specialists in oratory, who could read the discourses of speakers from the Commons and even the Lords in the pages of *Le Moniteur universel* and *Le Journal officiel*, and were sometimes personally acquainted with them. In a chapter on the Irish leader Daniel O'Connell, Cormenin compares British MPs and French deputies: 'While the one has a feeling for self-interest, calculation/ulterior motives or propriety, the other has a feeling for images, movements, coups and adventure'. He reactivates the topos of the opposition between British strength and French grace (Cormenin 1842 [1836]: 563–64). The admiration was sometimes offset with critical statements, as Frenchmen were then proud of their own parliamentary eloquence. François Guizot, then the French ambassador in London, ironically commented on the style of English parliamentary speaking in a letter he addressed to Princess de Lieven: 'Half of English eloquence is made up of "hear hears" and loud cheers' (8 April 1840, quoted in Vibert 2000: 238).

Throughout the century, parliamentary discourse shone out particularly when major political battles raged in connection with legislative-executive relations, majority-opposition rivalry, budgetary questions or religious matters. The controversies about the Revolution never ceased (Guislin 2005: 48ff). Almost a century after the storming of the Bastille, Georges Clemenceau mobilized all the resources of his sharp, rough, quarrelsome and feared eloquence – he was famous for his ability to bring down ministries from the platform – when, going back to the very foundations of the revolutionary era, he declared in the Chambre des députés: 'Whether we like it or not and whether we are shocked by it or not, the French Revolution is a landmark which remains fixed in the memories of us all', and he raises violent protests from the right-wing deputies (*Le Journal officiel*, 29 January 1891); ten years later (*Le Journal officiel*, 15 January 1901) Président du Conseil Pierre Waldeck-Rousseau proclaimed: 'You must choose either to support the Revolution along with its spirit or to support the counter-revolution against law and order'. From a political as well as from a rhetorical point of view, these conflicts were often parodical.

Some salient debates dealt even more directly with discursive logics: supporters of improvisation and an almost colloquial style (as in conversation or in the House of Commons) challenged what they considered to be the boring and obtuse tradition of reading speeches that followed rhetorical rules, especially those of the Latin tradition – the Greek tradition was regarded as freer. The terms of the debate were complex, as most of the orators who opposed classical rhetoric had themselves inherited it and practised it, and sometimes praised it: Victor Hugo, explaining in his *Etude sur Mirabeau* (1834) that rhetoric sterilized the actio, thirty years later voiced his admiration for 'those divine eclosions of the mind that the Greeks called Tropes' (William Shakespeare, 1864, quoted in Halsall 2001: 13–14). The question was far from over in the late nineteenth century, when Joseph Reinach declared that improvisation was 'the attribute, the difficulty, and the very beauty of the art of oratory' (Reinach 1894: III). The disappearance of the subject of rhetoric in lycées, at the very beginning of the twentieth century (1902), did not mean the end of the old tradition of parliamentary discourse.

Rhetorical and Oratorical Interdependencies: The Inside and the Outside

Throughout the nineteenth century, parliamentary discourse deeply influenced political life. Anthologies, collections of speeches by famous orators, treaties or school books (it is worth remembering that Reinach's book was primarily written for secondary school pupils) were complemented with portraits, sketches or caricatures of orators addressing assemblies, sometimes included in the above mentioned books, sometimes separate from them. It is easy to recollect dozens of images of 'Danton – or Lamartine, or Gambetta, or Jaurès – taking the floor' with an arm – usually the right arm – raised, their mouths open, their entire bodies committed to oratory. The centrality of the rostrum was affirmed in the activities of 'meetings', 'committees' and 'conferences' held in antechambers of the hemicycle. As early as 1815, a 'Comité des sept' was established by seven deputies to prepare debates; in the meetings of the so-called Molé conference (more precisely: Conférence de l'hôtel Molé), established in 1832, young (but rarely elder) men met, discussed and deliberated in a parliamentary way. In 1875 Labordère, the chairman of this conference, wisely advised the members who aimed at a brilliant career in politics: 'Grasp the series of facts he presents as the orator speaks, take in his arguments, extract the decisive or outstanding aspects, summarize the whole immediately so that it remains engraved in your mind' (quoted in Joana 1999: 145). The following year, the Molé conference and the Tocqueville conference merged and gave birth to the famous 'Molé-Tocqueville conference', called 'the Little Parliament'.

French parliamentary brilliance went hand in hand with the development of the press. Journalists, present in the galleries, reinforced the impact of parliamentary discourse. With ever greater efficiency, political newspapers not only spread and popularized debates, but engaged in oratory: if the press was much more than a mirror, it was because a 'journalistic eloquence' existed. 'The journalist's eloquence derives from his ability, within the context of the professional scenario that he excels at implementing, to combine both the skills of the political orator and the witty brilliance of the writer or the thinker' (Saminadayar-Perrin 2011: 680). Chateaubriand and Lamartine were not only outstanding writers and orators: they were deeply involved in journalism in newspapers or magazines (*Le Conservateur* for Chateaubriand, 1818–20; *Le Conseiller du Peuple* for Lamartine, 1849–51). Parliament and the press shared rhetorical devices, at least until the 1880s, and possibly even after. These interconnections contributed to the presence of literary universes in French parliamentary eloquence. Deputies and journalists conveyed in their discourses the idea of sovereignty, which increased throughout the nineteenth century.

French parliamentary eloquence was also deeply influenced by judicial eloquence throughout the nineteenth century. Quintilian's analyses of exordium, narratio, digressio etc., (*Institutio oratoria*, IV) were applied by deputies raising questions of truth and falsity, or justice and injustice in their speeches. Members of the legal professions such as barristers, solicitors, notaries, administrative officials, law teachers, judges and so on were omnipresent in this history of parliamentary discourse. Many of them were as much career politicians as jurists, and their influence is easily perceptible even when they did not predominate numerically. Pierre-Antoine Berryer was a leading monarchist lawyer and deputy; his major discourses were printed, some of them immediately, some in later miscellanies and anthologies. One hundred and seventy-seven of them are to be found in *Oeuvres de Berryer, Discours parlementaires* (five volumes, 1872–75). According to Cormenin, he can be compared only with Mirabeau and 'everything in him is eloquent' (1842: 473); he is a 'Legitimist Cicero' (Larousse 1867, 2: 612).

From the very beginning, the rhetoric of French parliamentarians was strongly influenced by the theatre. In 1914 as in 1789, the parliamentary session was often comparable to a stage performance. The devices used were not that different: many orators used the art of audience seduction in order to be heard and to convince. Many speeches were discursively constructed in the form of tirades, which displayed, once more, the close links between parliamentary discourse and literature. Moreover, since it was not forbidden to read speeches from paper – an important difference from Britain, for instance – it was easy to apply the classical oratorical rules. Orators – and not only writers and poets in the Chamber, like Chateaubriand, Lamartine or Hugo – frequently regarded their speeches as literary pieces that could be rewritten immediately afterwards, so that they would appear more elegant in the 'verbatim' records of *Le Moniteur universel* and *Le Journal officiel*. The speakers could be seen as actors, especially when grandiloquence prevailed and when political polarization was deep. Verbal and oratorical jousting were occasions for counterarguments and style in a way that reminds one of fencing (Guislin 2005: 42–43).

The architecture of assemblies encourages solemnity. In the plenary chamber of the Conseil des Cinq-Cents, 'The speaker's chair and the rostrum are located on the right of the chamber, often referred to by the Ancients as the proscenium' (*Le Moniteur universel*, 30 January 1798, quoted in Heurtin 1994: 120). In the Grand Théâtre de Bordeaux, where newly elected deputies used to meet after leaving Paris because of the advance of Prussian troops (1871), there was a platform for the orators on the forestage, while journalists and the general public sat together in the so-called *poulailler*, the 'hen house' gallery. The latter can be regarded as a rough equivalent of the Strangers' Gallery in the House of Commons, where an audience of visitors and members of the public at large expect British parliamentarians to enact a theatrically balanced shift between their public (institutional) role as representatives of a part of the electorate and their private (real-life) role as members of the electorate that they represent (Ilie 2003). In the French case, parliamentary theatricality has explicit cultural salience: according to Charles de Rémusat, one of the differences between French and British parliamentarians lay in the fact that 'members speaking without theatrical devices' was the rule in the Commons, which surprised French people (Rémusat 1959–67 [1867], 2: 167). This observation was further reinforced by Heinrich Heine in 1840: 'The representative and parliamentary system attracts the best actors among the French' (*Lutèce*, quoted in Mélonio 1998: 208).

Crossing Voices: Parliamentary Discourse Challenged

Even if constructive parliamentary debates with interventions pro et contra and rationally motivated decisions are the proclaimed ideal of parliamentarism, they were threatened by verbal excesses all through the nineteenth century. In this, ethos and logos were challenged by pathos. Insult, one of the key expressions of these excesses, is on the fringe of parliamentary practice. As has been pointed out by Ilie (2001), the principles of conduct in an institution such as parliament are often most clearly revealed through violations and disruptions of normative forms of politeness.

In France, from the Revolution years – Jean-Paul Marat attacking Elie Guadet by calling him *vil oiseau* (vile bird) (*Le Moniteur universel*, 10 April 1793) – to the fierce sessions of the very end of the nineteenth and the beginning of the twentieth century, the serenity of debates was interrupted by numerous attacks, mainly about matters of courage, truthfulness and patriotism. The turn of the century was, after all, the time of the Panama Scandal, the Dreyfus Affair, the separation of the church and the state, the

Clemenceau ministry and the rise of threats in pre-First World War Europe. Accusations of the period are exemplified by Georges Clemenceau's answer to a provocation by Paul Déroulède during the Panama Scandal: 'You are a liar and a coward! . . . the charlatan of patriotism' (*Le Journal officiel*, 19 June 1892). Such parliamentary insults are deliberately offensive rhetorical acts performed in a competitive institutional setting in order to stir up prejudices and create stereotypes by calling into question and undermining the adversary's position (Ilie 2004).

Not surprisingly, the oratory duel sometimes leads to actual fighting when words are no longer sufficient to restrain animosity. Representatives could be expelled from Chambers. This happened, for example, in the case of the Liberal deputy Jacques-Antoine Manuel in 1823 after his adversaries reacted violently to his speech: 'How can such horrid words possibly be uttered!' (*Le Moniteur universel*, 26 February 1823). There are also examples of general fighting in the hemicycle ('They call it a Chamber, but in reality it is nothing more than a kennel at feeding time', *Le Soleil*, 23 January 1898, at the height of the Dreyfus Affair, quoted in Bouchet 2010: 145). However, insults did not usually interrupt the sessions seriously, as often happens in the House of Commons (Ilie 2005). While most of the time the language of deputies was courteous and elegant during the Constitutional Monarchy, it became harsher in the Second and Third Republics. Systems of contention started to develop: there was a process of codification of parliamentary discipline during the second half of the nineteenth century, especially after the adoption of the parliamentary policy and procedures of the National Legislative Assembly in July 1849. From the Second Republic onwards, insults were deemed to be more and more outside 'the catalogue of legitimate parliamentary expressions' (Fayat 2000: 63–65).

It was the role of the Speaker to protect the Assembly from unbridled passions and, more prosaically, to encourage parliamentary ways of speaking, for instance by forbidding 'unparliamentary language' (*Le Moniteur universel*, 26 February 1850) or 'unparliamentary expressions' (*Le Moniteur universel*, 6 May 1850). In a similar way, official lists of unparliamentary words were recorded in the House of Commons (Ilie 2001, 2004). The Speaker was responsible for maintaining respect and reinforcing the limits of what was 'acceptable' (*Le Journal officiel*, 28 May 1900). He was supposed to hush 'mutterings, interruptions', 'lively protests' and 'tumult'. Eugène Pierre, in his *Traité de droit politique, électoral et parlementaire*, argued that the Speaker had to guarantee the precedence of reason over passion on the basis of parliamentary policy and procedures: 'Wherever men assemble there is a need for a law to protect each one of them from others' passions and above all their own' (Pierre 1893: no. 455).

The respectable nature of parliamentary discourse faced another challenge, related to the question of sovereignty and representation in the public sphere. The central role of the legislature – with its proclaimed discursive hegemony – was regularly contested from the outside: the assemblies were sometimes considered unable (or unwilling) to express the voice of the people. Occasionally, and for most of the early nineteenth century, vox populi could be heard for a moment: agitation in the public gallery and applause and shouts by men or women may interfere with debates. In the early phase of the Revolution, delegations representing political societies, national guards, Parisian revolutionary sections and the like came in to petition or read addresses, or sometimes even to sing. People assembled in the streets exerted pressure through political demonstrations. Invasions by outsiders as on 20 May 1795 or on 24 February and 15 May 1848 bear witness to the existence of an enduring tension. Evoking the invasion of 15 May 1848, Charles de Rémusat remembered a shoemaker criticizing Odilon Barrot and strangers sitting on the deputies' benches (Rémusat 1959–67 [1867], 10: 301–3).

As the voice of the people was sometimes relayed but more often reduced to silence, tensions with the world outside the hemicycle were manifested in the discordances with vox populi. These tensions also sometimes occurred in the ranks of the deputies themselves. During the Revolution, a passage 'from the language of rights to that of the people' was advocated by some of the leaders, but not by others (Guilhaumou 1989). The adoption of universal male suffrage in 1848 led to interesting reformulations as 'deputies' became 'representatives of the people'. In the first months of the Second Republic, there was a slight change in the parliamentary style: Charles Lagrange insisted on 'the simple language that I, as a man of the people, use' (25 August 1848); Deville asserted that he was an old soldier, 'not claiming to speak properly' (7 September 1848). However, the political evolution of the Assembly rapidly led to the restriction of suffrage and to the attenuation of dissenting voices.

By the end of the nineteenth century, some newly elected deputies, who were elected mainly by the workers and formed a socialist minority, tried unsuccessfully to import a different kind of language and a novel form of dress into the hemicycle. They sought to express their different identity, but they failed to exert any real influence. For example, Christophe Thivrier, elected in 1893, wore overalls. Jean Colly, elected in 1910, was very brash indeed when addressing Aristide Briand, the head of the government, in 1910 about a railway strike: 'Briand, Aristide, do you remember when I lent you a few francs to get a bite to eat?' (Quoted in Garrigues 2007). Throughout the nineteenth century, not only were most deputies well off, but they also often shared the same values, resembled one another and felt at ease together, speaking the same language. When some new groups entered the lower chamber, especially at the end of the century, their social origins – often middle class, including doctors of modest means, teachers, shopkeepers and low-ranking civil servants – did not change the rules: they understood they had better learn how to behave according to parliamentary rules, customs and ways of speaking.

Concluding Remarks

In nineteenth-century France, the influence of eloquence on legislative affairs and on political life is unquestionable: parliamentary discourse, reverberating all over French political culture, can be considered to have been a decisive agent in the parliamentarization of politics. After the First World War, the 'parliament of eloquence' (Roussellier 1997) maintained that general pattern. When he published his *Démosthène* in 1926, Georges Clemenceau shed bright light on the art of the Greek model but also on the French parliamentary eloquence of the Third Republic – especially his own. However, French parliamentary discourse can hardly be considered to have been a homogeneous category with specific oratorical rules. Its autonomy and centrality were relative. Outstanding debates with great orators were the exception, not the rule: thousands of anonymous deputies accompanied Mirabeau, Guizot and Jaurès. The sessions comprised multiple styles and idioms that may have been imported from other political or semi-political fields, from the British House of Commons, from the stage, journalism or literature. In fact, the discursive styles are highly contrasted: on one hand, the power of oratory was often emphasized, and on the other hand it could be vigorously challenged and its seductive power and limits criticized. Even Charles de Rémusat, a talented observer of political life, insistently pointed out in his *Memoirs* after a rich parliamentary career this 'singular and disappointing power of the word' (Rémusat 1959–67 [1867], 4: 457).

References

Primary Sources
Cormenin, L. de. 1842 [1836]. *Etudes sur les orateurs parlementaires*. Paris: La Nouvelle Minerve. (*Le Livre des orateurs* (1842) Paris: Pagnerre.)
Flaubert, G. 1972 [1869]. *L'Education sentimentale*. Paris: Gallimard.
Larousse, P. (ed.). 1867. *Grand Dictionnaire universel du XIXe siècle*, vol. 2. Paris: Larousse.
Le Moniteur universel, then *Le Journal officiel*.
Pierre, E. 1893. *Traité de droit politique, électoral et parlementaire*. Paris: Librairies-Imprimeries Réunies.

Reinach, J. 1894. *Le 'Conciones' français. L'Eloquence française depuis la Révolution jusqu'à nos jours*. Paris: Delagrave.

Rémusat, C. de. 1959–67 [1867]. *Mémoires de ma vie*, ed. C.H. Pouthas. Paris: Plon.

Secondary Sources

Bouchet, T. 2010. *Noms d'oiseaux. L'insulte en politique de la Restauration à nos jours*. Paris: Stock.

Fayat, H. 2000. 'Bien se tenir à la chambre. L'invention de la discipline parlementaire', *Jean Jaurès cahiers trimestriels* 153: 61–89.

Garrigues, J. (ed.). 2007. *Histoire du Parlement de 1789 à nos jours*. Paris: Colin.

Girard, L., et al. 1976. *La Chambre des députés en 1837–1839. Composition, activités, vocabulaire*. Paris: Publications de la Sorbonne.

Guilhaumou, J. 1989. *La Langue politique de la Révolution française. De l'événement à la raison linguistique*. Paris: Klincksieck.

Guislin, J.-M. 2005. 'L'Eloquence parlementaire aux débuts de la Troisième République', *Parlement(s)* 1(3): 39–60.

Halsall, A.W. 2001. 'La Rhétorique délibérative dans les œuvres oratoires et narratives de Victor Hugo', *Etudes Littéraires* 33(1): 13–26.

Heurtin, J.-P. 1994. 'Architectures morales de l'Assemblée nationale', *Politix* 26(7): 109–40.

Ilie, C. 2001. 'Unparliamentary Language: Insults as Cognitive Forms of Ideological Confrontation', in R. Dirven, R. Frank and C. Ilie (eds), *Language and Ideology, II, Descriptive Cognitive Approaches*. Amsterdam-Philadelphia: John Benjamins, pp. 235–62.

_____. 2003. 'Histrionic and Agonistic Features of Parliamentary Discourse', *Studies in Communication Sciences* 3(1): 25–53.

_____. 2004. 'Insulting as (Un)parliamentary Practice in the British and Swedish Parliaments: A Rhetorical Approach', in P. Bayley (ed.), *Cross-Cultural Perspectives on Parliamentary Discourse*. Amsterdam-Philadelphia: John Benjamins, pp. 45–86.

_____. 2005. 'Interruption Patterns in British Parliamentary Debates and Drama Dialogue', in A. Betten and M. Dannerer (eds), *Dialogue Analysis IX: Dialogue in Literature and the Media*. Selected Papers from the 9th IADA Conference, Salzburg 2003. Tübingen: Niemeyer, pp. 415–30.

Joana, J. 1999. *Pratiques politiques des députés français au XIXe siècle. Du dilettante au spécialiste*. Paris: L'Harmattan.

Mélonio, F. 1998. '1815–1880', in A. de Baecque and F. Mélonio (eds), *Histoire Culturelle de la France. Vol. 3: Lumières et liberté*. Paris: Seuil.

Roussellier, N. 1997. *Le Parlement de l'éloquence, la souveraineté de la délibération au lendemain de la Grande Guerre*. Paris: Presses de Sciences Po.

Saminadayar-Perrin, C. 2011. 'Avatars journalistiques de l'éloquence publique', in D. Kalifa et al. (eds), *La Civilisation du journal. Histoire culturelle et littéraire de la presse française au XIXe siècle*. Paris: Nouveau Monde Editions, pp. 667–90.

Starobinski, J. 1986. 'La Chaire, la tribune, le barreau', in P. Nora (ed.), *Les Lieux de mémoire, La nation – 3*. Paris: Gallimard, pp. 425–85.

Stein, M. 2007. *Un Homme parlait au monde. Victor Hugo orateur politique (1846–1880)*. Paris: Champion.

Vibert, A. 2000. 'L'Éloquence parlementaire sous la monarchie de Juillet (Guizot, Tocqueville, Thiers)', Ph.D. dissertation. Université Grenoble 3.

Thomas Bouchet, Ph.D., is Lecturer in Nineteenth-Century History at the University of Burgundy, France. His research interests concern mainly French political and social history from the Restoration to the Second Empire, with particular reference to the history of socialism, verbal insults in political confrontations and the history of parliamentary discourse. He is a member of the Centre Georges Chevrier.

Chapter 11

German Parliamentary Discourse since 1848 from a Linguistic Point of View

Armin Burkhardt

The history of German parliamentarism at the level of the federal state is much more complicated than in many other modern democracies (see Chapters 4 and 16 in this volume) – and so is the development of its typical language. The lack of continuity is the result of territorial fragmentation in the nineteenth century, the conservative attitude of the nobility and bourgeoisie during the Wilhelmine era, the emergence of nationalism and National Socialism with all their bitter consequences, and the division of the country after the Second World War. Considering the role communication in plenary sessions has to play within the respective political system and its internal organization and areas of responsibility, eight historical types of parliament can be distinguished. In what follows, the corresponding parliaments will be characterized with regard to the predominant linguistic features that reflect their general communicative design as a result and expression of the prevailing political system and its intrinsic conception of parliamentarism, their main political tasks, their relation to the relevant media and the communicative fashion of their time.[1]

Concentrating on the Paulskirche of 1848–49, the German Reichstag during the Weimar Republic and the Bundestag, the main features, linguistic means and communicative differences of debating in the German federal parliaments will be pointed out. Proto-parliaments and the non- and anti-democratic parliaments in German history will be described here only very briefly. As a general feature, it can be emphasized that German parliamentary debates are made up solely of verbal dispute and do not include, with very rare exceptions, the occurrence of physical confrontation.

The Paulskirche

Parliamentarism at the federal level in Germany began with the Revolution of 1848, which led to general (more or less) democratic elections and the opening of the Frankfurt Parliament. This existed from 18 March 1848 until the violent dissolution of the so-called Rumpfparlament (Rump Parliament) in Stuttgart by the military forces of the Old Regime on 31 May 1849. For the greater part of its existence, the plenary sessions were held in St Paul's Church (Paulskirche) in Frankfurt. As for the character of its plenary communication, the German National Constituent Assembly was a parliament of discussion – i.e., it widely fulfilled the ideal of 'government by discussion' as the main principle of parliamentary discourse: different opinions were discussed by almost party-independent MPs with the aim of mutual persuasion by almost party-independent MPs.[2] The first German attempt to establish a central democratic parliament failed, however, as the lack of power soon turned the work of the assembly into 'discussion without government'. Therefore, as a consequence of its often lengthy and academic discussions and in view of the many scholars who were among its members (e.g., Dahlmann, Gervinus, Moritz Mohl and Jacob Grimm), the German National Constituent Assembly was soon ridiculed as a 'Professors' Parliament' by the people. On the other hand, '[t]here was never a more learned parliament on earth' (Mann 1958: 210), and the formulation of the fundamental rights of the German people (*Grundrechte des deutschen Volkes*) has strongly influenced German constitutional discussions ever since.

The parliamentary debates in Frankfurt were controversial, sometimes polemic, but mostly argumentative from the beginning. Therefore, parliamentary discussion among the members, who were male without exception, was much less dispute than collective struggle to reach the best solution. Possibly due to the location, the absence of party membership and the lofty task of the assembly, the debates, with very few exceptions, were characterized by the extreme politeness and pathos of their tone.[3]

Instead of directly addressing a particular person by his name, the assembly adopted the British use of 'definite descriptions' that identified the respective MP by his constituency. Consequently, respectful expressions like *Herr Redner* (Mr Speaker) or *Vorredner* (previous speaker), *geehrter und berühmter Redner* (honoured and famous speaker) or *verehrtes* (honoured) or *verehrliches Mitglied* (venerable member) followed by the name of the respective constituency were used by the speakers. Thus, Robert Blum, the leader of the 'democrats' (Deutscher Hof), became the *'verehrtes Mitglied von Leipzig'*. As the constituency formula was preserved in confrontational contexts, it was even possible to propose 'that Mr. President should call to order the honoured member from Stade' (*daß der Herr Präsident das geehrte Mitglied aus Stade zur Ordnung ruft*; Paulskirche (PK) 1/116). These circumscriptions in the third person were used in order to address the MP in question only in his public role as a mandate holder and helped to avoid personal attacks or a direct public exposure of the addressee. This strategy is comparable to the use of the default form of address in the third person in the House of Commons, the role of which is to mark the institutional distance between parliamentarians and to mitigate the force of their face-threatening speech acts when counter-arguing and attacking their political adversaries (Ilie 2010).

Pathos may be determined as the essential stylistic feature of Paulskirche speech. This attitude, too, may have been caused by the ceremonial character of the environment, the exposedness of the rostrum and the fact that it was difficult for the speakers to make themselves heard in the huge plenary hall (with its seats for six hundred MPs and about two thousand spectators in the galleries) with their voice alone. Pathos is the impassioned and, therefore, connotatively overloaded way of arguing for a cause that has been recognized as correct, just and valuable by the speaker conceiving of himself as the mouthpiece of a presupposed common agreement on the relevant values. Grounded in emotion and politeness on one hand and elegant polemics on the other, it is not possible without an excessive use of rhetorical forms, the most important one being metaphor. Therefore, for example, the future state was metaphorized, in accord with the metaphorical concept 'the state is a building', not simply as a normal house, but as an imposing and sacral cathedral (*Dom*). Moreover, this metaphor was also applied to the German language, which is pathetically described as 'the bearer of our noblest life' (*Träger unseres edelsten Lebens*), conserving the 'shrines of our people . . . even in the period of deepest humiliation' (*Heiligthümer unseres Volkes . . . auch in der Zeit der tiefsten Erniedrigung*), and continues to live 'in the hymns of our poets' (*in den Gesängen unserer Dichter*). In the debates, this central metaphor was allegorically extended and repeated over and over again. Other typical semantic areas from which the basic metaphors were taken are, in addition to the traditional shipping, various forms of water: 'stream of democracy' (*Strom der Demokratie*), 'flood of restoration' (*Flut der Restauration*), 'swelling billows of absolutism' (*schwellende Wogen des Absolutismus*); and natural phenomena: 'avalanche of the red monarchy' (*Lawine der roten Monarchie*), 'political sky of spring' (*politischer Frühlingshimmel*) and 'sun of freedom' (*Sonne der Freiheit*).

Too strong an emphatic predilection for metaphors holds two dangers. First of all, there is the danger of overloading by allegorically continuing the metaphor, which may be illustrated by the following cryptic passage from a speech of Ludwig Simon (Deutscher Hof, then Donnersberg, the Left) with its rather obtrusive chain of weather metaphors:

Cold fogs have risen from the dim waters of 'Vormärz' diplomacy. If the power and warmth of the star of German unity and freedom is able to beat down and scatter these fogs, we will soon have blue sky and good weather . . . (PK 8/6134f)

The second danger of an emphatic abundance of metaphors consists in creating incompatible images – i.e., catachreses. Accordingly, Alexander von Bally (Café Milani, Conservative) once said in the debate about the report of the Navy Committee: 'Germany's wings, the pinions of which drink in the North and Baltic Seas and in the Mediterranean, want to raise Germany to unity' (*Deutschlands Fittiche, deren Schwungfedern in der Nord- und Ostsee und im mittelländischen Meere trinken, wollen Deutschland zur Einheit erheben*) (PK 1/312).

Apart from batteries of rhetorical questions and sequences of climaxes, parallelisms and other rhetorical figures, pathetic speeches tend to be dominated by the combination of evaluative attributive adjectives and nouns that connote value judgments. This may be exemplified by a quote from a famous speech of Wilhelm Jordan (Casino, then Landsberg, the Centre):

> The policy, I tell you, which calls out: release Poland whatever the cost is a policy of short-sightedness and self-oblivion, a policy of weakness, a policy of fear, a policy of cowardice. It is high time for us to wake up for once from this dreamy self-oblivion, in which we have continuously enthused about all possible nationalities while we ourselves have lain prostrate in ignominious bondage and have been kicked about by the whole world, to wake up to a healthy national egoism . . . (PK 2/1145)

The pathetic character of very many speeches in the Frankfurt Parliament was judged to be exaggerated even by contemporaries. In an article, published on the occasion of the fiftieth anniversary of the German Revolution, Hermann Wunderlich, one of the successors of the Brothers Grimm as an editor of *Deutsches Wörterbuch*, even spoke of the 'bombast' (*Schwulst*) (1898: 205) of many a speech.

From the beginning of the Frankfurt Parliament, interruptions were registered by the stenographers and they were part of the reports at all times. However, it may be taken as the effect of the huge interior of the church and the seriousness of the debates that interruptions were relatively rare, whereas the opposite can be said about the House of Commons where interruptions (both negative and positive) are a recurrent interactional phenomenon (Ilie 2005). In contrast to today's parliamentary practice the Paulskirche interruptions were short (they hardly exceeded one word), and they were mostly 'agreeing'/'disagreeing' or of the 'organizational/technical' kind. The expression of 'agreement' by shouting out 'Bravo!' is the most frequent type of interruption. Other forms of agreement are *Ja!*, *Ganz richtig!*, *Unterstützt!*, *Sehr wahr!*, *Sehr richtig!* and *Das ist sehr wahr!*. The very few 'disagreements' are mostly limited to a simple *Nein!*, *O nein!* or *Oh! Oh!*. About one third of the interruptions were directed at the Speaker. Very often these were requests regarding the organization of the debate: *Abstimmen!* (Call the vote!), *Schluß!* (Time!), *Reden, reden!* (Speak, speak!), *Vertagen!* (Prorogue!). Typically enough, calls of *Schluß!* and requests 'to come to the vote' are quite frequent (see Burkhardt 2004).

The generally discursive, well-mannered or even linguistically noble character of the Paulskirche debates did not exclude the emergence of at least one serious commotion. When the commission report about petitions of amnesty for political criminals was discussed, aiming mainly at the Baden revolutionary Hecker and his men, the MP Lorenz Peter Carl Brentano (Deutscher Hof, then Donnersberg, the Left) asks the suggestive question:

> Do you want to discriminate, against a Prince of Prussia, those who took up their arms in Baden? (*Wollen Sie die, die in Baden die Waffen ergriffen haben, zurücksetzen gegen einen Prinzen von Preußen?*) (PK 2/1438)

This provocative question, which alluded to the dubious role the 'Grapeshot Prince' (*Kartätschenprinz*) Wilhelm had played during the fighting at the barricades on 18–19 May 1848, led to disturbances and to a mutual exchange of insults and physical violence between the left and the right sides of the House, compelling the Speaker to end the session. And '[e]ven what is almost unimaginable in parliamentary life actually happened, namely that challenges to pistol duels were made in the Assembly and in the galleries' (*Sogar das im parlamentarischen Leben Unerhörte geschah, es wurden Forderungen zu Pistolenduellen in der Versammlung und auf der Tribüne gestellt*) (PK 2/1441). (For a more detailed description of Paulskirche communication see Burkhardt 2000: 83; see also Heiber 1953 and Allhoff 1975.)

As everywhere in politics, the Paulskirche debates were dominated by polarizing catchwords – i.e., the different groups and speakers advertised their opinions by using 'flag words' and fought against their political enemies by means of 'stigma words' (for the terminology and a typology of catchwords cf. Burkhardt 1998: 100; cf. also Hermanns 1994): *Demokratie* vs. *Absolutismus*; *Monarchie* vs. *Republik*; *Fürstenherrschaft* vs. *Volksherrschaft*; *Revolution, Bewegung, Fortschritt* vs. *Contrerevolution, Reaktion, Ruhe, Stillstand*; *Rechtsstaat* vs. *Polizeistaat*; *Geburtsaristokratie* vs. *Geld-* or *Geistesaristokratie*; *arbeitende Klassen* vs. *Capital*; *Conservative, Gemäßigte, Mitte* vs. *Radikale, Communisten, Sozialisten*; *Panslawismus* and *Wühlerei* (for a detailed description of the corresponding catchword family and its use and semantic change, see Burkhardt 2001) vs. *Deutschland* and *die deutsche Sache*; *echte Deutsche* vs. *Polenfreunde*; *Partikularisten* vs. *Unitarier*; *Einheit* vs. *Zerrissenheit*; *Großdeutschland* vs. *Kleindeutschland*.[4] *Volkssouveränität* (popular sovereignty) was a central flag word of the radicals, who understood it – in contrast to the stigmatized *Fürstensouveränität* (sovereignty of the princes) – as *Selbstherrschaft des Volkes* (self-government of the people), which is the expression of *Volkswillen, Willen des gesamten Volkes, der gesamten Menge* (the will of the [whole] people, of the masses), of *Volksmeinung* (people's opinion) or *Volksstimme* (people's voice) and based on the *Allmacht des Volkes* (omnipotence of the people) (see Grünert 1974: 215f).

As the kings and dukes, from the point of view of the monarchist Right, are ruling *in Übereinstimmung mit dem Willen des Volkes* (in correspondence with the will of the people) anyway, the monarchists only use *Volkssouveränität* as a stigma word that, therefore, is characterized negatively by means of adjectives such as *ausschließliche, absolute Souveränität* (exclusive, absolute sovereignty), *ausschließliche Volkssouveränität* (exclusive people's sovereignty), *absolute Volkssouveränität* (absolute people's sovereignty), *grenzenlose, absolute, unbedingte, ausschließliche Volkssouveränität* (unlimited, absolute, unconditional, exclusive popular sovereignty) as a sovereignty that is conceived wrongly (*falsch*), implying *einen falschen Begriff* (a wrong concept) of the sovereignty of the people. They speak of *omnipotente Volkssouveränitätstheorie* (omnipotent theory of people's sovereignty) and of the *omnipotentes Volkssouveränitätsaxiom* (omnipotent axiom of people's sovereignty) (Grünert 1974: 198). A thousand times 'high value words' like *Freiheit, Einheit, Vaterland* (freedom, unity, fatherland) were repeated, and, correspondingly, 'negative value words' like *Barbarei, Willkür* or *Terrorismus* (barbarism, arbitrary action, terrorism) that imply general dissent across party lines were used very often as well. (For a much more detailed account, see Grünert 1974.)

The German Reichstag and the Weimar National Assembly

The Erfurter Unionsparlament, Norddeutscher Reichstag and the German Reichstag until 1918 had resulted from free elections but were supplied only with limited competences (budget approval), exerted no direct influence on government formation, could be convened or dismissed by the head of state at any time and, despite several harsh controversies between the monarchist-conservative government and the Liberals and Social Democrats, were principally designed to serve as a forum for the discussion (and acceptance) of previously taken government decisions (for exemplary analyses, see Kalivoda 1988 and 1989; see also Chapter 4). Therefore, as none of these parliaments functioned as the main and most powerful constitutional organ representing the will of the people as the democratic sovereign, they may be called 'alibi parliaments'.

By contrast, the Weimar National Assembly, which elaborated the constitution of the Weimar Republic and the German Reichstag until 1933, was based on free, equal and secret ballot elections but dominated by ideological conflicts in the framework of which, in the debates, political opinions could only be discussed in an aggressive manner thereby limiting, as a consequence, the ability to compromise and allowing only unstable majorities. Therefore, both parliaments can be termed democratic 'working parliaments', or rather 'fighting parliaments'.

As a consequence of the November Revolution of 1918–19, women won active and passive voting rights and, therefore, entered the Reichstag, though still in a quite small number. This led to the fact that '*Meine Herren!*' was replaced by '*Meine Damen und Herren!*' as the general parliamentary form of address (though not adopted by some anti-feminist conservative male MPs). Both parliaments were characterized by ideological conflicts between the numerous parties, which in the course of time turned into an extreme tension between the left and the right, creating an irreconcilable conflict that increasingly dominated the discussions.

While the Weimar National Assembly still had its pathetic moments – and despite obvious ideological party antagonisms, particularly between monarchists, communists and genuine parliamentary democrats, and corresponding quarrels regarding certain specific topics and questions – it was still characterized by a general willingness to engage in constructive cooperation in order to produce a new democratic constitution as a positive result of its work, communication in the Reichstag became more and more confrontational and aggressive from one legislation period to the next (see Chapter 4). It mostly followed the discursive and institutional principles that had been developed in the Wilhelmine Reichstag, but under the pressure of the extremes it ended up witnessing hate speeches and rabble-rousing propaganda. On 5 February 1931, for example, instead of discussing and criticizing the government policy, the debate on the budget law was widely dominated by reciprocal reproaches, provocations and insults, particularly between Communists and National Socialists, as illustrated by the following quotations from the speeches of Ulbricht and Goebbels:

> Ulbricht (Potsdam) (KPD): . . . Mr. Goebbels has good reason to renounce speaking as the first speaker, for he is afraid that we will disprove and pick to pieces his hollow phrases and the lies he is constantly proclaiming in *Der Angriff* [a Nazi newspaper]. For weeks we have been asking him ten questions.

We asked him if it is true that the Nazis subsidize big industry, that they do not support any measure in favour of the unemployed, that, in fact, they supported all measures against the unemployed. Yes, it is true, and he is too cowardly to respond to these accusations from the Communist Party. (Deutscher Reichstag (DR) 3/685)[5]

Dr Goebbels (NSDAP): . . . By their being allies of international Marxism the bourgeois parties are no longer entitled to stand up in front of the nation as an interpreter of German nationalism. The bourgeois-liberal parties have made themselves slaves of international pacifism, and today they are merely the executive organ of international class struggle as it is conducted in the spirit of Marxism on the left and in the spirit of the bourgeoisie on the right . . . But decisions are made after divisions . . . This division is equivalent to an eradication of the international Marxist ideology of class struggle . . . The National Socialist movement makes itself the spokesman of the will of the people which demands that that shameless corruption that has spread through the offices and authorities since 1918 must be cleaned out . . . We know that the conquest of the state is achieved via the control of Prussia. We know that this shameless concubinage between the Centre and Marxism must be put an end to. (DR 3/693)[6]

It goes without saying that such aggressive and provoking speeches cannot pass without batteries of 'agreeing' (*Sehr wahr!*, *Sehr gut!*, *Bravo!*, etc.), 'disagreeing' (*Hört! Hört!*,[7] *Pfui!*, etc.) and 'insulting' interruptions (*Quatschkopf!*) (Windbag!) from the different sides and without a considerable amount of calls to order by the Speaker. The debates are characterized by the exchange of the predominant ideological flag and stigma words of the time: *Verelendung der werktätigen Massen* (impoverishment of the working masses), *Lohnraub* (wage theft), *Polizeiterror* (police terror), *Mordterror der Nationalsozialistischen Partei* (murderous terror of the National Socialist Party), *Faschist, Kommunist, nationalsozialistische Bewegung* (National Socialist movement), *zwölfjährige Tributpolitik* (twelve-year policy of tribute), *Steuerdruck* (tax pressure), *sozialreaktionäre Pläne* (social reactionary plans), *Staatsstreichpläne* (plans for a coup d'état), *internationaler Marxismus* and so on. Such debates are also characterized by frequent non-verbal expressions of agreement and disagreement like frenzied applause, laughter, tumultuous noise and collective booing, but contain very few sequences of dialogue (between speaker and shouter).

From Weimar via Pseudo-parliamentarism to the German Bundestag

After Hitler's seizure of power in 1933, the German Reichstag continued to exist as an institution. Except for the name, however, it had very little in common with a genuine parliament – it resulted from unfree and non-secret ballot elections and was convened only on strict orders to serve as a forum for extensive government policy statements by the self-appointed Fuehrer and for the pre-decided granting of prolongation of general powers for him to rule by edict. After the expulsion, persecution and often even physical elimination of the Communist and Social Democrat deputies, it only consisted of NSDAP party members who, in accordance with the Nazi family policy, were without exception male. As a consequence of the Reichstag fire, in which the original building was almost completely destroyed, the rare plenary sessions were held in the Kroll Opera House. The Nazi Reichstag was the self-contradictory case of a monological parliament that allowed only speeches by one single person and introductory and concluding statements by the Speaker, Hermann Göring. It was a 'parliament' in which not only the ordinary members but even the Speaker, who, according to the democratic parliamentary tradition, is obliged to observe neutrality, supported the dictator's aggressive hate speeches by consenting interruptions ('*Heil!*') and, therefore, the prototypical example of mock parliamentarism.

As a consequence of the Second World War, Germany was divided into two geographically and ideologically separate countries that belonged to different political blocks. The newly formed states, the Federal Republic of Germany (FRG) and the German Democratic Republic (GDR), were both keen to follow the parliamentary tradition, the first, however, did so by introducing a real democratic parliamentary system, the second by merely formally pretending to be a democratic republic with a parliamentary foundation.

The Provisional Volkskammer that worked out the constitution of the GDR and laid the basis for the future socialist state was already undemocratic in its composition and parliamentary procedures and unfree with regard to voting, which took the form of mere acclamation from the very beginning: in order to accept the constitution itself, the deputies in favour of the bill were asked to stand up by the Speaker while those against it were requested to 'make themselves felt' (see Burkhardt 2003: 72). And as it resulted from de facto unfree and non-secret ballot elections, the GDR Volkskammer (1949–89), in which different sections of the population (parties and mass organizations forced into line) got the chance to speak, albeit only to confirm government decisions that had already been taken before, may be called an 'acclamation parliament'. Its plenary sessions were relatively rare, and in them the political opinions of the Socialist Unity Party (Sozialistische Einheitspartei, SED) were continuously reiterated with abundant use of the corresponding ideological catchword vocabulary. Moreover, with very few exceptions (mostly in the first two legislation periods), they were absolutely uncontroversial. This can easily be detected from the meagre number of only 1,375 interruptions (almost all affirmative) in forty years, which corresponds to the output of about one day's debating in the German Bundestag.[8]

The Parliamentary Council that elaborated the Basic Law (*Grundgesetz*) of the Federal Republic of Germany was a proto-parliament that, installed by the three Western powers, was formed by elected members of the eleven West German *Landtage* and, therefore, did not result from general elections. However, its debates, though favouring joint decisions, were organized in a genuinely parliamentary way and mainly served the purpose of legally establishing a new political order and thereby preparing the work of a freely elected parliament. Such an assembly may be called an 'interim parliament'.[9] And, though for different reasons and on a quite different historical occasion, almost the same applies to the GDR Volkskammer during the revolutionary period from the memorable session on 13 November 1989, in the course of which the old GDR government was, as it were, interrogated by a self-democratizing parliament, to 7 March 1990, the day of its last session. This last period of the undemocratic GDR parliament may also be understood as an 'interim parliament', as it defined its main task as the democratization of the GDR by preparing free ballot elections (see Burkhardt 2003: 75).

The German Bundestag, however, which began its work on 7 September 1949, was a democratic parliament from the beginning. Its composition is based on free, equal and secret ballot elections, its plenary sessions are organized in such a way that political opinions and decisions are argued for and against in controversial debates and that the proper decision procedures (ballots) are respected. However, a real discussion with the purpose of mutual persuasion will hardly ever take place in it (except for so-called *Sternstunden* ('magic moments'), like the debates on abortion or on the future capital of the Bundesrepublik, when the group constraints were temporarily suspended), as the decisions actually have already been taken beforehand by the party executives or the parliamentary groups and committees. Thus, the plenary sessions have gradually turned into conferences in which the positions of the different groups, in an ultimate effort before the final decision is taken, are presented to the public in the shape of a parliamentary controversy after the internal discussions on the particular issue have been completed. As a consequence, the Bundestag may be termed a 'party parliament' or a 'display window parliament', but, considering its medial appearance, it might also be called a 'pseudo-public parliament' arranging its plenary sessions in a way that they seem to be real discussions.

Needless to say, within the debates from 1949 until today the orators have inevitably been making use of the catchwords that had been developed or are required in the respective discourse and by its subject. Flag words like *Sicherheitspolitik* (security policy), *Wiedervereinigung* (reunification) or *Betreuungsgeld* (care benefit) have been countered with stigma words like *Aufrüstungspolitik* (arming policy), *Anschluss* (joining – i.e., occupation) or *Herdprämie* (hearth bonus, which implicitly criticizes the fact that as a consequence of the new care benefit law mothers will stay housewives instead of working in a job), to give just a few examples. The catchwords that have been used in the course of the sessions since 1949 reflect the different public discourses within the Federal German society and have been described rather exhaustively by Stötzel and Wengeler (1995).

Much more interesting and characteristic than the vocabulary are the pragmatic features of the debates: the speeches are controversial and can also be polemic, particularly in the 1950s when there was much more confrontation between the parties, among them the communist KPD and a Social Democrat party that defined itself much more socialist than today. However, although speeches in the Bundestag can be polemical, aggressive and provocative, they hardly ever contain really vulgar forms of verbal abuse. Therefore, calls to order by the Speaker are mostly unnecessary, and they have become even rarer because so-called unparliamentary expressions like *Lüge/Lügner* (lie/liar) and *Heuchler* (hypocrite), which had to be avoided according to the accepted parliamentary usage and replaced with circumlocutions like 'not tell the truth', may now be used without being penalized by the Speaker (which does not mean, however, that they have become frequent).

Interruptions are quite common. It could be empirically proved that their frequency has continuously increased throughout the process of development from discussion parliament via working parliament to today's media-oriented display-window parliamentarism (see Burkhardt 2004: 411). On average, there is one heckle per minute. These have become longer than before and can consist of up to five complete sentences. They are mostly of the hint- or rather cue-giving 'memoranda' type, but especially the number of 'evaluatives' such as 'reproaches' or 'negative qualifications of the content' – *Quatsch!* (Rubbish!) – or 'of the person' – *Lümmel!* (Rascal!); *Quatschkopf!* (Windbag!); *Rotzjunge!* (Snotty-nosed kid!) – has increased considerably, serving to disturb the orator in developing his arguments and to provoke her or him into publicly unfavourable reactions. Sometimes, and indeed more and more often, a short verbal exchange takes place between the speaker and the heckler, as illustrated by the following example:

Daubertshäuser (SPD): ...
(... – Straßmeir (CDU/CSU): But this is twaddle!)
– But colleague Straßmeir, it isn't twaddle. You've just come from the Oktoberfest; that is why I forgive you this inept interjection. (Deutscher Bundestag [DB] 11/11823)[10]

In the analysis of such 'mini dialogues', which consist of 'interruptions' (or 'interim questions') and the corresponding speaker's reactions, it becomes quite obvious that the tool of the 'heckler's shout', which, in theory, could further the dialogical features of the debate, is actually used by the shouters to publicly ridicule the speakers and vice versa (see Burkhardt 2004: 602). The same applies to the institution of the interim question that was introduced in 1953 to further discussion and which is now mostly abused in order to disturb the speakers by asking pseudo-questions that sometimes do not even fulfil the requirement of using the syntactic form of a question (see Burkhardt 2004: 560). They are often mere statements, accusations, provocations or expressions of derision in disguise. Some of them are devoid of any serious content:

Dr George (CDU/CSU): Colleague Schreiner, are you prepared to admit that your biorhythm is a little less disturbed than ours, because you are an hour late for the session? (DB 10/6309)[11]

Frau Schoppe (the Greens): Walter, could you please ask Madam Speaker why she does not make sure that there is silence while you are speaking, as is the custom here?
(Laughter from CDU/CSU.)
Schwenniger (the Greens): Thank you for this suggestion. (DB 10/2444)[12]

On the other hand, it must be stressed that the creativity of the MPs has led to the emergence of special techniques of effectively formulating target-hitting interruptions. A very convincing example is the so-called 'sentence completion device' (in principle already known and discussed in conversational analysis), in which the sentence in question is completed in a way opposite to that in which the speaker her- or himself would have wanted to complete it, sometimes by effectively exploiting the infamous German verbal brackets:

Dr Wolfgang Schäuble (CDU/CSU): . . . the Federal Republic of Germany is a *xenophile* country.
(Freimut Duve, SPD: [has] been!) (DB 12/4211)[13]

Conclusion

From its beginnings in the Frankfurt Parliament up to the present day, German parliamentary language has undergone a lot of changes, especially with regard to the lexicon (i.e., of catchwords) and the introduction and use of pragmatic devices such as interruption, interim questions, calls to order and their different verbal techniques and forms of appearance. Step by step the original pathos of the parliament of discussion gave way to the omnipresent polemics of display-window parliamentarism. Under the influence of the audiovisual media, the debate gradually turned into a half-serious political show for the public in which even the dialogical means of interruption and interim question became perverted. Thus, the plenary debate in today's German parliamentarism can be seen as the stage-managed tip of the working parliamentary iceberg.

Notes

1 I would like to thank Rob Evans for his helpful corrections of my English.

2 A term that Carl Schmitt (1985 [1923]: 12ff, 43) apparently adopted from Walter Bagehot (1872).

3 Many MPs were loosely organized into so-called 'clubs', which were named after the Frankfurt pubs where the respective groups usually met.

4 Democracy vs. absolutism; monarchy vs. republic; the lords' reign vs. the people's reign; revolution, movement, progress vs. counter-revolution, reaction, quietude, standstill; state under the rule of law vs. police state; aristocracy of birth vs. aristocracy of money or intellect; working classes vs. capital; conservatives, moderates, centre vs. radicals, communists, socialists; panslavism and subversive agitation vs. Germany and the German cause; genuine Germans vs. friends of Poland; particularists vs. unitarians; unity vs. disunity; Greater Germany vs. Little Germany.

5 The German original runs: *Ulbricht (Potsdam) (KP): ... Herr Goebbels hat ja allen Grund, heute darauf zu verzichten, als erster Redner zu sprechen, weil er Angst davor hat, daß wir seine Phrasen, seine Lügen, die er permanent im „Angriff" proklamiert, widerlegen und zerpflücken. Seit Wochen haben wir dem Goebbels zehn Fragen gestellt. Wir haben ihn gefragt, ob es wahr ist, daß die Nazis die Großindustrie subventionieren, daß sie nicht eine einzige Maßnahme für die Erwerbslosen unterstützen, daß sie alle Maßnahmen gegen die Erwerbslosen unterstützt haben. Jawohl, es ist wahr, und er ist zu feige, auf diese Anklagen der Kommunistischen Partei zu antworten.* (DR 3/685)

6 The German original runs: *Dr Goebbels (NSDAP): ... Die bürgerlichen Parteien haben durch ihre Bundesgenossenschaft mit dem internationalen Marxismus das Anrecht verloren, als die Interpreten des deutschen Nationalismus vor die Nation zu treten. Die bürgerlich liberalen Parteien haben sich zu Hörigen des internationalen Pazifismus gemacht; sie sind heute die ausführenden Organe des internationalen Klassenkampfs, wie er links unter marxistischer und rechts unter bürgerlicher Prägung betrieben wird. ... Aber Entscheidungen fallen immer nach Scheidungen. ... Diese Scheidung ist gleichbedeutend mit einer Ausmerzung der international marxistischen Klassenkampfideologie. ... Die nationalso-*

zialistische Bewegung macht sich zum Wortführer jenes Volkswillens, der da fordert, daß aus der deutschen Demokratie jene schamlose Korruption ausgemistet wird, die sich seit 1918 in den Ämtern und Behörden breit gemacht hat. . . . *Wir wissen, daß die Eroberung des Reichs über die Eroberung Preußens geht. Wir wissen, daß dieser schamlosen Bettgenossenschaft zwischen Zentrum und Marxismus ein Ende bereitet werden muß.* (DR 3/693)

7   It corresponds to the British parliamentary 'Hear, hear!', but it is usually uttered as an expression of dissent.

8   Of these, 588 occurred during the first legislation period, 379 in the second, 286 in the third, and 48 and 57 in the fourth and fifth periods respectively. This negative trend continued: in the sixth legislation period only nine, in the seventh just seven and in the eighth only one interruption could be detected. From 1982 until 13 November 1989 there were no hecklers shouting in the Volkskammer at all (cf. Burkhardt 2004: 450). After the elections of 7 March 1990, the Volkskammer, which had now become a democratic parliament, continued to exist for only half a year, during which time it broadly followed the parliamentary forms of communicative behaviour of the German Bundestag, serving almost solely the purpose of bringing about the unification of the two German states and regulating this process by passing corresponding legislation. A parliament whose main task consists in its own dissolution might perhaps best be described as a 'self-liquidating parliament'.

9   As its main objective had been to prepare the elections for the National Constituent Assembly in Frankfurt, the Vorparlament, or 'proto-parliament', of Paulskirche may be defined as being already an interim parliament. For a detailed linguistic analysis of the Parlamentarischer Rat, see Kilian (1997).

10 The wording of the German original is:
    Daubertshäuser (SPD): ...
    (... – Straßmeir (CDU/CSU): Das ist doch dummes Zeug!)
    – Aber Herr Kollege Straßmeir, es ist nicht dummes Zeug. Sie kommen vom Oktoberfest; deshalb sehe ich Ihnen diesen unqualifizierten Einwurf nach. (DB 11/ 11823)

11 The German original, for comparison: *Dr George (CDU/CSU): Herr Kollege Schreiner, sind Sie bereit, zuzugeben, daß Ihr Biorhythmus etwas weniger gestört war als der Biorhythmus von uns, weil Sie eine Stunde später zur Sitzung kamen?* (DB 10/6309)

12 The original German passage runs: *Frau Schoppe (Die Grüne): Walter, kannst du bitte mal die Frau Präsidentin fragen, warum sie bei Deinem Beitrag nicht für Ruhe sorgt, wie das sonst üblich ist?*
    (Lachen bei der CDU/CSU.)
    Schwenniger (Die Grüne): Ich danke für diesen Impuls. (DB 10/2444)

13 The German original, for comparison: *Dr Wolfgang Schäuble (CDU/CSU):* . . . *Die Bundesrepublik Deutschland ist ein ausländerfreundliches Land.*
    (Freimut Duve, SPD: Gewesen!) (DB 12/4211)

References

Primary Sources

Deutscher Bundestag (DB), German Stenographical Parliamentary Protocols. Retrieved from http://pdok.bundestag.de/

Deutscher Reichstag (DR), German Stenographical Parliamentary Protocols. Retrieved from http://www.reichstagsprotokolle.de/index.html

Paulskirche (PK), German Stenographical Parliamentary Protocols of the National Assembly in Frankfurt am Main, 1848–49. Retrieved from http://daten.digitale-sammlungen.de/~db/ausgaben/uni_ausgabe.html?projekt=1182243493

Secondary Sources

Allhoff, D.W. 1975. *Rhetorische Analyse der Reden und Debatten des ersten deutschen Parlamentes von 1848/49. Insbesondere auf syntaktischer und semantischer Ebene.* Munich: Tuduv-Verlagsgesellschaft.

Bagehot, W. 1872. *Physics and Politics or Thoughts on the Application of the Principles of 'Natural Selection' and 'Inheritance' to Political Society.* London: H.S. King & Co.

Burkhardt, A. 1998. 'Deutsche Sprachgeschichte und politische Geschichte', in W. Besch et al. (eds), *Sprachgeschichte. Ein Handbuch zur Geschichte der deutschen Sprache und ihrer Erforschung.* 2nd edition. Berlin–New York: De Gruyter, pp. 98–122.

———. 2000. '"geredet, geträumt, gezögert, gezankt". Zur politischen Kommunikation in der Paulskirche', in K. Pape et al. (eds), *Sprache des deutschen Parlamentarismus. Studien zu 150 Jahren parlamentarischer Kommunikation.* Wiesbaden: Westdt. Verl., pp. 68–97.

———. 2001. '*Wähler, wühlen, Wühlerei.* Anmerkungen zu einer "Schreckwort"-Familie der 48er Revolution', in S.J. Schierholz (ed.), *Die deutsche Sprache in der Gegenwart. Festschrift für Dieter Cherubim zum 60. Geburtstag. In Zusammenarbeit mit Eilika Fobbe, Stefan Goes und Rainer Knirsch.* Frankfurt/Main–Berlin–Bern–Bruxelles–New York–Wien: Lang, pp. 57–67.

———. 2003. *Das Parlament und seine Sprache. Studien zu Theorie und Geschichte parlamentarischer Kommunikation.* Tübingen: Niemeyer.

———. 2004. *Zwischen Monolog und Dialog. Zur Theorie, Typologie und Geschichte des Zwischenrufs im deutschen Parlamentarismus.* Tübingen: Niemeyer.

Grünert, H. 1974. *Sprache und Politik. Untersuchungen zum Sprachgebrauch der 'Paulskirche'.* Berlin–New York.

Heiber, H. 1953. 'Die Rhetorik der Paulskirche', Ph.D. dissertation. Berlin: De Gruyter.

Hermanns, F. 1994. 'Schlüssel-, Schlag- und Fahnenwörter. Zu Begrifflichkeit und Theorie der lexikalischen "politischen" Semantik', in *Arbeiten aus dem Sonderforschungsbereich 245 'Sprache und Situation'*, no. 81. Heidelberg/Mannheim: Universität.

Ilie, C. 2005. 'Interruption Patterns in British Parliamentary Debates and Drama Dialogue', in A. Betten and M. Dannerer (eds), *Dialogue Analysis IX: Dialogue in Literature and the Media.* Selected Papers from the 9th IADA Conference, Salzburg 2003. Tübingen: Niemeyer, pp. 415–30.

———. 2010. 'Strategic Uses of Parliamentary Forms of Address: The Case of the U.K. Parliament and the Swedish Riksdag', *Journal of Pragmatics* 42(4): 885–911.

Kalivoda, G. 1988. 'Stilistik der politischen Ausgrenzung. Diskursstilistische Untersuchung am Beispiel der Sozialistengesetzdebatte des Deutschen

Reichstages von 1878', in B. Sandig (ed.), *Stilistisch-rhetorische Diskursanalyse*. Tübingen: Narr, pp. 269–84.

————. 1989. 'Rhetorik des Machtstaates. Untersuchung zum parlamentarischen Sprachgebrauch im Deutschen Reichstag am Beispiel der Flottendebatten von 1898 und 1900', in A. Burkhardt, F. Hebel and R. Hoberg (eds), *Sprache zwischen Militär und Frieden. Aufrüstung der Begriffe?* Tübingen: Narr, pp. 269–84.

Kilian, J. 1997. *Demokratische Sprache zwischen Tradition und Neuanfang. Am Beispiel des Grundrechte-Diskurses 1948/49*. Tübingen: Niemeyer.

Mann, G. 1958. *Deutsche Geschichte des 19. und 20. Jahrhunderts*. Frankfurt/Main: Büchergilde Gutenberg.

Schmitt, C. 1985[1923]. *Die geistesgeschichtliche Lage des heutigen Parlamentarismus*, 6th ed. Berlin: Duncker und Humblot.

Stötzel, G. and M. Wengeler. 1995. *Kontroverse Begriffe. Geschichte des öffentlichen Sprachgebrauchs in der Bundesrepublik Deutschland*. Berlin–New York: De Gruyter.

Wunderlich, H. 1898. 'Deutsche Redekunst im Jahr 48', in *Das litterarische Echo, Halbmonatsschrift für Litteraturfreunde* 1: 15 November.

Armin Burkhardt is Professor of German Linguistics at Otto von Guericke University Magdeburg, Germany, and was Chairman of the Association for the German Language (GfdS) from 2011 to 2015. His fields of expertise include semantics, lexicography, language philosophy, discourse analysis, text linguistics, German grammar, semiotics and *Politolinguistik*. He has published widely on German parliamentary discourse in a long-term perspective.

Chapter 12

Central and Eastern European Parliamentary Rhetoric since the Nineteenth Century

The Case of Romania and Poland

Cornelia Ilie and Cezar M. Ornatowski

Central and Eastern European parliamentary rhetoric reflects both the rich and varied local traditions and histories of the countries of the region as well as their shared historical experiences. The latter include imperialism (the Austro-Hungarian Empire, the Partitions of Poland and Romania), totalitarianism and authoritarianism (Fascism, Nazism, Soviet-style state socialism), as well as post-1989 democratic transitions. The countries of Central and Eastern Europe, as David Olson and Philip Norton point out, have 'endured the same domination for a part of the twentieth century, and are having to come to terms with the consequences of the end of that domination . . .' (2001[1996]: 3). It is a rich history, in the context of which parliament as an institution emerges in a dialectic between continuity and change. This dialectic in the case of Central and Eastern European parliaments – along with the chance to compare how different parliaments in the region responded to similar historical circumstances – offers a unique opportunity to examine the relationships between historical tradition, political context, parliamentary institutionalization and parliamentary discourse and rhetoric.

The growing interest in the rhetorical and discursive aspects of parliamentary practices in Central and Eastern European countries has lately materialized in both country-specific and comparative studies (Agh 1996; Olson and Norton 2001[1996]; Hogea 2010; Ilie 2010a, 2010b; Frumuşelu and Ilie 2010; Bruteig 2010; Ornatowski 2010; Olson and Ilonszki 2011). The aim of this chapter is to critically examine the rhetorical mechanisms underlying the historical processes of multilevel transformations that have taken place in the institutional practices and debating styles of the parliaments in Romania and Poland as opposite poles of the Central-Eastern European political spectrum, and as representative cases of parliamentarism operating under communism and post-communist reinvention. These countries embarked on the process of democratization at approximately the same time, but they had different starting points resulting from different parliamentary traditions, different legacies of communist-era legislatures, and different country-specific transitional circumstances. From the perspective of a conceptual history of parliamentary rhetoric, it is also significant to note to what extent each of the two parliaments displays instances of ideologically induced rhetorical distortion and recurrent linguistic anomalies (coined as 'langue de bois' by Thom 1987).

This particular approach, whose scope covers representative periods and moments of the two parliaments from the late nineteenth century up to the present day, offers deeper insights into the reconceptualizations underlying discourse-constituted correlations between political changes, institutional transformations and social tensions manifest at both macro and micro levels. It will become apparent that in the current post-communist period, as in the communist era, there is both divergence and convergence in the historical evolution of Romania and Poland with regard to the institutionalization of democracy, the policymaking structures and the relationship between the state and the civil society.

For the present study, the following questions are particularly relevant: How have the uses and interpretations of four central parliamentary concepts – deliberation, representation, responsibility and sovereignty – changed over the last two centuries in the Romanian and Polish parliaments? What are the most significant patterns of conceptual clusters and semantic shifts associated with the uses of the core parliamentary concepts in the two countries? To what extent are the semantic connotations of recycled key words and slogans rooted in culture-specific traditions of political rhetoric? When and under what circumstances did conceptual shifts occur and how did they impact parliamentary debate and argumentation structures? To what extent is it possible to identify similarities and differences related to the interplay of institution-specific, genre-specific, and language-specific constraints? We will start by exploring rhetorically representative stages in the evolution of the Romanian parliament, continue with an examination of rhetorically significant processes in the history of the Polish parliament, and end with some concluding remarks.

The Representative Historical Stages of the Romanian Parliament

To the complexity of post-communist tensions and challenges, Romania adds a picturesque set of paradoxes and profound disjuncture, which make it a fascinating case for anthropological study and research. It is a country with Latin roots and a Latin language, and yet with a predominantly Orthodox Christian religion. Hence, it has often been described as a Latin island situated in the middle of a vast Slav territory, and at a crossroads of ethnicities and influences that are in perpetual transition. The evolution of its parliamentary institution, whose origins go back to the second half of the nineteenth century, reflects in many ways a complex and tumultuous history. Following, as well as influencing, ongoing political events, the Romanian parliament has undergone several dramatic metamorphoses over time, which makes it possible to speak, in a historical perspective, not of just one Romanian parliament, but rather of 'Romanian parliaments'. Four major periods can be distinguished in the history of the Romanian parliament: (i) the first parliament (1864–1940); (ii) the suspended parliament (1940–44); (iii) the communist Great National Assembly (1944–89); and (iv) the post-communist parliament (since 1990).

The First Parliament – From Political Subordination to a Parliamentary Monarchy

A distinguishing feature of the first parliament consists in the decisive role it played in the development of two major historical processes in Romanian society, namely nation building and Westernization. The historical beginnings of this first parliament can be traced back to 1831, when a constitutional document, called the Organic Regulations, was adopted in Wallachia, one of the three Romanian historical principalities (together with Moldavia and Transylvania). This date is considered by the Romanian historian Lucian Boia (2001) as the landmark of Romania's process of Westernization and Europeanization in terms of institutional development, shared values and societal modernization. A year later, the same document was adopted in Moldavia, too. In this way, the Organic Regulations set the foundations for the parliamentary institution, as well as for a stronger connection between the Romanian principalities. The historical process of setting up the parliament of Romania asserted and reinforced, in rhetorically persuasive messages, the principle of national representation and sovereignty, which subsequently led to the union of two of the three principalities (Wallachia and Moldavia) in 1859. Prince Cuza's authoritarian Bonapartism became the catalyst of an alliance between the Liberals and the Conservatives, which served to safeguard genuine estate and political liberties. However, it was his forced abdication in 1866 that acquired the symbolic significance of a historic political change – which meant that the recruitment of a foreign prince became an available option for the political elite – as happened in Greece and Bulgaria.

Following a plebiscite on 10 May 1866, the German Carol of Hohenzollern Sigmaringen was sworn in as the Prince of Romania, marking the beginning of the constitutional monarchy. It is significant that the date of Romania's first constitution coincides with the beginning of the reign of King Carol I (1866–1914). The first Romanian Constitution of 1866 was inspired by the Belgian Constitution of 1831 and was promulgated by Carol I. It officially sanctioned the indivisible character of the Romanian state, which from then on was known as Romania (Carp 2002). As a result, Romania turned from an elective monarchy into a hereditary monarchy. The monarch opened and closed the sessions of parliament, which he could also convoke for an emergency session and which he could dissolve. Legislative power was exercised by the monarch and by the bicameral parliament (made up of an Assembly of Deputies and a Senate), while executive power was entrusted to the monarch, who exercised it through his ministers. In other words, the separation of powers did not apply in the Romanian parliament.

Parliamentary 'Consensus' by Default

According to this first constitution, parliamentarians were expected to register in advance if they wished to take the floor, and they were not supposed to be interrupted unless they exceeded the allocated speaking time or deviated from the main issue under discussion. Three types of oral parliamentary genres can be identified during this period: the discourse of address to the royal message, deliberative discourse and polemic discourse. In times of serious social-political changes, as Barbu Delavrancea (a famous writer and parliamentarian) remarked, the first genre was used by some MPs to express their confidence and hopes for the future, and by others to voice their apprehensions about it. Dissent was mostly manifested in the form of divergent political visions expressed in lengthy epideictic speeches or elaborate tirades, rather than pro et contra argumentation. The deliberative discourse genre, a prototypical instance of parliamentary debate, was instantiated in pro et contra interventions, while the polemic discourse was used exclusively in connection with interpersonal disputes, as, for example, when Mihail Kogalniceanu (a Liberal politician and several times Prime Minister of Romania between 1859 and 1865) attacked Dimitrie Sturdza (Minister of Public Instruction between 1859 and 1863, and member of the Liberal government) by making use of an ad hominem argument: 'Gentlemen, my understanding was that in this country the executive power is held by three ministers [he lists their names], but I was not aware that there is also a minister of public insults' (1883).

A tacit 'consensual' understanding gradually became the established practice, whose purpose was to 'balance' the political powers of the government with those of the parliament. This type of understanding was institutionalized as a consensus by default, which explains why it is almost impossible to find any strong disapprovals or negative points of view expressed against representatives of the government during the parliamentary proceedings of that period. This political compromise was also meant to avoid parliamentary disorder and too many disruptions or clashes during parliamentary debates. The Conservatives, who represented the great boyars, were forced to accept the rights claimed by the new emerging middle class, represented in parliament by the Liberals. Upholding the responsibility of the government towards parliament was considered the most adequate way of preserving the peaceful coexistence of the two main political parties. This politically odd situation was captured by Petre Carp (1837–1919), a Romanian statesman, political scientist and twice the country's prime minister, who summed it up in a witty rhetorical formulation: 'In Romania there are no parliamentary governments, but governmental parliaments'.

The most important challenge to the constitutional compromise of 1866, a constitutional structure that was (Western) European in its spirit and institution, may be found in the difference between the 'legal' and the 'real' country. This discrepancy was pointed out by Titu Maiorescu (1868), who described Romania as the juxtaposition of two different states, one modern and synchronized with the West, and the other rural with a limited franchise and still tied to traditional values. Since Romanians were still in the process of defining their collective identity, a recurrent theme in the debates during the first stage of the Romanian parliament was the idea of nation building and national unity. During the 1866–71 period, members of both chambers appear to have been convinced that majoritarian politics and the fragmentation of political parties must be categorically rejected in order to adequately realize representation. As has been pointed out by Marton (2009), 1866 – the year when a foreign prince (King Carol I) was invited to take the Romanian throne and a constitutional government was introduced – elevated the discourse of the 'unitary nation' to the rank of a state ideology, and it immediately became the hegemonic narrative. At the dawn of mass politics in Romania, the parliamentarians compensated for the late and weak statehood (with internal challenges and separatist movements, and reluctant international acknowledgment) with the patriotic rhetoric of national brotherhood and the exclusivist assertion of 'Romanianness'.

The Role of Parliament in Romania's Involvement in the First World War

During the period of the first parliament, 1915 marked a memorable year in the history of Romanian parliamentarism. The starting point and the central argument was a lively debate about Romania's position regarding the conflict that was changing the configuration of European states, the First World War. Romania's government under I.I.C. Brătianu first adopted a position of neutrality. However, the visions of integrating Transylvania (one of Romania's three historical provinces) into a unitary state divided public opinion. A majority of the political opposition and of the public argued in favour of Romania's involvement in the war alongside France, Britain and Russia. Another section of the opposition supported Romania's participation on the side of Germany, its traditional ally in the preceding decades. The debate, which played a decisive role in the country's political history, resulted in Romania abandoning its neutrality and joining the Entente in 1916.

According to Bălan (2005), three parliamentary speeches made in December 1915 are considered to have a particular historical and rhetorical value as they stand for three important elements: political power (represented by the Liberal Prime Minister I.I.C. Brătianu), civil society (represented by Nicolae Iorga, a famous extra-parliamentary militant politician, who favoured the unification of Romania's three historical provinces) and the political opposition (represented by Take Ionescu, the most influential Conservative politician at that time). These parliamentary speeches are essentially deliberative. As leader of the Conservative opposition party, Take Ionescu was famous for his brilliant interventions in parliament, where he used to challenge Prime Minister Brătianu:

> If you are really strong, then show the country that you are able to govern by means of liberal laws; but if you are not, then tell the country that you have changed your mind and you need restrictive laws. (Anastasie 2001: 23)

While the speakers disagreed about which side (the Triple Alliance or the Triple Entente Powers) to choose in joining the military conflict, all three shared the goal of national unity and a deep conviction that it was precisely their favoured allies who would be most supportive of the unification of the three Romanian provinces. The representative of the executive resorted to the argument of political responsibility – contrasted with the opposition's lack of responsibility – whereas the opposition made use of the argument of vigilance.

A Suspended Parliament and a Pseudo-parliament

During the interwar period, the parliament increasingly came under the control of King Carol II. In the Romanian parliament there was neither 'a majority' nor 'a minority', but there was a constant overwhelming governmental majority that reduced the opposition to powerlessness. This governmental majority in parliament was made up of one of the two ruling parties, which obtained power and organized parliamentary elections in turns (Dogan 1946). During this period, parliament never successfully developed autonomy, a failure that adversely affected the Romanian parliamentary culture. The autocratic regime of King Carol II was officially implemented through the 1938 Constitution. Two years later, on 5 September 1940, King Carol abrogated the constitution, and the activity of the Romanian parliament was suspended. Power was transferred to a military regime led by General Ion Antonescu, who ruled the country by decree until he was ousted on 23 August 1944. Immediately afterwards, under the pressure of Soviet and communist forces, parliament was reorganized as a unicameral legislative body, the Assembly of Deputies, which, according to the Soviet-style 1948 Constitution, was turned into the Great National Assembly (Marea Adunare Naţională), totally subordinated to the communist rulers. A populistic slogan became widely reiterated in official documents and meetings: 'Power in the hands of the people' (*Puterea in mâinile poporului*).

The Romanian communist-type of parliament can be appropriately defined as a 'pseudo-parliament' (Frumuşelu and Ilie 2010): although it theoretically had legislative power, its institutional role was limited to ratifying the decrees issued by the actually governing Council of State. There never were any debates in the Great National Assembly about any draft laws. Instead, its proceedings consisted exclusively of closely monitored interventions of 'the working people', who only reasserted 'the leading genius' and 'historic role' of the Communist Party. A typical parliamentary rhetorical style during the first communist period is illustrated by the following excerpt from a speech delivered at the inaugural session of the Great National Assembly by Vasile Luca, Finance Minister (1947–52) and secretary of the Central Committee of the Romanian Workers' (Communist) Party:

> The Great National Assembly distinguishes itself from all the previous parliaments we have had so far in this country, as well as from the Western bourgeois democracies. The Great National Assembly no longer represents the interests of the exploiting ruling class; it is made up of representatives of broad social strata – of the working class, the working agricultural class and the progressive intelligentsia. This is truly a people's parliament, in which reactionary ele-

ments will have very little to say through their few elected deputies. The Great National Assembly will hold short sessions and will discuss only fundamental problems, implementing the great reforms that our people are waiting for.

The message in the excerpt above is symptomatic of communist parliamentary rhetoric in that it reinforces the new politically endorsed hierarchical ranking of the social strata in society: first the working class, second the working agricultural class and third the progressive intelligentsia. Worth noting is that only a well-defined proportion of the intelligentsia – the 'progressive' one – is included among the social categories represented in the 'people's parliament'.

Unlike other communist-era parliaments, the Romanian Great National Assembly never developed autonomy from the Central Committee of the Romanian Communist Party. Thus, there was no deliberation in the Assembly, which was simply a facade helping to perpetuate the appearance of democracy – i.e., a 'pseudo-parliament' (a variant of the 'acclamation parliament' used in Chapter 11 to describe the GDR Volkskammer). Since all important political events, such as sessions of the Great National Assembly and Communist Party congresses, were carefully staged during the communist era, the role of the audience of deputies, or members of the Communist Party, was limited and totally controlled. To this should be added the overall suppression of individual expression and action during the period of Ceaușescu's personality cult, the rhetoric of which constantly reiterated the idea of the dictator as the glorious embodiment of the Communist Party and of the country as a whole, thereby aiming to programmatically instil an illusion of stability, predictability and continuity. A pervasive political control of language use involved a distorted representation of reality that was meant to inculcate stereotypical behaviour and action in language users. It is comparable to the linguistic manipulation practised by the Nazi regime, which was summed up by Goebbels thus: 'We don't speak in order to say something, but to obtain a sort of effect' (Ellul 1973: 10). The result was the proliferation of semantically anomalous key formulations – communist newspeak – as part of the official propaganda of communist indoctrination: 'We are building socialism and communism with the people and for the people. As I have mentioned on other occasions, we are moulding the new man for work and through work' (Ceaușescu 1979). A typical feature of these manipulative formulations is the recurring process of objectification and instrumentalization, whereby human beings and social actors are downgraded to the status of non-volitional or inanimate items (Ilie 1998, 2005). At the same time, the referential function of language is taken over by the imperative function, so that narratives and descriptions turn into unmistakable orders and prompts. The communist parliamentary discourse and behaviour reflected a coercion-based steering mechanism based on pre-established dogmatic notions, values and practices – a similar version to the Nazi 'mock parliamentarism' (see Chapter 11). In the Great National Assembly, the deputies did not speak on their own behalf, but on behalf of the same (communist) party and/or government. A recurrent rhetorical genre in parliament was the epideictic speech praising the 'superlative' qualities of the *conducător* (Ceauşescu). Applause occurred on command at pre-established moments during the reading out of carefully prepared, fully predictable and cliché-riddled speeches or reports. No spontaneous initiatives or speech acts were allowed, and the audience reactions were closely monitored (Frumuşelu and Ilie 2010). The deputies' well-rehearsed speeches employed a slimmed-down vocabulary (450–500 words, in contrast to the active vocabulary, which contains more than 120,000 words), loquacity (long, densely-structured phrases and clauses of more than 50 words), nominalizations (a tendency to change all parts of speech into nouns), verbs in the imperative as well as a disproportionate use of dichotomies or polarizations, such as socialism-capitalism, proletarians-imperialists, we-they/us-them (the others), old-new and past-present (Betea 2009).

Post-communist Parliamentary Democratization – Re-inventing Parliament

The political upheaval caused by the anti-communist revolutions and the collapse of communism created the necessity, and the opportunity, for political institutions such as parliament to reinvent themselves and for democratic practices to be relaunched and consolidated by promoting the values of human rights, freedom, solidarity and security. National parliaments became key political institutions during the post-communist process of democratic transition (Hibbing and Patterson 1994; Olson and Norton 2001[1996]; Maurer and Wessels 2006).

Post-communist parliaments, often characterized as 'parliaments in adolescence' during the first decade after the fall of communism (Mansfeldová, Olson and Rakušanová 2004), acquired institutional and operational maturity during the second decade as they continued to improvise and innovate (Olson and Ilonszki 2011). A number of similar processes of reinvention and reactivation of their respective parliaments took place, in different degrees, in several Central and Eastern European states. They consisted of (i) the removal of communist pseudo-parliamentary (in Romania) or quasi-parliamentary (in Poland) constraints; (ii) the reactivation of historical parliamentary practices, rituals and traditions; and (iii) the reinvention of new (post-communist) parliamentary norms and conventions. At the same time, the recently emerged democratic parliaments in the fledgling democracies of Central and Eastern Europe also displayed varying degrees of diversity. These countries embarked on the process of democratization at approximately the same time, but they had different starting points resulting from their different political cultures, different parliamentary traditions and different socio-historical circumstances. One basic element of difference concerns the ages of these parliaments: this can account for significant distinctions in the patterns of interaction and behaviour between older parliaments, such as the Polish Sejm, and more recent ones, such as the Romanian parliament. Another distinction regards the varying degrees to which each of these parliaments had served as 'pseudo-parliaments', such as the Romanian Great National Assembly (Ilie 2010b), and contributed to reinforcing totalitarian regimes (Ilie 1998). From the perspective of a conceptual history of parliamentary rhetoric, it is particularly relevant to examine the varying manifestations of rhetorical distortion of parliamentary discourses in different communist countries. This reveals huge linguistic anomalies such as *totalitäre Sprache* or *langue de bois* (Thom 1987) in all types of communication in the public sphere.

The collapse of Nicolae Ceauşescu's dictatorial regime during the dramatic events of December 1989 marked the beginning of a new political era in Romania and opened up the road for the return of democracy in that it paved the way for the organization of free elections, political pluralism, the separation of state powers and the rulers' accountability to the country's representative bodies. After the first free elections of 1990, Romania witnessed a gradual transition from totalitarian political rule towards a liberal democracy with a multiparty system. The country adopted a French-style semi-presidential regime, and its gradual consolidation as a democratic state was possible thanks to the recreation of the bicameral parliamentary system, which is enshrined in the country's new constitution, approved by referendum in 1991. At the same time, its interwar political tradition, on one hand, and its communist legacies, on the other, have had a significant influence on the post-communist process of parliamentary development (Roper 2004).

The institutionalization of the post-communist parliament in Romania has involved the emergence of new rules and regulations, in addition to the re-emergence of pre-communist political parties and parliamentary traditions. The field of legislation saw a redefinition of the concept of legislative institutionalization under the impact of EU institutions and policies (Chiva 2007). Plenary parliamentary sessions are now public, and thereby accessible to politically engaged citizens, who now have the possibility to voice their opinions by providing feedback on parliamentary decisions and by making petitions and proposals. The Romanian parliament has gradually become a central arena for negotiations and collective decision-making. This phenomenon of parliamentary reinforcement has prompted the development of new parliamentary roles and behaviours, practices and discursive conventions. Individual MPs have started to deliver improvised speeches in which they take a personal stand that often becomes a subject for deliberation. Moreover, parliamentarians no longer address an undifferentiated audience; rather they are keen to involve their co-parliamentarians and to engage in a real impromptu dialogue with fellow parliamentarians. This impromptu dialogue is initiated either by the listeners through interruptions and heckling, or by the speakers through well-targeted humorous and ironical interventions, as in the following excerpt where Laurențiu Nistor, a member of the Social Democratic Party (PSD), addresses sarcastic remarks to the former Romanian President Traian Băsescu (referring to his often reiterated slogan 'May you live well!' during the 2004 election campaign) and to Anca Boagiu, the former Minister of Transport and member of the Democratic Liberal Party (PDL):

> Laurențiu Nistor (PSD): May you live well, Mr. Băsescu, Sir! And you, Mrs. Boagiu (PDL), perhaps you could bestow some light on us, and enlighten us about how you have succeeded in accomplishing so many under-performances in such a short time?! Can you still see the light at the end of the tunnel? Be careful, that could be a torch-bearer – we know that locomotives are gradually disappearing and bound to turn into museum exhibits. (Romanian parliamentary debates, the Chamber of Deputies, 8 February 2011)

As in other post-totalitarian states (Ornatowski 2010), the occurrence and function of applause in the Romanian parliament have also changed from standing ovations carefully orchestrated during communist times to selective and politically prompted tokens of genuine appreciation, support and/or agreement. Some of the most radical changes have impacted on parliamentary rules of politeness, the most fundamental of which regards the completely changed forms of address, from the coercively imposed politically correct form *tovarăș/tovarășă* (comrade) to the commonly used polite form of address *domn/doamnă* (Mr/Mrs). The current register of parliamentary forms of address displays a wide range of rhetorically established honorific forms, which may be more or less ritualized. The choice of form depends primarily on the situational context, the status of the speakers involved and the issue under debate, all of which contribute to discursively constructing the targeted addressee(s), whether fellow party members or political opponents (Bruteig 2010). For example, unlike British MPs (Ilie 2010c), Romanian parliamentarians use their interlocutors' professional and academic titles whenever these can help to legitimize or dismiss specific viewpoints. Identity construction through discourse and metadiscourse has proved to be an essential part of the (re)construction of parliament as a democratic institution in post-communist Romania.

The Polish Parliamentary Tradition

The Polish Sejm provides an emblematic example of a Central/Eastern European parliament. Regarded as one of Europe's oldest legislative assemblies, it has been connected, at major stages of its development, to various nation-building and revolutionary projects. Throughout Poland's turbulent history, especially its recent history, the Sejm has exhibited both continuity and change, providing a case study for the relationship between parliamentary institutionalization, parliamentary rhetoric and political change.

Historically, the character of Polish parliamentarism has been shaped by two factors. One was the fact that by the sixteenth century the Polish monarchy had become electoral. The principle of election was formulated in 1506 in the conception of the 'Crown' as the state, separate from the person of the monarch (Gwiżdż 1997). In between reigns, the 'state' inhered in the Estates – the nobility and gentry – that comprised the 'political nation'. The other factor was the political empowerment of the gentry (Pol. *szlachta*) that accompanied the development of electoral monarchy. By the end of the sixteenth century, royal power was based on a contract between the monarch and the political nation, with the latter embodied in the Sejm. It was in effect the Sejm (in the form of an electoral parliament) that elected the monarch in exchange for specific privileges.

The political system of the polity that, following the Act of Union between Poland and Lithuania in 1569, became the Republic of the Polish Crown and the Grand Duchy of Lithuania (known also as the Republic of the Nobility) was characterized by decentralization and the diffusion of power (at a time when it was more typical for state power to consolidate). The 'jewel' of the 'democracy of the gentry', the very symbol of civil liberty, was the principle of liberum veto, which meant that any deputy simply by shouting 'I do not allow' could stop the proceedings and prohibit not only a single piece of legislation but also the entire legislative output of the Sejm (since all resolutions of a given Sejm were considered to be one package and were voted on together). Since the Sejm operated by consensus (which did not mean that everyone had to agree but that no one voiced a definite objection), debating in effect came down to trying to convince as many deputies as possible to back one's cause or embrace one's perspective by any available means, hoping that others would come round to one's view or at least refrain from a veto.

The foundation of the system was formed by the local assemblies, *sejmiki*, which met in churches or inns and elected two representatives to the General

Sejm and furnished them with detailed instructions. Proceedings at the sej-miki were lively and often included vituperation, invective, ridicule and even violence. In the seventeenth century, the political ideal of the Polish gentry was an orator at a provincial sejmik (Tazbir 1998).

Eventually, the centrifugal tendencies implicit in the system caused the liberty of the system to verge on anarchy. The late eighteenth century saw a movement for reform that resulted in the landmark Constitution of 3 May 1791. The constitution made the Sejm (defined as a permanently sitting, deliberative body designed to decide on public matters) the supreme political authority. The reform movement of 1763–91 marks the birth of what has been seen as modern Polish parliamentarism, while the 3 May Constitution became the touchstone of Polish parliamentarism, with the 'Four-Year Sejm' (1788–92), which enacted the constitution, known thereafter as the 'Great Sejm'. The Sejm became the symbol of collective identity and the guaran-tor of national sovereignty – an identification proclaimed in the adage 'The Republic [exists] as long as [there are] Sejms' (Pol. *Póty Rzeczypospolitej Póki Sejmów*) (Konarski 1760–63). Soon afterwards, however, the First Partition initiated the period of Poland's eclipse and eventual disappearance from the map of Europe for 127 years.

The Nineteenth Century and the Second Republic

The Polish nineteenth-century parliamentary experience was determined by the loss of national sovereignty. Polish involvement in representative govern-ment continued, however, through Polish deputies in the representative insti-tutions of each of the occupying powers: the Prussian Landtag, the Austrian Reichsrat and, after 1905, the Russian Imperial Duma. The experience of the deputies was shaped, on the one hand, by the memory of and allegiance to the native parliamentary tradition and, on the other hand, by both resistance and adaptation to the parliamentary and administrative traditions of a given regime. The experience of the Partitions confirmed the identification, in the Polish national consciousness, of parliamentary sovereignty with both politi-cal liberty and national sovereignty.

The revival of Polish statehood in November 1918 was followed quickly by a revival of the Sejm, which met on 10 February 1919. A resolution of 20 February 1919, referred to as the 'Little Constitution', made the initially unicameral Sejm the supreme power, sovereign over all other organs of state power. Subsequently, the Constitution of 17 March 1921 revived the Senate, reaffirmed the separation of powers, and declared that 'supreme power belongs to the people' – thus returning to the tradition of the Constitution of 3 May 1791, which was explicitly invoked in the Preamble.

In the immediate post-national-revival period (1919–22), the Sejm was the primary 'school of governing' for the newly independent multicultural, multi-religious and even multilingual country (Gwiżdż 1997). Debate was marked by conflicts between national minorities (which comprised one third of the population of the new republic) and social conflicts, especially between peasants and landowners. Language and behaviour in the chamber were confrontational, with invective, interruptions, backchannelling, unauthorized discussion among deputies, exclamations, merriment and other spontaneous, and often disruptive, forms of behaviour. Debating, however, was open and spirited, with many instances of political oratory in the best Ciceronian republican tradition.

The coup d'etat of 12 May 1926, however, initiated a shift in the political centre of gravity towards the executive. Echoing the authoritarian tendencies sweeping over much of Europe, parliamentary democracy began to be criticized for its 'fragmentation', party-dominated character, 'weakness' and 'ineffectiveness'. The new Constitution of 23 April 1935 decisively subordinated parliament to the president (who represented 'unified and indivisible power' and who was responsible only 'before God and history') and, in the second instance, to the government (declaring, among other things, that 'the functions of governing the state do not belong to parliament'), thus reversing both the historical tradition and the political order established in 1919.

The Nazi invasion of Poland on 1 September 1939 led to another loss of national sovereignty. With the government and most MPs in exile, the president dissolved the Sejm and Senate and ruled, for the duration of the war, by decree, advised by the 12- to 24-member National Council. With limited legislative prerogatives, the Council was primarily a forum for discussions on the future of the political system as well as for the president and prime minister to address the 'nation' under conditions of war and exile (Jankiewicz 1997).

Parliament under State Socialism

The state socialist system of government, which began to rule with the consolidation of the Soviet-style regime between 1947 and 1949, was characterized by the abandonment of the principle of separation of powers and by the unification of the legislative and the executive in pursuit of a unified state policy. Despite the characterization of the Sejm in the 'Stalinist Constitution' of 1952 as 'the highest organ of state power' and 'the highest body expressing the will of the nation, appointed to realize its sovereign rights', in practice parliament was reshaped to realize the one 'correct' political line represented by the Communist Party, which communist ideology assigned to play the 'leading role' in the state.[1] The reshaping of parliament in the image of the new political order took both institutional and rhetorical forms.

Parliament became unicameral. Parliamentary committees were made to correspond to government ministries. The traditional prohibition on holding several administrative posts simultaneously (*incompatibilitas*) was abandoned, and government officials (who typically were also party officials) became deputies and functionaries of parliament. After 1952, the Council of State took over many of the functions of parliament, including legislation (similar developments took place in other Central/Eastern European countries) and the decrees of the Council were often used to circumvent parliament.[2] The possibility of any political opposition in the chamber was precluded by the rule that candidates for membership had to be nominated by registered social and political organizations, while Article 72 of the 1952 Constitution forbade the existence of, or membership in, 'associations whose purpose or activity is contrary to the political and social system'.

The conduct of the proceedings also militated against debate and deliberation. The sequence of speakers (representatives of the 'ruling' party spoke first, followed by representatives of the 'allied' factions, then other MPs), combined with a lack of public coverage of the proceedings, privileged the dominant outlook and worked to discourage, isolate, and disarm any potential dissent. Discourse in the chamber became ritualized, ideologized, and declarative (or declamatory). It avoided personal commitments and opinions (including the use of personal pronouns, especially the first-person singular 'I', with a marked preference for the plural 'we'), and confrontational views (in effect, deliberation disappeared, since only 'pro' views were legitimate), while there were frequent references to (ideological) authorities. By the middle of 1949 (the year of the consolidation of Stalinism), any manifestations of deputies' independence and agency disappeared completely, along with interpellations, requests to speak, and direct exchanges between MPs. Henceforth, proceedings took the form of primarily epideictic speeches directed at the chamber in general.

Frumuşelu and Ilie (2010) refer to 'frozen pseudo-parliamentary' rhetoric: one that lacks any confrontation of ideas, debate, or criticism. For much of the state-socialist period, the Sejm was reduced to a 'core legitimizing function' (Olson and Norton 2001[1996]: 1); its legislative function 'in the final resort came down to giving the guise of state law to major political decisions, which were taken by the leadership *gremia* of PZPR (Polish United Workers' Party)' (Kraczkowski 1997: 301).[3]

It is not quite accurate, however, to describe the Sejm throughout the entire period of the 'Polish People's Republic' as a mere rubber stamp (Kraczkowski 1997). Traces of the parliamentary tradition remained in parliamentary terminology, symbolism, and ritual, while vestiges of genuine debate persisted in committees. The Sejm also reacted to important political events, such as the socio-economic crises of 1956, 1968, 1970 and 1980. On such occasions, rhetoric in the chamber changed, often dramatically. The voices of the few independent MPs, while tolerated mainly in order to maintain the fiction of freedom of speech, were also carefully attended to as genuine articulations and barometers of public sentiment.

During the last parliamentary term (1988–89) of the communist era, the routine of prepared speeches, applauding on cue and in unison, and unanimous voting began to give way to more agonistic relations in the chamber. In the closing speech of the term, the Speaker called on the chamber to 'reject . . . the principle of the one truth' and everything else 'contrary to democracy' (*Sprawozdanie Stenograficzne z VII sesji 50 posiedzenia Sejmu*, 30 May 1989, 94).

The revival of civil society during the period of the so-called 'First Solidarity' (August 1980–December 1981) and the creation by the opposition of what Adam Michnik referred to as the 'parallel state' in the second half of the 1980s saw the emergence of extra- and quasi-parliamentary assemblies, such as workers' councils, the First Solidarity Congress of September-October 1981, and the Citizens' Committee with Lech Wałesa (Pol. *Komitet Obywatelski przy Lechu Wałęsie*) in 1988 and 1989 (Michnik 1985). Such assemblies revived, or reinvented, many traditions of Polish parliamentarism, along with democratic forms of procedure and debate. A former Solidarity activist, in fact, mentioned to the present author that union meetings during the early 1980s resembled the sejmiki of the Golden Age, with bursts of spontaneous oratory, while 'democracy' was often identified with consensus.[4] Such quasi-parliaments – independent sites of political activity that recovered, or reinvented, parliamentary culture – functioned as training grounds for many future MPs. In fact, the Citizens' Committee, created in 1988 in the run-up to the Round Table Conference, played the role of the 'Sejm of independent Poland' during the last year of existence of the communist Polish People's Republic and constituted the nucleus of the future parliamentary opposition, becoming, after the watershed parliamentary elections of 4 June 1989, the major parliamentary club in the Sejm.[5] The Polish experience demonstrates the importance of such quasi-parliamentary forums in the revival, or development, of parliamentary culture.

The Third Republic: Parliament and Political Transition after 1989

The breakthrough parliamentary elections of 4 June 1989 ushered in the 'Contract' Parliament (Pol. *Sejm Kontraktowy*) – so called because its composition was the result of the political settlement reached at the 'Round Table' talks (6 February–5 April 1989) between the authorities and the opposition. Thirty-five per cent of MPs were elected freely and represented the political opposition. In the newly revived Senate, to which elections were fully democratic, 99 out of 100 senators represented the political opposition.

The result of the semi-free elections, which made it possible for many MPs to genuinely represent real constituents, was a shift in the relations of power in the chamber. The shift was captured in a quip by Jan Lityński, one of the newly elected opposition MPs, in a meeting in parliament between members of the opposition and representatives of the still-communist government soon after the transitional elections: 'The representatives of the people', Lityński quipped, 'greet the representatives of the authorities' (quoted in Dubiński 1999: 28). From the very first hours of the Contract Parliament, the 'representatives of the people' assumed rhetorical control of the proceedings. Invocations of representation became an explicit rhetorical topos; during the first debate of the new term, one MP opened her maiden statement with the words: 'I represent the people' [Pol. *społeczeństwo*] (*Sprawozdanie Stenograficzne z 3go posiedzenia Sejmu*, 10 July 1989, 76). Based on the new legitimacy derived from genuine representation, the members, led by opposition MPs, proceeded to transform the institution of parliament through discourse and rhetoric (see Ornatowski 2010 for a detailed analysis of the changes in the discourse and behaviour of MPs).

From the very first hours of debate, MPs acted on the assumption that parliament constituted the 'highest authority in the state these days' (*Sprawozdanie Stenograficzne z 3go posiedzenia Sejmu*, 10 July 1989, 69), in the words of one MP. The chamber's sovereignty was asserted through direct challenges to and interruptions of statements by officials of the executive, a shift in the rhetorical stasis in questions to officials that asserted the chamber's critical stance towards official pronouncements, as well as through non-verbal means such as whistles, heckles and backchannelling.

MPs also demanded a greater responsibility of the executive to parliament. 'To be able to have any kind of [meaningful] debate on the repair of the Republic,' one MP declared during the very first substantive debate of the term, 'we have to be familiar with and know everything the government does. [Only] then will our debates, our MPs' discussions on any matter be substantively meaningful' (*Sprawozdanie Stenograficzne z 3go posiedzenia*

Sejmu, 10 July 1989).[6] The government's responsibility to the chamber was elicited through questions and challenges to officials, as well as through a rapidly rising volume of interpellations, which had been virtually non-existent, although allowed, during communist times.

The new pluralism in the chamber resulted in a rhetorical shift towards argument, debate, and deliberation, especially as the Sejm found itself dealing with fundamental and highly controversial issues, such as socio-economic reform or a new constitution. The turn towards argument and oratory was reinforced by an awareness of an audience outside the chamber, since the proceedings, unlike in communist times, were now broadcast live and unabridged by the media.

Another important means of redefining political relations in the chamber was changes in forms of address. Pierre Bourdieu regards rules of politeness, including forms of address, as presupposing 'the implicit mastery, hence the recognition, of a set of oppositions constituting the implicit axiomatics of a determinate political order' (Bourdieu 1977: 218). The communist-era chamber used exclusively the form *obywatel poseł/obywatelka posłanka* (citizen deputy, male/female form). Over the initial weeks of the Contract Parliament, forms of address functioned as markers of political identification and differentiation, with practically all MPs representing the former ruling party initially using the old form (*obywatel/obywatelka*) and all opposition MPs using the ordinary polite form *pan/pani* (Mr/Mrs). Members of political factions formerly 'affiliated' with the ruling party were divided, some using one, some the other form, and some using both without any apparent consistency. For example, the Speaker (who was a member of the allied Polish Peasant Faction) in his inaugural speech used both, opening with the ordinary polite – and at the time politically novel – form and closing with the old form. Over time, increasing numbers of MPs switched to the ordinary polite form, and by the end of December 1989, six months into the term, the old form of address had disappeared completely. The timing of its disappearance was symptomatic: its last two recorded instances (from two diehard representatives of the former ruling party) occurred during the debate on the constitutional amendments that formally ended the Polish People's Republic and changed the name of the country to the Republic of Poland. The disappearance of the old form of address in the chamber thus literally coincided with the demise of one and the birth of another polity.

The Contract Parliament represented the second major moment of parliamentarization in Polish history. In his speech inaugurating the Contract Parliament, the Speaker referred to the constitutional moment in 1791, while in the speech concluding the term he compared its achievements to those of the 'Great Sejm', which enacted the Constitution of 3 May 1791

(Kozakiewicz 1992). During the political transition and throughout the first decade of political transformation, the Polish parliament – in its fundamental character as a forum of parley – played the key role in the process of rebuilding a democratic political culture (see Bruteig 2010 for the similar case of the Czech Republic). Two months into the term, one MP declared from the parliamentary rostrum: 'In this building a political game is taking place that increasingly resembles the rules of parliamentary democracy' (*Sprawozdanie stenograficzne z 3go posiedzenia Sejmu*, 24 August 1989, 95). By the end of the 1990s, as Bronisław Geremek, leader of the Citizen's Committee and of the parliamentary opposition during the Contract Parliament, noted, proceedings in the Sejm began to resemble the seventeenth-century Sejm of the Republic of the Nobility (*Rok 1989* [2008]).

Concluding Remarks

More than two decades of parliamentary rule in the post-communist states of Central and Eastern Europe have shown that parliamentary government and proportional representation have played a significant role in facilitating the development of a multiparty system as the main link between society and politics in these new democracies. The examination of the Romanian and Polish parliaments as representative cases indicates that the changes brought about by the new parliamentary institutions affect and are affected by the scope and depth of political reforms, the historically conditioned cultural values and the new institution-specific rules in each of the countries concerned (shifting role attributions, institutional power management, rhetorical deliberation styles).

In spite of a number of differences between the two parliaments, it is enlightening to find that in both cases discourse and rhetoric have a constitutive function (Ilie 2006). Contexts, including institutional contexts such as parliament, are not deterministic frameworks for discursive activity but 'dynamic structures' that are at least partially constituted by such activity: 'ongoingly constructed, updated and reconstructed' (van Dijk 2004: 350). While at the macro level parliamentarians are engaging in 'global acts, such as legislating and political governing', they constitute both the 'institution' of parliament itself and the broader political context of which this institution partakes (Ilie 2010c: 889). We treat 'constitution' in this context as an activity, an 'enactment arising in history', in Kenneth Burke's memorable formulation. Such acts of constitution involve an agonistic calculus of motives – that is, they appear as the outcome of an agonistic, and fundamentally rhetorical, process involving agents, purposes, agencies and so on. In this sense, constitution creates a particular kind of political community in history (Burke 1969 [1945]: 365).

Certain empirical evidence (Riggs 1998) has indicated that the new democracies that had chosen the parliamentary system of government had a considerably better chance to successfully consolidate their democratic development than those that had opted for a presidential system of government. Elgie and Moestrup (2008), focusing on semi-presidentialism (for example, in Romania and Poland), show that semi-presidential regimes can operate in quite different ways, some with very strong presidents, some with strong prime ministers and ceremonial presidents, and some with a balance of presidential and prime-ministerial powers. However, there seems to be a general agreement that post-communist constitutional design experiments generated a rich and diverse experience of institutional interactions in a large number of transitional polities (Protsyk 2011). It is therefore reasonable to conclude that the evolution of the post-totalitarian reconstruction of democratically functioning parliaments marked the transition from division (between Western and Eastern Europe during the Cold War) to integration into a new Europe of collaborative transnational interconnectedness.

Notes

1 The 1952 Constitution was formally in force until 1997, although constitutional amendments that changed the political system to a parliamentary democracy with separation of powers and made parliament sovereign and supreme were passed in 1989 and 1992. The party's 'leading role' in the state was explicitly added to the constitution in 1976.

2 As was the case with the imposition of martial law on 13 December 1981.

3 Yordanka Bruteig Madzharova (2010) points out that parliament plays an important role in the legitimization of political power, in addition to governing. In communist times, the legitimizing function dominated.

4 Zbigniew Bujak, personal conversation, 8 June 2010.

5 The phrase 'Sejm of independent Poland' was used by Stefan Bratkowski, as reported in 'Referat Programowy Departamentu III MSW na Odprawę Kadry Kierowniczej III w dniach 16-17.01.1989 przesłany przez Gen. Bryg. Krzysztofa Majchrowskiego komendantowi Wyższej Szkoły Oficerskiej MSW płk. Henrykowi Lewandowskiemu', in Jabłonowski, Stępka and Sułowski (2009: 37).

6 The phrase 'the repair of the republic'—frequently heard in Polish political discourse following the transition of 1989—echoes the well-known 1551 treatise 'On The Repair of the Commonwealth' (*De Republica Emendanda*) by Andrzej Frycz Modrzewski.

References

Primary Sources

Ceauşescu, N. 1979. *Raportul Comitetului Central cu privire la activitatea Partidului Comunist Român în perioada dintre Congresul al XI-lea şi Congresul al XII-lea şi sarcinile de viitor ale partidului* (19 noiembrie 1979). Bucharest: Editura politică.

Dubiński, K. 1999. *Okrągły Stół*. Warsaw: Krajowa Agencja Promocyjna.

Konarski, S. 1760–63. *O skutecznym rad sposobie albo o utrzymywaniu ordynaryinych seymow, częsc czwarta y ostatnia . . . Cz. 4.* Warsaw: w Drukarni J.K.Mci i Rzeczypospolitey u XX. Scholarum Piarum.

Sprawozdanie Stenograficzne z VII sesji 50 posiedzenia Sejmu. [Warsaw]: Sejm.

Sprawozdanie Stenograficzne z 3go posiedzenia Sejmu. [Warsaw]: Sejm.

Romanian Parliamentary Debates, the Chamber of Deputies, retrieved from http://www.cdep.ro/pls/steno/steno.stenograma?ids=6958&idm=1,007&idl=2

Rok 1989: Geremek Opowiada Żakowski Pyta, wyd. II rozszerzone. 2008. Warsaw: Agora.

Secondary Sources

Agh, A. 1996. 'Democratic Parliamentarism in Hungary: The First Parliament (1990–94) and the Entry of the Second Parliament', in D.M. Olson and P. Norton (eds), *The New Parliaments in Central and Eastern Europe*. London: Frank Cass, pp. 17–39.

Anastasie, I. 2001. *Take Ionescu*. Bucharest: Mica Valahie.

Bălan, N.A. 2005. *Discursul politic românesc*. Craiova: Editura Universitaria.

Betea, L. 2009. '"Limba de lemn" – de la Ceauşescu la Ion Iliescu', in I. Rad (ed.), *Limba de lemn în presă*. Bucharest: Ed. Tritonic, pp. 179–87.

Boia, L. 2001. *History and Myth in Romanian Consciousness*. Budapest: Central European University Press.

Bruteig Madzharova, Y. 2010. 'Czech Parliamentary Discourse: Parliamentary Interactions and the Construction of the Addressee', in C. Ilie (ed.), *European Parliaments under Scrutiny: Discourse Strategies and Interaction Practices*. Amsterdam and Philadelphia: John Benjamins, pp. 265–302.

Bourdieu, P. 1977. *Outline of a Theory of Practice*, trans. R. Nice. Cambridge: Cambridge University Press.

Burke, K. 1969 [1945]. *A Grammar of Motives*. Berkeley and Los Angeles: University of California Press.

Carp, R. 2002. 'Governmental Responsibility and Parliamentary Irresponsibility in the Romanian Constitutional Tradition', in M. Czobor-Lupp and J.S. Lupp (eds), *Moral, Legal and Political Values in Romanian Culture*. Washington, DC: Council for Research in Values and Philosophy, pp. 99–105.

Chiva, C. 2007. 'The Institutionalisation of Post-communist Parliaments: Hungary and Romania in Comparative Perspective', *Parliamentary Affairs* 60(2): 187–211.

Dijk, T.A. van. 2004. 'Text and Context of Parliamentary Debates', in P. Bayley (ed.), *Cross-Cultural Perspectives on Parliamentary Discourse*. Amsterdam and Philadelphia: John Benjamins, pp. 339–72.

Dogan, M. 1946. *Analiza statistică a 'democrației parlamentare' din Romania*. Bucharest: Editura Partidului Social-Democrat.

Elgie, R. and S. Moestrup (eds). 2008. *Semi-presidentialism in Central and Eastern Europe*. Manchester: Manchester University Press.

Ellul, J. 1973. *Propaganda: The Formation of Men's Attitudes*. New York: Vintage Books.

Frumușelu, M. and C. Ilie. 2010. 'Pseudo-parliamentary Discourse in a Communist Dictatorship: Dissenter Pârvulescu vs. Dictator Ceaușescu', *Journal of Pragmatics* 42(4): 924–42.

Gwiżdż, A. 1997. 'Sejm i Senat w Latach 1918–1939', in J. Bardach (ed.), *Dzieje Sejmu Polskiego*. Warsaw: Wydawnictwo Sejmowe, pp. 145–202.

Hibbing, J.R. and S.C. Patterson. 1994. 'The Emergence of Democratic Parliaments in Central and Eastern Europe', in G.W. Copeland and S.C. Patterson (eds), *Parliaments in the Modern World: Changing Institutions*. Ann Arbor, MI: University of Michigan Press, pp. 129–50.

Hogea, A. 2010. 'Coming to Terms with the Communist Past in Romania: An Analysis of the Political and Media Discourse Concerning the Tismăneanu Report', *Studies of Transition States and Societies* 2(2): 16–30.

Ilie, C. 1998. 'The Ideological Remapping of Semantic Roles in Totalitarian Discourse or How to Paint White Roses Red', *Discourse & Society* 9(1): 57–80.

_____. 2005. 'An Integrated Approach to the Analysis of Participant Roles in Totalitarian Discourse: The Case of Ceaușescu's Agent Roles', in L. de Saussure and P. Schulz (eds), *Manipulation and Ideologies in the Twentieth Century: Discourse, Language, Mind*. Amsterdam: John Benjamins, pp. 191–211.

_____. 2006. 'Parliamentary Discourses', in K. Brown (ed.), *Encyclopedia of Language and Linguistics*, 2nd ed., vol. 9. Oxford: Elsevier, pp.188–96.

_____. (ed.). 2010a. *European Parliaments under Scrutiny: Discourse Strategies and Interaction Practices*. Amsterdam and Philadelphia: John Benjamins.

_____. 2010b. 'Managing Dissent and Maximising Interpersonal Relations in Parliamentary Discourse', in C. Ilie (ed.), *European Parliaments under Scrutiny: Discourse Strategies and Interaction Practices*. Amsterdam and Philadelphia: John Benjamins, pp. 193–221.

_____. 2010c. 'Strategic Uses of Parliamentary Forms of Address: The Case of the U.K. Parliament and the Swedish Riksdag', *Journal of Pragmatics* 42(4): 885–911.

Jabłonowski, M., S. Stępka and S. Sułowski (eds). 2009. *Polski Rok 1989: Sukcesy, Zaniechania, Porażki, Częsc 2*. Warsaw: ASPRA-JR.

Jankiewicz, A. 1997. 'Rzeczpospolita bez Parlamentu: Organa Reprezentacji Politycznej w Latach 1939–1945', in J. Bardach (ed.), *Dzieje Sejmu Polskiego*. Warsaw: Wydawnictwo Sejmowe, pp. 205–29.

Kozakiewicz, M. 1992. *Byłem Marszałkiem Kontraktowego. . .* Warsaw: BGW.

Kraczkowski, R. 1997. 'Sejm w Okresie PRL', in J. Bardach (ed.), *Dzieje Sejmu Polskiego*. Warsaw: Wydawnictwo Sejmowe, pp. 265–306.

Mansfeldová, Z., D.M. Olson and P. Rakušanová (eds). 2004. *Central European Parliaments: First Decade of Democratic Experience and the Future Prospective*. Prague: Sociologický Ustav AV CR.

Marton, S. 2009. '"Subcontracting" Nation-Building: The Foreign Prince in the Romanian Parliament, 1866–1867', *Studia Politica* 9(2): 229–57.

Maurer, A. and W. Wessels (eds). 2006. *National Parliaments on Their Ways to Europe: Losers or Latecomers?* 2nd ed. Baden-Baden: Nomos Verlagsgesellschaft.

Michnik, A. 1985. 'On Resistance: A Letter from Białołęka 1982', in *Letters from Prison and Other Essays*, trans. M. Latynski. Berkeley and Los Angeles: University of California Press, pp. 41–63.

Olson, M.D. and P. Norton (eds). 2001[1996]. *The New Parliaments of Central and Eastern Europe*. London and Portland: Frank Cass.

Olson, D.M. and G. Ilonszki (eds). 2011. *Post-communist Parliaments: Change and Stability in the Second Decade*. New York and London: Routledge.

Ornatowski, C.M. 2010. 'Parliamentary Discourse and Political Transition: The Case of the Polish Parliament after 1989', in C. Ilie (ed.), *European Parliaments under Scrutiny: Discourse Strategies and Interaction Practices*. Amsterdam and Philadelphia: John Benjamins, pp. 223–64.

Protsyk, O. 2011. 'Semi-presidentialism under Post-communism', in R. Elgie, S. Moestrup and Y.-S. Wu (eds), *Semi-presidentialism and Democracy*. Basingstoke, UK: Palgrave Macmillan.

Riggs, F.W. 1998. 'Presidentialism vs. Parliamentarism: Implications for the Triad of Modernity', *International Political Science Review* 18(3): 253–78.

Roper, S.D. 2004. 'Parliamentary Development', in H.F. Carey (ed.), *Romania since 1989: Politics, Economics, and Society*. Lanham, Maryland: Lexington Books, pp. 159–77.

Tazbir, J. 1998. *Kultura Szlachecka w Polsce*. Poznań: Wydawnictwo Poznańskie.

Thom, F. 1987. *La langue de bois*. Paris: Gallimard.

Cornelia Ilie, Ph.D., is Professor of Business Communication in the College of Business, Zayed University, Abu Dhabi, the United Arab Emirates. She has previously worked as Professor of English Linguistics at Malmö University, Sweden. Her main research interests include the discursive practices of institutional dialogue – particularly in the media, political discourse and parliamentary debates – argumentation analysis and cross-cultural rhetoric. She is the founder of EPARDIS (Europe and Parliamentary Discourses), a cross-European network for the interdisciplinary study of parliamentary practices, and the President of ESTIDIA (European Society for Transcultural and Interdisciplinary Dialogue).

Cezar Ornatowski, Ph.D., is Professor of Rhetoric and Writing Studies at San Diego State University, the United States. His research interests include rhetoric and political transformation especially in Central/Eastern Europe, totalitarian and democratic rhetoric, strategic rhetoric and professional communication.

Part III

Parliament and Parliamentarism in Political Theory

Chapter 13

Political Theories of Parliamentarism

Kari Palonen

With Collingwood (1978 [1939]) we can ask which questions 'parliamentarism' has in various temporal and national contexts provided an answer to. Our thesis is that parliamentarism refers to a cluster of four concepts – representation, deliberation, responsibility and sovereignty – which call attention to different political questions. The political theories of parliamentarism refer to these four questions, but give them different weight and emphasis in different contexts.

The 'Alternatives' to Parliamentarism

In order to understand the parliamentary type of political theory better, I shall shortly take up various types of political theories against which it is offered as an alternative. The types indicate different forms of anti-parliamentary politics. They reject all parliamentary aspects only in extreme cases; on the other hand, they tend to give one type an interpretation that makes it possible to reject the others.

Parliamentary elements without representation are also present in debating societies, most prominently in the Oxford and Cambridge Union Societies. The members' associations do not claim to be representing anyone else, and therefore debating societies could serve as purer deliberative assemblies than the House of Commons, which provided the model for their procedures and debating practices (see Haapala 2012).

There also exists a variety of non-parliamentary models of representation. The estates, based on the social status of the 'electorate', are the classical example. The guilds and corporations representing specific interests such as professions or universities are examples of interest representation, as practised in independent medieval cities. A revival of this model replacing individual and equal suffrage and a deliberative parliament was proposed in early twentieth-century neo-corporatist theories, and attempts were made to implement it in Mussolini's Italy, Salazar's Portugal and in the Austrian Ständstaat of 1934–38 (Gusy 2008). Max Weber's *Wahlrecht und Demokratie in Deutschland* (1988 [1917]) contains an excellent polemic against *berufsständische Vertretung* and *Pluralstimmen* and their corporatist principles.

Jean-Jacques Rousseau's thesis (1966 [1762]) on the impossibility of representing the will of others (see e.g., Urbinati 2011) was used to reject representation as such. Moritz Rittinghausen (1851: 11–15) propagated the idea of 'direct government' after the French Revolution of 1848. The claim for specific non-individual workers' representation in the Assemblée nationale (see Proudhon 1977 [1865]) is a borderline case of interest representation. Like the corporatist models, it abrogates the free mandate to deliberate and accepts merely delegates of their *mandatants* (on Rittinghausen and *gouvernement simple* see Rosanvallon 2000: 157–173 and on the workers' candidates Rosanvallon 1998: 67–86).

The Paris Commune of 1871 took a further step against representation by rejecting the distinction between legislative and executive powers, which was claimed to be an advantage by Marx (1966 [1871]), among others. The commune model not only operated with the imperative mandate and revocation of the delegates by electors but also rejected the principle of responsibility by denying the very distinction between the parliament and the government. Furthermore, the commune was the model for the anarchist critique of parliamentary deliberation and representation (see e.g., Leverdays 1883).

A combination of the principles of the commune model with the Russian legislation against trade unions lies behind the soviet type of representation, which arose within the context of the 1905 Revolution in Russia. Developed out of strike committees, the soviets were based on industrial workplace representation, thus rehabilitating the Burkean 'congress of ambassadors' on a proletarian basis. The 'bourgeois' members in the workplace lost their vote on the same sort of grounds, as other opponents of universal suffrage excluded some sections of the population from the electorate, but with different categories of persons targeted (see Anweiler 1958). In the German Revolution of 1918–19 not only workers and soldiers but also farmers and officials had their own *Räte*. In the Bolshevik Revolution, the soviets were instrumentalized, and revocation and the purge of the 'bourgeois' were used against the opponents of the Bolsheviks. Left-wing communists, such as Otto Rühle (1970 [1924]), developed non-partisan soviets – *Arbeiterunionen* – in which deliberation and negotiation were also strongly rejected.

A common feature of all anti-parliamentary models is the tendency to base delegation on some allegedly 'natural' grounds that are beyond the choice of individuals, leaving nothing to deliberate in a parliament. The decisions are assumed to be based on the 'authentic experiences' of the delegates, and like expert bodies, such assemblies prefer acclamation to voting (cf. Schmitt 1970 [1928]). The epideictic acclamation model is exemplified in the pre-1918 Prussian-type government by officials, which excluded parliamentarians from government and governed without responsibility to the Reichstag (see the criticism of Weber 1988 [1918]).

The presidentialism of the Constitution of the United States (1789) for its part relies on 'checks and balances' and excludes parliamentary responsibility and sovereignty of the Westminster type. The Congress tends to understand itself narrowly as a legislature, not as a parliament. Epideictic rhetoric characterizes the presidential elections and the president's disputes with the Congress; for example, regarding his powers as commander-in-chief. The Congress has, however, a number of indirect parliamentary means to control the administration (see Kronlund 2013).

Restricting parliamentary sovereignty and favouring epideictic rhetoric at the cost of deliberative rhetoric exist in a semi-plebiscitarian regime, such as the Swiss system that has been in force since the mid-nineteenth century. Important parliamentary decisions must be ratified in a referendum, and this has, for example, made Switzerland the last European country to enfranchise women. Citizens' initiatives, which require one hundred thousand signatures, may also raise items onto the political agenda, which are finally decided in a referendum and not by parliament.

Common to expert decisions, referenda and presidential elections is the situation in which a given agenda excludes further deliberation and limits the vote to yes or no – to acclamation or rejection. The Swedish referendum on nuclear power in 1980 that allowed three alternatives is a notorious example that brought a non-conclusive result.

The deliberative practice of parliamentary procedures and the status of the parliamentarians as representatives both make the free mandate the core principle of parliamentary politics. Free speech, free and fair elections and parliamentary immunity also link representation and delegation closely together (on their origins see Hexter 1992). The lack of a government's responsibility to the parliament, a directly elected president and plebiscitary limits to parliamentary sovereignty prioritize epideictic rhetoric over deliberative. Constitutional courts also limit parliamentary powers of deliberation (for a critique, see for example Tomkins 2005).

The Historical Momentums of Parliamentarism across Europe

In the chapters on political theory, five examples of the parliamentarization of politics, its origins, obstacles and specific forms are presented in the form of five case studies. The studies presuppose the underlying constitutional and political histories as common knowledge and discuss how parliamentary politics has been conceptualized in their context. This section on the momentums of parliamentarization relies on these chapters, and it occasionally contains further speculation and links to the other chapters of the book.

The Westminster parliament is treated above by Paul Seaward and Pasi Ihalainen as the English/British version of parliament (Chapter 2). In this section, it serves rather as an historical approximation of the parliamentary ideal type of political action. From the point of view of political theory, the formation of a distinct parliamentary vocabulary with procedural instruments and practices distinguishes the Westminster parliament as a deliberative assembly from its predecessors and competitors. The procedure supports a parliamentary form of deliberative rhetoric. Many of the parliamentary concepts and procedural instruments were developed in the sixteenth and seventeenth centuries and the extension of their range of application was coordinated by John Hatsell's codifying work in the eighteenth century (see Palonen 2012).

The reforms of the nineteenth century, extending the basis of representation and enabling the government's responsibility to parliament, challenged parliamentary politics by increasing the amount and scope of the agenda items and the number of debaters. The tradition of a fair debate supported the parliamentarians' status as representatives, rather than mere delegates. Walter Bagehot's view of a responsible 'cabinet government' regards the core of a debating polity in general as lying in the parliamentary control of government. The increasing pressure on parliamentary time tended to reduce the responsibility to the parliament to a governmental technique, but in the British context new practices related to the fair distribution of parliamentary time made it possible to maintain and reinvigorate a political culture of deliberating pro et contra. Furthermore, the debates on parliamentary principles not only applied British parliamentary concepts and procedural instruments but also served as a model for other parliaments.

The momentum of the French Revolution for the political theory of parliamentarism is ambiguous. Certain aspects of procedure and debate cultures were adopted from Westminster (see Urbinati 2006, Roussellier 2005 and Gunn 2009), but Jeremy Bentham's *Tactics*, written for the French assembly, was viewed with suspicion, although it later became a well-known and widely translated document (see Bentham 1999 [1843]). What was not adopted in the French parliamentary culture was the Westminster principle of parliamentary sovereignty; rather the parliament was subordinated to the 'sovereignty of the people' (see e.g., Rosanvallon 1994 and 1998). This means, among other things, the priority of representation over deliberation, of the *nation une et indivisible* over debate pro et contra and a dissensus between perspectives as a condition of debate on items on the agenda and the fact that representatives are rather seen as delegates, *députés* (see Urbinati 2011).

The parliamentary traditions in Spain, Italy and Germany have been inspired by both French and British models, and conflicts between these are, as discussed in the articles of this volume, an inherent part of political debates in all three countries. For example, Gottfried Cohen (1861) criticized the tendency of the newly established German parliaments to follow the French rather than the British practice in their procedure and explained the Westminster practices to the German audience.

The contrast between parliamentary and anti-parliamentary politics has dominated Spanish politics for two hundred years. The Cadiz Constitution of 1812 replaced the old *Cortes* of the estates, but the traditionalist and corporative ideas of representation were re-activated after 1848 as well as in the dictatorships of the twentieth century. The parliamentarization of royal powers in 1837 was only partially successful, although parliamentary oratory played a crucial role in nineteenth-century Spanish politics. The restoration after the short-lived republic in 1874 managed to transmit the legacy of parliamentarism to the twentieth century, although it was criticized for corruption and party government.

In Italy, the criticism of the French Revolution aroused suspicions about parliamentarism and democracy in republican (Sismondi) and liberal (Rosmini) theories. The short-lived Roman Republic of 1848 was an exception, whereas the octroyed Savoyan Statuto Albertino was interpreted as either a constitutional or a parliamentary monarchy. Republicans such as Mazzini were opposed to parties as entities of antagonism, and Cavour's government used various means to get rid of the procedural constraints of parliamentarism. Various kinds of suspicion of parties and their divisive effects also characterize later parliamentarians and scholars, such as Orlando, Minghetti and Mosca, illustrating their indebtedness to the Francophone parliamentary culture. The traditions of anti-liberalism and anti-parliamentarism created legitimacy for the doctrine of a populist or mass democracy that gained support in Italy after the First World War.

Parliamentarism in Germany has likewise been the focus of political debate ever since the Revolution of 1848. However, proponents of parliamentarism, such as Mohl, Bernstein and Weber, all of them admirers of the Westminster type of parliamentarism, were for a long time a marginal minority. Nevertheless, adult male suffrage was established as a principle of representation on the national level in 1866, although different devices to replace both this form of suffrage and the Reichstag as the parliament were developed by right-wing politicians. Socialist thinkers' ambivalence towards parliamentarism has remained strong from the days of Marx down to the extra-parliamentary opposition of the 1960s, with Johannes Agnoli as its main theorist (see also Greven 2011). Striking similarities can be found in the identitarian structure of argumentation among anti-parliamentarians of the left and the right, such as Rosa Luxemburg and Carl Schmitt.

The momentum of parliamentarism under democratic conditions after the First World War (see Gusy 2008) was also followed in Germany and Italy, although under strong challenges from both traditional and new forms of anti-parliamentarism from the right as well as from the soviet model from the left. The Weimar Constitution also contains strong reservations about 'parliamentary absolutism' and includes an element of the U.S. type of presidentialism. In Spain, the momentum arrived only with the Second Republic of 1931. However, the 'revolutionary parliamentary democracy' failed to get anarchists, communists and socialists to support these principles.

In the post-war era, it is remarkable that the Italian revival of parliamentarism used to some extent the short-lived Roman Republic of 1848 as a model. In the German Basic Law of 1949 there are some interesting instruments intended to prevent the 'return of Weimar', in particular the principle of a constructive vote of non-confidence. Gerhard Leibholz's theory of *Parteienstaat* sees the stability of government as more important than the parliamentary freedom of the members.

Little theorization of parliamentarism was conducted in the post-war 're-parliamentarization' of politics in countries such as Germany, Italy or Austria, and this might be one reason why the parliamentary control of government and administration, strongly supported by Bagehot and Weber, has only marginally been on the agenda of debates about parliamentarism in those countries in the post-war period.

The same holds true for the second wave of re-parliamentarization, namely the end of authoritarian dictatorships in Greece, Portugal and Spain. The Spanish post-Franco constitution of 1978 is an example that has successfully legitimized parliamentarism and democracy, despite the fact that this has perhaps taken place at the expense of avoiding debate on the political costs of the preceding dictatorship.

International organizations, such as the League of Nations and the International Labour Organization, have had their own consultative parliamentary assemblies ever since the First World War. The European Parliament's origins were modest, and pro-parliamentary federalists lost the battle to the 'unionists', who stressed the primacy of the executive and intergovernmental structures. However, renaming the EEC Assembly as the European Parliament, the establishment of direct elections to it in 1979 and the treaties from Maastricht to Lisbon have strengthened its powers. Even so, the EU is far from sovereign or possessing a government responsible to the parliament, and aspects of presidentialism and executive federalism persist. Nonetheless, the control of the EP over other EU organs and its legislative powers over national parliaments has grown, and more recently the EP has exploited its parliamentary legitimacy in taking a stand on issues that are formally outside its remit.

Today all radical alternatives to parliamentarism have lost their legitimacy in Europe, although the powers and practices of parliament as an institution continue to be disputed. Disgust with parliamentary democracy has produced suggestions for supplementing election- and party-based parliaments with other forms of representation, new ways of controlling the representatives, elections by lottery or institutional occasions for citizens' deliberation (see Rosanvallon 2006; Brito Vieira and Runciman 2008; Hansen 2008; Buchstein 2009). The worth of such institutions remains contested. The jargon of 'deliberative democracy' fails to recognize the parliamentary procedure of debating as an historical paradigm of deliberation. The form of parliamentary sovereignty in which the citizens can be regarded as parliamentarians on the election day (Palonen 2010) also offers a reform perspective. The question remains: How does one create new occasions for citizens to engage in debating in parliamentary-style deliberative assemblies?

References

Primary Sources

Bentham, J. 1999 [1843]. *Political Tactics*. M. James, C. Blamires and C. Pease-Watkin (eds). Oxford: Clarendon Press.

Cohen, G. 1861. *Die Verfassung und Geschäftsordnung des englischen Parlaments mit Hinweis auf die Geschäftsordnungen deutscher Kammern.* Hamburg: Perthes-Besser & Mauke. Retrieved from http://books.google.fi/books/about/Die_Verfassung_und_Geschäftsordnung_des.html?id=IiNGAAAAcAAJ&redir_esc=y

Leverdays, E. 1883. *Les Assemblées parlantes. Critique du gouvernement représentatif.* Paris: Marpon et Flammarion.

Marx, K. 1966 [1871]. 'Der Bürgerkrieg in Frankreich', in I. Fetscher (ed.), *Marx-Engels-Studienausgabe IV.* Frankfurt/M: Fischer.

Proudhon, P.-J. 1977 [1865]. *De la capacité politique des classes ouvrières*, I–II. M. Leroy (ed.). Paris: Monde libértaire.

Rittinghausen, M. 1851. *La legislation directe par le people ou la veritable démocratie*. Paris: Librairie phalansterienne. Retrieved from http://books.google.de/books ?id=1Gxbcssy6lEC&printsec=frontcover&hl=de#v=onepage&q&f=false

Rousseau, J.-J. 1966 [1762]. *Du contrat social*. Paris: Garnier-Flammarion.

Rühle, O. 1970 [1924]. *Von der bürgerlichen zur proletarischen Revolution*. Berlin: Blankertz.

Schmitt, C. 1970 [1928]. *Verfassungslehre*. Berlin: Duncker & Humblot.

Weber, M. 1988 [1917]. 'Wahlrecht und Demokratie in Deutschland', in W.J. Mommsen (ed.), *Max-Weber-Studienausgabe* I/15. Tübingen: Mohr, pp. 155–89.

_____. 1988 [1918]. 'Parlament und Regierung im neugeordneten Deutschland', in W.J. Mommsen (ed.), *Max-Weber-Studienausgabe* I/15. Tübingen: Mohr, pp. 202–302.

Secondary Sources

Anweiler, O. 1958. *Die Rätebewegung in Rußland 1905–1921*. Leiden: Brill.

Brito Vieira, M. and D. Runciman. 2008. *Representation*. Cambridge: Polity.

Buchstein, H. 2009. *Demokratie und Lotterie*. Frankfurt/M: Campus.

Collingwood, R.G. 1978 [1939]. *An Autobiography*. Oxford: Clarendon Press.

Greven, M.Th. 2011. *Systemopposition*. Opladen: Barbara Budrich.

Gunn, J.A.W. 2009. *When the French Tried to be British: Party, Opposition and the Quest for Civil Disagreement 1814–1848*. Montreal: McGill-Queens University Press.

Gusy, C. (ed.). 2008. *Demokratie in der Krise. Europa der Zwischenkriegszeit*. Baden-Baden: Nomos.

Haapala, T. 2012. '"That in the Opinion of this House": The Parliamentary Culture of Debate in the Nineteenth-century Cambridge and Oxford Union Societies', Ph.D. dissertation. University of Jyväskylä. https://jyx.jyu.fi/dspace/bitstream/ handle/123456789/40560/978-951-39-4970-9.pdf?sequence=1

Hansen, M.H. 2008. 'Direct Democracy, Ancient and Modern', in K. Palonen, T. Pulkkinen and J.M. Rosales (eds), *The Ashgate Research Companion to the Politics of Democratization in Europe: Concepts and Histories*. Farnham: Ashgate, pp. 37–54.

Hexter, J.H. (ed.). 1992. *Parliament and Liberty*. Stanford: Stanford University Press.

Kronlund, A. 2013. 'Parliamentary Oversight of the Exceptional Situations in a Presidential System: Debating the Reassertion of the Constitutional Powers of the US Congress', Ph.D. dissertation. University of Jyväskylä. https:// jyx.jyu.fi/dspace/bitstream/handle/123456789/41511/978-951-39-5219-8_ vaitos25052013.pdf?sequence=1.

Palonen, K. 2010. 'The Parliamentarisation of Elections', *Redescriptions* 14: 133–56.

_____. 2012. 'Towards a History of Parliamentary Concepts', *Parliaments, Estates and Representation* 32(2): 123–38.

Rosanvallon, P. 1994. *La monarchie impossible. Les Chartes de 1814 et 1830*. Paris: Fayard.

_____. 1998. *Le people introuvable*. Paris: Gallimard.

_____. 2000. *La démocracie inachevée*. Paris: Gallimard.

_____. 2006. *La contre-démocratie*. Paris: Seuil.

Roussellier, N. 2005. 'The Political Transfer of English Parliamentary Rules in the French Assemblies (1789–1848)', *European Review of History* 12(2): 239–48.

Tomkins, A. 2005. *Our Republican Constitution*. Oxford: Hart.

Urbinati, N. 2006. *Representative Democracy: Concepts and Genealogy*. Chicago: University of Chicago Press.

_____. 2011. 'Representative Democracy and its Critics', in S. Alonso, J. Keane and W. Merkel (eds), *The Future of Representative Democracy*. Cambridge: Cambridge University Press.

Kari Palonen, Dr.Pol.Sc., is Professor of Political Science and Director of the Finnish Centre of Political Thought and Conceptual Change at the Department of Social Sciences and Philosophy at the University of Jyväskylä, Finland. Palonen has twice been an Academy of Finland Professor. He is the Editor of the journal *Redescriptions*. In his research he focuses on the history of politics as a concept, the methods of conceptual history and the political theory, rhetoric and conceptual history of parliamentarism.

Chapter 14

Thinking of Politics in a Parliamentary Manner

Perspectives on the Conceptual History of Parliamentarism

Kari Palonen

'Parliamentary politics' in this chapter refers to an ideal typical way of thinking and acting politically. In this sense, much of what 'takes place in parliaments' is not parliamentary, and the parliamentary form of politics can also be practised outside parliaments. The conceptual history of parliamentarism refers, accordingly, to the history of the ideal type, as a judgment of the parliamentary inventions and revisions of current practices.

In post-Second World War studies, 'parliamentarism' has frequently been reduced to the government's responsibility to the parliament in the minimal sense of the absence of non-confidence. This view allows the government to monopolize the parliamentary initiative and tends to reduce the parliament's role to one of ratification, to that of a 'rubber stamp' (see e.g., Soininen 2008). Instead of writing a genealogy of this parody of parliamentary realities, I intend to discuss the multifaceted character of parliamentarism by using mainly British examples as historically relevant ways of actualizing different aspects of parliamentary politics.

To each of the parliamentary dimensions – deliberation, representation, responsibility and sovereignty – we can construct counterpositions. The deliberative parliament is opposed by the silent, merely voting assembly and by one that reduces speaking to the rhetorical genres of applauding, jurisdiction or negotiation. Parliamentary representation contrasts with the delegate status of members, based on an imperative mandate or its surrogates, and by non-representative assemblies. The parliamentary responsibility of the government is opposed to procedures for electing and dismissing the government independently of a parliamentary majority. A parliament that lacks sovereignty may be one that has merely consultative powers or one whose decisions can be vetoed by the head of the state, a court or the electorate in a referendum or a superior parliament.

According to these criteria, it is obvious that it is in the Westminster parliament where most of the parliamentary innovations have first taken place. The Provisions of Oxford in 1258 regularized parliamentary practices: as Reginald Francis Treharne (1970 [1959]: 84) puts it: 'What had hitherto been merely an occasion was converted into a political institution, and a vague, untechnical colloquialism became a clearly defined and precise constitutional term'. In this line lies the regularization of Parliament, fought for in the struggles with the Tudor and Stuart kings, and affirmed in the Triennial Acts of 1641 and 1694 (see also Chapters 2 and 9 in this volume). After the Glorious Revolution, annual parliaments that regulated the country's finances became the rule. A further step in this direction was the doctrine of parliamentary sovereignty, first expounded by Blackstone (1753) and classically formulated by A.W. Dicey: 'The principle of Parliamentary sovereignty means neither more nor less than this, namely, that Parliament thus defined has, under the English constitution, the right to make or unmake any law whatever; and, further, that no person or body is recognised by the law of England as having a right to override or set aside the legislation of Parliament' (1961 [1885]: 39–40).

The free mandate for deliberation distinguishes a parliament from assemblies representing estates, soviets and corporative bodies. J.G. Edwards (1970 [1934]: 142) links it to taxation, representation and the full powers of Parliament during the years 1283–97 (see Post 1980 [1943]; Müller 1966). The free mandate was complemented with other forms of parliamentary freedom, namely free speech, free elections, and freedom from arrest (see Hexter 1992). Parliamentary freedom relates to the antithesis between freedom and dependence as a criterion of both deliberation and representation (see Skinner 2006 on the Levellers' criteria of a 'free man').

Procedure as a Criterion of Parliamentary Politics

A condition for parliamentary deliberation and freedom of the members lies in the formation of a distinct parliamentary procedure. For Thomas Smith, the parliamentary debate follows the Renaissance deliberative rhetoric of arguing in utramque partem. 'In the disputing is a mervelous good order used in the lower house . . . as he that speaketh with the bill, or he that spake against the bill, and gave this and this reason, [dothe not satisfie but I am of the contrary opinion for this and this reason.] And so with perpetuall Oration not with altercation, he goeth through till he do make an end' (Smith 1583: II.2). The notion of 'order' is here used in the distinct parliamentary sense of deliberating the item from opposite points of view following the rules of procedure.

In the seventeenth century, several detailed procedural tracts were published, based on a closer documentation of parliamentary records and arising out of the struggle with the Stuart kings. Henry Scobell, a Clerk of Parliament, distinguishes between parliamentary and unparliamentary speeches and gives priority to procedural questions of order: 'During any Debate, any Member . . . may rise up and speak to the Orders of the House, if they be transgressed' (Scobell 1656: 30–31). This illustrates a strong sense of parliamentary self-understanding. The deliberative dimension of parliamentary politics is deeply embedded in the procedure. The formation and extension of the procedural style of parliamentary politics provides a condition for free and fair deliberations that both in principle submit every motion to a confrontation with alternatives and regulate the debates between members and their parliamentary moves (see Palonen 2012).

The proceduralization of parliamentary deliberations created a vocabulary that included both new terms for parliamentary usages and gave concepts such as 'motion', 'amendment' and 'Speaker' a specific parliamentary sense. These intra-parliamentary concepts refer to parliamentary manners of proceeding in general and of conducting and regulating debates in particular. They form an inventory that the members have to learn in order to participate in the debates. I have divided the types of intra-parliamentary concepts into those that concern motions, order, time and the agenda, each of them having specific histories of their own at Westminster; for example, the term 'question' has had different parliamentary nuances at different stages of parliamentary history (Palonen 2012).

John Hatsell, a Clerk of Parliament, codified the parliamentary procedure and regularized the vocabulary in four volumes (1779–96, re-edited in 1818). The fair procedure of debating also protected Parliament against the government. Hatsell quotes a former Speaker, Arthur Onslow: 'That the forms of proceeding, as instituted by our ancestors, operated as a check and controul on the actions of Ministers; and that they were, in many instances, a shelter and protection to the minority, against the attempts of power' (Hatsell 1818 [1781]: 237). For Onslow and Hatsell, sticking to the procedure in itself guarantees the parliamentary character of the activities.

Jeremy Bentham's *Essay on Political Tactics* criticizes the conceptual and temporal non-separation of procedural items in French provincial assemblies in contrast to Westminster. Bentham offers an inventory of questions that can be presented on the parliamentary agenda as well as historical examples of controversies over the interpretation of parliamentary procedure itself. For example, he presents the following parliamentary 'evils': '1. Inaction. 2. Useless decision. 3. Indecision. 4. Delays. 5. Surprise or precipitation. 6. Fluctuations in measures. 7. Quarrels. 8. Falsehoods. 9. Decisions, vicious on account of form. 10. Decisions, vicious in respect of their foundation' (Bentham 1843: I.2 – no pagination in the Liberty Fund online edition). In this manner, he identifies the topics of procedural controversies: parliamentarians may judge existing regulations by these general principles, confront a rule with a principle or discuss which rule is relevant to the case in question. Josef Redlich (1905: 777–803) found in Bentham's *Tactics* the 'theory' of nineteenth-century Westminster procedure.

In his *Treatise*, Thomas Erskine May created the standard work of Westminster procedure, regularly updated from 1844 to the present. After the parliamentary reform of 1832, the number of items on the agenda multiplied and at the same time the loquacity of the members grew enormously, which put pressure on parliamentary time. For May, the main question was to retain the deliberative character of parliament under such conditions. He set the following criteria for the free and fair distribution of parliamentary time: 'That the debates upon each question shall be relevant and orderly – free from intemperance and personalities – fairly distributed among the Members who may be desirous of speaking and (so far as may be practicable) not unmanageable from their length, frequency, or repetition' (May 1854: 9). A fair redistribution requires a reorganization of debates: 'To limit the occasions for debate, without restricting its freedom; to discourage irregularities, in order to increase the opportunities for grave discussion; to organise the vast resources of Parliament, so as to diminish the labour and increase the efficiency of its deliberations – these are the ends to be accomplished' (May 1854: 46–47). In other words, May preferred to have thorough debates concentrated into the few situations provided for them.

May connected the 1882 reform of parliamentary procedure to rescuing parliamentary government and fair debate from the detrimental effects of obstruction resulting from the conditions of scarce parliamentary time. 'But in agreeing to these rules, the House clearly aimed at the correction and restraint of acknowledged abuses, without interfering with fair debate, or legitimate methods of opposition. A serious attempt has been made to rescue parliamentary government from its threatened paralysis' (May 1883: 384–85). He wanted to protect the House of Commons from its members' tendency to misuse the possibilities for parliamentary action by a fair distribution of parliamentary time. This should not, however, restrict the political imagination of members in interpreting the procedure. On the contrary, he admits: 'An ingenious orator may break through any rules, in spirit, and yet observe them to the letter' (May 1883: 367–68).

Bentham and May recognized that the Westminster procedure was inherently controversial with regard to which rules should be followed and how. The ability to initiate disputes over procedure has remained the main power share (in the Weberian sense of *Machtanteil*) of both oppositions and individual members against governments. In this sense the procedure serves as a guarantee of the possibility for a fair debate and the independence of the members.

Gilbert Campion, a twentieth-century Clerk of Parliament, insists on fair play as an underlying principle of parliamentary procedure and debate. Examples of its presence are 'the rules about motion . . . the rule which forbids an attack upon a Member unless he is given an opportunity to reply, or any personal charge being made unless it is explicitly formulated; the rules about notice, which guard against surprise and "slipping through" business' (Campion 1958: 51–52). The vocabulary of fair, fairness and fair play was used several hundred times in the procedural reform debate in the House of Commons in 1882 (see Palonen 2014). Fair play is not merely an ideal of the British political culture: it has been shaped by Parliament itself as a feature of an exemplary deliberative assembly, as a principle of its procedure and an inherent part of the rhetorical practice of debating.

The Parliamentary Variety of Deliberative Rhetoric

The Westminster procedure created specific conditions for parliamentary speaking and used Parliament as a basis for a new paradigm of deliberative eloquence, based on the rhetoric of debate. A major document focusing on the specific rhetoric of parliamentary debate in Westminster is William Gerard Hamilton's *Parliamentary Logick*, a collection of parliamentary maxims (published posthumously in 1808). Hamilton, who was an MP from 1754 to 1796, elucidated parliamentary dissensus as follows: 'The very nature of a disputable question is where some thing plausible or probable may be said on both sides' (Hamilton 1927 [1808]: 15). There were no indisputable motions: 'In the support of every principle and every measure there will be some excellencies and some defects; and their comparative merit, not their perfection, is the real question' (Hamilton 1927 [1808]: 60). For him '[r]hetorick is the power or faculty to consider in every subject what is therein contained proper to persuade' (Hamilton 1927 [1808]: 26), in other words, the art of debate. A crucial rhetorical scheme for him was paradiastole: 'Run a vice into a virtue; and vice versa' (Hamilton 1927 [1808]: 26). Hamilton's maxims transferred the dissensual rhetorical culture of the Renaissance to Parliament, and they clearly demonstrate that the parliamentary character of debates had transformed the rhetorical strategies of the members (see also Chapter 9).

Jeremy Bentham also defended the exclusion of written discourses as an advantage of the British parliament, which was also opposed to 'societies of academicians'. He eloquently praises parliamentary debate:

> the principal advantage of a national senate, and of public discussion, arises from that activity of mind, from that energy of feeling, from that abundance of resources, which results from a large assembly of enlightened men who animate and excite each other, who attack without sparing each other, and who, feeling themselves pressed by all the forces of their antagonists, display in their defence powers which were before unknown to themselves. (Bentham 1843: XI.4)

The collections of nineteenth-century parliamentary speech recognize the contemporary parliament as a new paradigm for a deliberative assembly. Thomas Browne argued: 'The Debates in our own Senate will furnish examples of this kind, in no respect inferior to the most admired productions of ancient Greece or Rome' (Browne 1808–10: 42–43). A nostalgia for the great speeches of the late eighteenth-century oratory in contrast with the emphasis on debating is, however, frequently visible in these works (e.g., Kenyon 1889: 43).

After the 1832 reform of parliamentary representation and the transition to a parliamentary government around 1835 (see Andrén 1947), an antiparliamentary reaction arose. Thomas Carlyle's *Latter-day Pamphlets* (1850) is the best-known British anti-parliamentary tract. He turns especially against Parliament's deliberative character: 'Your National Parliament, in so far as it has only that question to decide, may be considered as an enormous National Palaver existing mainly for imaginary purposes'. Deeds, not words, are his message: 'The State does not want vocables, but manly wisdoms and virtues: the State, does it want parliamentary orators, first of all, and men capable of writing books?' (Carlyle 1850). 'Rhetoric' and 'debate' were the main enemies of anti-parliamentarians of all colours.

Obviously replying to Carlyle, John Stuart Mill writes: 'Representative assemblies are often taunted by their enemies with being places of mere talk and "bavardage". There has seldom been more misplaced derision. I know not how a representative assembly can more usefully employ itself than in talk, when the subject of talk is the great public interests of the country' (1991 [1861]: 117). Mill regards talking as an ingenious instrument in the parliamentary control of the governmental business of 'doing': 'Such "talking" would never be looked upon with disparagement if it were not allowed to stop "doing"; which it never would, if assemblies knew and acknowledged that talking and discussion were their proper business' (1991 [1861]: 117). Parliamentary deliberations were especially valuable as interruptions in the government's and administration's business as usual.

Another defence of a deliberative parliament refers to the fact that it permits disputing without violence. According to Henry Grey, it is an achievement of 'Parliamentary Government, that it renders the contests of men for power as little injurious as possible' (Grey 1864: 24). This 'civilising' effect of Parliament on the political contest lies in 'the habit of Parliamentary debates . . . to raise these contests above those of a mere selfish and personal character' (Grey 1864: 35). Grey also defends the seven-year electoral term as 'favourable to its maintaining its proper character, as a deliberative assembly, instead of becoming an assembly of delegates . . . merely expressing the wishes of the several bodies of constituents by whom they are returned' (Grey 1864: 77).

In the twentieth century, the rhetoric of debate remains the focus of parliamentary politics. For example the former Irish parliamentarian John O'Connor Power defends the debating powers of Parliament: 'No man can gain the ear of the House of Commons . . . who is not a debater, no matter how skilful he may be in making an opening statement, or in the exposition of a complicated subject. The life of Parliament as a deliberative assembly, is in its debates' (Power 1906: 8).

Reforms of Parliamentary Representation

As a deliberative assembly, Parliament is based on the individual and equal status of its members, as affirmed in its procedure. Deliberation presupposes a readiness for persuasion by means of speeches, and this opportunity to make them excludes distinctions between parliamentarians. With regard to elections, Westminster has hardly been an ideal typical parliament, for the elections to the House of Commons divided the constituencies into counties, boroughs and universities. Parliament was assumed to represent 'virtually' different 'interests' of the country, not individual citizens.

Free, fair and competitive elections for parliament were rare in the eighteenth century and were based on different interests within a system of patronage (see Chapter 2). After the unsuccessful reform project of 1785 (see for example Steinmetz 1993), suffrage reforms were at the centre of British political debate. Jeremy Bentham argued for a 'virtually universal suffrage' in the name of the general interest and to obviate corruption and other 'mischiefs' based on privileges and vested interests. His model combines 'due dependence towards the constituents' with 'due independence as towards every other person' and excludes 'placemen' (office holders with particular interests) from suffrage. He further temporarily excludes minors and illiterates, remains ambiguous about the suffrage of women, soldiers and sailors and mentions other cases of 'appropriate probity and appropriate intellectual aptitude' (Bentham 1817: III–VII). His model does not necessarily break with interest representation; indeed, it could also be seen as an attempt to universalize it and exclude stagnating privileges.

J.J. Park, referring in his lectures to the Whig principles of the early nineteenth century, was perhaps the first scholar to speak of 'representative democracy' in English (see Park 1832; for uses in pamphlets after the French Revolution, see Ihalainen 2010, esp. 422–23, 428–29). William Gladstone turns the notion of 'capacity', developed by Guizot in France (see Rosanvallon 1992 and Chapter 3 in this volume), into a criterion of inclusion, although with a reservation: 'Every man who is not presumably incapacitated by some consideration of personal unfitness or of political danger is morally entitled to come within the pale of the Constitution' (1864: 19). Gladstone does not regard his 1866 reform proposal as democratic: 'If by democracy is meant . . . disregard of established distinctions of rank, forgetfulness of what our fathers have done for us, indifference or coldness to the grandeur of the inheritance we enjoy, then, gentlemen, I for one, and, I believe, all who I have honour to address, are in that sense enemies of democracy' (1866: 86). John Stuart Mill also well understood that 'this is not a democratic measure . . . It is not a corollary from what may be called the numerical theory of representation. It is required by the class theory, which we all know is the Conservative view of the Constitution' (Hansard, 13 April 1866).

Against Gladstone's proposal, Benjamin Disraeli defended the 'English' principle of representation for the 'House of Commons' and not the 'House of the People', representing different 'interests' and 'elements' but not 'numbers' in the House of Commons debate (Hansard, 27 April 1867). The following year Disraeli, as the minister responsible for the proposal, supported the vote for 'compound householders', which extended the franchise more than Gladstone's reform bill but did not break with the interest principle.

Robert Lowe transfers the ancient fears against 'democracy' to the principle of representation by referring to what he had learnt at Oxford in the 1830s about democracy as both 'a form of government in which the poor, being many, governed the whole country' (1867: 130) and a regime of flatterers: 'It is an old observation that every Democracy is in some respects similar to Despotism. As courtiers and flatterers are worse than despots themselves, so those who flatter and fawn upon the people are generally very inferior to the people, the objects of their flattery and adulation' (Lowe 1867: 150–51). James Bryce parodies the practice of the reform adversaries 'to call Plato and Aristotle as witnesses against democracy' as an expression of not understanding the distinction between direct and representative democracy (Bryce 1867: 252).

Opposed concepts of liberty were manifested in the 1866 suffrage debate. For Lowe, any form of government intervention always entailed 'a heavy sacrifice of individual liberty' (Lowe 1867: 9). For Gladstone the suffrage proposal contained a republican element: '[A]n immense value there is in the extension of the franchise for its own sake. Liberty is a thing which is good not merely in its fruits, but in itself' (Gladstone 1866: 59). John Bright supports the republican view by comparing the situation of the voteless men in Britain with that of the Russians: '[T]hose 84 [percent] might as well live in Russia, where there is no electoral system of parliament, or in those other countries, now very few indeed, in which Parliaments and representations are unknown' (Bright 1866: 29).

Political liberty was also prominent in debates on the enfranchisement of women, in which both the inclusion and the dependence argument were used. In the House of Commons, John Stuart Mill moved an amendment to Disraeli's Reform Bill, Clause 4 (Occupation Franchise for Voters in Counties): 'Amendment proposed, in page 2, line 16, to leave out the word "man," in order to insert the word "person," – (Mr. Mill,) – instead thereof' (Hansard, Committee of the Whole House, 20 May 1867). Mill's inclusion argument was 'to propose an extension of the suffrage which can excite no party or class feeling in this House'. He sees the absolute exclusion of women as a 'solitary case' in the British Constitution, leaving them without any chance to vote: '[N]either birth, nor fortune, nor merit, nor exertion, nor intellect, nor even that great disposer of human affairs, accident, can ever enable any woman to have her voice counted in those national affairs which touch her and hers as nearly as any other person in the nation' (Hansard, 17 May 1867).

The argument of dependence is not touched on in Mill's speech (unlike in Mill 1991 [1861]: 190–95, in which he is indebted to his wife, Harriet Taylor). Taylor's article 'The Enfranchisement of Women' refers to the inclusion of women, 'their admission, in law and in fact, to equality in all rights, political, civil, and social, with the male citizens of the community' (Taylor 1851: 289). However, the main point of her argument is that 'the worship of the custom is a declining idolatry' (Taylor 1851: 293–94). She compares the enfranchisement of women with other breaks with dependence:

> It [the world] is only now getting rid of monarchical despotism. It is only now getting rid of hereditary feudal nobility. It is only now getting rid of disabilities on the ground of religion. It is only beginning to treat any men as citizens, except the rich and a favoured portion of the middle class. Can we wonder that it has not yet done as much for women? (Taylor 1851: 294–95)

The enfranchisement of women was above all an unheard-of form of empowerment that would treat women, like other voters, as independent individuals.

The republican concept of liberty against dependence could be used for two opposing purposes. The Levellers used it in the 1640s as an argument against the enfranchisement of the dependent (see Woodhouse 1992 [1938] and Skinner 2006). Taylor, by contrast, regarded suffrage as a means to end other forms of dependence. The general question was whether enfranchisement was an appropriate means to end dependence or whether the status of independence must rather be a precondition of receiving the vote. Monks or soldiers might not be able to get rid of their situation of dependence with a vote, but the situation was different with the status of women.

For Mill, parliament was a government-controlling power (Mill 1991 [1861]: 97). The main dangers for a representative government were 'the low grade of intelligence among the representative body' and 'class legislation on the part of the numerical majority' (Mill 1991 [1861]: 144). Mill's remedy lay in the proportional representation that Thomas Hare had proposed (155–62), in literacy as a condition of enfranchisement (175) and in plural voting in non-plutocratic forms (181–86). The philosophical radicals campaigned against secret voting in the 1830s, but the late Mill turned against the 'Australian ballot': 'Exactly in proportion as the vote of the elector is determined by his own will . . . his position is similar to that of a member of Parliament, and publicity is indispensable' (Mill 1991 [1861]: 218; see Buchstein 2000). Mill takes the parliamentarian as a paradigm and regards the voter as if he were a member of parliament on the election day.

Parliamentary Government: Responsibility and Debate

The irreversible transition to the responsibility of the government to Parliament took place in Britain after the 1832 Reform Act. The main theorist of the British parliamentary 'cabinet government' is Walter Bagehot with his *English Constitution* (1867–72). The term 'cabinet' refers to the 'inner circle' of the government, which had existed unofficially since the eighteenth century. For Bagehot, '[t]he cabinet is . . . a board of control chosen by legislature out of persons whom it trusts and knows, to rule the nation' (Bagehot 2001 [1867–72]: 10). While, formally, the cabinet was a committee of Parliament, it could actually dissolve Parliament. In contrast to regimes based on the separation of powers, the English system was marked by a 'fusion' between legislative and executive power (Bagehot 2001 [1867–72]: 11).

For Bagehot, the cabinet system replaced the 'old opposition' between Parliament and government by the divide between the cabinet and opposition in parliament, 'the great school of popular instruction and political controversy' (Bagehot 2001 [1867–72]: 14). 'The nation is forced to hear both sides – all sides, perhaps, of all that what it is concerned' (ibid.). A crucial point is that the ministers could remain parliamentarians (Bagehot [1867–72] 2001: 18–19) and the 'House of Commons is an electoral chamber' (Bagehot [1867–72] 2001: 94), an assembly that elects and dismisses cabinets.

Bagehot was convinced of the link between a cabinet government and a debating parliament, as opposed to a presidential government. He writes: 'The distinguishing quality of parliamentary government is, that in each stage of a public transition there is a discussion; that the public assist at this discussion; that it can, through parliament, turn out an administration which is not doing as it likes, and can put in an administration which will do as it likes' (Bagehot 2001 [1867–72]: 223). In *Physics and Politics*, he speaks about the break with custom and the 'change from the age of status to the age of choice', including 'government by discussion' (Bagehot 1956 [1872]: 115).

Later authors on parliamentary government were less sure than Bagehot on the link between a parliamentary government and a deliberative assembly. The reduction of a parliament with a stable majority government into a ratifying and applauding assembly became one of the unintended consequences of the cabinet system. The obstruction campaigns led finally to giving the government a quasi-monopoly of parliamentary initiative (see Redlich 1905). Stricter party organization and cabinet discipline also tended to threaten the free mandate and the deliberative character of Parliament. Giving the government a monopoly of the parliamentary initiative would be pernicious 'both because it extinguishes the emulation of those whom it reduces to merely a negative part, and because it may retain the greatest talents in a state of inaction', as Bentham put it (1843: ch. VII).

In the twentieth century, many authors have claimed that the government's power over Parliament had continued to grow, restricting parliamentary control to that expressed in elections. Some of the Clerks of Parliament, however, considered that the dangers were overestimated. Courtenay Ilbert did not dramatize the party and constituency dependence: 'A member of parliament . . . is not a mere delegate or mouthpiece; he is a member of a body which is responsible for the interests of the country at large' (Ilbert 1911: 160). Similarly, Gilbert Campion saw that the government monopoly was exaggerated, and, despite stricter regulation of debates, both the opposition and the individual members had found new occasions for debating (Campion 1929: 85–92).

Campion further emphasizes the controlling power of parliamentary questions: 'It is modern and affords a useful method of supervising the administration of the Government' (1929: 124). He also regards May's proposal for the reform of the Westminster committee system as an efficient method of parliamentary scrutiny: '[I]t has aimed at making them miniature Committees of the Whole House, with a shifting rather than permanent personnel, who are not likely to develop a specialist point of view, but rather to judge the matters that come before them much as the House itself would' (Campion 1929: 207). He emphasizes continuity in the debating and controlling powers of Parliament in the course of the democratization of Parliament: 'Parliament has kept more than lost of its original character throughout the transition from seventeenth and eighteenth century aristocracy to twentieth century democracy' (Campion 1953: 11).

The Parliamentary Culture of Politics

In the opinion of the public, in Britain, too, the parliament has lost its central role in the polity. Numerous authors have written on the 'decline' or 'eclipse' (Lenman 1992) of Parliament. Such theses depend on the perspective. If we include the procedural and rhetorical aspects of deliberation in the concept of parliamentarism, the theses of decline can be disputed.

The debate dimension was crucial, for example, for Ivor Jennings, writing during the Second World War: 'The democratic process is a process of constant argument over different opinions. The House of Commons begins the public debate which is carried on by the weekly journals of opinion and the monthly reviews. From there it percolated into the leading articles and thence into the railway carriage, the factory and the office' (Jennings 1941: 65; see also Barker 1942: 206–21; for the views of Laski and Oakeshott, see Soininen 2008). This view of the centrality of the House of Commons no longer appears plausible, but Jenning's debate-centred view of politics indicates the presence of a substrate for a parliamentary type of political culture, which has been strongest in Britain.

In the nineteenth century, James De Mille, a Canadian professor of rhetoric, put the point of parliamentary politics in a nutshell: 'The aim of parliamentary debate is to investigate the subject from many points of view which are presented from two contrary sides. In no other way can a subject be so exhaustively considered' (1878: 473). The parliamentary deliberation pro et contra is both a methodological principle of a rhetorical vision of knowledge for which the consideration of opposed perspectives is a condition for understanding the question at all, and a principle of political judgment for weighing the alternatives in a debate based on parliamentary procedure.

Max Weber formulated the same point in his procedural revision of the concept of 'objectivity' into a principle that in the human sciences the controversy between opposed perspectives – '*daß es um die regulativen Wertmaßstäbe selbst* gestritten *werden kann und* muß' (Weber 1973 [1904]:

153) – forms the very core of understanding (see Palonen 2010). Here the procedure of the British parliament serves as a model for the rhetorical means of parliamentary control of the knowledge of officials (Weber 1988 [1918]: 235–48). Defending parliamentarism means above all defending its procedural and debating characteristics.

References

Primary Sources

Bagehot, W. 2001 [1867–72]. *The English Constitution*. Cambridge: Cambridge University Press.

_____. 1956 [1872]. *Physics and Politics*. Boston: Beacon Press.

Barker, E. 1942. *Reflections on Government*. Oxford: Oxford University Press.

Bentham, J. 1817. 'Plan of Parliamentary Reform', in *Collected Works of Jeremy Bentham*, vol. 3. Retrieved from http://oll.libertyfund.org/title/1922/115261

_____. 1843. 'An Essay on Political Tactics', in *Collected Works of Jeremy Bentham*, vol. 2. Retrieved from http://oll.libertyfund.org/title/1921/113915

Blackstone, W. 1753. *Commentaries on the Laws of England in Four Books*, vol. 1. Retrieved from http://oll.libertyfund.org/simple.php?id=2140

Bright, J. 1866. *Speeches on Parliamentary Reform*. Manchester: Heywood.

Browne, T. 1808–10. *The British Cicero or a Selection of the Most Admired Speeches in the English Language*, vol. 1. Retrieved from http://www.archive.org/stream/britishcicerowi00browgoog

Bryce, J. 1867. 'The Historical Aspect of Democracy', in *Essays on Reform*. London: Macmillan, pp. 239–78.

Campion, G.F.M. 1929. *An Introduction to the Procedure of the House of Commons*. London: Allan & Co.

Campion, G. 1953. 'Parliament and Democracy', in G. Campion et al. (eds), *Parliament: A Survey*. London: Allen & Unwin, pp. 9–36.

_____. 1958. *An Introduction to the Procedure of the House of Commons*. London: Macmillan.

Carlyle, T. 1850. *Latter-day Pamphlets*. Retrieved from http://www.gutenberg.org/dirs/1/1/4/1140/1140.txt

De Mille, J. 1878. *Elements of Rhetoric*. Retrieved from http://www.archive.org/stream/elementsrhetori01millgoog

Dicey, A.W. 1961 [1885]. *An Introduction to the Study of the Law of the Constitution*. London: Macmillan.

Gladstone, W.E. 1864. *Speech of the Chancellor of the Exchequer on the Bill for the Extension of the Suffrage in Towns. 11 May 1864*. London: Murray.

_____. 1866. *Essays on Parliamentary Reform*. London: Murray.

Grey, H.G. 1864. *Parliamentary Government Considered with Reference to Reform*. Retrieved from http://www.archive.org/stream/parliamentarygo00greygoog

Hamilton, W.G. 1927 [1808]. *Parliamentary Logic*, with an Introduction and Notes by Courtney S. Kenny. Cambridge: Heffer.

Hansard 1803–2005, retrieved from http://hansard.millbanksystems.com/

Hatsell, J. 1818 [1781]. *Precedents of Proceedings in the House of Commons; with Observations*. Vol. II. Retrieved from http://www.archive.org/stream/ precedentsofproc02hats

Ilbert, C. 1911. *Parliament, Its History, Constitution and Practice*. Retrieved from http://www.archive.org/stream/parliamentitshis00ilbeiala

Jennings, W.I. 1941. 'Parliament in Wartime IV', *Political Quarterly* 12(1): 53–65.

Kenyon, F.G. 1889. *Comparison of Ancient and Modern Political Oratory*. Oxford: Blackwell.

Lowe, R. 1867. *Speeches and Letters on Reform*. London: Bush.

May, T.E. 1854. *The Machinery of Parliamentary Legislation*. Reprinted from the *Edinburgh Review* of January 1854 with a letter from the author. Retrieved from http://www.archive.org/details/machineryofparli00mayt

———. 1883. *A Treatise on the Law, Privileges, Proceedings and Usage of Parliament*. Retrieved from http://www.archive.org/stream/treatiseonlawpri00maytrich

Mill, J.S. 1991[1861]. *Considerations on Representative Government*. New York: Prometheus Books.

Park, J.J. 1832. *The Dogmas of the Constitution*. London: Fellowes.

Power, J.O. 1906. *The Making of an Orator. With Examples of the Great Masterpieces of Ancient and Modern Eloquence*. New York: Putnam & Sons.

Scobell, H. 1656. *Memorials of the Method and Manner of Proceedings in Parliament in Passing Bills*. Retrieved from http://gateway.proquest.com.ezproxy.jyu.fi/ openurl?ctx_ver=Z39.88-2003&res_id=xri:eebo&rft_id=xri:eebo:image

Smith, T. 1583. *De Republica Anglorum*. Retrieved from http://www.constitution. org/eng/repang.htm

Taylor, H. 1851. 'Enfranchisement of Women', *Westminster and Foreign Quarterly Review* 54: 289–311.

Weber, M. 1973 [1904]. 'Die "Objektivität" sozialwissenschaftlicher und sozialpolitischer Erkenntnis', in *Gesammelte Aufsätze zur Wissenschaftslehre*. Tübingen: Mohr, pp. 146–214.

———. 1988 [1918]. 'Parlament und Regierung im neugeordneten Deutschland', in *Max-Weber-Studienausgabe* I/15. Tübingen: Mohr, pp. 202–302.

Woodhouse, A.S.P. (ed.). 1992 [1938]. *Puritanism and Liberty*. London: Dent.

Secondary Sources

Andrén, N. 1947. *Den klassiska parlamentarismens genombrott i England*. Uppsala: Almqvist & Wiksell.

Buchstein, H. 2000. *Öffentliche und geheime Stimmabgabe*. Baden-Baden: Nomos.

Edwards, J.G. 1970 [1934]. 'The Plena Potestas of English Parliamentary Representatives', in E.B. Fryde and E. Miller (eds), *Historical Studies of the English Parliament*: vol. 1, *Origins to 1399*. Cambridge: Cambridge University Press, pp. 136–49.

Hexter, J.H. (ed.). 1992. *Parliament and Liberty*. Princeton: Princeton University Press.

Ihalainen, P. 2010. *Agents of People: Democracy and Popular Sovereignty in British and Swedish Parliamentary and Public Debates 1734–1800*. Leiden: Brill.

Lenman, B. 1992. *The Eclipse of Parliament*. London: Arnold.

Müller, C. 1966. *Das imperative und freie Mandat*. Leiden: Sifthoff.

Palonen, K. 2010. *'Objektivität' als faires Spiel. Wissenschaft als Politik bei Max Weber*. Baden-Baden: Nomos.

_____. 2012. 'Towards a History of Parliamentary Concepts', *Parliaments, Estates and Representation* 32(2): 123–38.

_____. 2014. 'Fair Play and Scarce Time. Aspects of a Procedure Reform Debate in Westminster in 1882', in K. Palonen, J.M. Rosales and T. Turkka (eds), *The Politics of Dissensus*. Santander and Madrid: Cantabria University Press and McGraw-Hill, pp. 327–348.

Post, G. 1980 [1943]. 'Plena Potestas and Consent in Medieval Assemblies', in H. Rausch (ed.), *Grundlagen der modernen Volksvertung I*. Darmstadt: Wissenschaftliche Buchgesellschaft, pp. 30–114.

Redlich, J. 1905. *Recht und Technik des Englischen Parlamentarismus*. Leipzig: Duncker & Humblot.

Rosanvallon, P. 1992. *Le sacre du citoyen*. Paris: Gallimard.

Skinner, Q. 2006. 'Rethinking Political Liberty', *History Workshop Journal* 61: 56–70.

Soininen, S. 2008. 'Rubber Stamp or a Stage of Debate? Approaches to Parliament in 1930s and 1940s British Political Theory', in S. Soininen and T. Turkka (eds), *The Parliamentary Style of Politics*. Helsinki: The Finnish Political Science Association, pp. 61–81.

Steinmetz, W. 1993. *Das Sagbare und das Machbare*. Stuttgart: Klett-Cotta.

Treharne, R.F. 1970 [1959]. 'The Nature of Parliament in the Reign of Henry III', in E.B. Fryde and E. Miller (eds), *Historical Studies of the English Parliament:* vol. 1, *Origins to 1399*. Cambridge: Cambridge University Press, pp. 70–90.

Kari Palonen, Dr.Pol.Sc., is Professor of Political Science and Director of the Finnish Centre of Political Thought and Conceptual Change at the Department of Social Sciences and Philosophy at the University of Jyväskylä, Finland. Palonen has twice been an Academy of Finland Professor. He is the Editor of the journal *Redescriptions*. In his research he focuses on the history of politics as a concept, the methods of conceptual history and the political theory, rhetoric and conceptual history of parliamentarism.

Chapter 15

Theories of Representative Government and Parliamentarism in Italy from the 1840s to the 1920s

David Ragazzoni and Nadia Urbinati

The history and development of parliamentarism in Italy started in the shadow of the French Revolution. It was beset by one persistent problem, which, with the exception of some isolated intellectuals (principally Carlo Cattaneo, the leader of republican federalism), spanned the entire ideological spectrum: how to avoid and contain the growth and influence of political parties and create a national elite that would be able to overcome factional interests. The Italian history of parliamentarism shows the difficult metabolism of political pluralism and the persistent conviction that healthy politics is defined by concord and consensus rather than accommodation and compromise.

Dissatisfaction with parties took the direction of a strong aversion to the democratic element that parliament embodied since it was based on individual suffrage. Suffrage, it was thought, would open the door to the 'masses' and to social interests in the life of the state, which to both liberal and conservative leaders and scholars alike meant anarchic destabilization. Dilacerating conflicts, it was held, would be the fatal effect of democratization (De Sanctis 1970: 175).

Building National Unity, Countering the Revolution: Representative Government before 1861

Constitution and Representation: In the Shadow of the French Revolution

The legacy of the French Revolution, which in Italy produced both the diffusion of Jacobin republicanism and the welcoming of the Napoleonic conquest (to many Italian intellectuals it meant the liberation from ancien régime powers like the Bourbon Realm of Naples or the Catholic Theocracy of Rome), is the starting point for any meaningful reconstruction of the history of parliamentarism and the idea of representative and constitutional government as a legitimate form of state power. The notion and project of democratic citizenship took root in the years that followed the French Constitution of 1795, the impact of which on Italian political movements of emancipation was profound and easily detectable both in the work of Giuseppe Mazzini and his followers and in the Constitution of the Roman Republic of 1849, to the drafting of which Mazzini himself contributed. Between 1796 and 1799, a rich literature inspired by French revolutionary ideals circulated widely in Italy, aimed at making *libertà, eguaglianza, sovranità popolare, democrazia* and *virtù* the components of a republican popular education (Guerci 1999; for the Neapolitan Revolution, see Rao 2012).

On the one hand, the terms 'democracy' and 'representative democracy' started circulating as synonyms and became the object of a clash of interpretations between revolutionaries and counter-revolutionaries, republicans and moderates. Followers of Jean-Joseph Mounier, Emmanuel-Joseph Sieyès and Jacques Mallet du Pan employed the term 'representative democracy' to mean a moderate regime, implying containment of the popular element, and therefore opposed to 'pure democracy'. The principle of the division of labour served in this case as a justification for the separation within the nation of 'two peoples' – 'the producers' and 'the auxiliaries', the former being a class of citizens who made the laws for all and the latter those who obeyed them (Sieyès 1985: 106, 75; see Bastid 1970). On the other hand, the followers of Condorcet and Brissot turned to political equality as the condition for creating the representation of the nation and insisted on the abolition of the census as a prerequisite of political inclusion, and on the institution of primary assemblies in which the selection of candidates and the discussion on the decisions by the representative assembly could be publicly held. In their opinion, the words 'democracy' and 'representation' had the potential to reconcile broader participation with the parliamentary system.

These French debates had an enormous impact in Italy through the circulation of innumerable pamphlets and 'republican catechisms'. For instance, in an anonymous dissertation titled 'Sul governo che conviene all'Italia' (1796), the author used the terms 'representative democracy' and 'elective aristocracy' interchangeably. He associated this form of government with a constitutional republic as theorized by Gaetano Filangieri and Montesquieu: a moderate government that could remedy the ancient defects of democracy – i.e., anarchy and the potential for the despotism of the assembly. Constitutionalism and representation were thus the invaluable contributions of the French Enlightenment and the Revolution to the renaissance of democratic ideals in Italy. For moderate authors, representative government did not entail universal suffrage based on equal citizenship, but a government to be selected by citizens on the basis of their property and interests. The existing representative governments were in fact aristocratic republics (like Holland, Venice or Switzerland). 'Representative democracy', wrote an Italian republican in 1798, 'not well known by the ancients, is a government in which the people, who are aware of their sovereignty and who exercise it [through suffrage], elect in common *comitia* and assemblies their magistrates and representatives, through whom they govern according to the law established by the general will of the nation' (Ganzetti 1999 [1798]: 421).

Taming Democracy: The Construction of Representative Government and the Rejection of Terror

With the end of the Napoleonic Empire and up until the debacle of the republican and democratic revolution of 1848–49, the Italian debate about the forms of government soon evolved into a debate on the best form of national unification. The implementation of representative government took place in many Italian states in the years between the Congress of Vienna (1815) and the 1848 upheavals. With the exception of the anarchists, who became active only after the unification of the country, the first half of the nineteenth century should be seen as the age of the celebration of representative government with the parliament as its core institution and the constitution as its ordering instrument. Like in France, in Italy, too, Jean-Jacques Rousseau was a symbol of both the trajectory of representative revision and of the endorsement of popular sovereignty and his work served as a starting point for the ideas of moderate and radical thinkers. However, the Terror provoked a wave of reaction against democracy and Rousseau's doctrine of popular sovereignty among both republicans and conservatives. The successful endorsement of representative government by Italian scholars in some Italian states (in particular Sardinia, which was ruled by the Savoy monarchy) occurred within this ideological framework, which was profoundly anti-democratic.

Yet both republican and conservative thinkers argued that the 'obscurantism' of ancien régime politics must be ended, and emphasized their break with the radical interpretation of the principles of the 1789 Revolution. Two examples can elucidate this phenomenon: the republican Simonde de Sismondi and the moderate liberal theologian Antonio Rosmini; as different as they were in many important respects, they proposed to free the idea of good government (whether republican or monarchical) from Rousseau's egalitarian premises. Both of them regarded representative government as the only legitimate form, and their liberal projects met on some important issues, such as the questioning of the myth of popular sovereignty, the rejection of the democratic centrality of legislative power, the proclamation of the priority of private property and the promotion of social pluralism. For Sismondi, 'republicanism' was identical to constitutionalism and an answer to the emergent democratic transformation of society thanks to its ability to moderate equality, divide and bridle popular sovereignty and contain the immoderate and homogeneous propensity of 'assemblearism'. In his view, the modern threat to liberty did not originate from the power of either the few or the one. Instead, it originated both from the power of the many and from the majoritarian principle. Like Hegel, Sismondi thought that it was possible to contain democracy by constitutionalizing social pluralism and opposing individualistic equal suffrage. 'All free governments should give a part of sovereignty to both the ignorant and the learned, and balance each of these two great classes with one another' (Sismondi 1965 [1801]: 131; Sismondi 1847: 289–92).

The target of Sismondi's corporatist republicanism was Rousseau's theory that linked liberty and equality: *La liberté ne peut subsister sans l'égalité* (Rousseau 1964: 391). Sismondi thus revived the classic republican theme of the inability of the people to recognize and want what was in their own best interest, and in consequence the need for some gens éclairs – that is, virtuous, honest and competent political leaders who could channel people's anti-absolutist passions towards constitutional liberty (Sismondi 1965 [1801]: 101; 1815: 49). 'True' liberty consisted in the 'equilibrium of powers, which alone can preserve the constitution and save society from dangerous convulsions' and 'the tyranny of popular assembly' (Sismondi 1965 [1801]: 98; Sismondi 1815: 10). It seemed possible only in a society which, as suggested by Montesquieu, was composed of 'diverse classes' and which 'multiplied' the criteria for the distribution of suffrage (Sismondi 1965 [1801]: 129, 124). Accordingly, the republican Sismondi produced a counterargument against democracy that was no less devastating than the argument made by reactionary and conservative thinkers like Joseph de Maistre and Edmund Burke.

Rosmini's conceptualization of representative government was similar to that of Sismondi. Rosmini restated Burke's dualism between constitutions that are modelled through gradual changes (thus conducive to freedom) and constitutions that are the immediate creation of the will of the people (thus conducive to democracy or tyrannical majoritarianism). According to Rosmini, the objective of constitutionalism should be to emancipate politics from the two radical vices of French-type constitutions: political justice and a notion of property rights that derived from the political constitution rather than existing prior to it. Limiting the power of parliament was the goal of moderate constitutionalism. This could be obtained by adopting bicameralism and ascribing the promulgating power to the sovereign (in order to both temper hastiness and ensure more impartial decisions). As a matter of fact, parliaments represented not the people but the nation, the name of a conglomerate of different interests and classes, as Sismondi, too, had expounded (Rosmini 2007: 5–7). This corporatist interpretation of parliamentary politics was Rosmini's strategy for disassociating representation from popular sovereignty. 'The legislative chambers have the power to discuss and to vote on the laws, which have to be submitted, once a majority in both chambers is obtained, to the ratification of the king, who can grant or refuse his sanction at his discretion' recited one of the articles of Rosmini's constitutional model, the principal argument of which was that parliament had a natural propensity to expand its power since it was the locus of rhetoric – the game of words that demagogues would use to unleash an 'irrational and animal instinct' in the people in order to obtain electoral support (Rosmini 2007: 103–4).

1848–49: Regime Bifurcation

The Radicals and the Roman Republic of 1849: The First Italian Experiment in Representative Democracy

Unitarian republicans and federalist republicans were, perhaps more than the conservatives, conscious of and attentive to the impact of constitutional and representative government on the existing political order, both national and international. Giandomenico Romagnosi, who shared with Sismondi a strong opposition to the French model of the republic, wrote in his masterpiece *La scienza delle Costituzioni* (published posthumously in 1850) that 'the mutual action of foreign states in Europe is ceaseless and is parallel to the birth and the daily life of each of us' (Romagnosi 1850: 478). The construction of states of almost equal power (*egual potenza*) was the condition for a new European order after the decline of the myth of a 'universal monarchy' (Romagnosi 1850: 382).

The Roman Republic of 1849 was the first Italian experiment in representative democracy. It was founded on the ideal of a new international order made of republican governments seeking peace. It also set the basis for modern constitutionalism and would later inspire the members of the Constitutional

Assembly of 1946–47 as for two pivotal concepts: sovereignty as a legitimate force of consent 'springing' from the people and manifesting itself through state institutions (an elected assembly, the executive and the judiciary), and the notion of the people as a collective of electors who enjoyed an equal right to vote. The majority age was the only limit, and for the first time in Italy, women were recognized as equal citizens. (The constitutional text we refer to is available in *Le Costituzioni Italiane* – Acquarone, d'Addio and Negri (eds) 1958: 614–19.) In its short life – just a few weeks – the Republic of Rome shone out as an advanced model of a leaderless parliamentary democracy that was founded on a democratic revolution and had a democratically elected convention in charge of writing the constitution (which was approved unanimously almost on the very same day that the Republic was overthrown by the army of the French Republic). The constitution defined citizenship, set the rules that should govern both social and public relations, proclaimed basic social rights like health care and housing, declared its autonomy from the Church and instituted the rule of law and habeas corpus. Moreover, the Roman Republic committed itself, to paraphrase Immanuel Kant, to respect humanity and peace, domestically and universally, and interpreted 'pure democracy' as a parliamentary form of government based on equal suffrage rights. The outcome of a popular uprising by the people of Rome, this constitution, in the drafting of which an unprecedented number of intellectuals were involved, was regarded by its contemporaries as the actualization of Giuseppe Mazzini's vision of democratic self-determination and the most advanced expression of democracy in modern Europe.

Mazzini's innovations were of paramount importance with regard to eighteenth-century republicanism and concerned the very concepts of government, liberty and society that were part of the republican tradition. Indeed, the theories of political representation and constitutional government that Mazzini inherited were strongly inimical to factions and parties, and yet Mazzini made the republican ideal into a party programme aimed at obtaining an electoral advantage in the political competition. His elaboration took place at a time when parliamentary politics started to shape political languages and goals. Mazzini was with no doubt one of the most important European protagonists of the parliamentary transformation of revolutionary ideals in the years between 1848 and the Commune of Paris (Mastellone 1994: Chapter XIV).

The Monarchical Constitution and the Making of Representative Government

At the other end of the political spectrum, pre-unitary Italy had its first experience of representative government based on a written constitution in the crucial years around 1848. The Statuto Albertino was conceded (*octroyé*) by King Charles Albert of Savoy to his subjects of the Kingdom of Sardinia (Piedmont, Liguria and Sardinia), and it shaped the Italian state until the end of the Fascist regime and the subsequent creation of a democratic constitution in 1946–48. Most importantly, it provides a strategic observation point from which to view some major problems that characterized the evolving trajectory of political representation from a constitutional to a parliamentary monarchy in Italy. The formula 'monarchic representative government' (Art. 2) that was applied to the Kingdom of Sardinia first, and from 17 March 1861 on to the Kingdom of Italy as a whole, neatly summarizes the variety of backgrounds that informed the moderate minds authoring this text (see Ullrich 1999).

The Statuto was neither the creation of a revolutionary, popular constituent power nor the result of a gradual transformation: it was in accordance with neither the French nor the English model. Originally drafted in French and only subsequently translated into Italian (Ullrich 1999: 131, note 5), it was ratified during the rapid development of events in France in January and February 1848 (Negri and Simoni 1989: 399) precisely in order to fight the nightmare of the Revolution (for further details, see Perticone 1960; Ghisalberti 1999: 25–50, 113–28; Rebuffa 2003; Colombo 2003). The design of the Statuto was significantly inspired by the French Charte constitutionnelle of 1830, the Belgian one of 1831 and the contemporary creation of the Tuscan Constitution, and it creatively combined all these models while substantially revising their overall architecture. Ignoring the Spanish Constitution of Cadiz (1812) owing to its strongly progressive features (e.g., restraints on monarchical power, unicameralism, broad suffrage), the Statuto displayed a number of significant French echoes, such as silence about specific procedures of constitutional revision. In particular, the Consiglio di Conferenza, which authored the text, looked at the French constitutional movement on two levels: it identified the source of the constituent power with the person of the king and declared Catholicism 'the only Religion of the State', thus rephrasing the wording of the 1814 Charte. Moreover, the institutional design of 'a full system of representative government' resembled the French Charte of 1830 with regard to the role of the king and his executive power. At the same time, the Statuto differed from the quasi-contemporary republican Roman experiment, since it located the legislative power in 'the king and [the] two chambers' and stipulated that the First Chamber should be composed of lifetime members nominated by the king and the Second be elective 'on the basis of property qualification'.

The Janus-faced nature of the representative government outlined in the Statuto was also reflected in the two diverging interpretations that immediately developed about it. While one stressed its monarchic-constitutional dimension, the other emphasized its monarchic-parliamentary features. The latter, explicitly defended by Cavour, was soon to prevail both in practice and in scholarly debates, highlighting the democratic legitimacy of the elected chamber as a crucial step towards progressive politics at both the institutional and the societal level. At the other end of the spectrum, Cesare Balbo (the first constitutional Prime Minister after the octroi of the Statuto) interpreted the new representative government along the lines of a *monarchia costituzionale pura*. In his 1857 treatise *Della Monarchia Rappresentativa*, he provided an interesting interpretation of the word 'representative', which was not to be confused with 'parliamentary'. Heavily influenced by Benjamin Constant, Balbo feared parliamentary despotism and the passive acquiescence of the king in equal measure: instead, a neutral constitutional throne was expected to minimize the clash between ministerial and assembly claims and to authoritatively embody the superior interest of the state. In this way, he emphasized the unifying role of the monarch against the potential tyranny of the assembly and the traditional threefold division of government branches.

In Europe, the repression of republican and democratic revolutions induced the established regimes to promote anti-constitutional policies. This was not, though, the road taken by the Savoyard monarchy, which maintained the Statuto throughout the complex process of national unification and the wars of independence. However, the hitherto unopposed supremacy of the king was to be progressively reduced in the following decades: the gradual development of a robust parliamentary government confined royal power to the spheres of foreign affairs and the military to a sort of 'enclave of the *monarchia costituzionale* within the *régime parlementaire* of liberal Italy' (Ullrich 1999: 153).

Parliamentarism under Siege

Early Criticism

The legacy of 1848–49 was equivocal. On one hand, Italy had enjoyed an experience of a constitutional regime, republican or monarchical, and the perspective of the unification of the country thanks to the leading role of the Savoy monarchy. On the other hand, the discussion on the form of the unity (whether federal or unitary) and the role of the Church of Rome in the unification process (whether hostile or moderately favourable) did not converge towards a common interpretation. In this climate, the early parliamentary experiment in the Kingdom of Sardinia was accompanied by strong criticisms, some of which were similar to those that would emerge before fascism.

Even before it established itself at the national level, parliamentarism was already under attack.

The most influential voice in this pre-unitary and stormy reception of parliamentary representation was that of Vincenzo Gioberti, a priest and patriot and the author of important texts in which he called for a new Italy made up of a confederacy of states under the hegemony of the Church, a project known as *neo-Guelfismo* (from the pro-papist movement in the medieval communes of early humanism). In his *Del Rinnovamento morale e civile d'Italia* (the edition we quote from is Gioberti 1851), Gioberti argued for the need to rephrase the language of representation and restate the role of parliamentarism. He condemned the predominant haggling behaviour of elected representatives, driven by rhetoric and convenience rather than virtue and intellectual sharpness. Contemporary deliberative assemblies, Gioberti argued, followed the logic of circumstances and lacked any far-sighted vision; they were characterized by a plebiscitarian form of consent manifested, for example, in frequent strategic interruptions, hectic applause and muddled shouting that impeded any systematic discussion of relevant issues and rather resembled the squawking (*uccellare*) of aggressive birds (Gioberti 1851: 283–94). In order to counter such a degeneration, he emphasized the essential contribution of a free press as a source of civic education, for he believed that only when coupled with a sound process of opinion formation through the everyday reading of newspapers across the kingdom could parliamentary representation be sustained and empowered.

With historical and comparative acumen, Gioberti invoked the ancient Roman Senate and the English parliament of his time as positive models of representative government because of their capacity to moderate the passions of the many through the sound political judgment of the few (see Gioberti 1851: 274–76). Moreover, he vehemently criticized the quest for unanimity that often adversely affected parliamentary politics: he defended conflict and dissent as crucial features of any healthy political body, for no agreement could be made without an open clash of ideas. The uncontested unity of deliberative institutions might produce positive outcomes in stormy, revolutionary times, but its achievement should never become either a precondition or a systematic goal of parliamentary activity. To amend what he perceived as the main flaw of legislative assemblies – i.e., their legicentrism – he conceived of parliament as a checking or containing body exercising a 'negative' power of surveillance and suggested a de-structuring of its system into several deliberative bodies within each of the two chambers (cf. Gioberti 1851: 283–94).

The Equivocal Parliamentarism of Cavour

After 1861, the republican understanding of representative government was definitively overthrown by the liberal consolidation of the parliamentary state through the activities of Camillo Benso, Count of Cavour (1810–61; for an extensive overview of the literature on Cavour, see Mack Smith 1957). Although he has been unanimously regarded as the champion of parliamentarism in the transition from a pre-unitary to a unitary Italy, his conceptualization of the role, functions and limits of parliament has never been the topic of systematic attention by the many biographers and scholars who have investigated his diaries and parliamentary speeches (1848–61). An extensive reading of Cavour's *Diaries* shows that his political theory of parliamentarism was highly influenced by European liberalism: from the early 1830s on, he was a voracious reader of seminal authors such as Tocqueville, Constant, Cousin, Smith, Ricardo, McCulloch, Bentham and J.S. Mill, who are often cited in his letters. He also admired the constitutional theory of Pellegrino Rossi, whose lectures at the Collège de France he personally attended, and the unfinished *Histoire du Gouvernement Parlamentaire en France* by Duvergier de Hauranne, one of the leading liberals of the July Monarchy. At the same time, however, his practice of parliamentary politics was inspired by Palmerstone and Gladstone, who together with Peel, Wellington and Grey he pointed out in his parliamentary speeches as a positive example to imitate. (On this discrepancy between the Cavourian theory and practice of parliamentarism and its sources, see Salvadori 2011: 71–111.)

One fear constantly ran through Cavour's overall understanding of representative government: that of the tyranny of factions and the weakening of the 'constitutional throne' under the assault of 'extremist', 'unconstitutional parties' (i.e., reactionary and ultra-democratic ones). Whenever he employed the word 'party' in an institutional context, it was always in a pejorative sense. In his moderate outlook, the partial claims of different political forces by definition conflicted with the radical reforms that were needed. Only one 'party' was tolerable in his eyes: the vast moderate majority of the parliamentary assembly, constantly absorbing the growth of any rival alternative and acting within the boundaries of the Statuto. Thus, he imposed an artificial unity on the parliament and constantly pursued a 'parliamentary alchemy' (Mack Smith 1957: 45) with the specific intention of countering all radical oppositions from clericalism to republicanism. He intentionally used the term 'sect' when viscerally criticizing the Mazzinians and underlining their fanatic devotion to their leader and their lack of any robust political plan (Cavour 1969 [1857–58]: 189–92 [session MCXLIV: 16 April 1858]). For, when 'donning the colours of factions' (Cavour 1932 [1850–51]: 71 [session LVII: 7 March 1850]), no constitutional representative government, he argued, can develop a far-sighted project but only a sequence of small, incomplete and 'homeo-pathic' reforms (Cavour 1932 [1850–51]: 79 [session LVII: 7 March 1850]).

Although Cavour claimed to 'live in a time of publicity and parties' (Cavour 1933 [1851]: 289 [session CLV: 22 April 1851]), he constantly took precautions to disarm any potential antagonism and implement his mono-party idea of parliament. Therefore, following the ever-changing political needs of the moment (a practice that became known as *connubio* (matrimony, union)), he systematically created and dissolved majorities, even resorting to extra-parliamentary means. His inclination for breaking up parliamentary debates, together with his daring, Machiavellian conception of politics, made Cavourian parliamentarism an early and contested example of charismatic leadership. His faith in the crucial role of representative figures more than in the contribution of representative institutions led his contemporaries to warn him about the risk of parliamentary atrophy and has caused a number of scholars to describe his actions as 'Caesarism'. 'Moral dictatorship' and 'dic-tatorial politics' are in fact just some of the expressions used to label Cavour's behaviour towards parliament (a very personal form of parliamentarism often dismissed as 'Cavourism'; see Rusconi 2011). As Mack Smith has argued, the Cavourian understanding of representative government embodied a huge 'paradox' in the foundation of modern Italy: that 'the victory of constitu-tional Piedmont depended on the pseudo-dictatorship of a genuine liberal', an original scar on the face of Italian parliamentarism, open to subsequent involutions (Mack Smith 1957: 42).

A Parliament of or without Parties?

The Infiltration of Parties into the Administration: The Critique of Marco Minghetti

After the first two decades of the parliamentary experiment, which took place within a state structure that was strongly marked by centralization in the wave of the administrative reform of 1865, the emerging problem that Italy had to face was that of party corruption. The first leader who denounced it as a degeneration of parliamentary life was Marco Minghetti, a former prime minister, in his capital book titled *I partiti politici e la ingerenza loro nella giustizia e nell'amministrazione* (1881). Minghetti argued that the intrusion of political parties into the administration would be fatal to the stability of the state system because their only aim was that of acquiring or preserving electoral power; however, a good government required justice in the sense of impartiality. It was essential to devise remedies to solve this problem in order to preserve parliamentary government and a legitimate state. The point Minghetti raised concerned the kind of degeneration that was to be expected from a mixed government based on elections, assuming that none of the ancient and modern theories of the degeneration of the political bodies (from Aristotle and Polybius to Machiavelli) would hold true in this case. Since representative government is government by opinion, the question is how to make the multiplicity of parties functional within the administration and then how to reach a compromise that serves the general interest of the country. The problem was both one of lobbyism, involving a violation of the equality of the subjects, and one of corruption, related to the use of state power by parties in order to increase their influence by other means than electoral support.

Referring to Lord Brougham, Minghetti acknowledged the importance of party pluralism and saw electoral competition as the means for the selection of the best candidates. However, he distinguished between good and bad partisanship. Partisanship was good as long as it allowed for the emergence of groups that were open to change and facilitated the selection of the most highly qualified deputies. It was bad when it made competent behaviour irrelevant and increased the fatal tendency of parties to interfere in public administration. Administration, he argued, falls within the domain of impartial justice, but it also involves decisions regarding the concrete needs of local and national communities. That was precisely why it required both high-quality public servants (competence) and honesty and transparency in the use of financial resources.

However, what Minghetti identified as the locus of the potential degeneration of parties was not the parliamentary model per se but the continental design of the state, with its plan for social policies and the strong administration of society. As he showed through a detailed comparative analysis of patronage in the United States, Britain, Germany and France, the continental paradigm was more conducive to corruption as it involved parties in administration. Minghetti's criticism was also oriented by the belief that the consolidation of parliamentary government would alleviate radical partisanship and bring parties closer to one another. By the same token, he thought that public discussion in society would help to overcome divisions and to increase reasoned deliberation. Partisan views seemed thus to betoken an as yet undeveloped political life. Along with Mill, Minghetti regarded a lively public forum and freedom of opinion as basic conditions for a form of politics that was capable of gradually becoming less partisan and more able to hold representative institutions in check (see Valitutti 1966: 265–67).

After Minghetti, the issue of the proper role of political parties dominated the public debate at the end of the nineteenth century (see Gherardi 1986 and Compagna 2001). Here, priority will be given to the work of two Sicilian figures of unitary Italy, Gaetano Mosca and Vittorio Emanuele Orlando, who both acknowledged the problematic developments of political associations and organized elites as well as party bureaucracy as distinctive features of late nineteenth-century parliamentarism.

Gaetano Mosca: Political Parliamentarism without Parties

The crisis of the Cavourian model and the critique of the liberal ideal of reconciling the clash of social interests through political parties at the institutional level found its most eloquent expression in the work of Gaetano Mosca, the first theorist to attempt to analyse scientifically the formation, selection and change of the political class and to develop an early critique of parliamentarism and government by consent through electoral competition. He also brought to its radical conclusion Minghetti's critique of the colonization of the state by political parties. We give him primacy over the other two most acute elitist critics of the parliamentary system – Vilfredo Pareto and Robert Michels – precisely because of the systematic attention he devoted to the relation between representative politics and its corrosion through the practice of 'parliamentarianism', a term which he employed to denote a corrupted ideology rather than an institutional form of representation and to which he ascribed the pejorative meaning of elective corporatism. For, as he argued both in *Sulla teorica dei governi e sul governo parlamentare* (1884) and *Le Costituzioni moderne* (1887), the usual perspective that is applied to the functioning of parliamentary politics has to be reversed. What typically occurs is not that the electors choose their deputies, but exactly the opposite: the deputy makes his electors vote for him through a systematic process of moral suasion that is conducted by a restricted number of organized minorities over the passive, politically unorganized and profoundly uninterested majority of citizens. As a result, parliamentary politics not only proves to be the grave of any Rousseauian, democratic myth of popular sovereignty, but also annihilates the project of checks and balances derived from Montesquieu within the framework of representative government (Mosca 1982 [1923]: 210–24). Furthermore, contrary to what Cavour had written in 1848, the Chamber of Deputies proved to be founded upon a sort of new 'natural law': intellectual mediocrity, moral corruption and the absolute primacy of private and corporate interests over the pursuit of the public good. According to Mosca, in a parliamentary system everyone is encouraged to favour those who share their same parental, ideological and/or economic affiliations, without any idea of accountability and responsiveness of representatives to their constituencies. This is why the most brilliant minds and active characters of the nation will 'always be left outside the doors of the Chamber' (Mosca 1982 [1923]: 210–24), with long-lasting implications for the quality of governmental activity.

However, Mosca never identified 'parliamentarianism' with representative government based on parliamentarism: the former was rather understood as a degeneration of the latter, a step back towards the corporation- and class-based system that had been typical of medieval Europe. At this level, political parties were deleterious, although they embodied the human tendency to organize and institutionalize the asymmetry of power that intrinsically pertained to any political order, as he would later explain in his *Elementi di Scienza Politica* (1923).

Vittorio Emanuele Orlando: *Juridical Parliamentarism without Parties*

The parliamentary system theorized and defended by Vittorio Emanuele Orlando throughout the 1880s stemmed from the ideas developed by Minghetti and Mosca about the role of parties and their relation to the state administration and institutional assemblies. At the same time, however, he went beyond them to provide the last significant endorsement of parliamentarism before its tragic collapse in the 1920s.

Unlike Mosca, who theorized a political parliamentarism without parties, Orlando developed a juridical parliamentarism without parties (see Compagna 2003: 113–39), a perspective that directly derived from his understanding of the relationship between the state and society. In fact, he firmly believed that a correct analysis of parliamentary settings had to be confined to the state and the institutional domain, whereas associations, movements and parties played a meaningful role in the sphere of society, as he also argued in the 1885 essay *Della resistenza politica individuale e collettiva*. Unlike Mosca, he thought that parliamentarism bore no responsibility for the moral and political degeneration of the Italian state. In the 1884 essay *La decadenza del sistema parlamentare*, Orlando (1884a) critically discussed some of the most relevant and recent voices in the anti-parliamentary literature of his time, Ruggiero Bonghi and Mosca in particular (Bonghi 1884; Mosca 1884). As Fulvio Tessitore (1963: 120) argued, the young Sicilian jurist did not agree with the pessimistic, 'catastrophic' view of the effects of parliamentarism held by both Bonghi and Mosca: rather than representative institutions per se, the interaction between political corruption, the socio-economic crisis and intellectual decay – he wrote – must be held responsible for the many fragilities of unitary Italy in the early 1880s.

However, Orlando also admitted that Italian parliamentarism was unique in terms of its genesis and subsequent development. He referred to Britain, the cradle of parliamentary traditions, in particular, to highlight the defective nature of parliamentarism in Italy: unlike the British people, the Italians had not developed the habit of representation through a gradual evolution of their institutional design. A jigsaw puzzle of local realities assembled by the visionary efforts of Cavour, unitary Italy had 'transplanted' the representative institutions that the English people had created, experienced and improved over centuries.

Again in the 1884 review of Adolphe Prins's *Démocratie et le régime parlementaire*, Orlando (1884b) distinguished the world of parties and movements from that of the state and its institutions and outlined a reconciliation between the rule of law and the parliamentary system that was systematically developed in the 1886 essay *Studi giuridici sul governo parlamentare*. In this latter work, he proceeded from a juridical perspective to argue that the powers and competences of the parliament had to be coordinated together with those of the state and limited by the royal prerogative. His reinterpretation of parliamentarism was thus meant to redefine and defend the function of parliamentary institutions in an attempt to preserve both the authority and the unity of the state.

However, Orlando's 1884 prophecy about the long-term collapse of the parliament and the appearance of a deus ex machina who would 'take the helm of the State' proved to be dramatically true. The leader who was about to emerge, though, was not a new charismatic parliamentary dictator à la Cavour. His name was Benito Mussolini, and he strategically monopolized liberal institutions to get rid of electoral representation, inhibit party pluralism and progressively annihilate parliamentarism.

The Crisis of Representative Government

Throughout the first two decades of the twentieth century, Santi Romano and Benedetto Croce critically elaborated on the need to preserve the unity of the sovereign state in relation to the fragmentation of social interests. On the other hand, liberals and radical socialists, Piero Gobetti and Antonio Gramsci in particular, pinpointed the inability of the liberal state that had been inherited from the nineteenth century to fulfil its promises, namely, to ensure both stability and the rule of law in the context of extended universal suffrage and a mass society. In the years that followed the First World War, the attack against the parliamentary regime emerged as a common denominator among both scholars and political actors (cf. Chapters 4 and 16). In that situation, which Gramsci would later refer to as one of 'catastrophic equilibrium' (the same words that Karl Marx used to denote the condition that prepared for the coup of Napoleon III), the advent of fascism, which Benito Mussolini justified as the restoration of state authority in a situation of emergency, turned out to be the occupation of the state by one party and, in turn, the death of parliament itself. The populist solution that fascism imposed on the country ended the first period of the representative system in Italy and interrupted the long-term project of democratizing its institutional system.

It is no oxymoron to suggest that the doctrine of a populist or mass democracy that emerged in post-First World War Italy belongs to the tradition of anti-liberalism and anti-parliamentarism that developed as a reaction against the French Revolution. This genealogy finds a brilliant confirmation a contrario in the work of one of the early critics of representative and parliamentary politics, Gaetano Mosca. In his last speech as a senator in parliament on 19 December 1925, Mosca accused fascist populism of burying liberty and the democratic procedures that protected it under the pretext of recovering the 'true' will of the people against parliament and its pluralistic fragmentation. 'I should not have thought it possible,' he said, 'that I would be the one to deliver the funeral oration on the parliamentary regime . . . I, who have always taken a harsh attitude toward it, I am today obliged to lament its departure . . . One may say in all sincerity: the parliamentary regime was better' (included in Mosca 1949, cited from Meisel 1985: 225–26). The replacement of the Chamber of Deputies with one made up of fasci and corporations and vested with legislative power from 1939 to 1943 was both the epilogue of the long-term attempt that unitary Italy had pursued to disassociate representative government from individual political equality and the developments of parties as interest groups, on one hand, and the tragic revelation of the frailties that Italian liberalism and its institutional creation had thus far incubated, on the other.

References

Primary Sources

Acquarone, A., M. d'Addio and G. Negri (eds). 1958. *Le Costituzioni Italiane*. Milan: Comunità.

Balbo, C. 1857. *Della Monarchia Rappresentativa in Italia: Saggi Politici*. Florence: Le Monnier.

Bonghi, R. 1884. 'Una questione grossa – La decadenza del regime parlamentare', *Nuova Antologia*, 1 June 1884.

Cavour, C. 1932 [1850–51]. *Discorsi parlamentari*, vol. II. A. Omodeo (ed.). Florence: La Nuova Italia.

_____. 1933 [1851]. *Discorsi parlamentari*, vol. III. A. Omodeo (ed.). Florence: La Nuova Italia.

_____. 1969 [1857–58]. *Discorsi parlamentari*, vol. XIV. A. Saitta (ed.). Florence: La Nuova Italia.

De Sanctis, F. 1970. *I partiti e l'educazione della nuova Italia*. N. Cortese (ed.). Turin: Einaudi.

Ganzetti, A. 1999 [1798]. 'Il giovane instruito ne' principj e ne' doveri di cittadino', in L. Guerci (ed.), *Istruire nelle veritá repubblicane: La letteratura politica per il popolo nell'Italia in rivoluzione (1796–1799)*. Bologna: Il Mulino, pp. 403–467.

Gioberti, V. 1851. *Del Rinnovamento morale e civile d'Italia*, vol. 2. Paris-Turin: Giuseppe Bocca.

Minghetti, M. 1881. *I partiti politici e la ingerenza loro nella giustizia e nell'amministrazione*. Bologna: Zanichelli.

Mosca, G. 1884. *Sulla teorica dei Governi e sul Governo parlamentare*. Rome: Statuto.

_____. 1887. *Le Costituzioni moderne*. Bologna: Zanichelli.

_____. 1949. *Partiti e sindacati nella crisi del regime parlamentare*. Bari: Laterza.

_____. 1982 [1923]. *Scritti Politici, vol. II: Elementi di scienza politica*. Turin: Utet.

Negri, G. and S. Simoni (eds). 1989. *Lo Statuto Albertino e i lavori preparatori*. Rome: Colombo.

Orlando, V.E. 1884a. 'La decadenza del sistema parlamentare', *Rassegna di scienze sociali e politiche* 1(2): 589–600.

_____. 1884b. 'Recensione a "la démocratie et le régime parlementaire" di Adolphe Prins', *Rivista Critica delle Scienze Giuridiche e Sociali* 2: 338.

_____. 1885. *Della resistenza politica individuale e collettiva*. Turin: Loescher.

_____. 1886. 'Studi giuridici sul governo parlamentare', *Archivio giuridico* 36: 521–86.

Romagnosi, G. 1850. *La scienza delle Costituzioni*. Florence: A Spese Degli Editori.

Rosmini, A. 2007. *The Constitution under Social Justice*. Trans. Alberto Mingardi. Boston: Lexington Books.

Rousseau, J.-J. 1964. 'Du contract social', in B. Gagnebin and M. Raymond (eds), *Oeuvres completes*, vol. 3. Paris: Gallimard, pp. 436–470.

Sieyès, E.-J. 1985. *Ecrits politiques*. R. Zapperi (ed.). Paris: Vrin.

Sismondi, J.-C.-L., Sismonde de. 1965 [1801]. *Recherches sur les Constitutions des peoples libre, texte inédit*, with an introduction by M. Minerbi. Geneva: Droz.

_____. 1815. *Examen de la Constitution française*. Paris: Treuttel et Wurtz.

_____. 1847. 'On Universal Suffrage', a translation of 'Du Suffrage Universel. Extrait de la Revue Mensuelle d'Economie Politique' (March 1834), in M. Mighet (ed.), *Political Economy, and the Philosophy of Government: A Series of Essays Selected from the Work of M. de Sismondi*. London: Chapman, pp. 289–92.

Secondary Sources

Bastid, P. 1970. *Sieyès et sa pensée*. Paris: Hachette.

Colombo, P. 2003. *Con lealtà di Re e con affetto di padre. Torino, 4 marzo 1848: la concessione dello Statuto albertino*. Bologna: Il Mulino.

Compagna, L. 2001. 'Alle origini della partitocrazia', in V. Olita (ed.), *Marco Minghetti e le sue opere. Atti del Convegno di Società Libera (Bologna, 11 novembre 2000)*. Milan: Società Aperta, pp. 63–80.

_____. 2003. *Parlamentarismo antico e moderno*. Palermo–Syracuse: Lombardi.

Gherardi, R. 1986. *Introduzione*, in M. Minghetti, *Scritti politici*. Rome: Presidenza del Consiglio dei Ministri.

Ghisalberti, G. 1999. *Stato, Nazione e Costituzione nell'Italia contemporanea*. Naples: Edizioni Scientifiche Italiane.

Guerci, L. 1999. *Istruire nelle verità repubblicane. La letteratura politica per il popolo nell'Italia in rivoluzione (1796–1799)*. Bologna: Il Mulino.

Mack Smith, D. 1957. 'Cavour and Parliament', *Cambridge Historical Journal* 13: 37–57.

Mastellone, S. 1994. *Il progetto politico di Mazzini (Italia-Europa)*. Florence: Olschki.

Meisel, J. 1985. *The Myth of the Ruling Class*. Ann Arbor: University of Michigan Press.

Perticone, G. 1960. *Il Regime Parlamentare nella storia dello Statuto Albertino*. Rome: Edizioni dell'Ateneo.

Rao, A.M. 2012. 'Republicanism in Italy from the Eighteenth Century to the Early Risorgimento', *Journal of Modern Italian Studies* 17(2): 149–67.

Rebuffa, G. 2003. *Lo Statuto albertino*. Bologna: Il Mulino.

Rusconi, G.E. 2011. *Cavour e Bismarck. Due leader fra liberalismo e cesarismo*. Bologna: Il Mulino.

Salvadori, M.L. 2011. 'Il liberalismo di Cavour', in U. Levra (ed.), *Cavour, l'Italia e l'Europa*. Bologna: Il Mulino, pp. 71–111.

Sul governo che conviene all'Italia. 1796. Anonymous dissertation.

Tessitore, F. 1963. *Crisi e trasformazione dello Stato. Ricerche sul pensiero giuspubblicis-tico italiano tra Otto e Novecento*. Naples: Morano.

Ullrich, H. 1999. 'The Statuto Albertino', in H. Dippel (ed.), *Executive and Legislative Powers in the Constitutions of 1848–49*. Berlin: Duncker & Humblot, pp. 129–61.

Valitutti, S. 1966. *I partiti politici e la libertà*. Rome: Amando.

David Ragazzoni is a PhD student in Political Theory in the Department of Political Science at Columbia University, New York. His research sits at the intersection of political theory and the history of political thought, with a specific focus on theories and critiques of representative government and democracy in the nineteenth and twentieth centuries. He is currently working on an intellectual history of partisanship in modern Europe and America.

Nadia Urbinati, Ph.D., is Kyriakos Tsakopoulos Professor of Political Theory in the Department of Political Science at Columbia University, New York. She specializes in modern and contemporary political thought and the democratic and anti-democratic traditions. Her main works have discussed the principles and genealogy of representative democracy, populism and plebiscitary democracy, and the long-term history of democracy. She has written on the political thought of Condorcet, John Stuart Mill, Piero Gobetti and Giuseppe Mazzini, among others.

Chapter 16

Parliamentarism and Democracy in German Political Theory since 1848

Dirk Jörke and Marcus Llanque

In this chapter we sketch the main theoretical contributions to the German debate about parliamentarism and democracy from the middle of the nineteenth century up to the second half of the twentieth century. In the first section, we distinguish three constitutive strands of the German debate for the discussions that have been conducted since the second half of the nineteenth century: a conservative apology of the existing monarchical principle (Friedrich Julius Stahl), a liberal justification of parliamentary government (Robert von Mohl) and the Marxist debate about the prospects and threats of representative democracy for socialist politics (Karl Marx, Karl Kautsky, Eduard Bernstein and Rosa Luxemburg).

In the second section we trace the further development of this tension in the Weimar Republic on the basis of two prominent political theorists, namely Max Weber and Carl Schmitt. Both have enormously influenced not only the German but also the international debate about the relationship between parliamentarism and democracy.

The German discussion after the Second World War was at first dominated by a liberal advocacy of the concept of representative democracy. We will sketch this line of thought in the third section on the basis of Ernst Fraenkel's theory of pluralism. However, during the highly politicized times of the late 1960s, the leftist criticism of parliamentarism returned. The central contribution of this criticism was *Die Transformation der Demokratie* (1967) by Johannes Agnoli, who argued that representative democracy only depoliticizes the main conflict of capitalist societies, namely that between labour and capital.

The Debates of the Nineteenth Century

Owing to the comparatively late establishment of parliamentary government in German history (see Chapter 4), the discussions about its vices and virtues have been vehement. Many German political thinkers regarded the relation between parliamentarism and democracy as problematic if not contradictory at least until the middle of the twentieth century. In the debates of the second half of the nineteenth century, the proper seat of representation was highly contested, the alternatives being the parliament or the monarch. Conservative thinkers like Friedrich Julius Stahl criticized parliamentary government for its strong connection with the democratic idea. Stahl distinguished between a monarchical principle, which he regarded as the only legitimate government and a parliamentary principle with its '*bloß numerischer Volksrepräsentation*' (mere numerical popular representation) and its 'Western origins' (Stahl 1927 [1845]: 5). He especially complains that ministers are responsible only to the random majorities in parliament. He also criticizes the separation of powers and the corruption that, according to Stahl, is a constant feature of parliamentarism. However, Stahl does not reject the idea of a representative assembly altogether. He postulates a *reichsständische Verfassung* (constitution of the imperial estates) that would guarantee the representation of the people through the estates. According to Stahl, an assembly of the elite of all estates could claim to truly represent the complete nature of the people (Stahl 1878: 318). Indeed, Stahl was a typical conservative in assuming that there was a higher organic order besides the aggregation of the individual will. Stahl was eager to emphasize that this assembly should not be understood as an expression of popular sovereignty and that the estates should not be considered mandatories of the people. Therefore, the main function of this assembly of the estates was to mediate between the king and the people. Its competences also included the right to approve taxes and laws. Nevertheless, the right to appoint the government and to formulate laws remained in the hand of the king. 'The prince being the very power itself, does not divide himself' (Stahl 1869: 319). Accordingly, this corporate and limited understanding of representation was still compatible with the monarchical principle.

By contrast, liberal thinkers like Robert von Mohl stressed the necessity and the legitimacy of a parliamentary government (see von Beyme 2009: 325–28). Only a year after the publication of *Das monarchische Prinzip*, Mohl published, without knowing the work of Stahl, an article comparing the representative systems of Britain, France and Germany (von Mohl 1966 [1846]). Mohl admired the British parliamentarian government with the cabinet's strong dependency on both houses. Against this background, he criticized the dualism between the parliament and the government that was typical of most of the German states. The effect of this dualism was to consolidate the backwardness not only of the political system but also of the whole society. He mentions, for example, the weakness of public opinion and the incompetence of many state officials resulting from the widespread practice of nepotism.

Mohl articulated his strong support for parliamentary government in Germany in *Das Repräsentativsystem, seine Mängel und Heilmittel* (1852). In this influential article, Mohl turned against Stahl – albeit without mentioning him – and his monarchical principle. He especially doubts Stahl's claim that a parliamentary government would foster demagoguery and corruption. On the contrary, Mohl argued that constant alternations of the government and the opposition had a moderating influence on the representative assembly. What prevented the opposition from making senseless statements in the chamber and concomitantly instilling false ideas in the minds of the public was the ever-present possibility that it could assume power at any time. At this point, the opposition would be obliged to realize in practice what it had been contemplating in theory before (von Mohl 1966 [1852]: 159).

According to Mohl, the parliamentary principle primarily meant that the government was formed from the majority of the assembly and secondly that the parliament had the right to formulate laws and to approve the budget of the state. The main achievement of such a parliamentary system would be to overcome the dualism between the prince and his governmental power on one side and the representative assembly on the other.

However, for Mohl, parliamentarism did not include democracy. On the contrary, he was a strong opponent of universal suffrage, which he equated with the emergence of 'communism'. He argued for a limited franchise as the precondition of a wise parliamentary system. To bypass the proletariat would be unjust as well as imprudent. However, it would also be unreasonable to give them the majority that, in fact, they could claim on the basis of a head count (von Mohl 1966 [1852]: 198f; cf. von Mohl 1966 [1869]: 274–75). This plea for a limited franchise was a typical liberal stance in the nineteenth century. Mohl also argued for some kind of professional or special representation that should be organized in a complex system of representative assemblies to represent special interests in society like those of trade, industry and agriculture, as well as those of the churches and universities. Furthermore, these assemblies should also delegate deputies to a general assembly (*Gesamtvertretung*). It is, however, not clear how this system was to be connected to the electoral system, which in itself was very complicated in Mohl's outline.

Among socialist thinkers, Karl Marx was one of the critics of parliamentary politicking. In *The Eighteenth Brumaire of Louis Bonaparte* (1852), he sketches the political struggles that had led to the coup d'état of Louis Bonaparte. According to Marx, one of the main causes of the end of the Second French

Republic was the fact that the bourgeoisie feared a socialist revolution. Parliamentarism turned into a double-edged sword for the French bourgeoisie, as universal suffrage had provided the opportunity for a socialist majority. Therefore, in order to stabilize their economic dominance, the bourgeoisie had sacrificed representative government: 'Thus the industrial bourgeoisie applauds with servile bravos the coup d'état of December 2, the annihilation of parliament, the downfall of its own rule, the dictatorship of Bonaparte' (CW 11: 179).

However, parliamentarism also slowed down the socialists' efforts to take over the state, as Marx demonstrated in sketching the change of the left towards a non-revolutionary socialist party, which tried to transform 'society in a democratic way', claiming that this was 'a transformation within the bounds of the petty bourgeoisie' (CW 11: 130). Marx shows in detail and not without some malice the constraints of the parliamentary style of politics for socialist aims. He mentioned in particular the corrupting effects of parliamentary means on socialist politicians. Certainly, according to Marx, the coup d'état was mostly the result of the failure of the bourgeois factions to handle Louis Bonaparte. Nevertheless, the Social Democratic politicians were authoritarians, too. Thus, one can see in *The Eighteenth Brumaire* an early criticism of parliamentarism as a tool for socialist politics. Marx even criticized universal suffrage, which had hitherto been regarded even by him as an essential instrument for the socialist transformation of society. However, the success of Louis Bonaparte in the plebiscite on 21 December 1851 showed that the correlation between democracy and socialism could not be taken for granted. As long as the consciousness of the underprivileged classes was captivated by religious and bourgeois values, universal suffrage would only reinforce the capitalist structure. Louis Napoleon's coup d'état cooled down enthusiasm for parliament as the natural instrument for modernizing any political system, not only in Germany but also in other European countries (Llanque 2008: 367–70).

Marx continued this criticism of parliamentarism as a mere bourgeois form of democracy in 'The Civil War in France' (1871). The parliamentary republic under the presidency of Louis Bonaparte was 'a *régime* of avowed class terrorism' (CW 22: 329); the Empire was the only feasible government at a time when the bourgeois had already lost the ability to rule society and the working class was not yet ready for this task. Twenty years later, the French working class not only gained power – even if only for a few weeks – but also found a political form that satisfied socialist expectations: the Paris Commune. 'The rural communes of every district were to administer their common affairs by an assembly of delegates in the central towns, and these district assemblies were again to send deputies to the National delegation in

Paris, each delegate to be at any time revocable and bound by the *mandat impératif* (formal instructions) of his constituents' (CW 22: 332). The core institutions of such a council democracy were the imperative mandate, revocation, rotation and the abolition of the separation of powers. For Marx, this form of direct democracy was not only a true socialist conception of democracy but also a model for large nation states like France, England and Germany.

However, Marx corrected his appraisal of the Commune shortly after writing his article in 1872 in a speech about the International Working Men's Association in The Hague, he conceded that in England, America and Holland the working class could attain their aims peacefully by parliamentary means (MEW 18: 160; CW 23: 254).

Social Democratic thinkers like Karl Kautsky and Eduard Bernstein also favoured the adoption of parliamentarism, hoping that through universal suffrage a socialist change could be realized. In Kautsky's *Parlamentarismus und Demokratie* (1893), in particular, one can find a democratic justification of parliamentarism. This small book harshly criticizes Moritz von Rittinghaus's model of direct democracy (see Rittinghausen 1893). According to Kautsky, the idea of direct democracy was appropriate for the Swiss cantons, but it was not feasible in a large nation state such as Germany due to its complex structure. In addition to that, Kautsky emphasized the possibility of effective control of the state administration by parliamentarians, especially those belonging to the opposition (1911 [1893]: 83). The most positive aspect of a parliamentary system, however, was that it helped the emergence of a modern political party system, which in a more direct form of democracy would not be the case. Since antagonistic classes existed in modern industrial societies, this was particularly relevant, because, according to Kautsky, only Social Democratic parties were able to organize the working class. In other words, a parliamentary system with universal suffrage would lead to a strong and well-organized working class. A system of direct democracy would only reproduce the class structure, as it would give the backward population of the rural areas too much weight. Kautsky's commitment to parliamentary democracy, therefore, was mostly instrumental; he considered the expansion of the franchise to be the best way towards a socialist society. A parliament with universal suffrage would be a battlefield for the class struggle (*Schlachtfeld für den Klassenkampf*) (1911 [1893]: 62). This was indeed crucially different from the liberal concepts of representation and parliamentary government. However, it was also different from the more moderate and even more liberal ideas of Eduard Bernstein.

Bernstein contemplated a reconciliation of liberalism and democracy, meaning a parliamentary government with universal suffrage on one side and the limitation of the majority principle through liberal rights that bind the majoritarian will on the other. He especially criticized direct democracy and argued for a separation of powers and the rule of law. Thus, one can say that it is in Bernstein's *Die Voraussetzungen des Sozialismus* (1899) where we can find, for the first time in the German context, the modern concept of liberal democracy with its core institutions like universal suffrage, parliamentarism, separation of powers, the rule of law and, last but not least, a social welfare system. Bernstein summarized his credo in the following words: 'Democracy is both means and end. It is a weapon in the struggle for socialism, and it is the form in which socialism will be realized' (1993 [1899]: 142).

As it is well known, Bernstein and Kautsky's flirtation with parliamentarism in general and with liberalism in particular was not approved by all leading thinkers of the socialist movement. One of the harshest critics of parliamentarism from a socialist perspective was Rosa Luxemburg. Even if she had flirted in some of her early writings with the idea of a socialist transformation of society through universal suffrage (1982 [1899]: 432f), during her career as a political activist she became more and more convinced that the socialist transformation of society was most effectively blocked by parliamentary politicking. Luxemburg developed a twofold criticism in her influential article *Sozialdemokratie und Parlamentarismus* (1904). Firstly, she regarded parliamentarism as an outdated relic of the struggle between the bourgeoisie and feudalism. At the beginning of the twentieth century, these struggles terminated in a compromise between these two classes. According to Luxemburg, the parliamentarian compromise reflected the social compromise between feudal and bourgeois forces in society and was a significant factor in the further decline of parliament (1979 [1904]: 449). Consequently, parliament had lost its main function and developed into an 'automatic "yes" machine' (*automatische Jasagemaschine*) (1979 [1904]: 447). Indeed, one can find in this small article many of the arguments that Carl Schmitt twenty years later famously advanced against the liberal concept of parliamentarism. Luxemburg sketched a decline in the political culture of parliamentary debates by arguing that only 'window speeches' were made, owing to the fact that the crucial decisions were taken elsewhere, and that the real disputes no longer took place in the parliament but behind closed doors, where the party leaders conducted their horse trading. In a word, parliament was no longer the place for public deliberation and political decision-making.

Her second line of criticism against parliamentarism referred not to its decline but to its effects on the Social Democratic Party. Luxemburg's argument was based on the experience of the transformation of the French Socialist Party from a revolutionary force into a bourgeois faction. When the Socialist Party joined the government, the result was not a socialist transformation of society but an artificial extension of the rule of the bourgeois class. In short, in parliament, even socialists preferred to uphold democracy than to instigate a revolution (Luxemburg 1979 [1904]: 452). Therefore, Luxemburg rejected the hope of Bernstein and Kautsky that a socialist, or at least a social democratic, transformation of society could be attained through parliamentary means. However, in 1904 she did not reject parliamentarism altogether. Together with an intensification of the political struggle in the working environment and in the streets, parliament could be seen as a useful stage for socialist agitation. She pleaded for an incitement of the class struggle, inside and outside parliament, instead of replacing it by parliamentarism (1979 [1904]: 453).

In the highly politicized atmosphere of the November Revolution, her verdict on parliamentarism as a strategy for the Social Democratic Party is harsher; she calls it a 'cloud cuckoo land' (*Wolkenkuckucksheim*) (1974 [1918]: 462). In her last writings, Luxemburg pleads for a republic of councils as a socialist alternative to parliamentarism. However, her ideas about this political form are not elaborated on to any great extent. Furthermore, as it is well known, the workers' and soldiers' councils that were established in some German cities in the chaos after the capitulation in the First World War and the end of the monarchy failed to survive.

The Weimar Debates

In the Weimar Republic, both theoretical and political debates about the relationship between parliamentarism and democracy reached a new stage. Particularly in the works of Max Weber and Carl Schmitt, new and very influential theories were formulated. Weber is famous for his efforts to establish a responsible government based on parliamentarism and universal suffrage. Although in 'Parlament und Regierung im neugeordneten Deutschland' (1918) and in 'Wahlrecht und Demokratie in Deutschland' (1917) he emphasized that parliamentarism and democracy were not the same and in the past often had been opposed to each other, he nevertheless argued for a simultaneous strengthening of both forces as a precondition of a modernization of German politics.

Does Weber mean by 'democracy' a form of popular rule? His essay 'Wahlrecht' (1917) is founded on the radical equality of citizens, on the principle that votes are counted and not weighted. His plea for individual and equal suffrage is a radical stand against corporatist ideas (*berufständische Vertretung*, sometimes translated as 'occupational corporations'). For Weber, 'berufständische Vertretung' was an application of corporatism to parliament that gave representatives of social and economic interest groups mandates in the assembly according to their 'objective' weight in society instead of taking into account the number of individuals voting for them. To some extent, these proposals echoed Hegelian ideas in the *Rechtsphilosophie*, where the philosopher had discussed corporations composed of actors in civil society as representing the real life of social activities as an alternative to representation based on an artificial concept of representation in which individuals were regarded as independent atoms. During the First World War, when both liberal and left-wing politicians and intellectuals demanded the democratization of the political system, the defenders of the ancien régime used the concept of the 'berufsständische Vertretung' as an institution in order to remain as close as possible to the old system. By contrast, Max Weber put the case for the concept of representation based on individual franchise, claiming that the social reality was already too complex for it to be duplicated in the parliament according to a corporate scheme. He pleaded for an equal vote as the best option for representing the social reality without being too static to prevent any change (Weber 1994: 88–97).

The main point of Weber's pamphlet on parliamentarism is his opposition to universal bureaucratization as a major world trend, which he sought to counterbalance. In the German Empire, the government had been based on the rule of officialdom without ministers being responsible to the parliament. For Weber, a parliament could above all provide a counterweight to the everyday rule of bureaucracy. Weber writes:

> First and foremost, modern parliaments are assemblies representing the people, who are *ruled* by means of bureaucracy. It is, after all, a condition of the duration of any rule, even the best organised, that it should enjoy a certain measure of inner assent from at least those sections of the ruled who carry weight in society. Today parliaments are the means whereby this minimum of assent is made manifest. (1994: 165)

Parliaments elected by universal suffrage provided for the citizens a minimum share in politics and could create professional politicians to control the rule of the unelected officials. The political leadership was always conducted by few persons; this could not be eliminated, but it could be held in check by parliament and the voters.

Weber saw a second positive feature of parliamentarism in its ability to allow opposing political camps to make compromises, which attests to the integrative power of a democratic parliament: 'This is the specific function performed by parliaments: to make it possible to achieve the "best" solution (relatively speaking) by a process of negotiation and compromise . . . Nothing else can replace this purely technical superiority of parliamentary legislation' (1994: 128).

The third aspect of a democratic parliamentary system consisted in its ability to ensure the selection of qualified political leaders through the contest in parliament as well as through their engagement in election campaigns. Weber hoped that by means of a dual strategy of democratization of the electoral law and the establishment of parliamentary government the quality of the political cadre would rise. Already in his Freiburg inaugural lecture he had complained about the poor quality of politicians in Germany. He subsequently reiterated this charge again and again. Against the background of a looming defeat in the First World War, this motif occurs increasingly in his political writings. In 'Parlament und Regierung im neugeordneten Deutschland' (1918), Weber argues that the low quality of the political elite can be traced back not only to the inheritance of Bismarckian authoritarianism but also to the backwardness of German parliamentarism with its specific mixture of impotence and the dominance of notables. In order to overcome this backwardness, he pleaded for the adoption of British parliamentarism in Germany, too. However, the new constitution of the Weimar Republic did not fulfil Weber's hopes. In 'Politik als Beruf' (1919), he complained that the outmoded structures of the German party system and the associated political practices had only changed externally, not in their essential characteristics. The old political elite was successfully holding on to power while the truly qualified candidates had been repulsed through intrigues and the political machinations of cliques. According to Weber, the main cause of this failure was the rejection of the majority vote system. One can see his concept of the plebiscitarian presidency with his emphasis on charismatic nature, which he discussed in his last writings in response to the above mentioned shortcomings.

Whether this model shows at least some kind of congeniality with the anti-liberal and anti-parliamentary ideas of Carl Schmitt (for the relationship between Weber and Schmitt, see Mommsen 1974; Anter 2006; Breuer 2006) has been the subject of considerable discussion. Weber stressed an 'anti-authoritarian' interpretation of the charismatic nature of elected leaders (see his article 'Die drei reinen Typen legitimer Herrschaft' in Weber 1985 [1922]: 487–88). Most plausible, however, is the assumption that he did not intend to displace parliamentary government in favour of charismatic elements but rather to establish a balance between both features of modern mass democracies (Llanque 2007).

Certainly it was Carl Schmitt who formulated the harshest criticism of parliamentarism and liberalism in the German context. The central topic of a small book from 1919 is the inability of Romanticism to make a clear decision (Schmitt 1998 [1919]). According to Schmitt, compromise is only a stopgap, which he tries to replace with an understanding of politics based on decisionism.

In 1923 he published *Die geistesgeschichtliche Lage des heutigen Parlamentarismus* (English translation, *The Crisis of Parliamentary Democracy* [1988]), in which he systemized his attacks against liberalism and representative democracy. His starting point was a sharp distinction between parliamentarism and democracy: 'The belief in parliamentarianism, in government by discussion, belongs to the intellectual world of liberalism. It does not belong to democracy' (1988 [1923]: 8). Referring to Rousseau, Schmitt develops an interpretation of democracy as the identity of the ruler and the ruled. According to his understanding of democracy, the will of the people is not formulated through discussion in parliaments but through a spontaneous acclamation of the political leader. The precondition of this concept of democracy is, as Schmitt argued in a famous quote, 'first homogeneity and second – if the need arises – elimination or eradication of heterogeneity' (1988 [1923]: 9).

However, this distinction between democracy and parliamentarism was only a preparatory step. The main topic Schmitt deals with in this book is the historical backwardness of parliamentarism. In order to demonstrate this, he constructed an ideal type of parliamentarism, which he found in the nineteenth-century model of a parliament of dignitaries. There were two core principles of this concept, namely publicity and deliberation: 'What was to be secured through the balance guaranteed by openness and discussion was nothing less than truth and justice itself. It was believed that naked power and force . . . could be overcome through openness and discussion alone, and the victory of right over might achieved' (1988 [1923]: 49).

According to Schmitt, the equation of parliamentarism and a deliberative search for truth and justice was already an idealization in the days of Francois Guizot (see Chapter 3), and it was not entirely appropriate for the realities of politics in mass democracies. He maliciously describes a political system that, owing to a party government and the concomitant repeal of the separation of powers, has lost its original liberal character. Now decisions are taken behind closed doors, and big capitalist interests dictate the rules of the game. Even if the reference to capitalist interests reminds one to a certain extent of Luxemburg's criticism, his purpose was different. Schmitt's criticism of parliamentarism was directed against the constitution and political culture of the Weimar Republic with the aim of establishing an authoritarian system capable not only of overthrowing the liberal-democratic order but also of leading Germany towards new glory.

In 1931 Schmitt tried to legitimate the presidential system of the last years of the Weimar Republic. He again regarded the existing party state as contradicting the liberal idea of representation and government through discussion. In the *Reichspräsident*, on the other hand, he saw a guardian of the constitution (*Hüter der Verfassung*), a neutral power above party politics. In his model, the Reichspräsident represents and ensures the unity of the state against the pluralistic factions of society (Schmitt 1996 [1931]). However, as Schmitt had already argued in *Die geistesgeschichtliche Lage des heutigen Parlamentarismus*, a powerful president, even some form of dictatorship, does not necessarily involve the end of democracy if one regards democracy as the identity of the ruler with the ruled. The demos should no longer elect their representatives but only applaud the decisions of the leader.

Schmitt's political theory was, of course, highly controversial. Richard Thoma elaborated one of the first criticisms of Schmitt's interpretation of liberalism and parliamentarism (1925). Referring to the work of Hugo Preuß, Friedrich Naumann and Weber, he demonstrated that Schmitt's reconstruction was one-sided and antiquated. Instead of sketching a comprehensive account of parliamentarism, he complained that Schmitt 'singles out only the side of parliamentarism that is already mouldy and neglects all the others' (1969 [1925]: 56). It was also an oversimplification when Schmitt equated the end of democratic discussion with the pre-eminence of the parties. Rather, the democratic process had shifted to the electoral campaign. This meant that decisions about central issues were not made in parliament but were formed in and through elections.

The Debates of the Bonn Republic

It is no surprise that after the Second World War the discussion about parliamentarism and democracy in West Germany concentrated on the so-called 'Special Path' (*Sonderweg*). One of the most profound contributions to this debate can be seen in the work of Ernst Fraenkel, who, after his return from exile, became one of the founding fathers of political science in Germany. During the 1950s and 1960s, Fraenkel developed a pluralist theory of democracy that has many similarities with Robert Dahl's concept of 'polyarchy'. Fraenkel argued in an article with the programmatic title 'Historische Vorbelastungen des deutschen Parlamentarismus' (1960) that in Germany a delegation theory of representation had dominated not only theoretical debates but also the actual political culture. According to Fraenkel, this concept of representation stood in conflict with the need to find compromises between the different social groups, in particular between labour and capital and the different religious sectors of society. He wrote: 'Continental parliamentary thought, including German, is based on the rejection of the idea that parliament could be the place where the pluralist forces of society can find a balance' (1991: 33). Against this continental theory, Fraenkel called for the adoption of the Anglo-American concept of parliamentarism with the free mandate as its cornerstone. For him, this concept of parliamentarism in combination with a pluralistic understanding of society was the sine qua non of a stable Western democracy.

Fraenkel opposed ways of thinking that threatened to depart from the Western form of parliamentarism; for instance, that of Gerhard Leibholz with his idea of the *Parteienstaat*. The Basic Law (*Grundgesetz*) of 1949 gave the parliamentary reality of party politics a legislative acceptance by claiming a prominent role for political parties: 'Political parties shall participate in the formation of the political will of the people' (Basic Law, Article 21, paragraph 1). The founders wanted to prevent further debate about the mere acceptability of political parties, reacting to Weimar debates in which the very legitimacy of parties had been questioned. The interpretation of that provision started a fierce debate about the nature of political parties in relation to parliamentary democracy in the 1950s and 1960s. Gerhard Leibholz believed that political parties were replacing the people in terms of democratic political philosophy (Leibholz 1951). He argued that the role of the people, which in Rousseau's democratic theory had been to realize the general will, could today only be attributed to parties. Hence, the classical doctrine of the free mandate of representatives had to be replaced by a doctrine that took the strong ties between representatives and political parties into account. The only provision for parties replacing the democratic people in this way was a guarantee that there would be an efficient democratic bottom-up organization within the parties themselves. Fraenkel criticized Leibholz for what he believed to be a revival of Rousseau and his idea of the general will, which seemed to re-emerge in Leibholz's concept of the *Parteivolk* (Fraenkel 1991: 87f).

Fraenkel's admiration of the British parliamentary system was shared by many political scientists of the first post-war generation like Arnold Bergstrasser, Kurt Sontheimer and Kurt Kluxen. However, a short work by Johannes Agnoli, a colleague of Fraenkel at the Otto-Suhr-Institut in Berlin, challenged this liberal consensus. In the highly politicized times of the late 1960s, Agnoli published together with Peter Brückner *Die Transformation der Demokratie* (1967). Agnoli's contribution, in particular, has fast become a kind of bible of the anti-parliamentary left in West Germany. Agnoli's main criticism is that parliaments only whitewash the antagonistic structure of modern democracies, namely the fundamental conflict between labour and capital. Agnoli, following Schmitt and other critics of liberal parliamentarism like Gerhard Leibholz, describes a transformation of classical parliamentarism with legislative competences into a model where the main function of the parliament is to produce some pseudo-democratic legitimization. According to Agnoli, it is pseudo-democratic because the crucial decisions are not taken in the parliament but in oligarchic circles out of the public view. Furthermore, it is also pseudo-democratic because one of its most important functions is to simulate a true democratic process. Agnoli tries to show how the political system of liberal democracies in general and parliaments in particular reinforces the capitalist order by creating the impression of an open political agenda. In reality, according to Agnoli, the main structures of societies are not open to political contestation. Thus, the parliament only creates the illusion of democratic decision-making, and it is above all for that reason that parliament still plays a crucial role in capitalist societies, namely an ideological one: for him parliament is only a tool to disguise interest-based politics as constitutionally valid (2004 [1967]: 69).

Reacting to this fundamental criticism of parliamentarism, Fraenkel and other liberal political scientists have accused Agnoli of using Schmittian arguments and of becoming an advocate of leftist totalitarianism. And, of course, in the academic world this criticism of Agnoli's work succeeds. At least up to the end of the 1980s, the liberal conception of parliamentarism dominated the German discussion, although in the context of the new social movements there was strong criticism of parliamentary democracy and, to some extent, the old debate between direct and representative democracy was revived in the late 1970s and early 1980s (Llanque 2011; see also Chapter 4 in this volume). However, the German mainstream political view was rather sceptical of the strengthening of direct decision-making.

There are some signs that this position has changed in recent years. Many scholars claim that contemporary democratic systems are becoming post-parliamentary if not post-democratic. The basis of these theories is, on one hand, the growing importance of supranational and transnational decision-making bodies and, on the other hand, the increase in so-called public-private policy networks. Both tendencies threaten to weaken the competence of elected parliaments (Jörke 2005; see also Chapter 18 in this volume).

What is to be learned from the German development of parliamentary thought? The modern theory of parliamentarism is mostly based on the Anglo-Saxon paradigm. Against this background, the German case seems odd in many ways. German theories of parliamentarism not only provide an example of an exception to the Western model, but they also provide alternatives to it, at least in the realm of ideas.

References

Primary Sources

Agnoli, J. 2004 [1967]. *Die Transformation der Demokratie*. Hamburg: Konkret Literatur Verlag.

Bernstein, E. 1993 [1899]. *The Preconditions of Socialism*, trans. H. Tudor. Cambridge: Cambridge University Press.

Fraenkel, E. 1991. *Deutschland und die westlichen Demokratien*. Frankfurt am Main: Suhrkamp.

Kautsky, K. 1911 [1893]. *Parlamentarismus und Demokratie*, 2nd ed. Stuttgart: J.H.W. Dietz Nachf.

Leibholz, G. 1951. 'Parteienstaat und repräsentative Demokratie', *Deutsches Verwaltungsblatt* 66: 1–8.

Luxemburg, R. 1982 [1899]. 'Sozialreform oder Revolution', in *Gesammelte Werke 1.1*. Berlin: Dietz, pp. 369–445.

_____. 1979 [1904]. 'Sozialdemokratie und Parlamentarismus', in *Gesammelte Werke 1.2*. Berlin: Dietz, pp. 447–55.

_____. 1974 [1918]. 'Nationalversammlung oder Räteregierung', in *Gesammelte Werke 4*. Berlin: Dietz , pp. 462–65.

Marx, K. and F. Engels. 1975ff. (CW). *Collected Works*. Moscow: Progress Publishers.

_____. 1956ff. (MEW). *Marx-Engels-Werke*. Berlin: Dietz Verlag.

Mohl, R., von. 1966 [1846]. 'Über die verschiedene Auffassung des repräsentativen Systems in England, Frankreich und Deutschland', in K. von Beyme (ed.), *Politische Schriften*. Cologne and Opladen: Westdeutscher Verlag , pp. 47–84.

_____. 1966 [1852]. 'Das Repräsentativsystem, seine Mängel und die Heilmittel', in K. von Beyme (ed.), *Politische Schriften*. Cologne and Opladen: Westdeutscher Verlag, pp. 118–226.

_____. 1966 [1869]. 'Allgemeines Wahlrecht', in K. von Beyme (ed.), *Politische Schriften*. Cologne and Opladen: Westdeutscher Verlag, pp. 265–75.

Rittinghausen, M. 1893. *Die direkte Gesetzgebung durch das Volk*, 5th ed. Zurich: Verlag der Buchhandlung des Schweizerischen Grütlivereins.

Schmitt, C. 1998 [1919]. *Politische Romantik*, 6th ed. Berlin: Duncker & Humblot.

_____. 1988 [1923]. *The Crisis of Parliamentary Democracy*, trans. Ellen Kennedy. Cambridge, MA: MIT Press.

_____. 1996 [1931]. *Der Hüter der Verfassung*, 4th ed. Berlin: Duncker & Humblot.

Stahl, F.J. 1927 [1845]. *Das monarchische Prinzip. Eine staatsrechtlich-politische Abhandlung*. Berlin: Weltgeist Bücher.

_____. 1878. *Die Staatslehre und die Principien des Staatsrechts*, 5th ed. Tübingen and Leipzig: Mohr.

Thoma, R. 1969 [1925]. 'Zur Ideologie des Parlamentarismus', in K. Kluxen (ed.), *Parlamentarismus*. Cologne and Berlin: Kiepenheuer & Witsch, pp. 54–58.

Weber, M. 1971 [1917]. 'Wahlrecht und Demokratie in Deutschland', in J. Winckelmann (ed.), *Gesammelte politische Schriften*, 3rd ed. Tübingen: Mohr, pp. 245–92.

_____. 1971 [1918]. 'Parlament und Regierung im neugeordneten Deutschland', in J. Winckelmann (ed.), *Gesammelte politische Schriften*, 3rd ed. Tübingen: Mohr, pp. 306–443.

_____. 1971 [1919]. 'Politik als Beruf', in J. Winckelmann (ed.), *Gesammelte politische Schriften*, 3rd ed. Tübingen: Mohr, pp. 505–60.

_____. 1985 [1922]. 'Über die drei reinen Typen legitimer Herrschaft', in J. Winckelmann (ed.), *Gesammelte Aufsätze zur Wissenschaftslehre*, 6th ed. Tübingen: Mohr, pp. 475–488.

_____. 1994. *Political Writings*. P. Lassmann and R. Speirs (eds). Cambridge: Cambridge University Press.

Secondary Sources

Anter, A. 2006. 'Max Weber und die parlamentarische Demokratie der Bundesrepublik Deutschland', in K.-L. Ay and K. Borchardt (eds), *Das Faszinosum Max Weber: Die Geschichte seiner Geltung*. Konstanz: Universitätsverlag Konstanz, pp. 353–73.

Beyme, K. von. 2009. *Geschichte der politischen Theorien in Deutschland 1300–2000*. Wiesbaden: Verlag für Sozialwissenschaften.

Breuer, S. 2006. *Max Webers tragische Soziologie*. Tübingen: Mohr Siebeck.

Jörke, D. 2005. 'Auf dem Weg zur Postdemokratie', *Leviathan* 33(4): 482–91.

Llanque, M. 2007. 'Max Weber and the Relation between Power Politics and Political Ideals', *Constellations* 14(4): 483–97.

_____. 2008. *Politische Ideengeschichte. Ein Gewebe politischer Diskurse*. Munich and Vienna: Oldenbourg.

_____. 2011. 'Otto Kirchheimer und die sozialistische Verfassungslehre', in R. von Ooyen and F. Schale (eds), *Kritische Verfassungspolitologie. Das Staatsverständnis von Otto Kirchheimer*. Baden-Baden: Nomos, pp. 69–86.

Mommsen, W.J. 1974. *Max Weber und die deutsche Politik 1890–1920*, 2nd ed. Tübingen: Mohr Siebeck.

Dirk Jörke, Dr. phil., is Professor for Political Theory and the History of Political Ideas at Technische Universität Darmstadt, Germany. His research interests are the history of political thought and democratic theory. He has published on American pragmatism, political anthropology and the history of democratic thought.

Marcus Llanque, Dr. phil., is Professor of Political Science, University of Augsburg, Germany. He specializes in democratic theory, republicanism, the history of political thought, constitutional theory and human rights. His major works have focused on the German debate on democracy during the First World War and the Weimar Republic and on the relationship between classical republicanism and the modern constitutional state.

Chapter 17

Parliamentarism in Spanish Politics in the Nineteenth and Twentieth Centuries

From Constitutional Liberalism to Democratic Parliamentarism

José María Rosales

We promised that all political families could have a place in parliament, and on Wednesday they can obtain one. I think the Spanish political map has already been drawn and we can begin to build on it. This Spain, which politically belongs to all of us, should also begin to be ours socially, economically and culturally.

— Adolfo Suárez's televised end-of-campaign address, 14 June 1977

The Spanish transitional prime minister lacked democratic credentials. A regime insider, he was appointed to introduce political changes that were calculated to secure continuity. During his first term in office, from 1976 to 1977, he maintained a fragile balance between the dictatorship's old guard and a defectively organized opposition. Endorsed with a disputed legitimacy, he succeeded in transforming the entire edifice of political institutions. The previous democratic experiment some forty years earlier had ended in disaster. Few believed that the parliament, the Cortes, could really become a democratic institution.[1] Yet it re-emerged as the centre of an all-embracing political transformation.

This chapter presents an overview of parliamentarism in Spain.[2] By examining two centuries of political history it first documents the early parliamentary debates on the enactment of a liberal constitution and its political consequences. Even if the path of the 1812 constitution turned out to be fraught with setbacks – as it only came into force intermittently, from 1812 to 1814, 1820 to 1823 and 1836 to 1837 (Tomás Villarroya 1981: 27–30) – the Cadiz debates began an unexpected process of parliamentarization of politics that was further consolidated in the course of the nineteenth century. The adoption of parliamentary procedures was initially contested in the Cortes by non-liberal representatives as a foreign import, deemed incompatible with the country's historical constitution and its traditional style of politics.

The medieval and modern Cortes were a 'congress of ambassadors', to use Edmund Burke's insightful expression, the monarchy sharing power with the landed nobility and the Catholic Church (see the historical surveys by Martínez Marina 1813 and Fernández Martín 1885: 77–129, 184–211). Hence only the transitional (Regency) 1834 Royal Statute, in force until 1836, was a real foreign import, although it had a lasting impact. The Statute marked the end of absolutism and introduced the basic features of a representative system, such as direct elections, bicameralism and parliamentary control of government (Tomás Villarroya 1981: 44–46). Thus a tentative experiment gradually outlined the practices and institutions of parliamentarism, most notably with the establishment of a party system that turned the traditional estate-based Cortes into a modern parliament.

Second, the chapter recounts a selected sequence of constitutional debates that represented breakthroughs in the political transformation of Spain in conjunction with the constitutions of 1812, 1876, 1931 and 1978.[3] Every new constituent moment resumed the discussion on the polity of the state, be it a monarchy or a republic, a tension that remained unbroken until a reformed parliamentary monarchy was adopted by the 1978 constitution. Moreover, every new constituent moment became a chance to revamp the system of institutions with the aim of addressing unsettled problems. However, the most relevant aspect of constitutional debates is that a comparative overview of them reveals a meaningful, albeit irregular (Romeo 2002) parliamentariza-tion of Spanish politics, which belies the traditional view of Spain as a late-comer in the continent's political modernity (see López Pina 1994).

Third, the chapter argues that the history of Spanish parliamentarism can be illuminated through the lens of constitutional debates. They allow us to examine the discussion about ultimate political issues and show parlia-mentary activity in its most critical moments. More interestingly, the con-stitutional focus is repeatedly resumed in remarkable parliamentary debates throughout the different legislative periods. Parliamentary politics cannot be reduced to constitutional politics, but it makes sense to survey its history against the political horizon that each new constitution outlines. Conversely, exploring Spanish politics through the lens of parliamentarism brings into focus disregarded aspects of political history, such as the debates surrounding the rise and fall of governments, viewed both from inside the parliament itself and from the wider public sphere created by the press.

The Promise of Early Parliamentarism

The 1808 French invasion of Spain, taking place after the rupture of a previous alliance between the two countries and initiating one of the last phases of the Napoleonic Wars, was bravely contested. Ferdinand VII was forced to abdicate in connection with the invasion. By 1810 a neutralized government managed to reorganize itself into a Central Council (*Junta Central*) made up of the provincial administrative juntas, and it appointed a Regency Council that convened 'national representatives from both hemispheres' (i.e., representatives from Spanish possessions in the New World) at the 'General and Extraordinary Cortes' in the city of Cadiz. Their assignment was to draft a new constitution. The project went through although the summons was not answered by all political leaders, their loyalties being divided between supporters of absolutism, advocates of a British-inspired constitutional government and the *afrancesados*, opposed to the invasion but seeking a French-inspired form of constitutionalism (Fernández Martín 1885: 239–354; Morán Orti 1991).

For about eighteen months after 24 September 1810, while the country was embroiled in the War of Independence, the Cortes convened until a new constitution was adopted on 19 March 1812. Representatives met 98 times in 1810, 361 times in 1811 and 79 times in 1812, totalling 538 parliamentary sessions. The constitution that was finally adopted had distinctive features of both British and French parliamentary traditions, such as the separation of powers, constitutional monarchy, the principle of national sovereignty, and the recognition of basic civil liberties. The principle of representation followed the French model, whereas parliamentary immunity, debating procedures and committee work mostly followed the practice of the British parliament (see the historical review by Fernández Sarasola 2012: 15–118). The innovations were so broad in scope that, given the country's political instability, the new constitution paved the way for a delayed process of political changes. The solemn proclamation and swearing in of the Cortes neither hid the fragile confidence representatives had in the regency nor underestimated the threat of the invasion.

In his closing speech, the Speaker (*Presidente del Congreso*), Vicente Pascual Esteban, recalled the regency's duty to protect the constitutional order: '[The Cortes] cannot but remind [the Regency] that the happiness of the nation is entrusted to their hands', a nation that 'will eternally bless the names of its regents if they do not do or allow the least damage to this beneficial law';

otherwise, 'in the unlikely case of failing in such a sacred duty imposed by God and the fatherland, they will be held most strictly responsible' (DSCGE, 19 March 1812: 2950). In his response, the President of the Regency, Joaquín de Mosquera y Figueroa, renewed his oath of allegiance and acknowledged the dire situation of the 'beleaguered nation' and its determination to 'fight with one hand and write laws with the other' (DSCGE, 19 March 1812: 2950).

The breadth of the debates was only matched by their intensity, which was echoed in a myriad of gazettes, pamphlets and newsletters, many of them established in the heat of political events. Compared to the late eighteenth-century press, the new journalistic writings were not just a means of political enlightenment for the general public but rather partisan accounts of proceedings. In March 1812, with the noted exception of the Cadiz-based, pro-absolutist *Diario de la Tarde*, most periodicals endorsed the constitution (see e.g., *El Conciso*, 20 March 1812: 1–8), though there were critical reservations about the regency's constitutional loyalty, expressed for instance by the London-based liberal paper *El Español* (30 March 1812: 329–44).

While the draft constitution was being debated, a companion document was written to justify the envisaged changes. The three parts of the *Preliminary Speech*, collectively authored by the Constitutional Commission but mainly written by Agustín de Argüelles, were gradually read, alongside the draft articles in the Cortes in August, November and December 1811. Although it tried to underline the legacy of Spain's constitutional tradition, '[e]verything the Commission offers in its draft is already present, in the most authentic and solemn way, in the different Spanish legislative bodies' (De Argüelles 1981 [1811]: 67; ref. DSCGE, 18 August 1811: 1651), it openly endorsed parliamentary innovations such as the separation of powers and the overriding of royal sovereignty, which would have been unimaginable achievements only a few years earlier. 'The absolute freedom of the discussions', it acknowledged, 'has been made possible by parliamentary immunity (*la inviolabilidad de los diputados por sus opiniones en el ejercicio de su cargo*) and by banning both the king and his ministers from influencing deliberations by their presence' (De Argüelles 1981 [1811]: 87).

After the constituent period, there came the test of whether the parliamentary system would work. Activity was resumed, still in the extraordinary sessions of the Cortes, from 1 April 1812 until 20 September 1813, and then in two ordinary sessions from 1 October 1813 to 10 May 1814, when the Cortes was dissolved. The equivocal return of King Ferdinand VII, ostensibly in support of the constitutional regime, resulted in the suspension of the 1812 constitution. Parliamentary sessions, most of which had dealt with military operations, followed by debates on overseas policy, had been permanently compromised by the war. However, the inaugural session of the

1813 legislative period fully complied with the Cortes bylaws by appointing fourteen commissions aimed at addressing and reforming the main legislative areas (CAS, 1 October 1813: 9–10). The parliamentary activity proved that the Cortes was a working parliament, albeit one beset with gloomy prospects.

The agenda of the last session was surprisingly dealt with as usual (CAS, 9 May 1814: 349–53). In less than four years, the parliamentary activity of the Cortes had left a remarkable imprint on the country's political culture. The background of the Spanish uprising against Napoleon arguably explains the 'acceleration' of changes, observable in both the system of institutions and the rise of a new political language (La Parra 2012). Parliamentarians certainly played their part and became active in the emerging publicistic sphere, thus setting a precedent for the characteristic behaviour of leading political representatives (Sierra 2010: 32–33).

Constitutional Liberalism and Parliamentary Politics

Politics was no longer the exclusive province of lawyers. Other professionals and, above all, intellectuals were elected as members of parliament. Besides, the influence of constitutional liberalism and parliamentarism that inspired the liberation from France was also instrumental in the Central and South American wars of independence from the decaying Spanish Empire (Breña 2012), which also may explain why the American constitution was rarely invoked in the Cortes of Cadiz (De la Guardia 1996: 215–18). Parliamentary politics was only resumed six years afterwards, during the so-called 'Liberal Triennium' from 1820 to 1823. Significantly, the first session proceeded in a climate of normality (DSC, 26 June 1820: 1–4). Furthermore, this happened in spite of its acknowledged interim position, which gave the parliamentary debates an air of patriotic provisionality.

As agreed by the Cortes, before the expected restoration of absolute monarchy, parliamentary sessions were suspended in Madrid on 23 March 1823, to be resumed on 23 April in Seville and later in Cadiz. When the parliament moved, the official parliamentary archives were looted, then fragmentarily reconstructed and the documents reprinted in gazettes (Argüelles 1858). Manuel Flores Calderón, the Speaker, ironically recalled how '[a]mid huge obstacles . . . we have again disappointed the whole of Europe by peacefully moving from the shores of the Mazanares [the river running through Madrid] . . . to the wide, pleasant and delightful plains of the Guadalquivir, leading *liberty* in triumph' (*Gaceta Española*, Seville, Cortes, 24 April 1823: 1). The parliamentarians' resistance was valiant. Some months afterwards, Flores Calderón, no longer the Speaker, would reformulate Argüelles's proposal regarding the defence of the constitutional order: 'I ask the Cortes to solicit the government to publish their decision to continue the defence and the communications justifying this decision (*Gaceta Española*, Cadiz, Extraordinary Cortes, 12 September 1823: 441). It was one of the last proposals the Extraordinary Cortes approved.

By 1833 the first liberal state had been administratively established, again under a regency. The Cadiz constitution was reinstated in 1836, replacing the Royal Statute, although the latter remained in force until 1837. From then on, conservative, liberal and republican governments followed one another in three new constitutional periods, beginning respectively in 1837, 1845 and 1868. After many traditionalists had gradually embraced moderate views of liberalism in the form of a constitutional monarchy, reactionary Carlists remained the sole advocates of absolutism. Despite the fact that the 1837 constitution promoted the executive into almost a cabinet government (Arts. 58 and 72) and counterbalanced the royal power with the Cortes in the appointment of ministers (Art. 47; see Tomás Villarroya 1981: 60–61), parliamentarism had been only partially adopted. The 1845 constitution maintained the doctrine of double confidence, granting both the king and Cortes authority to sanction government policies (Arts. 12 and 43). It was certainly a diminished constitutional monarchy, in which the king, while not being actually a *pouvoir modérateur*, retained ample powers, which proved a delaying factor in the process of parliamentarization (Marcuello Benedicto 2005: 6–8, 23–33).

However, both friends and foes of parliamentarism learned its conventions, tellingly revising the political vocabulary (Rico y Amat 1855), and very early on conservative, formerly anti-parliamentary politicians excelled as newly minted parliamentarians (see Rivera García 2014). The Cortes became the scene of a revamped form of adversarial politics: fierce but enlightened. Juan Donoso Cortés's defence of Prime Minister Ramón María Narváez's Cortes-sanctioned suspensions in 1848 of constitutional guarantees to neutralize popular uprisings in major cities is eloquent:

> Liberty does not in fact exist in Europe: the constitutional governments that formerly represented it have everywhere become, gentlemen, but the frame of a lifeless skeleton . . . the question lies not, as said earlier, between freedom and dictatorship; if it were so, I would vote for freedom, like all who sit here. However, the question is this, and I conclude: namely choosing between insurrection dictatorship and government dictatorship . . . between sabre dictatorship and dagger dictatorship: I choose sabre dictatorship as it is the nobler one. (DSC, 4 January 1849: 172)

Following the parliamentary period inaugurated in the 1840s, the dethroning of Isabella II in the Glorious Revolution of September 1868 began the so-called 'Democratic Sexennium' that led to the proclamation of Spain's First Republic in February 1873. It was a time of audacious legal changes and of intense political debates marking a recasting of the party system. Parliamentary addresses had by then established themselves as a political genre. Some were published independently soon after their delivery in the Cortes, such as the famous speech of Emilio Castelar on 20 June 1870 denouncing the maintenance of slavery: 'Wake up, Spanish legislators, and make the nineteenth century, you who can consummate it, the century of the definitive and total emancipation of all slaves' (Castelar 1870: 48). However, slavery was only abolished in Puerto Rico in 1873 and in 1880 in Cuba.

Parliamentarism in Non-liberal Times

Though the First Republic was proclaimed by the Cortes, the form of the state was never constitutionalized. Its short life, marked by a series of unstable republican federal governments, ended in 1874 with a military reinstatement of the Bourbon monarchy. This second restoration was skilfully negotiated by the leader of the Conservative Party, Antonio Cánovas del Castillo, who later on as prime minister was instrumental in convening members of most parties to prepare a draft constitution. Politics, Cánovas argued, 'requires a series of constant transactions, from the highest to the lowest [levels], without limits', but it was, he claimed, the only option for governments in order to avoid revolutions (Cánovas del Castillo 2002 [1876]: 602).

Elected by universal male suffrage in January 1876, as granted by the 1869 constitution, the Cortes ratified the new constitution on 30 June (Tomás Villarroya 1981: 103–5). Sovereignty was shared by the king and the Cortes (Art. 18). However, the monarchy was held in abeyance by a subtle scheme of checks and balances that made the establishment of representative government possible. Ministers, for example, even if directly appointed by the king, were responsible to the Cortes and were the agents of the king's rulings (Art. 49). Furthermore, the constitution acknowledged a number of civil and political rights (Arts. 1–17) akin to other liberal constitutions of the time.

What is more relevant to understanding the political significance of the Restoration is that it extended, under a liberal regime, the legacy of parliamentarism into the twentieth century (Cabrera 1998; Dardé 2003). Its most distinctive feature was a consensual form of politics that Cánovas had envisaged in the 1880s by sealing an alliance with the leader of the Liberal Party, Práxedes Mateo Sagasta, to secure their alternation in government and in opposition. Neutralizing the role of the opposition, the flexibility of the 1876 constitution allowed each party in government enough space to accommodate the constitutional order to its own policies.

Shortly before being elected a representative of the Republican Party, Gumersindo de Azcárate, a law professor, had written some gloomy pages on 'parliamentary corruption' (*corruptelas parlamentarias*), denouncing the fact that in practice the Spanish parliamentary regime had become 'a new form' of 'personal government', in which 'party leaders are like temporary Caesars and dictators who succeed each other in power' (Azcárate 1931 [1885]: 104). Playing with legal norms, party machineries had bred an 'oligarchy of notables' (Azcárate 1931 [1885]: 106). Further critical remarks were made by another professor of law, Adolfo Posada, in one of the most pertinent treatises on Spanish parliamentarism: 'In a word, for it is a mystery to no-one that whatever happens in parliament looks in general theatrical: it is the performance of a comedy before the country, a comedy that everybody acknowledges as such, a comedy that goes on impassively' (Posada 1891: x).

Posada's analysis, particularly with regard to the party system, resembles the contemporary accounts of Bryce, Ostrogorski and Michels. His discussion of parliamentary immunity, defiantly abused by the political class, is a fine comparative study of the inner tension of parliamentarism (Posada 1891: 136–98). Spain is presented as a 'clinical case' that reproduces the typical troubles of parliamentary regimes from electoral corruption to clientelism, inefficient control of the executive, a lack of representativeness and, finally, its bureaucratic drift (Posada 1891: 58–73). His study partly continues Azcárate's somehow pre-Weberian reflections on the vocation and the professionalization of politics (Azcárate 1931 [1885]: 239–55).

For more than forty years, the system of institutions was smoothly instrumentalized, and only in the second half of the period did a challenging political dissent begin to rise. Left-wing and republican parties were in a minority in the Cortes, and that alone sufficed to explain the reaction. The latter years of the regime were times of economic downturn and social discontent. Along with the unrest in the military, they became a catalyst for a new coup. General Primo de Rivera's dictatorship would last from 1923 to 1930. Its trial-and-error appointments of civilian governments turned into a failed search for social legitimation, highlighted by the drawbacks of improvised economic policies, and the final recourse to bringing the monarchy back in 1930, which was resorted to only in order to anticipate an inevitable regime change and calculated as a supervised gambit to keep the status quo.

A Revolutionary Parliamentary Democracy

Aimed at paving the way for favourable general elections in May, the municipal elections held on 12 April 1931 led unexpectedly to a triumph of the republican parties in all major cities, which was perceived by the monarchic government as a warning of a pressing need to hand over power. Within two days, Spain's Second Republic was proclaimed (Payne 1993: 23–35). A provisional government, formed from a revolutionary committee, called a general election for 28 June and took on the task of drafting a new constitution. It was passed on 9 December, establishing Spain as 'a democratic republic of workers' (Art. 1) and bringing back a unicameral parliament (Art. 51; see Fernández Sarasola 2008). Constituent sessions were held from 27 August to 8 December. Two debates are especially representative of the political moment, namely the discussion on women's suffrage and the debate on regional autonomy. The former opened the way for the democratization of politics. The latter anticipated what would become one of the most puzzling issues of Spanish democracy.

> If Spanish women were all workers, if Spanish women had attended the university and were emancipated in their conscience, I would stand up today before the whole Chamber to ask for the vote for women. Yet at this moment I stand up to say precisely the contrary . . . [to propose] either the conditionality of suffrage or its postponement; I think its postponement would be more beneficial. (DSCCRE, 1 October 1931: 1352)

These were the words of Victoria Kent, a prominent socialist. They were responded to by Clara Campoamor, member of the Radical Party and the Constitutional Commission: 'I . . . understand the torture of her [Kent's] mind in arriving at the unpleasant situation of denying woman's basic capability' (DSCCRE, 1 October 1931: 1352), adding: 'I feel myself . . . to be first a citizen and then a woman, and I consider that it would be a profound political mistake not to grant that right to women, to the women who hope and trust in you . . . Do not commit a historical mistake that you will never cease to regret by leaving women out of the Republic' (DSCCRE, 1 October 1931: 1354).

Article 36 of the constitution read: 'Citizens of either sex, above twenty-three years of age, will have the same electoral rights as determined by the law.' The discussion ran almost parallel with the deliberations on the structure of the state. Article 1 defined Spain as an 'integral State compatible with the autonomy of its municipalities and regions'. However, the debate on regional autonomy, conceived as an optional form of decentralization, was easily connected with the federal question. It was interpreted in secessionist terms for misleading reasons, observed José Ortega y Gasset, a representative of the liberal *Agrupación al Servicio de la República* (Grouping at the Service of the Republic), arguing:

We cannot settle the issue of the reform of Spain, particularly because of the problem posed by Catalonia, in terms of sovereignty but by searching for a less formidable area, the area of the widest but strictest autonomy [. . . which] offers an unlimited horizon of freedom. (DSCCRE, 25 September 1931: 1257)

A Statute of Autonomy for Catalonia would be approved by the Cortes on 9 September 1932. During its parliamentary passage, Prime Minister Manuel Azaña acknowledged (or wished to think) that once the constitution was passed in parliament, 'there would be no possible prejudice about a likely dispersion of Spanish unity' (DSC, 27 May 1932: 5866). Secession was not a looming threat although it added to the many challenges the new regime faced. The most important of these was violence. The passing in October 1931 of the Law in Defence of the Republic granting the Provisional Government supra-constitutional powers to curb 'aggression against the Republic' (Art. 1) was justified as being a temporary measure. However, it remained in force until the even more disquieting Law on Public Order replaced it in July 1933.

The constituent process led to a doomed parliamentary life for the constitution. Once approved, the constitution was questioned by all political parties and selectively used by the twenty-six governments that ruled the Republic, first by six centre-left governments from 14 April 1931 to 8 October 1933 to advance a revolutionary legislative agenda aimed at revising the country's economic and social conditions, church-state relations and the role of the military. It was next questioned by ten centre-right governments from 16 December 1933 to 30 December 1935 with the aim of restoring law and order while keeping most of the reforms. Finally, when the Civil War broke out in July 1936, it was questioned by ten Popular Front governments from 19 February 1936 to 5 April 1938. The war ended in April the following year.

Especially in the third phase, parliamentary polarization was violently reflected outside the Cortes. Popular Front governments were opposed in the Cortes by CEDA, the Spanish Confederation of Autonomous Right-Wing Parties (*Confederación Española de Derechas Autónomas*), and were they significantly weakened by internal splits in their coalition, above all by the rupture between socialists and republicans that marginalized the gradualists on both sides. In the streets, they faced the unrest of fascist groups, such as the *Falange Española*, and paradoxically some of their own allies, namely the socialist General Union of Workers (UGT).

Some of the leaders of both the UGT and the Socialist Party backed the use of violence to advance reforms and to counteract political adversaries (see Casanova 2010: 125–49). Compared to the anarcho-syndicalism of the National Confederation of Workers (CNT), this kind of counter-parliamentary action proved lethal for the republic. The anarchists had refused to cooperate with the regime right from its uncertain beginnings. They had been the 'vanguard' of the opposition against the dictatorship between 1923 and 1930, and for the two previous decades they had violently challenged the Restoration regime. As early as 12 May 1931, the Barcelona-based periodical *Solidaridad Obrera* claimed: '[T]he current Government is no longer a revolutionary government, it has become another liberal government of the monarchy'. Even while admitting that 'The constituent Cortes is the product of a revolutionary fact', the CNT followed its own revolutionary paths through strikes and land seizures, which were brutally repressed, 'in order to intervene' in Spain's social and political problems: '[T]his is our apoliticism or, better, our anti-parliamentarism' (CNT 1931: Art. 8). It was a principled position: 'We are against the constituent Cortes as we are against any oppressive power. We keep up our war against the state. Our mission, sacred and high, is to educate the people so that they understand the need to join us, with full awareness, and to attain our total emancipation through social revolution' (CNT 1931: Art. 8.1).

It took the Civil War to change the anarchists' anti-political creed and methods (González Calleja 2008: 105–7). With their militancy growing, anarchist regional federations had seized virtual control of the countryside through their system of cooperatives. Out of these, thousands of workers organized themselves into militias that made up for the many weaknesses of the Republican Army, although they ultimately shared the same fate. In November 1936 four CNT members were appointed as ministers.

The 'frustration with the parliamentary system' (Payne 2006: 118–39) arose from a disgraceful combination of irresponsible leadership in both the government and the opposition parties. They lacked the nerve to consistently defend the reformist progress of parliamentary democracy and resorted to violence in order to repair their own political incompetence. Indeed, they allowed their sister organizations to act freely until they finally lost authority and the ability to control the outbreaks of violence in their own ranks. The last general elections of February and May 1936 (Villa García 2009: 423–27) and the turbulent parliamentary sessions that followed further revealed the incapacity of the constitutional regime to prevent the war.

In July 1939 the Franco regime abolished the parliamentary system, although it kept the names of the institutions for tactical reasons A so-called 'organic democracy' was established in an attempt to rhetorically refurbish the corporatist state with the aim of re-establishing diplomatic relations, which, however, did not begin to happen until the 1960s. The electors were granted a symbolic participatory role in plebiscites, a distinctive feature of fascist regimes, while the corporatist representatives played according to the parliamentary rules in a dissimulating way for nearly four decades.

Building a Parliamentary Democracy

Against early expectations of the 1977 Law for Political Reform, Prime Minister Adolfo Suárez succeeded in gathering the support of most political parties for his proposal to turn the transitional parliament into a pluralist arena (Fuentes 2011: 213–78). The experiment worked. In his response to interpellations after his new victory in the general election of March 1979, Suárez stated that he felt no shame about the political path that he had taken: 'I have worked to turn an authoritarian system into a democratic one, mostly relying on the laws that are available to implement political change' (DSC, 30 March 1979: 126).

Spain's parliamentary monarchy, the state polity adopted by the 1978 constitution, conjured up an ominous vision of past military-monarchy alliances. The uncertainty lasted until a coup was defeated in February 1981. By then, basic institutional changes had been carried out, and the mirage of a return of the 1930s regime had vanished. The 1977 democracy was in fact a new endeavour, not the recovery of a repressed, dormant heritage. Compared to the parliamentary events of the 1930s, the constituent Cortes of 1977–79, and the ensuing democratic period, 1979–82, left a series of edifying debates that offered the public a new form of parliamentary politics in action.

Passionate as they were, the debates manifested tenable forms of partisan dissent that helped channel pluralism into the nascent party system. A ceaseless, ideological and highly diverse body of legislation emerged from the hectic parliamentary activity: plenary sessions alternated with continuous committee sittings, parliamentary group meetings were reinstated, and the Cortes Bulletin uninterruptedly published the government's answers to the opposition representatives' written questions. The debating revived the features of enlightened disputes, accompanied as they were by scholarly and comparative references, since the new parliamentarians, albeit with some exceptions, had to prove that they possessed a fluent command of the language of parliamentary democracy. This they certainly did, but even so it was a formal change that required a diligent self-re-education. Theoretically, the constituent debates gave the impression that the political class was coming of age. The vocabulary of rights and freedoms re-politicized the language of politics (De Santiago Guervós 1992: 63–70). The state broadcasting system became truly public, and restrictions on the freedom of the press were lifted, thus contributing to a prolific politicization of the public space. For decades Spaniards had been clandestinely politicized and thereby fragmented along ideological lines. Suddenly they gained a new conception of political debating that forced previous enemies to share the same political space.

The 1977–78 constituent debates grew out of an irreconcilable diversity of views on how the state should be organized, but they also made clear the need to agree on negotiating halfway positions. Around three decades afterwards, the constitutional consensus began to reveal signs of weariness, and claims for reform were on the rise. In the historical perspective, however, the new democracy has produced the country's longest period of democratic stability. For the first time in history, representatives in parliament have embodied the majority will to embark on a conciliatory political project. However, memories of the 1936–39 Civil War lived on and more than six decades afterwards took centre stage in politics. It was assumed that the inevitable new beginning entailed an unprecedented process of political re-learning. Few anticipated that it was going to involve different generations for so long. Over time, parliamentary politics has established itself even though it has lost the original appeal that it possessed in the early years of democracy. On the other hand, this may also be a sign of its durability.

Notes

The following abbreviations have been used: Diario de Sesiones de las Cortes Generales y Extraordinarias (DSCGE) (1810–12); Cortes: Actas de las Sesiones (CAS) (1813–14); Diario de las Sesiones de Cortes (DSC) (1820 to the present); Diario de Sesiones de las Cortes Constituyentes de la República Española (DSCCRE) (1931).

1 The Cortes are not courts of justice but the national legislative assembly, which for most of its history in the past two centuries has been bicameral, the exceptions being the constitutions of 1812 and 1931. *Congreso de los Diputados* (literally the Congress of Deputies) is Spain's current lower chamber of parliament and the Senate (*Senado*) the upper chamber. *Diputado* or *diputada* is the Spanish name for a member of parliament.

2 This chapter is part of the Civic Constellation Project (Spain's National Research Fund, FFI2011–23388).

3 The Journals of the Spanish Parliament (*Diario de Sesiones*) are available in different collections. For 1810–73, see the Journal of Debates: Cádiz: Fundación Centro de Estudios Constitucionales 1812, www.constitucion1812.org/listado_completo. asp?tipo_libro=3. For 1810 to the present, see the Journal of Debates (historical series and contemporary legislative periods available in DVD-ROM. Madrid: Congreso de los Diputados. 2000–). For 1977 to the present, see the following digitized archive: www.congreso.es/portal/page/portal/Congreso/Congreso/Publicaciones

References

Primary Sources

Argüelles, F. 1858. 'Preliminary Note', in _Diario de las Sesiones de Cortes celebradas en Sevilla y Cádiz en 1823_. Madrid: Imprenta Nacional, pp. i–ii.

Azcárate, G. de. 1931 [1885]. _El régimen parlamentario en la práctica_. Madrid: Sobrinos de la Sucesora de M. Minuesa de los Ríos.

Cánovas del Castillo, A. 2002 [1876]. 'Discurso en Cortes' (5 June), in J.M. Cuenca Toribio (ed.), _La oratoria parlamentaria española. Una antología_. Madrid: Boletín Oficial del Estado-Centro de Estudios Políticos y Constitucionales, pp. 581–602.

Castelar, E. 1870. _Abolición de la esclavitud_. Madrid: Imprenta de J.A. García.

CNT. 1931. 'Proceedings of the CNT's Third Congress'. Madrid, 11–16 June 1931. Retrieved from http://es.wikisource.org/wiki/III_Congreso_de_la_CNT

De Argüelles, A. 1981 [1811]. _Discurso preliminar a la Constitución de 1812_. L. Sánchez Agesta (ed.). Madrid: Centro de Estudios Constitucionales.

Fernández Martín, M. 1885. _Derecho parlamentario español_, vol. 1, _Introducción_. Madrid: Congreso de los Diputados.

The Journals of the Spanish Parliament (_Diario de Sesiones_). See Endnote 3 for details.

Martínez Marina, F. 1813. _Teoría de las Cortes_, vol. 1. Madrid: Imprenta de D. Fermín Villalpando.

Posada, A. 1891. _Estudios sobre el régimen parlamentario en España_. Madrid: Biblioteca Económica Filosófica.

Rico y Amat, J. 1855. _Diccionario de los políticos, o Verdadero sentido de las voces y frases más usuales entre los mismos_. Madrid: Imprenta de F. Andrés y Compañía.

Secondary Sources

Breña, R. 2012. 'Presentación: Las independencias americanas, la revolución española y el enfoque atlántico', _Historia y Política_ 24: 11–22.

Cabrera, M. (ed.). 1998. _Con luz y taquígrafos. El Parlamento en la Restauración (1913–1923)_. Madrid: Taurus.

Casanova, J. 2010. _The Spanish Republic and Civil War_, trans. M. Douch. Cambridge: Cambridge University Press.

Dardé, C. (ed.). 2003. _La aceptación del adversario. Política y políticos de la Restauración, 1875–1900_. Madrid: Biblioteca Nueva.

De la Guardia, C. 1996. 'La Revolución americana y el primer parlamentarismo español', _Revista de Estudios Políticos_ 93: 205–18.

De Santiago Guervós, J. 1992. _El léxico político de la transición española_. Salamanca: Universidad de Salamanca.

Fernández Sarasola, I. 2008. 'Cortes', in J. Fernández Sebastián and J.F. Fuentes (eds), _Diccionario político y social del siglo XX español_. Madrid: Alianza, pp. 312–22.

_____. 2012. _Reglamentos parlamentarios (1810–1977)_. Madrid: Iustel.

Fuentes, J.F. 2011. _Adolfo Suárez. Biografía política_. Barcelona: Planeta.

González Calleja, E. 2008. 'Anarquismo', in J. Fernández Sebastián and J.F. Fuentes (eds), *Diccionario político y social del siglo XX español*. Madrid: Alianza, pp. 100–9.

La Parra, E. 2012. '"Presentación" to Dossier "La Guerra de la Independencia"', *Ayer: Revista de Historia Contemporánea* 86: 13–24.

López Pina, A. (ed.). 1994. *Democracia representativa y parlamentarismo: Alemania, España, Gran Bretaña e Italia*. Madrid: Servicio de Publicaciones del Senado.

Marcuello Benedicto, J.I. 2005. 'Gobierno y "parlamentarización" en el proceso político de la Monarquía constitucional de Isabel II', *Revista de Estudios Políticos* 130: 5–33.

Morán Orti, M. 1991. 'La formación de las Cortes (1808–1810)', *Ayer: Revista de Historia Contemporánea* 1: 13–36.

Payne, S.G. 1993. *Spain's First Democracy: The Second Republic, 1931–1936*. Madison: The University of Wisconsin Press.

_____. 2006. *The Collapse of the Spanish Republic, 1933–1936: Origins of the Civil War*. New Haven: Yale University Press.

Rivera García, A. 2014. 'Nineteenth-century Spanish Counter-revolution: The Critique to Liberal Parliamentarism and the Praise of the Traditional Constitution', in K. Palonen, J.M. Rosales and T. Turkka (eds), *The Politics of Dissensus: Parliament in Debate*. Santander and Madrid: Cantabria University Press and McGraw-Hill, pp. 127–48.

Romeo, M.C. 2002. 'Parlamentarismo', in J. Fernández Sebastián and J.F. Fuentes (eds), *Diccionario político y social del siglo XIX español*. Madrid: Alianza, pp. 495–501.

Sierra, M. 2010. 'The Profession of Deputy: The Idea of Political Representation in Liberal Spain', *Parliaments, Estates and Representation* 30(1): 31–40.

Tomás Villarroya, J. 1981. *Breve historia del constitucionalismo español*. Madrid: Centro de Estudios Constitucionales.

Villa García, R. 2009. 'The Failure of Electoral Modernization: The Elections of May 1936 in Granada', *Journal of Contemporary History* 44(3): 401–29.

José María Rosales, Ph.D., is Associate Professor of Moral and Political Philosophy at the University of Málaga, Spain. His research focuses on democratic theory, political philosophy and the history of political thought. He has edited books on nationalism, citizenship, democratization, and parliamentarism and democratic theory. He is a board member of Concepta – International Research School in Conceptual History and Political Thought.

Chapter 18

Towards a Political Theory of EU Parliamentarism

Teija Tiilikainen and Claudia Wiesner

Since all EU member states are defined as representative democracies, debating the political theory of EU parliamentarism involves, strictly speaking, the entire multilevel system of the EU and therefore the member states and their parliaments as well. This chapter will concentrate on the EU level only and discuss the role of the European Parliament in the EU's political system. First of all, the history of parliamentarism at the EU level and its conceptualization will be outlined. Secondly, the chapter will discuss the character of the EU's political order and the particular role of the EP in it. The third section of the chapter will discuss the particular features of the EP as a parliament.

The Conceptual and Political History of the European Parliament

The idea of creating a European parliament, one would perhaps assume, is a rather natural outcome of the endeavour to create a unified Europe. A closer look at both the conceptual and political history behind EU integration and the development of the European Parliament reveals that this is not the case. While the conceptual history behind the EP is vaguer than one would have thought, its political history is not.

The conceptual history of European integration started several centuries ago. For a number of thinkers after Dante, a unified Europe was a kind of utopia that would guarantee peace in Europe. However, there were two different directions of argumentation that developed over time. The first aimed at a balance of power of sovereign nation states; the other had a stronger normative background and conceptualized Europe as a supranational and later also an explicitly democratic federation.

During the Second World War and right after it, there developed two types of political activist groups, both of which wanted to make European integration a reality but disagreed over the democratic federation concept and the balance-of-power issue. Their conflict and its outcome predetermined the development of parliamentarism in the EU for several decades (see Wiesner 2014c).

The 'European federalist' associations, founded in relation with the resistance against national socialism and fascism, advocated the democracy concept and played the main role in advancing European integration between 1940 and 1945 (for a description of the groups, see Lipgens 1977: 545). The federalists believed that a democratic European federation that was supreme over the nation states was the only way to ensure the progress of peace and freedom in Europe. The guiding principles should be democracy, civil liberties and rights, pluralism, decentralization and federalism. A parliament did not predominantly figure in these concepts, except for the idea that a European constitutional council should be held and a vote on the constitution of a European federation be taken (Czuczka 1947; Schenck 1947; Kövér 1947a, 1947b; Lipgens 1977: 43, 109, 292, 514).

The alternative balance-of-power conception of a united Europe was adopted by the 'European Unionists', represented in the United Europe Movement (UEM) founded in 1947. Their idea, too, was to safeguard peace in Europe and create a unified Europe, but they wanted it to consist of sovereign nation states that would be coordinated by a European Council of the member states (similar to, but not to be confused with today's EC). Hence, a parliament had no role in this conception either. The Unionists mobilized the new leaders of the European nation states and the media in support of their ideas (Niess 2001: 126).

The Unionists prevailed in the struggle of integrative concepts: the founding of the European Coal and Steel Community (ECSC) in 1952 and the application of the 'Monnet method' of integration were based on the unionist perspective. Integration was to be fuelled by the member states and their economic and political self-interests. Nevertheless, the ECSC together with the Common Assembly already contained the rudiments of a parliament: it was founded in 1952 and consisted of seventy-eight delegates of the – then only six – member states' parliaments. It did not have law-making powers.

However, the political and democratic face of European integration remained a key question. It was already back on the agenda in the 1952 and 1953 debates on a European Community of Defence and a European Political Community. The respective concepts explicitly foresaw the creation of a two-chamber parliament, one chamber to be directly elected and the other to be based on the Council. A draft constitution had even been developed on the initiative of the ECSC Foreign Ministers (Europäische Politische Gemeinschaft 1953). However, the entire project fell apart when the French National Assembly did not ratify the project of a Treaty on a European Community of Defence in a 1954 vote. Afterwards, European integration was, for many years to come, based on the two pillars of intergovernmental cooperation and economic integration, even though politicians, in particular EP parliamentarians, advanced proposals for EU democratization several times (European Parliament 2009: 99, 111).

Nevertheless, the EP gradually evolved as a result of the establishment of the European Economic Community (EEC) in the Treaty of Rome in March 1958. The former 'Common Assembly' of the ECSC became the 'European Parliamentary Assembly', created as a result of the Treaty of Rome. In 1962 it changed its name to 'the European Parliament'. However, these name changes did not affect its powers or composition: for many years the EP remained a representative body consisting of delegates from the member states' parliaments and having mere consultative competence (European Parliament 2009: 13). A decisive exception was the right (already granted to the ECSC Common Assembly) to censure the Commission and force it to resign.

The question of the political and democratic integration of the European Economic Community (EEC) came back on the agenda in the 1970s, and with it the role of the EP. Conceptualizations of EP reforms and parliamentarism in the European Community, together with steps to realize them, were for the most part closely related at that time. The development of the EP was impressive, showing as it did a dynamism fuelled by political struggles, strategic and rhetorical moves and political 'windows of opportunity'. A decisive step was taken when the EP obtained budgetary power. The Treaties of Luxembourg (1970) and Brussels (1975) gave the EEC a budget of its own for the first time – and the EP in some areas shared a say on it with the Council. The Treaty of Brussels even gave the EP the right to reject the budget by a two-thirds majority of its members (European Parliament 2009: 16, 61, 145).

The introduction of a direct election procedure for the EP in 1979 was the next decisive step. There had been a provision in the Treaty of Rome demanding direct election to the EP in due course, but its realization was related to a political window of opportunity. It was claimed that European integration had been in a crisis since the second half of the 1960s. The EEC was criticized for being too bureaucratic and for lacking democratic legitimacy. In this context, the EP's indirect legitimation by delegates from national parliaments was also debated: MEPs were rarely appointed from opposition parties in the member states, and since they were also MPs in their home countries, MEPs could only spend a limited amount of time at the EP. This situation led to several reform proposals to strengthen the EP. Valéry Giscard d'Estaing, who was elected President of France in 1974, supported direct election and consequently in December 1974 in Paris the Council decided that it should be introduced. After a lengthy process of approval in the member states, the first direct EP elections took place from 7 to 10 June 1979, and 410 MEPs were elected (European Parliament 2009: 35).

The direct election did not immediately change the EP's formal powers, but it did strengthen the parliament's institutional role and its legitimacy, and it brought a new dynamism: 185 million EEC citizens had taken part in the election, and the polling rate was almost 63 per cent. The first strategic institutional move the EP took afterwards was the rejection of the 1980 draft budget in December 1979 (European Parliament 2009: 37).

In the following years, the EP used such moves over and over again to influence the institutional dynamics of the EU system in its favour (for a detailed account, see Wiesner 2014b). Since 1990, framework agreements have defined the relationship between the EP and the Commission. They demonstrate the growing influence of the EP, and also the increasing responsibility of the Commission to it. The EP has become more and more an independent political actor and a counterpart of the Council and the Commission. The EP's powers have also been increased by all the treaty changes of the 1990s and 2000s, as will be explained later.

The Political System of the EU

Towards Parliamentarism or Presidentialism?
The EU's political system must also be perceived from the perspective of the initial plans for European integration. The main goal was to gradually establish a European federation, which has been reflected ever since in the main contours of the union's political system. The establishment of the EU's political system followed the federal model of government in the sense that the union's political bodies were planned to form a layer of federal government above the member states (Monnet 1978; Cardozo 1989). The EU's overall political rule clearly represents, first of all, a system of cooperative federalism where no clear-cut division of power between the two levels of government exists but where the state-level actors and the federal-level actors both have legislative powers in most policy fields (Elazar 2001; Dann 2003).

The present European Parliament has legislative powers equal to those of the Council. The Commission represents an EU-level government and performs the same kind of tasks as national executives, while the provisions of the treaties require that it be responsible for its actions to the EP. The Council, which was supposed to evolve gradually into the EP's second chamber, has only very slowly adopted this line of development, as the member states have been reluctant to decrease their own powers.

An analysis of the formal powers granted to the EU bodies in the Lisbon Treaty must start by seeking to understand their roles and mutual relationships by using the regime model that seems to provide the best framework for this. However, the union appears to fit neither the category of parliamentary rule nor the U.S. type of presidential system based on a separation of powers between the main political bodies. In fact, the division of powers in the EU seems to follow a regime model that has gained ground among European political systems more generally: a semi-presidential system. Semi-presidentialism is a polity that falls between parliamentarism on one hand and a separation-of-powers system on the other. It combines a parliamentary government with the powers of another fairly independent executive instance: the president (Sartori 1994; Duverger 1980).

The EU's political system consists firstly of a parliamentary government, of which the cabinet – that is, the Commission – is accountable to the European Parliament. The election of the Commission does not, however, follow normal parliamentary practices as this task is still strongly in the hands of the member states. The formal possibilities of the EP to dismiss the Commission have been limited for many years by a rule according to which a vote of censure can only be applied to the entire Commission and not to single members of it. However, the role of the Commission as a political government has gradually been strengthened. In accordance with the Lisbon Treaty, the results of the EP elections must be taken into account when electing the President of the Commission. The latter also has the right to ask individual commissioners to resign.

While the Council has in general been treated as the other partner of the union's dual executive (Hix 2005: 31), here we would like to offer that role to the newly institutionalized European Council. Owing to the institutionalization of the EC in the Lisbon Treaty and the creation of a permanent presidency, this body has taken a much firmer grip on the union's executive powers than the former summit meetings held under the rotating presidency were able to do. The formulation of the EC's remit as being to 'provide the Union with the necessary impetus for its development and define the general political directions and priorities thereof' gives it a strong executive mandate, particularly when complemented with the powers it possesses in the nomination of the Commission and in the Common Foreign and Security Policy (CFSP).

The Council is, to a large extent, independent of the EP in the sense that it can define the guidelines for the union's policies without taking heed of the EP's view or its political constellations. In most policy fields, the implementation of these guidelines is, however, firmly dependent on the parliamentary machinery – that is, on the Commission and the EP. The other side of the coin consists of the fact that the Commission is accountable to the EP and to the EP alone. In semi-presidential systems, the president usually takes his legitimacy from some other source than the Parliament and, according to Sartori's criteria for semi-presidentialism, the president is elected by a popular vote for a fixed term of office. The Council essentially gets its legitimacy from the member states, and the political considerations about whether its permanent president should be elected through a direct vote must be understood against this background (Hix 2002).

The contours of semi-presidentialism have become stronger both through the deepening and the extension of the parliamentary rule and through the simultaneous reinforcement of the Council. We can thus talk about a simultaneous accentuation of parliamentarism and presidentialism. The two parts of the executive come together in the European Council (EC), of which the President of the Commission is a member. The EC's presidential characteristics are further emphasized through its role in the nomination of the latter. In spite of the fact that the EC can neither dismiss the Commission nor its President, its proposal is still the key factor in the nomination procedure.[1]

The Council has clearly been developing in the direction of a second chamber of the legislature, a role that was accentuated further by the Lisbon Treaty.[2] In many other matters the Council carries executive competence, but here, too, changes have taken place in favour of the EC on one hand and the new High Representative for Foreign Affairs and Security Policy on the other. It should be noted that the EC defines the strategic guidelines both for the EU's external relations and in the area of freedom, security and justice (TEU, Art. 10b, and TFEU, Art. 61A) and consequently also provides the political framework for the Council's actions. The plurality of functions given to the High Representative again emphasizes his or her role in the leadership of the CFSP.

One of the most important executive functions remaining in the hands of the Council is the role it takes in the Union's system of executive federalism (Dann 2003). The Council's role as the meeting point between the two levels of government stresses its executive functions, as it provides an important forum for coordination and consensus- building between the two levels.

The EP within the Framework of Semi-presidentialism

The EP's powers have been constantly reinforced in the EU's institutional setting, where the elements of presidentialism presented above currently create obvious constraints on any further development in the direction of parliamentarism. There is, however, another distinction that has to be made for further study of the EP's role. The division of parliaments into debating parliaments and working parliaments is closely linked with the categories of government presented above (in the sense used by Dann 2003). The concept of a debating parliament tends to characterize parliaments in a parliamentary system. It stresses the parliament's close political connection with the government, the relationship between the government and the opposition, and activities in the plenary format.

A working parliament, on the other hand, emphasizes the institutional framework of a parliament over the political one. The parliament forms an institutional counterweight to the executive bodies in a separation-of-power type of system. The emphasis lies in its legislative proceedings and committees rather than in the political struggle with the government. As semi-presidential systems include elements of both parliamentary and presidential systems that must be seen as affecting the role of parliament from the outset, parliaments in such systems could be expected to represent a hybrid of the two models.

The EP's powers are mainly legislative, and its way of dealing with them clearly follows the model of a working parliament. Firstly the development towards one main legislative procedure – known as the 'ordinary legislative procedure' – and the extension of it to most legislative fields has clearly strengthened the independence of the EP's mandate. When the EP's formal powers were smaller, it often adopted a strategy of blocking or slowing down legislation in order to win concessions (Farrell and Héritier 2003: 587). Along with the increase in the use of the ordinary legislative procedure, the emphasis has moved to the early stages of the process, with the EP trying to engage in informal negotiations and arbitration with the Council. Consequently, the number of legislative acts adopted on the basis of a first reading has increased remarkably.

The internal working mechanisms in the EP have also changed. There seems to be wide agreement about the reinforced powers of the parliamentary committees and the role of the rapporteurs (Benedetto 2005; Settembri and Neuhold 2009; Ripoll Servent 2009). The relationship between political groups and committees seems to be the most important internal axis of power in the EP at the moment. The establishment of EU-level political parties has strengthened the party-political dimension in the union's political system in spite of the fact that the parties do not fully correspond to parties at the national level either in their organization or with respect to their political programmes.[3] EU-level parties influence the union's decision-making both through informal and formal channels, the latter being strongly centred around their political groups in the EP. As the EP's focus in legislative matters has moved to the parliamentary committees, it is through these committees and the key functions of committee chairpersons and rapporteurs that political groups now exert power (Mamadouh and Raunio 2003).

In the Lisbon Treaty, the EP's legislative powers were strengthened with new budgetary powers and a more formalized role in amending the fundamental treaties (formalization of the convention mechanism). It seems that in this role the EP fulfils the criteria of parliamentarism much better than in its political control of – or interaction with – the executive. These are prerogatives that are emphasized in the model of a debating parliament.

The roots of a debating parliament lie in the principle of parliamentary control of the executive. In the EU's case, this principle was already confirmed in the initial treaties that entitled the EP to dismiss the Commission by a vote of censure. The recent treaty changes have also created an indirect possibility for the EP to force individual commissioners to resign, if necessary.

Constant amendments boosting the EP's role in the process of nominating the Commission have equally underlined the value of the principle of parliamentary control. The EP's role in the nomination procedure has been systematically strengthened, with the Lisbon Treaty taking it one further crucial step forward.

The EU's government comprises numerous legal and institutional preconditions of the parliamentary control of the executive. Within the framework of semi-presidentialism, however, this control only applies to one part of it. Another constraint relates to the lack of a party government. The Commission possesses the critical functions of a political executive and acts in legal and institutional terms under the formal responsibility of the EP. The political content of this responsibility is, however, seriously hampered by the Commission's character as an independent body without the normal characteristics of a parliamentary government.[4]

In terms of fully fledged parliamentarism, parliamentary rule at the EU level would mean that the EP controlled the Commission's political agenda from the point of view of a government programme based on the electoral campaigns of the ruling parties. As the normal political connection is lacking in the relationship between the Commission and the EP, this relationship can only be of a quasi-parliamentary nature. In this respect, too, some changes have, however, been made with the effect of reducing the Commission's status as an independent body and rather giving it a parliamentary executive position. These changes have, above all, been directed at the role of the President of the Commission, whose post became highly partisan as a result of the Lisbon Treaty (TEU, Art. 9D, 7), which in practice demands that the President come from the party group that wins the elections. Together with the duty of the President to ask a commissioner to resign if the EP so requires, this emphasizes the President's role as a political guarantor of the Commission.

These practices try to balance the lack of political government and get the best out of parliamentarism in these conditions. The EP's approval of the Commission (college) is preceded by hearings of the individual commissioners. This practice and the approval itself are well compatible with the logic of parliamentary responsibility. However, the lack of political programmes – either electoral or for the cabinet – leads to the parliamentary approval focusing on the personal qualifications and backgrounds of the candidate commissioners rather than on their political views. And this remains the major focus of the EP's control of the Commission throughout the electoral period.

Relations between the EP and the Commission do not fully correspond to the concept of a debating parliament. There are, however, political projects in preparation that would deepen the partisan relationship between them. The first is the proposal for a new electoral law for the European Parliament that would lead to the election of twenty-five MEPs from a transnational list of candidates (see European Parliament 2012b). This change would promote the formation of political parties and other movements at the European level. For the time being, however, it is unclear whether the proposal will get the necessary support of the member states and the EU institutions. Every now and then another proposal is made concerning the composition of the Commission from persons who have been elected to the European Parliament. This amendment would essentially change the role of the European elections and enhance the parliamentary connection between the Commission and the EP, as the former EP Speaker, Jerzy Busek, suggested.

How to Theorize the EP Today?

Political thinking on the EP also has to take into account its particularities. The core argument in the rest of this chapter is that the European Parliament, which is still often criticized for being a deficitary parliament, possesses certain special features and plays a key role in democratizing the EU's institutional system.

The EP as a Deficitary Parliament?
Despite the impressive development of the EP, it has for several years occupied a central part of the argument concerning a democratic deficit in the EU. In several contributions during the last twenty years, critics have described the EP's law-making competence as limited compared to that of a fully fledged national parliament in a parliamentary system, since it does not possess the right to initiate new legislation (this argument has become partly obsolete since the Lisbon Treaty, as the EP may now by a majority vote

compel the Commission to present a legislative proposal: TFEU, Art. 225), and its legislative competence does not extend to all policy fields. Another point of criticism is that in practice twenty-eight different national voting procedures take place in the EP elections, even though the treaties set general rules for them. Moreover, the fact that there are no EU-wide candidate lists has been criticized. At times it has also been argued that these factors add to the problem that EU citizens feel they are not involved in the affairs of EU and EP politics and thus create a 'mental distance' between the represented and the representatives (for an overview of the current state of the art in the democratic deficit argument, see Føllesdal and Hix 2006: 535; European Parliament 2009: 27, 129; for earlier contributions see e.g., Scharpf 1995, 1998; Kielmannsegg 1996, 2003; Føllesdal and Koslowski 1997).

It is important to emphasize five points in connection with these criticisms. As has been argued in the earlier sections of this chapter, firstly several of these criticisms result at least partly from the special features of the EU institutional system. Secondly, different political traditions give rise to different judgments of the EP. It is a key argument in German debates, for example, to criticize the EP's lack of power in foreign and security policy by contrast with German parliamentary culture (Wiesner 2014a).[5] Thirdly, as will be argued in the following, several particularities result from the EP's role as a parliament in development in the EU (European Parliament 2009: 289), which itself is a political system in the making. Thus it is important to take into account not only the formally ratified powers of the EP, but also those that it has acquired through political struggles and which have not (yet) been formally ratified or confirmed by treaties (see below). Fourthly, a justified picture must take into account the EP's particular features, and especially the EP's role in democratizing the EU institutional system. Finally, the EP shows some specific characteristics with regard to the key dimensions of parliamentarism – deliberation, representation, sovereignty and responsibility – that should also be taken into account.

Representation, Sovereignty, Responsibility and the Free Mandate in the EP

Deliberation, representation, sovereignty and responsibility can be distinguished as core dimensions of parliamentarism. The EP presents a particular picture with regard to these dimensions.

Deliberation in the EP is, on one hand, shaped by the EP's characteristics of a working parliament, to which the EU's character as a polity in the making also contributes. In the EP, unique forms of parliamentary working routines have developed, among them cooperation across party camps (Görlach 2002). MEPs also traditionally use the fact that they work on legislative initiatives and/or policy fields to strengthen their role in the EU institutional system. By using their expertise, they impose themselves as equally strong sparring partners with the Commission and the Council, even in areas where MEPs have no decision-making prerogative. In these cases, for example in connection with extensive hearings in the area of the CFSP, the EP uses its characteristics as a debating parliament – i.e., the classical parliamentary practice of speaking pro et contra, to take a stand.

Representation in the EP is, as has been said, based on a direct, free and secret ballot. To what extent it is also equal might be subject to discussion, since the twenty-eight member states organize the EP elections nationally, which leads to small differences in voting times and dates. Moreover, MEPs are still elected from twenty-eight national lists of candidates. In the last EP election in 2009, most of the larger party families in the member states published integrated EU-wide election programmes. These were, however, not followed to an equal extent by all the national parties (see Sigalas, Mokre and Bruell 2011). Finally there is the fact that, for example, a Maltese MEP represents 82,520 Maltese inhabitants, whereas a Spanish MEP represents 917,060 Spanish citizens. The EU average is 678,904 inhabitants per MEP (Bundeszentrale für politische Bildung 2012). These differences reflect the fact that the logic of representation in the EP is, in practice, based on both EU citizens and the EU member states, even though the Lisbon Treaty only states that the EP is a body of representatives of EU citizens (TEU, Art. 14). Given this unstated representation of all member states in the EP, the differences in the weighing of the votes vis-à-vis the citizens cannot be cured by simply introducing a voting system in which each vote has equal weight – in such a system the large member states would have by far the most MEPs, while Malta would have difficulties in obtaining a seat at all.

The sovereignty of the EP has reached a high level thanks to the Lisbon Treaty, which names the co-decision procedure the 'ordinary legislative procedure', and in this respect the EP's decision-making competence now seems to be rather similar to that of parliaments in parliamentary systems, even though some national parliaments also possess more competence in the area of foreign and security policy than the EP. The EP's role in legislative initiatives and its influence on the government can rather be compared to those of parliaments in presidential or semi-presidential systems.

The de facto EU government, the Commission, has relatively high responsibility to the EP because the EP votes on the EU budget, it approves a new Commission and the Commission's annual activities, it can pass a vote of no confidence in a serving Commission, it can in practice force individual commissioners to resign, and it can reject individual candidates for a new Commission. The crisis mechanisms in the current financial predicament, however, must be regarded as having a very deleterious effect on the position of the EP. They have created a new intergovernmental structure around the European Stability Mechanism (ESM), which in practice excludes the EP from decision- making and political control in connection with the handling of the financial crisis. The powers of decision-making in the financial crisis are located in the Commission and the Council as well as in institutions such as the European Central Bank and the International Monetary Fund (for a detailed discussion, see Wiesner 2012b).

With regard to the responsibility of the MEPs towards EU citizens, the biggest problem is the fact that one single MEP represents so many citizens. In practice, the MEPs' offices and teams are prepared to handle this task, and they, like the EP ombudsman, also deal with the citizens' enquiries and questions. Thus the problem might be partly related to an insufficient awareness of EU citizens' rights vis-à-vis the EU and the EP in particular – even if knowledge about the EP seems to be growing slowly (Bullmann 2005). This insufficient knowledge has created a fertile ground for populist criticism (which has arisen in some EU countries in recent years) that the EP is too expensive and that MEPs are using their allowances in a wrong or even fraudulent way.

The EP as a Special Parliament

The EP is a special parliament in several respects; firstly for its multilingualism. The fact that the EP consists of MEPs of 28 EU member states speaking 24 official languages allows for 552 language combinations which means that the EP's multilingual parliamentarism is dependent on an army of translators and interpreters. There are clear standards for translations, and the translators are monitored strictly (European Parliament 2012a).

The EP does not have a classical government-opposition divide. This is partly related to the fact that for many years the EP's main political counterparts were the Commission and the Council (Görlach 2002). Before Lisbon, several different decision-making procedures existed for the EP, ranging from co-decisions to hearings. In practice (not formally) this meant that a two-thirds majority was necessary in all procedures except co-decision, since the EP majority had to be large if it wanted to have any influence at all against the Commission and the Council. Thus, cooperation across party camps was necessary. Since Lisbon, with co-decision becoming the standard, apart from some exceptions, divisions on several levels (parties, ideologies, policies, languages, regions, etc.) have become more important. However, this does not mean that a classical government-opposition divide has developed, since it is simply not yet necessary that the EP majority vote for and support a government: the party that wins the EP elections does not establish a government, even if it has greater influence on the nomination for important posts like the Commission President.

The free mandate thus seems to be in a better state in the EP than in several national parliaments in parliamentary systems. Even if there is strong party discipline in the groups, and despite the ongoing formation of EU-level political parties, MEPs in general are still more independent of national parties than their national counterparts. The role of the whip is also reduced, since a whip serves to avoid shifting majorities and thereby enable government stability in parliamentary systems. On the negative side, the MEPs' greater independence (and hence the increased weight of the individual MEP) makes them a more important target for lobbyists than national MPs.

Unsurprisingly, MEPs often consider themselves an EU avant-garde (Pekonen 2011) with a mission to broaden the EP's competence and strengthen its role – despite a growing number of EU-critical and EU-sceptical parties and groups being represented there. This also means that the relationship between many of the representatives in the EP and the electorates they represent is a singular one: on average they are (much) more pro-integrationist than the inhabitants of their home countries. The pro-EU attitude of most MEPs has a long tradition, and in consequence the EP has often functioned as a think tank for developing and pushing forward ideas for EU democratization. It was, for example, from the EP that the first ideas for a treaty change emanated several decades ago in the 1980s in what was then the EEC, followed by the ideas for an EU constitution in the 1990s (European Parliament 2009: 20, 111).

The EP as an Agent of EU Democratization

In many respects, the EP acts as an agent of EU democratization. First of all, it contributes to the politicization of the EU in manifold ways – be it by its institutional power struggles or by creating awareness of and positive or negative reactions to EU politics and policies, as in the case of environmental problems in the Ebro Delta and the human rights problems that the population of Kurdish origin faces in Turkey (Wiesner 2007: 179; European Parliament 2005b). The EP ombudsman is responsible for taking action in cases where EU citizens feel aggrieved by EU authorities. The EP has on at least one occasion become the target of an EU-wide demonstration; this was related to a directive on services in February 2006, when forty thousand participants came to Strasbourg (Wiesner 2012a; Gewerkschaft Erziehung und Wissenschaft 2012).

Secondly, the EP deliberately and continually tries to broaden the limits set by the EU institutional system. Prime examples of the EP's strategies are the events surrounding the resignation of the Santer Commission and the nomination of the Prodi Commission in 1999–2000, as well as the nomination of the Barroso Commission in 2004–2005: MEPs, using first of all their budgetary rights, helped to force the Santer Commission to resign because of intransparency and allegations of fraud. Later, using their right to approve a new Commission, the MEPs forced the newly nominated candidate for the Commission presidency, Romano Prodi, to allow hearings of individual candidate commissioners before the EP in 1999 and 2000 as a condition of approval of the Commission. The hearings lasted several days and there was strong pressure on Prodi. He assured the MEPs that in the future he would take seriously any demands for the demission of a commissioner issued by the EP, and also take serious account of its ideas when drafting law initiatives. These events created new institutional routines that were later fixed in a framework agreement in 2000 (European Union 2001).

In 2004, when the first Barroso Commission was nominated, the hearings led to a change of two candidate commissioners because the MEPs refused to approve them (see in detail Wiesner 2014b). The hearing procedure is thus a highly effective power: MEPs in practice may reject individual candidates even if according to the treaty they can only vote for the Commission as a whole. Furthermore, the political struggles around the Barroso Commission also strengthened the right of the MEPs to force individual commissioners to resign, which was again established in the following framework agreement in 2005 (European Parliament 2005a).

Conclusion

It has been argued in this chapter that the EP should be analysed in a way that takes into account its particularities. As a parliament in the making, it has a specific role in democratizing the EU representative institutional system. The contours of a semi-presidential regime serve as a good framework for analysing the powers of the EP. Like other parliaments in semi-presidential systems, the EP interacts with a dual executive, the Commission and the Council, with its parliamentary mandate being clearly circumscribed by the existence of the latter. From the point of view of semi-presidentialism, the EP differs from other parliaments mainly because of its more limited possibilities to control the parliamentary government – i.e., the Commission.

Furthermore, the discussion here has emphasized the thesis that, in several areas, the EP exhibits numerous other special features: it is a parliament in development, and it is also an agent of EU democratization. Many of the powers the EP acquired in political struggles were not formalized at first, or were regulated in 'grey documents' like the framework agreements, so the focus of analyses on the EP should be widened to include these areas as well.

The dynamism of the EP's development shows clear similarities with the development of parliaments in the first waves of the representative democratization of nation states. At present, it is obvious that the EU financial crisis constitutes both an 'open space' for new changes in EU democratization and a critical moment – the current tendencies may lead in the opposite direction as well.[6]

Notes

1 An interesting combination of parliamentarism and presidentialism characterizes the rules of nomination, as the EC, taking into account the EP elections (TEU, Art. 9D, 7), proposes a candidate for the presidency of the Commission, who is then elected by the EP. If the proposed candidate does not gain a sufficient majority, the EC must come up with a new proposal.

2 TEU, Art. C, 8 divides the Council's competences into legislative competences and others and requires that each Council meeting be divided into two parts accordingly. As the treaty subordinated a number of new legislative fields to the ordinary legislative procedure, it in practice decreased the Council's power over these issues.

3 The development of European political parties has taken place gradually in close interaction with the powers and rules of procedure of the EP. Following the incorporation of the 'party article' (TEU, Art. 191) ('Political parties at the European level are important as a factor for integration within the Union. They contribute to forming a European awareness and to expressing the will of the citizens of the Union'), the Socialist, Liberal and Christian Democrat federations established new and more cohesive party organizations. Later, other parties did the same, and all of them have reinforced their links with the party groups in the EP (Hix 2005: 187).

4 The critical treaty provisions have more or less remained in the same form since the Maastricht Treaty. The Lisbon Treaty defined the Commission's independence in the following way (TEU, Art. 9D, 3): 'In carrying out its responsibilities the Commission shall be completely independent. Without prejudice to Article 9E(2), the members of the Commission shall neither seek nor take instructions from any Government or other institution, body or entity'.

5 The background to this criticism must be seen in the experience of two World Wars being instigated by Germany, and the new tradition in the Federal Republic of Germany of ensuring democratic control over military activities through the German Bundestag. The German Basic Law even contains a prohibition against a war of aggression led by Germany. This tradition led to widespread German criticism of the EP as deficient because the EP does not possess a similar competence.

6 Prodi had been nominated by the European Council heads of state, as is always the case with both the Commission President and the commissioners. The EP approves these candidates but cannot present its own candidates.

References

Primary Sources

Bullmann, U. 2005. Rollen und Strategien des EP. Interviewed by Claudia Wiesner. Gießen.

Bundeszentrale für politische Bildung. 2012. 'Stimmengewichtung im europäischen Parlament'. Retrieved 24 May 2012 from www.bpb.de/system/files/pdf/AEN30Q.pdf

Czuczka, R. 1947. 'Grundsätzliches zum Kongress einer Europabewegung', *Die Friedens-Warte* 3: 176–78.

European Parliament. 2005a. 'P6_TA(2005)0194 Framework Agreement on EP-Commission Relations and European Parliament Decision on the Revision of the Framework Agreement on Relations between the European Parliament and the Commission (2005/2076 [ACI])'. Retrieved 8 May 2012 from http://www.europarl.europa.eu/sides/getDoc.do?pubRef=-//EP//NONSGML+TA+P6-TA-2005-0194+0+DOC+PDF+V0//EN

————. 2005b. 'Report on the Deliberation of the Committee on Petitions during the Parliamentary Year 2003–2004, 2004/2090(INI)'. Retrieved 28 November 2005 from http://www.europarl.eu.int/omk/sipade3?PUBREF=-//EP//NONSGML+REPORT+A6-2005-   0040+0+DOC+PDF+V0//EN&L=EN&LEVEL=2&NAV=S&LSTDOC=Y

————. 2009. 'Building Parliament: 50 Years of European Parliament History 1958–2008'. Retrieved 8 May 2012 from http://www.abgs.gov.tr/files/ardb/evt/1_avrupa_birligi/1_1_tarihce/50_years_of_european_parliament_history.pdf

————. 2012a. 'Multilingualism in the European Parliament'. Retrieved 12 December 2013 from http://www.europarl.europa.eu/aboutparliament/en/007e69770f/Mehrsprachigkeit.html.html

————. 2012b. Constitutional Affairs Committee, EP, 26 January 2012. Retrieved 14 October 2013 from http://www.europarl.europa.eu/meetdocs/2009_2014/documents/afco/am/883/883266/883266de.pdf

European Union. 2001. 'European Parliament/Commission Framework Agreement C5-0349/2000'. Retrieved 8 May 2012 from http://eur-lex.europa.eu/LexUriServ/LexUriServ.do?uri=OJ:C:2001:121:0122:0126:EN:PDF

Europäische Politische Gemeinschaft. 1953. 'Entwurf zu einem Vertrag über die Satzung der Europäischen (Politischen) Gemeinschaft (EPG)'. Retrieved 5 February 2013 from http://www.politische-union.de/epg1.htm

Görlach, W. 2002. Rollen und Strategien im EP. Interviewed by Claudia Wiesner. Frankfurt.

Kövér, J.F. 1947a. 'Der Föderalismus als Kraftquelle der politischen Entwicklung', *Die Friedens-Warte* 4–5: 306–12.

————. 1947b. 'Die föderalistische Bewegung auf neuen Bahnen', *Die Friedens-Warte* 3: 170–76.

Monnet, J. 1978. *Memoirs*. London: Doubleday & Company.

Schenck, E., von. 1947. 'Europa und die Sicherung des Weltfriedens', *Die Friedens-Warte* 1–2: 131–37.

Treaty of the European Union (TEU): European Union. 2010. 'Consolidated Treaties. Charter of Fundamental Rights'. Retrieved 5 February 2013 from http://book shop.europa.eu/is-bin/INTERSHOP.enfinity/WFS/EU-Bookshop-Site/en_ GB/-/EUR/ViewPublication-Start?PublicationKey=QC3209190

Treaty on the Functioning of the European Union (TFEU): European Union. 2010. 'Consolidated Treaties. Charter of Fundamental Rights'. Retrieved 5 February 2013 from http://bookshop.europa.eu/is-bin/INTERSHOP. enfinity/WFS/EU-Bookshop-Site/en_GB/-/EUR/ViewPublication-Start? PublicationKey=QC3209190

Secondary Sources

Benedetto, G. 2005. 'Rapporteurs as Legislative Entrepreneurs: The Dynamics of the Codecision Procedure in Europe's Parliament', *Journal of European Public Policy* 12(1): 67–88.

Cardozo, R. 1989. 'The Project for a Political Community (1952–54)', in P. Roy (ed.), *The Dynamics of European Union*. London and New York: Routledge.

Dann, P. 2003. 'European Parliament and Executive Federalism: Approaching a Parliament in a Semi-parliamentary Democracy', *European Law Journal* 9(5): 549–74.

Duverger, M. 1980. 'A New Political System Model: Semi-presidential Government', *European Journal of Political Research* 8(2): 165–87.

Elazar, D.J. 2001. 'The United States and the European Union: Models for their Epochs', in K. Nicholaidis and R. Howse (eds), *The Federal Vision: Legitimacy and Levels of Governance in the United States and the European Union*. Oxford: Oxford University Press, 31–53.

Farrell, H. and A. Héritier. 2003. 'Formal and Informal Institutions under Codecision: Continuous Constitution-Building in Europe', *Governance* 16: 577–600.

Føllesdal, A. and S. Hix. 2006. 'Why there is a Democratic Deficit in the EU: A Response to Majone and Moravscik', *Journal of Common Market Studies* 44(3): 533–62.

Føllesdal, A. and P. Koslowski (eds). 1997. *Democracy and the European Union*. Berlin: Springer.

Gewerkschaft Erziehung und Wissenschaft. 2012. 'Dienstleistungsrichtlinie'. Retrieved 13 June 2012 from http://www.gew.de/Dienstleistungsrichtlinie.html

Hix, S. 2002. 'Why the EU Should Have a Single President and How She Should be Elected', Paper for the Working Group on Democracy in the EU for the UK Cabinet Office, London, October 2002.

————. 2005. *The Political System of the European Union*. London: Palgrave.

Kielmannsegg, P.G. 1996. 'Integration und Demokratie', in M. Jachtenfuchs and B. Kohler-Koch (eds), *Europäische Integration*. Opladen: Leske + Budrich.

————. 2003. 'Integration und Demokratie', in M. Jachtenfuchs and B. Kohler-Koch (eds), *Europäische Integration*. Opladen: Leske + Budrich.

Lipgens, W. 1977. *Die Anfänge der europäischen Einigungspolitik 1945–1950*. Stuttgart: Klett.

Mamadouh, V. and T. Raunio. 2003. 'The Committee System: Powers, Appointments and Report Allocation', *Journal of Common Market Studies* 41(2): 333–51.

Niess, F. 2001. *Die europäische Idee*. Frankfurt: Suhrkamp.

Pekonen, K. 2011. 'Members of the European Parliament as Delegates and Parliamentarians', in C. Wiesner, T. Turkka and K. Palonen (eds), *Parliament and Europe*. Baden-Baden: Nomos.

Ripoll Servent, A. 2009. 'Playing the Co-decision Game: Is the European Parliament Striking a Balance between Liberty and Security?', Paper prepared for the UACES conference, 3–5 September 2009, Angers.

Sartori, G. 1994. *Comparative Constitutional Engineering: An Inquiry into Structures, Incentives and Outcomes*. Basingstoke: Macmillan.

Scharpf, F.W. 1995. 'Föderalismus und Demokratie in der transnationalen Ökonomie', *Politische Vierteljahresschrift* (Sonderheft 26): 211–35.

————. 1998. 'Demokratische Politik in der internationalisierten Ökonomie', in M.T. Greven (ed.), *Demokratie – eine Kultur des Westens?* Opladen: Leske und Budrich.

Settembri, P. and C. Neuhold. 2009. 'Achieving Consensus through Committees: Does the European Parliament Manage?', *Journal of Common Market Studies* 47(1): 127–51.

Sigalas, E., M. Mokre and C. Bruell. 2011. 'Supranational Elections in the Making? European Election Manifestoes and Campaigns in Austria', in C. Wiesner, T. Turkka and K. Palonen (eds), *Parliament and Europe*. Baden-Baden: Nomos, pp. 165–80.

Wiesner, C. 2007. *Bürgerschaft und Demokratie in der EU*. Münster: LIT.

————. 2012a. 'Bürgerschaft, Demokratie und Gerechtigkeit in der EU', in R. Kreide, C. Landwehr and K. Toens (eds), *Demokratie und Gerechtigkeit in Verteilungskonflikten*. Baden-Baden: Nomos, pp. 185–210.

————. 2012b. 'Ist die Finanzkrise auch eine Demokratiekrise? Eine Diskussion aus politikwissenschaftlicher Sicht', *Zeitschrift für Vergleichende Politikwissenschaft* 2: 187–206.

————. 2014a. *Demokratisierung der EU durch nationale Europadiskurse. Strukturen und Prozesse europäischer Identitätsbildung im deutsch-französischen Vergleich*. Baden-Baden: Nomos.

————. 2014b. 'The European Parliament as Special Parliament and Political Actor: Dissensus, Debate and Deliberation as Tools', in K. Palonen, J.M. Rosales and T. Turkka (eds), *The Politics of Dissensus: Parliament in Debate*. Santander and Madrid: Cantabria University Press and McGraw-Hill, pp. 101–24.

————. 2014c. 'From Safeguarding Peace in Europe to Financial Crisis: Old Questions and New Challenges of European Integration', in C. Wiesner and M. Schmidt-Gleim (eds), *The Meanings of Europe*. London: Routledge, pp. 91–106.

Teija Tiilikainen, Dr.Pol.Sc., is Director of the Finnish Institute of International Affairs in Helsinki and Editor-in-Chief of the *Finnish Journal of Foreign Affairs*. Her areas of expertise include European integration, the political institutions of the European Union, the Common Foreign and Security Policy, the European security policy system and Finland's foreign and security policy. She has recently published on the European Parliament and works on subjects such as European political cultures and the formation of political identities.

Claudia Wiesner, Dr.Rer.Pol., is Acting Professor at Philipps-Universität Marburg, and a Docent and Senior Research Fellow at the Finnish Centre of Political Thought and Conceptual Change, University of Jyväskylä, Finland. Her main research interests include comparative research on the European Union multilevel system; conceptual history, democratic theory and their contemporary implications; and comparative studies in civic culture, government and policy implementation.

Epilogue

Some Challenges to Parliamentarism

Kari Palonen

Compared with the interwar period (see e.g., Gusy 2008), we are not really facing a 'crisis of parliamentarism' today. In Western Europe the central political role of parliaments is recognized everywhere, and the principles of parliamentary representation, responsibility and deliberation are widely shared. Nonetheless, parliamentary politics today faces a number of challenges, some of them old, others more recent, which may require some rethinking of parliamentary practices. I shall discuss here some politically important examples from a conceptual historical perspective.

The old challenges can be divided into four types: (i) the extension of the agenda and scarce parliamentary time; (ii) the governmentalization of parliamentary agenda setting; (iii) the election and party-dependence of parliament; and (iv) the reduction of the parliamentary timetable. We can add two more recent challenges: (v) counter-bureaucratization from within, and (vi) inter-parliamentarization, both by-products of the actual success of parliamentarism. There are, of course, also other problems that classical parliaments have not dealt with so well, such as the representation of genders and small minorities, but they cannot be discussed within the confines of this chapter.

The Fair Distribution of Parliamentary Time

The democratization of parliament and the parliamentarization of government have politicized parliament itself in terms of the growing number of items on the agenda. They have also raised the public's expectations that the members should participate in debates. The continuing growth of the parliamentary agenda is a consequence of a parliamentarization and democratization of politics that could hardly have been avoided. Parliaments have to learn to protect themselves against their own success and to hold the activity of their members in check in order to prevent the paralysis of the entire institution.

The challenge lies thus in learning to cope with this constantly growing agenda in the face of scarce parliamentary time. One possibility lies in extending the parliamentary concept of fair play to a fair distribution of parliamentary time (see Chapter 14). The loquacity of members can be countered by reinterpreting freedom of speech to concern the content and presentation of speeches but not their length in order to ensure a fair distribution of time between members. The application of the principle of fair play between different items, however, requires various measures ranging from delegation to committees, using rotation or lottery in the selection of the motions for the agenda and sharing of motions between the lower and higher levels of parliamentary types of assemblies, to debating the content of the agenda itself instead of allowing the government or party leaders to determine it. This would require a lot of parliamentary imagination.

The Politics of Agenda Setting

A second topos that challenged parliamentarism in the nineteenth century and still does today concerns the governmentalization of parliamentary agenda setting without it being submitted to effective parliamentary control and debate. Walter Bagehot's nineteenth-century vision of the cabinet as an executive committee of parliament (see Chapter 14) underestimated the government's agenda-setting power. The reduction of parliamentary politics to a game between government and opposition tends to turn parliamentary speaking into an epideictic form of ratification or non-ratification of government measures. The deliberative dimension of parliamentary politics presupposes a degree of independence of parliament from the government-opposition divide within it.

The current Westminster procedure, however, provides occasions in which individual backbenchers initiate the debate. Griffith and Ryle consider this 'second confrontation' in parliament as 'equally important although less obviously manifested and usually less fiercely demonstrated' than the divide between government and opposition. They regard 'members without executive responsibilities [. . . as] free to criticize ministers or their department' (Griffith and Ryle 2003: 14). With a two-dimensional view on disputes between parliamentarians, the authors recognize that '[i]t is to a large extent the historical, constitutional confrontation between Parliament (answerable to the people) and the Executive appointed by the Crown' (Griffith and Ryle 2003: 14; see also Chapter 2).

Elections, Parties and Parliament

Parliamentary elections and government formation can hardly be realized otherwise than on a partisan basis whereby votes are counted and not weighted (see Weber 1988 [1917]: 167–70). The elective and representative quality of parliament has, however, frequently turned into a dependence not only of the composition of government but also of the politics of parliaments on election results. 'Popular sovereignty' has been given an anti-parliamentary interpretation; for example, in Carl Schmitt's (1970 [1928]) insistence that parliament, unlike referenda or presidential elections, dissolves the 'unity' of the people. In contrast, we could interpret parliamentary sovereignty to include elections as a medium for transferring parliamentary dissensus and debate to the citizens (see Palonen 2010). Even if they are elected on a partisan basis, the members face the questions on the parliamentary agenda as individuals; they speak as individuals and cannot delegate their vote to others even when they are members of the same party. In the procedural terms of a deliberative assembly, every debate, speech and vote is a chance to revise the parliamentary distribution of power.

However, parties are necessary mediators and simplifiers of parliamentary politics, and a member must carefully consider when, where and how to express dissent with his or her own party. The members' chances of re-election remain in the hands of the parties, although the grip of the party apparatus on parliamentarians has declined somewhat. The improved investigative, supportive and personnel resources of both parliaments and their members have also weakened their non-electoral dependence on the party leadership and apparatus.

The Parliamentary Timetable

Debating a motion in a parliament does not, strictly speaking, happen on a singular occasion but rather over a series of occasions and includes different perspectives in plenum or in committee. The key parliamentary procedures, such as moving, seconding, putting a question, speaking pro or contra the motion, amending, adjourning and moving a question of 'order' are all temporal operations. They concern the present, future and past of parliamentary politics, and the spending of precious parliamentary time. The debate itself provides occasions for sudden insights for or against the motion but also requires time to reflect on the arguments, to construct objections or to invent dissensual arguments.

There is also a temporal subtext in parliamentary debates. The moves of members are separate, successive, non-simultaneous and irreversible: in the parliamentary agenda, motions are either transferred forward on their parliamentary journey or not, and frequently never come to the vote. With the growing pressure on parliamentary time, this complex parliamentary temporality is submitted to simplifications, such as constraints on the time for debate (*clôture*) and the allocation of a maximum time for a motion (*guillotine*).

The dedication of an extensive amount of time to debating pro et contra remains, nonetheless, a major political advantage of parliaments. They are well equipped against pressures to 'accelerate' proceedings but still able to make urgent decisions in a 'parliamentary' manner. Even so, parliaments sometimes too easily give in to the demands of institutions and practices for which time is merely a matter of consumption without duly recognizing the temporal subtext as an asset of parliamentary politics.

Counter-bureaucratization

The Westminster tradition sees parliament as an institution that controls government and administration. Max Weber insists that, while bureaucracy is indispensable in the modern state, the tendency towards bureaucratization is a major danger to individual freedom and parliamentary politics (Weber 1988 [1918]: 222–23). He proposes ingenious rhetorical instruments for enabling parliamentary control of the rule of officialdom (Weber 1988 [1918]: esp. 235–37) and supports strengthening the powers of professional parliamentarians and providing them with staff and apparatus of their own (Weber 1988 [1918]: 244–47).

By comparison with governmental bureaucracy, the existence of parliamentary staff constitutes a modest form of counter-bureaucracy. Nonetheless, we cannot exclude the possibility that through it the bureaucratic mentality is creeping into parliaments. The parliamentary officials – unlike the EU Commission, for example – can hardly claim to represent a Hegelian 'objective spirit' that is above politics. However, the growth of the staff might render parliamentarians dependent on them. The parliamentarians' pro et contra thinking remains largely alien to their staff, who may be unable to assist in speculation about alternatives or in provoking dissensus and debate. The staff might turn into a Trojan horse of bureaucratization inside parliaments, in particular if its members do not have any parliamentary or proto-parliamentary experience acquired in municipal or student politics.

Inter-parliamentarization

One of the greatest challenges and opportunities for parliamentary politics today is the advent of inter-parliamentary politics. The British parliamentary sovereignty of a single parliament, which has the last word in politics, has encountered a limit as a result of devolutions and EU membership. In federal polities the regulations between the federal and the 'member state' levels, as well as between a directly elected parliament and the federal chamber, are detailed, albeit regularly controversial.

All local, regional and 'federal state' parliaments or parliament-analogous assemblies provide occasions for a number of citizens to act politically in representative and deliberative assemblies. There is today a danger that fewer citizens may have the opportunity to experience such parliamentary ways of acting politically, as decentralization, devolution and the localization of politics has not been realized in parliamentary forms.

From this perspective, moves towards the parliamentarization of the European Union are of great interest. The dominant view regards the nation states as primary, quasi-natural entities that 'lose sovereignty' in the Union, irrespective of its degree of parliamentarism. In contrast, we can construct an ideal type of parliamentary institution for the Union, in which the application of the parliamentary principles of deliberation, representation and responsibility independent of the political levels is the main point.

Despite its member-state-based electoral districts, the European Parliament provides a unique example of a supranational parliament. In its procedures, the EP corresponds to a full parliament of equal members who speak and vote as individuals. Neither the party lines nor the government vs. the opposition divide are as manifest as in national parliaments (see Chapter 18). Even so, the power struggles between deliberating and negotiating assemblies remain rather weakly regulated, both within the EU institutions and in their relations to national parliaments and governments.

We can, however, at least place the inter-parliamentary relationships between parliamentary-type assemblies from the municipal to the European level on the agenda of political and scholarly debates. The opportunity to do so lies not merely in the distribution of time and resources between political levels but also in enabling second-order debates between deliberative assemblies without intervention by governments. In particular, this can take the form of defending or expanding debate-based parliamentary politics on all political levels against governmental, administrative or juridical models of dealing with questions.

The 'challenges' discussed here are by-products of the successes of parliamentarism; therefore, they are not insurmountable but require both parliamentary imagination and self-restraint against excessively mechanical applications of parliamentary principles.

References

Primary Sources

Schmitt, C. 1970 [1928]. *Verfassungslehre*. Berlin: Duncker & Humblot.

Weber, M. 1988 [1917]. 'Wahlrecht und Demokratie in Deutschland', in W.J. Mommsen (ed.), *Max-Weber-Studienausgabe* I/15. Tübingen: Mohr, pp. 155–89.

Weber, M. 1988 [1918]. 'Parlament und Regierung im neugeordneten Deutschland', in W.J. Mommsen (ed.), *Max-Weber-Studienausgabe* I/15. Tübingen: Mohr, pp. 202–302.

Secondary Sources

Griffith, J.A.G., and M. Ryle. 2003. *Parliament: Functions, Practices and Procedures*, 2nd ed. by R. Blackburn and A. Kinnon. London: Sweet & Maxwell.

Gusy, C. (ed.). 2008. *Demokratie in der Krise. Europa in der Zwischenkriegszeit*. Baden-Baden: Nomos.

Palonen, K. 2010. 'The Parliamentarisation of Elections', *Redescriptions* 14: 133–56.

Index